Cockatoos ...getting started

John Coborn

Contents

Photographs: David Alderton, Dr. Allen, Glen S. Axelrod, Dr. H. R. Axelrod, Joan Balzarini, M. Bonnin, John Daniels, Michael DeFreitas, Kerry V. Donnelly, Isabelle Francais, Ralph Kaehler, S. Kates, Don Mathews, Horst Muller, Frank Nothaft, Robert Pearcy, Fritz Prenzel, L. Robinson, San Diego Zoo, R. Small, Carol Thiem, T. Tilford, Vogelpark Walsrode

© T.F.H. Publications, Inc.

Distributed in the UNITED STATES to the Pet Trade by T.F.H. Publications, Inc., 1 TFH Plaza, Neptune City, NJ 07753; on the Internet at www.tfh.com; in CANADA by Rolf C. Hagen Inc., 3225 Sartelon St., Montreal, Quebec H4R 1E8; Pet Trade by H & L Pet Supplies Inc., 27 Kingston Crescent, Kitchener, Ontario N2B 2T6; in ENGLAND by T.F.H. Publications, PO Box 74, Havant PO9 5TT; in AUSTRALIA AND THE SOUTH PACIFIC by T.F.H. (Australia), Pty. Ltd., Box 149, Brookvale 2100 N.S.W., Australia; in NEW ZEALAND by Brooklands Aquarium Ltd., 5 McGiven Drive, New Plymouth, RD1 New Zealand; in SOUTH AFRICA by Rolf C. Hagen S.A. (PTY.) LTD., P.O. Box 201199, Durban North 4016, South Africa; in JAPAN by T.F.H. Publications. Published by T.F.H. Publications, Inc.

MANUFACTURED IN THE
UNITED STATES OF AMERICA
BY T.F.H. PUBLICATIONS, INC.

Introduction

Female Citron-crested Cockatoo, *C.s. citrinocristata*. The sexes of most cockatoo species can be distinguished from examining the color of the eye. A brownish-red colored eye denotes a female. A solid black eye is typical of the male.

Cockatoos are unique members of the parrot family that, in the wild, are found exclusively in Australia and some of the nearby islands. There are some 17 species and numerous subspecies, all of which exhibit characteristic erectile crests used to express emotional or sexual excitement.

Ever since the first Europeans discovered the Spice Islands and Australasia in the 17th and 18th centuries, cockatoos have been popular as pets for their intelligence, ability to mimic, bizarre appearance, and color. Their exotic mystique has also made them coveted prizes of the aviculturist, all the more so since the ban by Australia on the export of all native wildlife to other parts of the world.

The natural attributes of cockatoos give them instant appeal to people who may never have kept a bird before. However, possessing a cockatoo as a pet can have distinct disadvantages and these should be fully understood before a bird is obtained. The volume of their voices is amazingly loud, especially when heard at close quarters, and the natural repertoire of most species is a series of harsh screeches and screams, especially emitted when a bird is bored through lack of company. They may scream all day until their owner gets home and this can lead to complaints from the neighbors. Cockatoos are, therefore, not suited for people who are absent from the home for most of the day as they require a great deal of attention and company.

The housing of cockatoos is more expensive than that of the smaller parrotlike birds (e.g., lovebirds, budgerigars, and cockatiels) due to their size and destructive powers. Timber frameworks will be destroyed by their powerful beaks in no time at all, so metal or metal-lined structures have to be used. A pet cockatoo should be kept in a strong metal cage, and the bird must be let out in a room for exercise at regular intervals. Unless you keep very close watch on the bird, your furniture, house plants, and other items will soon be chewed up.

All the disadvantages described may make it appear that the author is trying to dissuade people from buying a cockatoo. Well, maybe he is. Unless you are absolutely sure that you have the time, the patience and the ongoing enthusiasm to care properly for your bird, you should not acquire a cockatoo, but remain content with a canary or a budgie. However, for those enthusiasts with the right attitude, cockatoos are highly entertaining and give an enormous amount of pleasure.

After keeping a pet cockatoo for a time, some enthusiasts really get the avicultural bug and would like to turn their hand to cockatoo breeding. This constitutes a real challenge as, outside Australasia, most species are relatively inaccessible and expensive. In addition, most cockatoo species cannot exactly be classified as "easy" breeders. Successful cockatoo breeding can be an extremely profitable business and the author knows people who make a good living from doing just that. However, do not expect it to be easy and be prepared for numerous setbacks and heartbreaks before you finally get the "knack" and become successful.

Goffin's Cockatoo, *Cacatua goffini*. The Goffin's Cockatoo makes for a very comical pet. This smaller sized species proves to be very agile and loves to play in amusing ways with its owner.

This little book is intended to introduce the reader to the fascinating world of cockatoos and to help him decide whether he would like to keep one as a pet or attempt to breed them. All the necessary information on selection, housing, feeding, general maintenance, and breeding management are covered in brief but concise detail. This information should allow the prospective keeper of cockatoos to start his new hobby with confidence and, hopefully, lead him into many years of the pleasure that these outstanding birds can provide.

The Lesser Sulphur-crested Cockatoo, *Cacatua sulphurea*, is very fond of fruits and vegetables. Apples and fresh coconut are two of their favorites.

Cockatoo Natural History

Although not very attractive because of the naked, blue-skinned eye ring that appears swollen, the Bare-Eyed Cockatoo, *Cacatua sanguinea*, is the best talker of the cockatoo family.

People who are interested in cockatoos are usually interested in birds in general and this chapter is intended to introduce the reader very briefly to bird evolution, classification, and general biology, thus providing background information for a discussion of cockatoos in particular.

BIRD EVOLUTION

Evolution of life on the planet earth is a very complex subject and, although generations of scientists have spent a great deal of time studying it, the surface of the subject has, so to say, barely been scratched. The word "evolution" has several meanings, but for our purpose we can take just one of the definitions given in the dictionary. To evolve means to "gradually arise" which is the operative phrase. However, gradually arising can almost be regarded as an understatement when we consider that the gradual arising of higher forms of life from the lower ones has taken hundreds of millions

The crest of the Moluccan Cockatoo, *Cacatua moluccensis*, is salmon-colored and varies in intensity. This creates an unusual color contrast to the rest of the body and a truly beautiful creature.

of years. Prior to the middle of the nineteenth century, man had some very odd ideas about evolution, until a certain British scientist by the name of Charles Darwin (1809-1882) expounded a theory of evolution by natural selection in his book *The Origin of Species* published in 1859. At the time, a great deal of controversy arose as many people were unable to imagine life originating other than by divine forces. However, in the intervening time, fossil evidence and modern methods of research have proven that the theory is mostly correct.

It is generally accepted that the birds (and the mammals) arose from various groups of primitive reptiles. A simple theory as to how the birds arose is as follows: At the time when the highest form of life on earth was reptilian, certain small lizardlike reptiles, which were vulnerable to larger carnivorous ones, would have taken refuge in trees in order to escape from them. Of course, the predators were not happy with this state of affairs, so they also developed sufficiently to be able to chase their prey up into

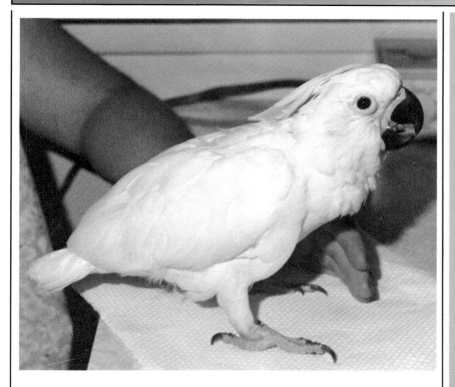

Baby Citron-crested Cockatoo, *Cacatua citrinocristata*. Each cockatoo has its own particular characteristics; they are all as individual in their personalities as any humans might be.

tree branches. The prey developed still one step further by learning to escape by leaping from one tree to the next or to the ground. Those which were too slow in doing this quickly became victims. It follows that those with the most convenient weight and shape were able to leap further and faster than the others, which gradually became extinct. From generation to generation, piece by piece, those little mutations which were favorable to the survival of the species gradually developed; digits became longer and webbed, flaps of skin gradually formed along the body and the leapers became parachutists and gliders, being able to cover considerable distances through the air.

The power of flight had already been developed by the invertebrates (insects), but the requirements of flight in the vertebrates were more complex. Due to their heavier build, they had greater problems in overcoming the pull of gravity. The flying vertebrate reduced its weight by developing hollow, air filled bones and the strength of the wings had to be great enough to support the whole body. It

had to have powerful forelimb muscles to operate the wings, which meant that the breast bone had to be enlarged for the attachment of these muscles.

The first vertebrate animals with the complete power of flight were the flying reptiles known as pterosaurs which appeared in the early Jurassic period about 190 million years ago. A large number of fossil species have been described, most of which are relatively small but some had a wingspan of 15 meters (50 feet) or more! Their skeleton was superficially birdlike but they are believed to have lacked feathers and to have been "cold-blooded."

The pterosaurs became extinct toward the end of the Cretaceous period (about 70 million years ago). It is thought that these flying reptiles were unable to withstand competition from the birds, which began to evolve in the late Jurassic period (about 140 million years ago) and had reached a high state of development and diversity by the end of the Cretaceous period. Like the pterosaurs, the birds probably arose from arboreal reptiles, but there is no fossil evidence to prove a connection between the two. The birds evolved in a different way. The reptilian body scales developed into feathers, which not only assisted in the power of flight, but also insulated the body from heat loss, thus increasing the metabolic rate, thereby making more energy available and increasing efficiency.

Fossil remains of birds are scarce, but what are considered to be the oldest fossil birds were found in the Jurassic-aged Solnhofen limestone of Bavaria, Germany. The fossil bird was named *Archaeopteryx lithographica* which literally means "ancient winged-creature, etched into stone." Although its anatomy was very similar to certain fossil reptiles, the presence of obvious feathers resulted in its being classified as a bird.

Unfortunately, good fossils of birds are few and far between. The fragile bones and the feathers tend to be poorly preserved and the remains of a bird seldom had time to be completely petrified before it decomposed completely. From the Cretaceous period to the present time, an era of about 65 million years, very few fossil birds are known, making it almost impossible to prove the

Opposite: The Black Palm Cockatoo, *Probosciger aterrimus*, is the largest parrot in Australia and New Guinea and is among the largest member of the parrot family.

Young Yellow-tailed Black Cockatoos, *Calyptorhynchus funereus*, have bright, yellow cheek patches, darker legs, and have fewer yellow markings on the feathers of the neck than adults.

path of evolution from the early to the modern birds; most of our knowledge of this subject is pure but logical theory. With the enormous variety of bird life on earth today, one can imagine that the evolution of the present forms was a long and complicated process. Differences in habitat led the birds into becoming one of the most diverse classes of modern vertebrate animals, with almost 8,500 living species (outnumbered as a vertebrate class only by the teleost fishes) inhabiting almost every corner of the earth, from the oceans to the mountain peaks, and from the equatorial rain forests to the polar regions. Adaptations to the enormous diversity of habitat have led birds to develop a staggering array of forms, colors, and habits. As examples, take the huge flightless ostrich of the African savannah and the tiny hummingbirds of the Americas, the almost totally aquatic penguins of the Antarctic and the majestic eagles of the mountain peaks.

One relatively small group of birds, with which we are here concerned is the order Psittaciformes, which comprises a single family, the Psittacidae, containing some 328 species in 77 genera. The cockatoos, of which there are only 17 species, are sometimes classified as a family in its own right (Cacatuidae) or, probably more correctly, as a subfamily of the Psittacidae (Cacatuinae). To help better understand how the cockatoos fit into the complex structure of evolution, it is worth taking a brief look at classification.

CLASSIFICATION OF COCKATOOS

Early natural historians had a great deal of difficulty in categorizing the vast numbers of living things on this planet, particularly those which resembled each other in form or color, or which were closely related. As Europeans began to discover territories further and further away from their homelands, the numbers of hitherto unknown species of animals and plants found became greater and greater. Due to language barriers and the considerable volume of material being sent back to the museums and universities of Europe, one can imagine that utter confusion soon arose and the need for a logical and international system of scientific classification became apparent. It was the Swedish biologist Karl von Linne, generally known as Linnaeus (1707-1778), who eased the situation by devising the first "logical" system of classification in his work *Systema Naturae*.

Known as the *binomial system* of nomenclature, every plant and animal species known was designated with a double name, the first being the *generic* name, the second being the *specific* name. As Latin was the language used mainly by international scholars at the time, it was this language that was most often used for the binomials, but a fair proportion of Greek and

Eleonora Cockatoo, *Cacatua galerita eleonora*. This subspecies of cockatoo is often referred to as a Medium Sulphur-crested.

other languages may appear in zoological nomenclature. Taking a simple example, the Greater Sulphur-crested Cockatoo has been given the scientific name *Cacatua galerita* (literally translated *Cacatua* is a latinization derived from a native word "kakadu" for the bird and *galerita* means "rustic" probably in the sense of "country living"), the first name, being the genus to which the species belongs and the second name, being the species itself. Other species in the particular cockatoo genus have the same generic name but, obviously, a different specific name (e.g.,

Cacatua moluccensis, Cacatua alba, Cacatua sanguinea).

Just as one or more species are placed in a genus, genera are placed in families, orders, classes, etc., in ascending order, based on differences and similarities. In some difficult cases of classification, additional categories such as subfamilies or infraorders may be used, these often being based on the judgment of a particular author. The science of the classification of living organisms is known as *taxonomy*, and those who study this discipline are called taxonomists. Due to the complexity of life forms, it is inevitable that difficulty may be experienced in classifying certain creatures which are similar to each other. Controversy frequently occurs among taxonomists as to how a particular species should be classified. However, there is an international body known as the IUZN (International Union for Zoological Nomenclature) which tries to strike a happy medium among the ideas of taxonomists throughout the world.

Some species, with a wide distribution or living on separate islands, form

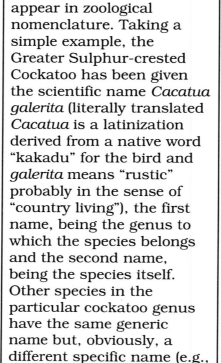

Moluccan Cockatoo, *Cacatua moluccensis*. Besides having an impressive appearance, cockatoos are valued by fanciers as gentle and good natured creatures that can be tamed easily.

distinct geographical races. These races exhibit slight differences to each other but the differences are not sufficient to warrant separate specific classification. Such cases are therefore relegated to *subspecific* rank and a third name is added to the binomial, making it effectively a *trinomial*. For example, the standard Australian Greater Sulphur-crested Cockatoo becomes *Cacatua galerita galerita*, while the New Guinea race of that species is designated *Cacatua galerita triton*.

BIOLOGY OF THE COCKATOOS

As we have seen, cockatoos belong to the family Psittacidae (parrotlike birds) in the order Psittaciformes, although some authors classify them in a family of their own (Cacatuidae). In this work, we will regard the cockatoos as being a subfamily (Cacatuinae) of the parrotlike birds. Parrotlike birds are mainly arboreal (with a few exceptions) and range in size from the tiny pygmy parrots (*Micropsitta*), 10 cm (4 in) in length, to the huge Hyacinthine Macaw (*Anodorhynchus hyacinthinus*) with a length of 92 cm (36 in). The family

Psittacidae contains about 328 species in 77 genera which have a pan-tropical distribution. They are particularly numerous in the Australasian region where in fact all of the 17 or so species of cockatoo are found.

Cockatoos are typically parrotlike and, although they may lack the variety of colors seen in their parrot relatives, they are nonetheless spectacular in their livery of white, black, or pink, depending on the species. Typical

Major Mitchell's Cockatoo, *Cacatua leadbeateri*. All cockatoos breed in hollows of tree trunks or similar places. They clear out and enlarge decayed or damaged trunks to the desired size with their powerful bills.

identification features of the parrots are a relatively sparse plumage with hard and glossy feathers. The beak is short, stout, strongly hooked, and, in most cases (especially in cockatoos), immensely powerful. The beak is used to crack open hard seeds and nuts, to dig up roots and tubers, to strip bark from trees and to enlarge nesting cavities. In addition, the beak is used as a sort of third limb, for clambering about in the foliage of trees. The upper mandible can be raised by a lever mechanism of bones, when the lower jaw is depressed, giving parrots an extremely efficient feeding apparatus. Cockatoos are largely herbivorous, feeding on a range of seeds, grains, nuts, foliage, bark, roots, and tubers. There is evidence to suggest that a certain amount of insect food is also ingested, either deliberately or accidentally.

The legs are relatively short and the feet have a unique arrangement of toes shared by relatively few other bird families. Being zygotactylous, the two outer toes point to the rear, while the two inner toes face the front. This not only gives the parrots a very efficient means of perching and climbing; it enables the foot to be used to pick up items of food and hold them to the beak while feeding. The wings are relatively short, broad, and rounded and the flight is usually fast, with down-curved wings.

Cockatoos are typified by having an erectile crest, which is used to express mood. The crest is raised when the bird is excited (territorially or sexually) or frightened. Some species have spectacular crests, while in others, the crest is

Goffin's Cockatoo, *Cacatua goffini*. All species of cockatoos are very protective of their nest, especially if they have young.

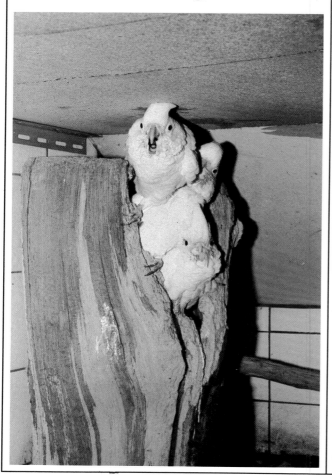

The Triton Cockatoo, *Cacatua galerita triton*, seems to be extremely talented and entertaining. Its talent includes dancing up and down while flapping its wings and bobbing its head, and whistling all the while.

relatively short. Cockatoos usually inhabit open woodland, where there are adequate trees for nesting. Like most parrots, cockatoos nest in tree holes, and no nest, as such, is constructed, although enlargement of the interior of the hollow may result in a bed of wood chips in the base. The eggs of all species are invariably pure white and ellipsoidal, and numbers laid range from one to six, depending on the species. The newly hatched young are naked, later downy, and tended by both parents.

Many cockatoo species are gregarious outside the breeding season and, in Australia, some species may assemble in flocks of a thousand or more, but groups of 40 or 50 birds are more common. Such groups of some species can be extremely damaging to cultivated crops, resulting in organized culling procedures. Fortunately, most species exist in sufficient numbers in the wild, rendering them relatively safe from extinction.

Housing

Due to their relatively large size, powerful beaks and a tendency toward destruction, cockatoos (and other large parrots) require more substantial accommodation than most other types of cage or

Moluccan Cockatoo, *Cacatua moluccensis.* When excited, these cockatoos have a habit of raising their crests, stamping their feet, and clacking their bills. They also have the incredible ability to fluff their feathers so much that they appear to be double their original size.

aviary birds. Types of accommodations range from single cages for the pet cockatoo to various indoor and outdoor aviaries for breeding purposes.

CAGES

Although a pet cockatoo will do quite well in a cage, it will still need to be let out into the room for exercise at regular intervals. A typical parrot cage is suitable for a cockatoo and such cages are available in various patterns and price ranges. It is not really necessary to purchase an expensive cage with numerous dust-catching embellishments. These will only detract from the appeal of the bird itself and make cleaning more work. A simple, box-type cage made from galvanized steel wire is all that is required. The corner uprights and the horizontal bars are usually of about 3 mm thick wire, while the main vertical wires of the cage are about 2 mm thick and set about 1.5 cm apart, to allow for maximum view. The wires are welded together to form the main body of the cage.

The floor of the cage should be made of sheet metal, usually aluminum or galvanized steel. The sides of the floor are bent upward to form low walls about 5 cm (2 in) high. This stops most of the food waste, grit, etc., from falling out onto the floor and forms a sort of framework into which the wire part of the cage is fitted. The cage and the floor are attached by clips, so that they can easily be separated for cleaning purposes. The cage will usually have a ring in the center of the top, so that it may be suspended from a strong ceiling hook, or from a special cage stand.

A single access door is set approximately in the middle of the cage front. The door may be on a spring-controlled hinge so that it is self-closing, or it may be a sliding door. A vertical sliding door, which drops downward to close is probably the best to use for cockatoos, which soon discover ways of opening other types of doors, even if they have a "secure" catch. If the bird can let itself out, you will certainly not want it to do this when you are out and unable to keep an eye on it; a mischievous cockatoo can do an enormous amount of damage in a very short time!

The dimensions of the cage will depend on the species of cockatoo being kept. For example, the minimum dimensions for a

The Gang-gang Cockatoo, *Callocephalon fimbriatum*, is one of the most unique cockatoos and also one of the rarest in captivity.

cage for a Lesser Sulphur-crested Cockatoo should be 55 x 55 x 65 cm high (approx. 21 x 21 x 25 in), while a cage for a Greater Sulphur-crested Cockatoo should be at least 5 cm (2 in) greater in each dimension.

A single perch is usually set about half way up the height of the cage and clipped onto the cage wire at each end. Perches are generally made of hard, ridged plastic or hardwood. Although plastic is probably more hygienic and less likely to be chewed up, the author favors hardwood, which is more natural and probably easier on the soles of the bird's feet. Although hardwood perches are eventually chewed up, they are relatively inexpensive to replace and the bird will derive some enjoyment from gnawing at them. The perch should be placed far enough from the walls of the cage so that the bird does not touch the wire with its feathers when perching, otherwise there is the possibility that they will soon become soiled or damaged. Particular care should be taken to ensure that it is set low enough so the bird's erect crest does not touch the wire of the top of the cage for similar reasons. The diameter of the perch should not be less than 2 cm (.75 in), preferably a little more for most species.

The only other important furnishings for the cage are food and water containers. These are best made from metal (galvanized steel, stainless steel or aluminum), earthenware, or porcelain. Plastic containers are useless for cockatoos as they will soon chew them up.

The floor of the cage may be covered with clean, coarse sand. It is possible to purchase special "bird sand" from your avicultural supplier. This is not only sterile, but some brands contain mineral grit which is a valuable additive to your bird's diet. The bird sand is relatively inexpensive and will soak up droppings, water spillages, etc., making it easy to clean the cage floor. A fair layer should be placed on the floor of the cage and this should be changed as soon as it gets soiled, preferably daily. In some cages is easy to remove the cage top and place it on the floor while the bird is sitting on the perch, so that you can clean the base. The sand can be removed with a scraper and tipped away (add it to your compost heap). Some cockatoo owners like to cover the cage floor with paper to keep it clean, but if you own a cockatoo that does not soon rip the paper into very fine shreds and scatter them all over the floor, you are very lucky indeed. About once per week, the floor should be scrubbed with warm water and detergent, rinsed thoroughly and dried before being replaced. Perches, feeding pots, and the cage body should also be thoroughly cleaned at regular intervals.

CAGE SITING

Where you place your cockatoo cage should be carefully considered. Cockatoos come from (usually) warm, sunny climates and certainly enjoy a certain amount of sunlight. However, this does not mean that you should place the cage in the full glare of the sun, especially in front of a glass window, where the heat will be magnified. There should always be a part of the cage that is shaded, so that the bird can get into a cooler spot if it so wishes. Unfiltered sunlight is much better and extremely beneficial to the birds; on

The cockatoo's destructive nature requires that they have either ample time outside of their cage or have plenty of toys to keep them busy when inside.

Ducorps's Cockatoo, *Cacatua ducorpsii*, is very prolific and can be seen daily in its homeland; however, few are known of being kept in captivity.

warm spring, summer, and fall days, the cage may be placed outside on the balcony or in the garden in a partially shaded position. One method of ensuring adequate shade is to clip a cloth over half of the cage, so that the bird can "sunbathe" as it wishes.

Indoors, a cage must be placed in an area that receives adequate ventilation but, at the same time, is not in cold drafts. A continual cold draft which a bird is unable to avoid will soon reduce its resistance and sickness will arise. Do not place the cage where it is subjected to excessive cooking fumes or tobacco smoke; this can also be distressing to the bird.

THE "T" PERCH

Certain enthusiasts like to keep their cockatoo at semi-liberty on a "T" perch. Some cockatoos are not inclined to wander too

much (especially if the wings are clipped), but others will need to be restricted in their movements.

The "T" perch itself consists of a pole on a heavy base with the perch at the top of the pole at a height of about 120 cm (4 ft). Food, water, and grit containers are usually affixed to the perch itself. A variation on the "T" perch is a stout, natural branch, attached firmly to a heavy base. A piece with several branches will give your bird additional exercise as it clambers about. With a little imagination, one can come up with a veritable array of ladders, platforms, see-saws, etc., all designed to give your cockatoo plenty to occupy it. Of course, timber structures will soon be chewed to pieces but they are usually inexpensive to replace. Siting of "T" perches is as described for cages.

AVIARIES FOR COCKATOOS

Aviaries come in many shapes and sizes. They may be purchased in prefabricated form or, if you are a handy person, you can construct your own. Constructing your own gives one an extreme sense of satisfaction in a job well done. The structure of aviaries for cockatoos (and other large parrots) must be much stronger than that required for most other kinds of birds. The strong psitticine beaks are well-suited to unwelcome carpentry, so timber on the inside of frameworks must be well-protected. A single, pet cockatoo can be kept in a small, all metal aviary. Some of these are supplied with wheels so that you can easily move the aviary in or outdoors depending on the weather. Such a cage is usually about 180 cm (6 ft) high and 90 cm (3 ft) square. The advantage of such an aviary over a cage is that the bird will get much more exercise clambering about and additional perches can be added.

For breeding cockatoos, a large, preferably outdoor aviary is essential. Before installing an aviary a few important points should be considered. The size will depend on the amount of available space. Ensure that you are not contravening any local council planning by-laws. Discuss the aspects of installing an aviary with your family and neighbors. In particular, ensure that the aviary will not encroach on the view or take light away from your neighbors' property. Remember that cockatoos are noisy birds with extremely raucous calls and, understandably, some people are not overly fond of the noise. In metal cages and aviaries, the birds can also make quite a noise just by clambering around on the wire. It is best to discuss all your intentions with the appropriate people and get their approval before you go ahead, rather than risk having to remove an expensive and unpopular aviary at a later date. In general, it can be stated that a cockatoo aviary is more suitable for owners of large gardens than those with a small backyard and close neighbors (unless your neighbors are extremely understanding!).

The position of the aviary will depend on the climate. If you live in a temperate region with cold winters, it is best to place the aviary against a south-facing wall (of course, in the southern hemisphere, the opposite will prevail) to protect the inmates against the bitter northerly and north-easterly winds. In such areas, a strong draft-and-damp-proof shelter will also have to be constructed. Those who are lucky enough to live in sub-tropical or tropical climates have a greater range of possibilities with their aviary siting, but provision should be made to protect it from strong winds, rainstorms, and excessive sunlight. Protective screens can be installed by using timber windbreaks or by planting the area with suitable hedging. With a little careful and artistic planning, it is possible to create an extremely attractive aviary area. For ambitious enthusiasts who have the space and finances to breed several species or have several breeding pairs of a particular species, the first aviary should be so constructed that further aviaries can be added as required.

If you allow your cockatoo outdoors, it is important that your neighbors not mind the amount of noise that the bird is capable of making. It can be quite deafening and bothersome.

Sulphur Crested Cockatoo, *Cacatua galerita galerita*. Cockatoos are notorious wood chewers. A playpen made of PVC piping would last longer than one made of wood.

It is best to select a flat area for your aviary or, if this is not available, level off an area of an appropriate size. Unless your aviary is going to be very large (the larger the better for breeding cockatoos) it is best to arrange for the floor to be solid concrete or stone slabs. Although grass looks attractive, it harbors parasites and, in addition, the birds will soon uproot it all. This, coupled with a few downpours of rain, will convert your beautifully grassed enclosure into a muddy quagmire in a short space of time!

Rather than have your aviary frame directly in contact with the ground (causing wood rotting or metal corrosion through dampness, and easy access for vermin), it is advisable to mount it on a low concrete-block or brick wall. Aviary panels in metal or wood can be purchased ready made or you can make your own. Metal panels can be made from steel pipe, angle iron or angle aluminum. The frames can be drilled and bolted together and the aviary wire may be welded or attached with metal strips and bolts. All metal should be treated with a good quality rust or

corrosion inhibitor, primed, and painted (preferably a dark color to reduce glare). Timber frameworks are more attractive but must be protected on the inside or the birds will make short work of them. It is best to use 75 x 75 mm (3 x 3 in) timber for corner posts and 75 x 50 mm (3 x 2 in) timber for the intermediate framework. The aviary wire mesh should be attached to the *inside* of the framework and covering the timber. Drilled metal strips are then screwed to the inside of the framework, covering the mesh and protecting the wood.

The minimum sized aviary for a pair of cockatoos should be 3 m (10 ft) long by 1.5 m (5 ft) wide by 2 m (6.5 ft) high. In addition, an enclosed shelter (in cold climates) or a partially covered area (in warmer climates) should be at least 1.5 m square and 2 m high (5 x 5 x 6.5 ft).

Having decided on the size of your aviary (and ascertained the size of panels if you are purchasing them), mark out the area and dig a trench around the aviary (and shelter) perimeter, ensuring that the exact perimeter line is in the center of the trench. A trench 30 cm wide and 25 cm (12 x 10 in) deep should be adequate. Estimate levels by banging wooden pegs into the base of the trench and, using a spirit level and a straight edge, ensure that the tops of all pegs are at the same level. Fill in the trench with concrete (made from 1 part cement, 2 parts builders' sand, and 4 parts clean gravel), and stamp it down to the level of the tops of the pegs. This will give you a constant level of concrete foundation all around. Allow 24 hours for the concrete to set before building your brick wall cemented together with mortar (1 part cement to 4 parts builders' sand). This can be built around the whole of the enclosure (flight and shelter) to a height of 3 cm (12 in). Long bolts or steel lugs can be cemented into the joints at the top of the wall, to which your framework will be attached later. After building the wall, small aviaries can have a layer of hard core placed and rammed on the floor, before covering with a 5 cm (2 in) layer of concrete. Be sure that you leave a drainage hole in one corner and slope the floor gently towards this. The floor of the shelter part can be raised so that it is level with the top of the wall and

Opposite: The pastel beauty of the Major Mitchell's Cockatoo, also known as the Leadbeater Cockatoo, *Cacatua leadbeateri*, is breathtaking, and the coloring of the crest feathers is unlike that of any other Cockatoo species.

The red band on the tail feathers of the Red-tailed Black Cockatoo, *Calyptor-hynchus magnificus*, is present only in the male which is predominantly black in color.

a sheet of polyethylene or other damp proofing material placed under it. This will ensure permanent dryness once the shelter is built.

After all the cement and concrete has thoroughly set, the framework for the shelter can be bolted onto the wall. The shelter may be clad with tongue-and-groove boarding, ship-lap, weather board, or other treated durable material. Adequate windows should be provided as birds do not like entering dark areas (other than nest boxes) during the day. The roof should overhang the structure and preferably slope away from the aviary. It is best to install a gutter and drain pipe to carry rainwater away from the roof. The roof itself should be covered with a suitable roofing material, ranging from bituminous felt to roof tiles, depending on how ambitious you are and how much you can afford. If transparent, synthetic roofing materials are used, care should be taken to install extra ventilation facilities within the shelter, as oven-like conditions can prevail in hot weather.

Next, the aviary wall panels should be bolted to the walls of the flight and finally, the roof panels are added. Galvinized weldmesh is probably the best type of material to use on the flight. A strong gauge 2.5 cm (1 in) mesh is ideal (if you are likely to have trouble with mice, it is better to use 12 mm (0.5 in) mesh). If you have a large aviary and shelter, it is best to have the entry door via the shelter. This way the shelter doubles as a safety porch to prevent the escape of nervous birds. Otherwise, a separate safety porch will have to be built outside the flight. This allows you to enter one door and close it before entering the actual flight door, thus preventing escapes.

Finishing-off procedures include lining the shelter with plywood or hardboard and ensuring that there are no parts sticking out where the birds can start gnawing with their beaks. They are unable to gain access on a totally flat area, but joints and corners should be covered with aluminum strips. The inside walls can then be painted with a light-colored, nontoxic emulsion paint to enhance available light and to

A Moluccan Cockatoo, *Cacatua moluccensis* will rarely bite, even a wild caught one. They try to ward off danger with their defense mechanisms first; they fluff up, clack their beak, hiss, and stomp their foot.

The Umbrella Cockatoo, *Cacatua alba*, is a very gentle bird and is among the easiest of all cockatoos to tame.

facilitate the cleaning procedure. If enough space is available, it is best to enlarge the size of the shelter, incorporating a service corridor. This way, you can enter the shelter and inspect your birds through the wire of their indoor flight without disturbing them; you will have room for storing food and equipment, etc., and somewhere dry to work during inclement weather. If you intend to build a battery of aviaries, the shelters may be attached

and the service corridor can run along the width of them. If windows are installed in areas to be occupied by birds, they must be protected with mesh frames on the inside, to prevent birds flying into the glass and injuring themselves, and also to allow the windows to be opened in hot weather for extra ventilation.

The birds will enter and leave the shelter to the outdoor flight by means of a pophole. For most cockatoo species, the pophole should not be less than 30 x 30 cm (12 x 12 in). The pophole should be situated fairly high up on the wall of the shelter and a shelf should be fitted at its base to allow birds to land and take off as they use it. A sliding door (useful if birds are to be caught up or separated for any reason) should be fitted into grooves along the sides of the pophole and this can be operated by a chain from outside the aviary, somewhat in the manner of a portcullis. If the sliding door is made from a heavy piece of sheet metal, it is most unlikely to jam in the runner. Alternatively, the door to the pophole can run horizontally across the opening and be operated with a rod through the aviary wire. When opening and closing such doors, great care should be taken to ensure birds are not caught in the mechanism. Some fanciers like to shut their birds in the shelter at night. While this is not a bad idea for the cold winter nights, it is not recommended during the breeding season as the birds will be disturbed, and they will usually want to start foraging about in the flight at dawn. If you have a battery of attached aviaries,

The Citron Cockatoo, *C.s. citrinocristata*, is slightly larger than the Lesser Sulphur-crested Cockatoo. They are not as readily available as the Lesser, but are very close in personality comparison.

it can be useful to have additional controlable popholes leading from one flight or shelter to the next. This will facilitate moving or catching up birds when this is necessary.

HEATING AND LIGHTING

Although most cockatoo species are extremely hardy and theoretically will survive even the coldest of winters, provided they have an adequate diet and dry, damp-proof accommodation, it is advisable to provide them with enough heat in their shelter to ensure a frost-free environment. Small, inexpensive, electric tubular heaters are ideal. Your avicultural supplier will be able to advise you on the best system to use for your situation. Control of temperature with a thermostat will help keep electric bills down.

Lighting is a different matter and the very short winter days in some of the colder climates will give the birds insufficient time to take their full quota of food before darkness sets in. When breeding, in particular, the birds should have at least 12 hours of light per day in which they can perform the essential duties in rearing their young. In most shelters, a single fluorescent tube, preferably of the "daylight" type, can be used in the mornings and in the evenings to artificially extend the hours of daylight. With a little expense one could install a system of automatic time switches and dimmers which will provide an almost natural, automatic system of lighting, including "dawn" and "dusk."

AVIARY DECORATIONS

Due to the unfortunate destructive habits of cockatoos, it is almost impossible to have an attractively decorated and planted aviary as one can have with finches or softbills. All plants would be destroyed almost immediately and the birds soon dig up any turf on the aviary floor. Instead of decorating a cockatoo aviary, one should turn more to neatness and cleanliness. The advantages of a solid concrete floor have already been discussed and a couple of heavy rocks can be added for decorative purposes. In addition, adequate natural perches should be provided in the form of natural branches from nonpoisonous trees and shrubs. These will soon be whittled away by the birds, but they can be

Opposite: The Goffin's Cockatoo, *Cacatua goffini*, is one of the more inexpensive species of cockatoos and is quite a good talker with an excellent personality.

replaced easily and (usually) cost free. Beware of poisonous trees such as laburnam, yew, or oleander. If unsure about the qualities of a certain tree, don't use it, and to be on the safe side, use branches of fruit trees, or those of oak or beech. Bizarre shaped branches can be arranged attractively in the aviary but must be securely affixed to prevent the possibility of their falling down and injuring the birds. Bark, leaves, and buds may be left on but it is advisable to scrub the trunk and hose it down with clean water to remove

Umbrella Cockatoo, *Cacatua alba*. In comparison to other parrots, cockatoos breed well in captivity.

The beak of the Lesser Sulphur-crested Cockatoo, *Cacatua sulphurea*, is actually larger than that of the Greater Sulphur-crested which is a much larger bird!

any hazardous pollutants (wild bird droppings, insecticides, etc.) before using it in the aviary.

Instead of a plain water dish, a specially constructed pond, perhaps surrounded with rocks and clean shingle, can provide an attractive focal point in an otherwise bare aviary. It is easy to construct such a pond by cementing a number of natural rocks together and to the concrete floor in a three-quarter circle. A sheet of waterproof plastic is then placed flat in the center of the circle, with the edges coming part of the way up the rocks. A large dollop of (not too wet) cement mortar is then placed on the plastic and worked outwards with a trowel until a basin-like structure has been formed in the rocks and the plastic is totally covered with cement. At the side where there are no rocks (usually at the front) the cement is simply made into a low lip to retain the water. When the cement is partially set, it can be smoothed over with a soft handbrush to remove all the imperfections left by the trowel. The depth of the water should not be greater than 7.5 cm (3 in) in case of accidents. Although cockatoos do not bathe very often (they prefer to allow their plumage to be wetted by rain), they will use the pond for drinking water. The water should be changed daily by sweeping it out over the cement lip with a stiff broom. A high powered hose will clean the pond, the rocks, and aviary floor at regular intervals. In cold winters, it is best to empty or cover the pond and supply water in a more conventional container in case an over enthusiastic bird wets its plumage and gives itself hypothermia when it returns to the cold wind. The pond should, of course, be sited in an open part of the aviary and not under a perch where it would soon become fouled with droppings.

AVIARY MAINTENANCE

All timber used in aviary construction should receive a good coating of wood preservative, paying particular attention to those parts which will be generally inaccessible once the aviary is built (inside joints and the bottoms of frames, inside the wall cavity of the shelter, etc.). This will not only protect against wet or dry rot, but also against termites (white ants) or other wood borers. It is possible to purchase wood preservatives in various colors which, once dry, are relatively inoffensive to birds. These compounds are more attractive on timber than paint as they enhance, rather than hide the grain of the timber and are less stark in appearance. A new timber aviary should be given a good coat of preservative at the outset and should not require maintenance for at least two years. When applying wood preservative to aviaries, you should not introduce or reintroduce your birds until the fluid is completely dried out. The birds can be removed to cages or to a spare aviary for the duration of the maintenance.

All metal used in aviary construction should preferably be resistant to corrosion (aluminum or treated galvanized steel, rust inhibitor, etc.). In addition, corrodible metals

should receive a regular coat of good quality enamel type paint (nontoxic). Always be sure that there are no sharp or jagged edges of metal or wire on which the birds could injure themselves.

In addition to daily feeding, cleaning and inspection, a thorough cleaning of the flight and shelter should be made once per week (except during breeding, when it may be advisable to forgo major cleaning until the young are safely reared). All sand, droppings, and other mess should be cleaned off the floor and walls; perches should be scrubbed and wiped down with soapy water. At 12-month intervals, the shelter should be more thoroughly cleaned out and washed down with a solution of bleach in warm water, followed by a thorough rinse with clean water. The bleach will kill off any germs or parasites which are lurking in the cracks and crevices. When the walls have dried, a new coat of emulsion paint may be applied if necessary. Ventilate thoroughly and be certain that everything has dried out before the birds are allowed back into the shelter. It is best to do such work on a warm day, outside the breeding season.

One problem which frequently occurs in indoor flights and birdrooms is a continual build-up of dust consisting of fine particles of the food, sand, droppings, and feathers. If this dust is allowed to build up, it can have a detrimental effect on the birds as it is stirred up every time they fly and then remains lingering in the air. Unchecked, it can cause asthma and other respiratory problems (sometimes to the keeper as well as the birds). A moderately recent innovation in aviculture is the negative air ionizer which effectively kills off airborne organisms and causes dust to settle quickly. Working by electricity, an ionizer is inexpensive to buy, cheap to run, and a definite advantage to both the birds and their keeper due to a vastly improved environment. Your avicultural supplier will be pleased to advise you on the merits of an ionizer.

Opposite: The Umbrella Cockatoo, *Cacatua alba*, is a completely white bird except for a yellow suffusion under the wing and tail feathers.

Feeding

Being largely herbivorous, cockatoos are not difficult to feed. Providing they are given a balanced diet and are kept in hygienic conditions your birds should thrive. One may ask, what exactly is a balanced diet? All kinds of animals specialize in eating a certain selection of foods; there are carnivores, omnivores, and herbivores; there are those which subsist mainly on fish and others that live mainly on grass. In order to remain healthy, all animals, whatever they mainly eat, must have in their diet all of the basic dietary constituents of proteins, carbohydrates, fats, vitamins, mineral salts and the ever-important water. An infinite variety of invertebrates, fishes, amphibians, reptiles, birds, and mammals all require a steady supply of these basic dietary constituents if they are to remain successful as individual species and they have to get them from somewhere. In fact, if you think about it, there is not a single living organism which does not need other organisms for food. Many animals have become specialized in the way they seek a sufficient variety of food to provide them with a balanced diet. Consider the vast number of differently shaped avian bills, each of which has evolved to exploit a particular range of food items. As indicated earlier, the powerful, hooked beak of the cockatoo is fashioned to crack seeds and nuts, to strip bark, and to dig up roots and tubers. With a combination of its practical beak and sensitive tongue, the cockatoo is able to remove the nutritious kernels from seeds and to discard the husks. By gathering a variety of foods, the wild cockatoo is able to ensure that it receives a balanced diet. Let us now take a brief look at the basic dietary constituents and discuss their individual merits.

PROTEINS

These consist of chains of amino acids and are essential for the structure and function of all living organisms. Individual protein types may consist of just a few or many different amino acids, each forming structural substances such as albumins, globulins, and protamines, all of which are

Opposite: At a very young age, the Lesser Sulphur-crested Cockatoo, *Cacatua sulphurea*, has a generally white plumage color.

Although they have a very sharp point at the end of their beak, the Black Palm Cockatoos, *Prosciger aterrimus*, are very gentle, and generally do not bite.

basic building ingredients of the living cells. Proteins are not only concerned with the growth, repair, and replacement of body tissues; particular kinds of proteins are responsible for various metabolic functions and these include enzymes, antibodies, and hormones. Proteins are important for efficient digestion; without them the system would be unable to convert ingested foods into the essential dietary constituents. The main source of protein for cockatoos are the various seeds which are fed to them.

CARBOHYDRATES

These can be divided into two main groups: the water soluble sugars (monosaccharides and disaccharides) and the insoluble starches (polysaccharides), all of which are important in producing energy and thus body heat. The greater part of a cockatoo's diet should consist of carbohydrates which are found in almost every item of food offered to them.

FATS

These help to keep the body warm and act as a

food reserve should times become difficult (i.e., during a long period of drought) or should extra energy be required at particular times (i.e., during the breeding season). Fats may be ingested directly from oils contained in the seeds, or excess carbohydrates may be converted into them. Fat cells are stored in the subcutaneous tissue and act as an insulator against heat loss and may act as shock absorbing tissue. Excessive aggregations of fat cells lead to obesity and its attendant problems, so a certain amount of care should be taken in the selection of seeds given to the birds.

VITAMINS

While proteins, carbohydrates, and fats are required in large amounts in the diet and are thus known as *macronutrients*, vitamins and minerals are required in minute quantities and are thus known as *micronutrients*. In spite of the small quantities required, one must not underestimate the importance of the micronutrients. Vitamin A helps fight diseases, particularly those of the respiratory tract. The vitamin B-complex promotes healthy growth,

assists in the function of the nervous system and enhances the condition of the plumage, as well as increases the efficiency of the digestive system. Vitamin C is regarded as being unnecessary to birds. Vitamin D is important to the growth and repair of bone and the lack of it can lead to rickets in young birds. Vitamin E is important for muscular coordination and a lack of it in a gravid hen will lead to abnormal development of the embryos. With the exception of vitamin D all of the essential vitamins are contained in a variety of good quality seeds and grains which are fed to cockatoos. Vitamin D is produced in the body but cannot be produced unless

The soft mixture of pastel pink and gray coloring of the Rose-breasted Cockatoo, *Eolophus roseicapillus*, is most appealing and makes this species one of the most desirable of all.

The Greater Sulphur-crested Cockatoo, *Cacatua galerita galerita*, is one of the highest priced species of white cockatoos. The light blue eye ring and bright yellow crest, contrast so beautifully with the immaculate white plumage that it is truly a very desirable bird.

the skin or plumage receives a certain amount of ultraviolet radiation contained in natural sunlight. It is therefore important that birds be allowed to receive as much natural sunlight as possible.

MINERALS

The inorganic elements, in the form of mineral salts, perform a wide variety of functions within the body. Some appear to act in a similar manner to vitamins, as enzyme activators, while others have more basic structural or physical functions. Most of the essential elements are contained in sufficient quantities in the normal food. Calcium and phosphorus however, in conjunction with vitamin D, are important in bone formation, the prevention of rickets and, in particular, the formation of healthy egg shells in the gravid hen. As calcium and phosphorus are not normally contained in sufficient quantities in organic foodstuffs, wild birds supplement their diet with calcareous grit. Our captive birds must be provided with these minerals in supplementary form. as there is no way of telling exactly the micronutrient content of individual foodstuffs (without expensive bio-chemical analysis). It is advisable to give your birds a proprietary vitamin/ mineral supplement in case certain essential constituents are contained in insufficient quantities. Supplements are available in fluid or powder form and the former may be dissolved in the drinking water while the latter (probably better) is mixed into the food in very small quantities. Your avicultural supplier will be able to advise you of the type of vitamin/mineral substances available and their particular merits. Quantities should be administered as recommended on the manufacturer's instructions. It is not easy to give an overdose of vitamins or minerals but one should work in "drops" or "pinches" rather than in larger quantities.

As mentioned above, the most important minerals are probably calcium and phosphorus. Phosphorus is contained in grit, mineral supplements, or mineral blocks; calcium can be found in cuttlefish bone. This is one of the finest sources of calcium for birds and may be given crushed or, preferably, in a solid piece; one can purchase a special holder for cuttlefish bone which can be clipped to the wire of the cage or aviary.

Cuttlefish bone may be obtained from your petshop or, if you are lucky enough to live near the seashore, you may be able to collect your own. In the latter case, the bone should be scrubbed, soaked in clear, running water for about 24 hours and then dried out before being given to the birds. This removes pollutants and excessive sea-salt.

WATER

Although it may seem obvious that cockatoos require clean, fresh water at all times, a few words about this essential commodity will not go amiss. It is said that water forms more than 90% of the bulk of all living organisms and, if you were able to remove all of the water from your cockatoo for example (not suggesting, of course, that one should try it!), you would be left with a little pile of dust. Without water, all of the other ingredients of a balanced diet would be useless. Water forms the greater part of the blood which transports nutrients in solution around the body; it is required to keep the internal organs lubricated, and it acts as a cooling agent when hot conditions prevail.

Tap water, rainwater, or well water should be quite all right for your birds. If it is safe for us to drink it, it will be safe for the birds. In the cage, water is offered in small open containers, preferably of galvanized or stainless steel. The container is usually clipped onto the wire to prevent the bird from overturning it. In the aviary, a heavy drinking font or a small concrete pond may be provided. Drinking fonts

Your cockatoo's health is directly related to the diet it receives. For optimum health, fresh water and a variety of foods should be supplied on a daily basis.

Goffin's Cockatoo, *Cacatua goffini*, does not sport a very large crest as most of the other cockatoo species do. Its crest only stands about ¾ inch off of its head when erected.

may be of metal or a combination of glass and metal and they operate on a siphon system. The advantage of a drinking font is that it will hold a fair amount of water and have a relatively small drinking aperture (which keeps the water clean longer than in a more convenitonal container). Open water containers must be cleaned and replenished with fresh water at least once per day. Water fonts must have the water changed daily and the interior should be scrubbed out with a brush at least once per week. Remember that polluted water is a potential health hazard and can often be blamed for enteric infections.

SEED FOR YOUR COCKATOO

Seeds form the major part of the pet cockatoo's diet. Most cockatoo species are relatively easy to feed in captivity and should thrive, providing you give them suitable variety plus supplements. Most pet

shops sell "parrot mixtures" consisting of various seeds, usually approximately equal parts of wheat, sunflower seed, sorghum, and maize, with lesser quantities of barley, oats, canary seed, and millet. Such a variety of seeds is adequate as a staple diet providing vitamin/mineral supplements and additional fruit/vegetables are given.

If you keep a number of cockatoos, it is more economical to buy your seeds separately, in bulk. Pet shops are wonderful sources for this type of purchase. However, this would be impractical for the owner of a single pet bird, and a pre-mixed parrot food will be better to purchase. If you buy your seed in bulk, mixtures can be made up as necessary. One advantage is that mixtures can be varied depending on the time of the year. During the breeding season and the molting period, for example, oil and protein-rich seeds can be increased and carbohydrate-rich seeds reduced.

The following mixtures will be found suitable for most of the more common cockatoo species:

Normal seed mixture to be given most of the year:

20% Wheat
20% Sunflower Seed
20% Sorghum
15% Maize
15% Barley
5% Oats
2% Millet
2% Canary Seed
1% Hemp

Seed mixture during breeding and molting period:

12% Wheat
25% Sunflower Seed
15% Sorghum
15% Maize
15% Barley
10% Oats
2% Millet
2% Canary Seed
4% Hemp

Sunflower seeds contain a high proportion of oil and should not be fed in greater quantities than those shown above as too much can lead to obesity. Sunflower seeds are grown commercially for oil production used in such commodities as margarine and cooking oil. However, they are also rich in protein and in sensible quantities an excellent food for cockatoos. Sunflower seeds come in various strains, including white, striped and black. The white variety is preferable as it has a relatively low fat content and has a proportionately higher protein content.

In recent years, pine

Opposite: The Leadbeater Cockatoo, *Cacatua leadbeateri*, does not make a good pet unless it is obtained when it is extremely young or hand-raised.

nuts have become a popular food for cockatoos and they are available from specialist suppliers in most countries. They are as good as, if not better nutritionally than, sunflower seeds and can be supplied occasionally instead of sunflower seeds because they are rather expensive. It is best not to supply them all of the time. They are more natural than sunflower seeds and will be eaten greedily by most species of cockatoo. Peanuts are also a popular food to some birds but may be ignored by others. Peanuts are also high in oil content and should be given sparingly, perhaps four or five per day, a few more for breeding birds. Other kinds of nuts, including walnuts, brazils, almonds, hazel-nuts, macadamias, etc., can be given sparingly as special treats.

FEED CONTAINERS

Dry seed mixtures are best placed in special, clip-on food containers and, in the case of cages, these are usually supplied complete with a means of holding them securely. In the aviary, it is best to use relatively large and heavy dishes of metal or earthenware. They should be of such a weight that the birds cannot pick them up and throw them about or a lot of seed will be wasted. Alternatively, smaller dishes can be used which are attached to the aviary wire near the end of perches. Food dishes are best placed off the ground and under some sort of cover. A large, vertical tree stump, cut off level at the top, makes a good, solid stand for a food container. Small seeds, such as millet and canary are best given separately in smaller dishes; otherwise they will be lost in the bulk of the larger seeds. As cockatoos remove the husks from the seeds before they eat the kernels, many of the husks will fall back into the food container and eventually cover the untouched seed. Some birds, particularly new, or nervous ones, will then be unable to find the whole seed and will go hungry. It is important to make certain that the husks are removed from the surface at regular intervals. By blowing across the top of the seed, you will scatter most of the light husks from the container. Inspect the seed containers twice each day, removing husks and replacing seed as necessary.

The Gang-gang Cockatoo, *Callocephalon fimbriatum*, is one of the most sought after species of cockatoos due to its unusual appearance, beautiful colors, and terrific personality.

A distinguishing feature of the Triton Cockatoo, *Cacatua galerita triton*, is large, scallop-shaped feathers throughout its body.

SOAKED SEED

In the wild, cockatoos do not necessarily eat ripe, dry seeds all of the time; a large part of their diet must consist of unripe seeds or those which have fallen to the ground and begun to germinate. For a change (especially during the breeding season or during the molt), your birds can be given seed which has been soaked in water. Prepare only enough seed which can be used immediately, as it quickly sours and could cause upsets to the birds' digestive systems. Take a quantity of your usual seed mixture, place it in a container and add cold water until the seeds are waterlogged. Place the container in a warm place and leave it to stand for about 24 hours; then rinse it thoroughly under a running tap (preferably through a strainer) and shake out the excess moisture. Further moisture can be removed by wrapping it in absorbent paper towels for a few minutes. The soaked seed is then placed in a separate dish and given to the birds. Not only do most birds love this change, it is also extremely good for them. As the seed is soaking, the various processes which cause it to germinate will begin. During germination the biochemical composition of the seed changes; the protein content increases and the levels of the B-complex vitamins rise, a useful addition to the diet, especially during breeding. When cockatoos are rearing young, soaked seed is more quickly partially digested and more nutritious to the young when they are fed by regurgitation. Soaked seed should never be left in the cage or aviary for more than a few hours; if given in the morning, any uneaten seed should be removed in the evening and discarded; a fresh supply can then be made for next time.

White-tailed Black Cockatoo, *C.f. baudinii.* It is amazing to note the contrast in popularity between the white and black cockatoos. White cockatoos are in much greater demand among would-be pet owners.

GREENFOOD

In addition to seeds, various greenfood, fresh vegetables and fruit should be supplied in conservative quantities at regular intervals. Greenfood is a valuable source of vitamin A, as well as significant amounts of vitamins B1 and B2. Spinach is particularly high in these vitamins and should be given when available. Some wild-growing "weeds" and seeding grasses can also be offered in season. Dandelions (including the flowers and the roots), chickweed, shepherd's purse, groundsel, thistle heads, and plantains are all useful items. The type of wild foods available will of course vary depending on the area in which you live. It is wise to visit other aviculturists in the vicinity and see what wild foods are being offered. Even food generally collected for poultry or rabbits may be

Opposite: Red-vented Cockatoo, *Cacatua haematuropygia*. The beauty of these birds lies in their impeccably neat and clean looking plumage. Because of the way their feathers are kept, the red around the vent contrasts so well that it looks impeccable.

useful to try on your cockatoos. One word of warning however, when collecting wild food, be sure that it is not polluted with traffic fumes, insecticides, herbicides, or the droppings of domestic or wild animals. All such foods should be given fresh, and removed when they start to wilt.

Various items from the vegetable garden can be tried; fresh peas (and the pods) can be given and some cockatoos will like to nibble at cabbage, cauliflower, broccoli or brussels sprouts. Lettuce is usually taken readily, but this does not have a very high nutritional value. Small pieces of raw root vegetables such as kohlrabi, turnip, parsnip, and carrot can be given occasionally. Carrot in particular is a valuable food, high in fiber and vitamin A.

Berries and fruits of various kinds can be given in season. Blackberries, black and red currants, and grapes can be given as tidbits, while a slice of apple or pear may not go amiss. Some birds are fond of more tropical fruits such as mangoes, bananas, and figs. Dried fruits such as raisins, and dates may also be tried. Not all birds will eat everything you offer,

but there is no harm in experimenting.

ADDITIONAL FOODS

Although pet cockatoos will do very well on the range of the foodstuffs already described, they will soon learn to eat many other items which we also eat. They will enjoy receiving an occasional treat, and you will enjoy giving it to them. However, bear in mind that a treat is a treat only, and remember that too much of what we like is almost always bad for us; this applies to our pets too. When giving them treats, make sure it is in sensible quantities. Cockatoos usually enjoy sweet things like various confections and sweet meats, cakes, and cookies. They may like to try jam or cream cheese on bread or toast. They may eat boiled potato, boiled rice, or rice pudding. It does no harm to give these items and others you may want to experiment with in small, occasional quantities. An item which a bird is particularly fond may be used in training it to do tricks or to talk.

GRIT

All birds require grit to aid digestion and to provide extra valuable trace elements to the diet. As

cockatoos devour many hard seeds, grit is especially important to them. In the wild, the birds swallow small stones, pieces of shell, etc., and these sit in the birds' gizzards. The gizzard is an efficient grinding machine with muscular walls which push a mixture of grit and food about, thus reducing the food to a fine mush which then passes on into the gut for further digestion. Some kinds of grit are partially soluble and will eventually dissolve, provided the bird is receiving valuable minerals in its diet. Other kinds of grit may not be soluble, but even these will eventually be ground away by the action of the gizzard,

so a fresh supply of grit must always be provided.

Grit may consist of crushed stones, fine shingle, crushed sea shells, etc. It is best to purchase commercially prepared bird grit which often contains additional minerals, but there is no harm in collecting shells from the beach, washing them thoroughly and then pounding them into a suitable size. Eggshells are also useful to mix in with the grit; these can be baked in the oven until they are brittle (but not burnt) and then crushed. Grit may be offered in a container, or simply sprinkled on the floor of the cage.

PELLET FOOD

In recent years, various companies have developed pelleted food consisting of crushed grain, grass meal, fish meal, etc., plus additional supplements. Theoretically, these pellets contain all that is required for a balanced diet and, other than water, are all the birds require to keep them fit and healthy. However, such a diet can be boring and monotonous to a pet bird so it is suggested that, if pellets are used, they be given only two or three times per week, with a more varied diet on other days.

Most birds, including cockatoos, relish millet spray, but it should only be used as a treat, not as a primary source of nutrition.

The Pet Cockatoo

By far, the largest number of cockatoos kept in captivity are household pets. Most species are suitable as pets and, providing they are given the necessary care and attention, will soon become tame, trusting, and highly entertaining. Cockatoos are very intelligent when compared with other birds, and some species can be taught to perform simple tricks and to repeat words. Compared with a dog or a cat, a cockatoo is cheaper and easier to maintain in a confined space, so is more suitable for a small apartment (however, do not forget to take the noise factor into consideration). If a cockatoo is to be left on its own for long periods each day, it should not be purchased. They are gregarious creatures by nature, and in view of their intelligence, are likely to become bored or will pine under such conditions. This often results in unpleasant vices like feather-plucking. A cockatoo should be regarded as a companion that requires a great deal of attention.

SELECTION OF A PET COCKATOO

In selecting a pet cockatoo, a factor even more important than the species is that you find a bird that is very young. An even better pet is one that has been hand-reared; such birds have no fear of humans and are the best subjects for taming and training. However, even some older birds will settle and become tame if treated gently and kindly. In some countries where wild cockatoos live, young birds are collected from nests when just about half grown, then hand-reared before being exported to petshops throughout the world. Although relatively expensive, hand-reared birds are, without doubt, the best bet for somebody seeking a cockatoo which ideally will develop into a cherished, entertaining, tame, and talking individual. In view of the fact that cockatoos are extremely long-lived, it is much more satisfactory to wait for a suitable bird of known age, rather than

The Greater Sulphur-crested Cockatoo, *Cacatua galerita*, has a very elegant appearance even when its crest is not extended.

buying the first one that is seen, however strong the temptation.

SETTLING IN AND TAMING

Having acquired a young cockatoo, it should be placed in its cage and left quietly to settle into its new environment. If possible, the food offered should be similar to what was provided at its previous home. It is important, in these early stages, to disturb the bird as little as possible. Do not startle it with sudden movements; do not allow children to poke and scream at it; keep other pets away from it; and do not invite all your friends and neighbors in to admire it until it is thoroughly settled. Be mindful that the bird is feeding properly; difficulties may sometimes occur with birds which have been hand-reared and have not been thoroughly weaned. In such cases, it may be necessary to continue to hand-rear it for a time.

There are no hard and fast techniques for taming a cockatoo except that the process should be carried out with patience, love, and kindness. Shock tactics will only make a bird more nervous. In the first instance, the pet can be encouraged to take tidbits in the form of fruit or nuts, through the bars of the cage. The young bird may refuse them at first, but with patience, it should soon start to take such offerings. The next step is to offer it tidbits inside the cage. Although cockatoos can give a nasty bite with their powerful beaks, they rarely do so unless actually being physically restrained. Most cockatoos hate being picked up and you must train the bird to sit on your arm or shoulder of its own accord.

After the bird is satisfactorily taking tidbits from the hand, you may attempt to stroke it. Slow, deliberate movements will help to overcome the bird's nervousness, and on no account should the hand be pulled away rapidly. You can gently scratch the breast with the finger, pushing gently through the feathers as if preening (as cockatoos preen each other naturally). If the bird remains distressed or nervous, do not continue but wait until the next day to repeat the procedure. After a few days the bird will begin to realize that you do not intend it any harm and will allow you to scratch it on most parts of its body, even raising its wings or crest so that you can scratch it on the sides or top of its head.

Most cockatoo cages are too small to house a cockatoo on a permanent basis and the bird should be allowed out of its cage for exercise, preferably everyday. It is a good idea to have a "T" perch, in

The variation of coloring among Moluccan Cockatoos, *Cacatua moluccensis*, is due to the diet of the birds and to geographical differences. Variations in size are also, generally due to geographical differences.

addition to the cage. If you have a perch which separates from the stand, you can encourage the bird to climb onto this for removal from its cage.

Otherwise, you can use a pair of thick, leather gloves and encourage the bird to sit on your hand. The gloves are necessary to protect you from bites,

Cockatoos are generally affectionate birds that will provide their owners with a lifetime of companionship if properly cared for.

should you have to restrain the bird.

The gloved hand is stretched slowly along the perch and the bird's feet are first gently stroked. You may have to do this several times until the bird gets used to it. It is gradually encouraged to grip your gloved fingers with its toes by pushing them gently against its lower breast. At first the bird may grip with one foot and then let go again when it realizes what is happening. Eventually it will sit on your hand and you can slowly withdraw your pet from its cage.

It is best for your bird to have the flight feathers of one wing clipped initially, so that it does not fly about in a panic and cause damage to both itself and your furniture. Wing clipping should be carried out by an experienced aviculturist, your supplier, or a veterinarian.

Once out of the cage, the bird can be encouraged to climb onto your shoulder. During these training sessions, talking to the animal in a soft voice will tend to reassure it so that it does not panic. The bird can be placed on a "T" perch, or on the back of a chair. Many birds have a favorite place on which they will sit when let out into a room and will make

straight for this when let out of the cage. The favorite position of the author's Greater Sulphur-crested Cockatoo is on the handlebars of his son's bicycle, although he frequently has to be scolded to prevent him nibbling the plastic off the brake cables.

Cockatoos often seem to enjoy spending time in a certain position and will sit for hours on a chairback or somewhere similar taking a great interest in what the family is doing. To protect your carpet from droppings, you can place a sheet of newspaper under its perch. Eventually your cockatoo will lose all fear of you and will climb onto your arm or shoulder whenever you want. The bird may even come to you when called, especially if you offer a choice tidbit.

When a bird is let out in a room, you must be sure to keep an eye on him at all times. Not only can he be destructive to your furniture, he could endanger himself by nibbling at live electric wires (the TV cable, for example) or eating potentially poisonous house plants or other items. Be sure that all windows and doors are closed to prevent escape, and keep other pets such

Opposite: The Moluccan Cockatoo, *Cacatua moluccensis*, is a natural "show off" and loves to be the center of attention at all times.

The Goffin's Cockatoo, *Cacatua goffini*, is a very docile species of cockatoo. They are capable of much comical mimicry, become extremely tame, and make excellent pets.

as cats and dogs out of the room. The windows are best covered with net curtains, to prevent your bird from attempting to fly through the glass and injuring himself.

TEACHING TO TALK

Most cockatoos are able to learn to repeat words. Some seem more adept than others and it is largely a matter of luck, coupled with the patience of the owner as to how many words and phrases the bird will eventually have in its vocabulary. It is said that male birds make far better mimics than females but this is not always the case and some hen birds develop large vocabularies. In any case, if you obtain a young bird, it is often very difficult to distinguish the sex and many a talking "male" cockatoo has surprised its owner by suddenly laying an egg!

Successfully teaching a cockatoo to talk is largely a matter of repetition. It is best to start with a single word or phrase and wait until the bird is familiar with this before proceeding with the next; otherwise the bird is likely to become

confused and get all his phrases muddled. An ideal word to start with is the bird's name. It is best to choose a fairly short and distinct name such as "Billy" or "Charlie" or "Chico." Many people call a cockatoo "Cocky" but please try and be a little more original! You can already start to teach your bird to talk, even as you are getting it finger tame. Repeat his/her name slowly and distinctly every time you go near the bird; in a week or so he should learn to repeat it. Some birds learn faster than others so do not be disappointed if you do not get immediate results. As soon as he has learned his name, you can start teaching other phrases. Word association is a useful method of getting your cockatoo to say appropriate things. For example, when you draw your curtains at night, say "good night" and when you open the curtains in the morning, repeat the phrase "good morning." The bird should soon learn to reiterate these phrases. A vocabulary gradually can be built up in this way, providing that all of the learned phrases are continually repeated. Some specialist companies have produced cassette tapes designed to teach parrots and cockatoos to talk, but these are usually of little value unless the owner is present to reinforce the lessons being taught.

TEACHING TRICKS

With patience, you can train a cockatoo to perform simple tricks and party pieces. Most people have seen the "circus" cockatoos which ride little bicycles, use miniature roller skates and walk tightropes. One good trick to teach a brid is to pick up objects such as coins and place them in a container. Some birds can be taught to whistle tunes and to "conduct" with one of their feet. Tricks are taught with kindness, patience, and rewards of tidbits; never by force or punishment. A bird which is forced or punished will just become frightened and nervous, and will learn nothing.

A Selection of Species

There are 17 species of cockatoo and some of these are further divided into geographical races or subspecies. The species most often sold as pets include the Greater Sulphur-crested Cockatoo, *Cacatua galerita*, the Lesser Sulphur-crested Cockatoo, *C. sulphurea* and the Moluccan Cockatoo, *C. moluccensis*. Most other cockatoo species are suitable as pets provided young specimens are obtained. Every attempt should be made to breed the rarer species. The following text describes all cockatoo species. Those which are more commonly kept are covered more extensively than others due to the fact that more information on their captive care is essential.

Palm Cockatoo— *Probosciger aterrimus*

Length: 58-68 cm (23-27 in)

Description: The only species in the genus, but several subspecies have been described. General color is black with a steel gray tinge, more pronounced on the much elongated, narrow, and lanceolate crest feathers and on the wing feathers. The bare facial patch is deep red. The elongated upper mandible is black, the lower mandible, slate gray. The legs and feet are blackish, the iris brown. The sexes are similar in appearance but the female may be smaller with a smaller bare facial patch and bill. Juveniles differ from adults in being more dusky black in coloration and the under feathers may be tipped with yellow.

Range: New Guinea, Aru Islands and the extreme tip of Cape York Peninsula in Australia.

Habitat and Habits: A tropical rain forest species which usually roosts singly on the often dead, upper branches of tall trees at the forest edge. The birds assemble in parties of about six in the morning and feed communally. The diet consists of seeds, nuts, fruits, and buds, usually taken from the crowns of trees. Call consists of shrill whistles to harsh screeches.

Captive Care: Due to its rarity, it is usually only seen in zoological

collections. The Black Palm should have a relatively large proportion of fruit and nuts in its diet. It is probably more suitable for breeding attempts in aviaries rather than as a single pet.

Breeding: Has been bred in captivity a few times. Nests in a hollow tree trunk or nest box; sometimes lines nest with splintered twigs. A single egg is laid and incubated for about 34 days by the female. The young fledges in 14-16 weeks.

Red-tailed Black Cockatoo—*Calyptorhynchus magnificus*

Length: 50-61 cm (20-24 in)

Description: There are five species of "black" cockatoos in the genus *Calyptorhynchus*. The male Red-tailed Black Cockatoo is generally black with a greenish gloss. There is a broad band of bright red near the end of the tail feathers, except for the two central tail feathers which are black. The iris is dark brown and the naked skin around the eye dark gray. The bill and the legs and feet are steel gray. The female's plumage is brownish black with yellow speckles on the upperside, and yellow bands on the underside. The tail band is yellow merging into orange.

Juveniles are similar in appearance to the females.

Range: Has a very wide range in the Australian continent. Largest populations in Northern Territory and Queensland. Isolated populations in central, southeastern, and western Australia. Several subspecies have been described.

Habitat and Habits: Found in a range of habitats and is the only species in the genus to occur in the drier, pastoral districts, where it may assemble in flocks of 100 or more. In forested areas, it occurs in smaller family groups. They are highly nomadic and, in some areas, may only be seasonally present. Its main diet is seeds from various species of *Eucalyptus*. The voice consists of a harsh, grating, single note.

A female Red-tailed Black Cockatoo, *Calyptorhynchus magnificus*, attains numerous yellow spots on the head and neck as well as on the crest.

Captive Care: Pairs are suited to a large aviary. Hand-reared males make the best pets and become tame and trusting. Captive specimens have reached an age in excess of 50 years. They do well on the usual cockatoo diet of mixed seeds and supplements.

Breeding: Has been bred in captivity. In the wild, they nest in hollow limbs from 2-30 m (6-95 ft) above the ground. A large nest box is required in captivity. The nest may be lined with wood chips. One, rarely two, white eggs are laid and these are incubated by the female for about four weeks. The young fledge in 10-12 weeks.

White-tailed Black Cockatoo—
Calyptorhynchus baudinii

Length: 55-60 cm (22-24 in)

Description: The male is dusky black, the feathers edged with off-white, giving a scalloped appearance. There are off-white patches on the cheeks. There is a broad, white band near the end of the tail, but the two central tail feathers are all black. The eye is dark brown and the naked skin surrounding the eye is pink. The relatively long, slender bill is steely gray. The legs and feet are dark brown. The female is similar, except that the cheek patches are larger and whiter; the bare skin around the eye is dark gray and the feet are a fleshy-buff color. Immature specimens are similar in appearance to the females, but male youngsters have smaller cheek patches.

Range: Extreme southwestern Australia.

Habitat and Habits: During the breeding season, it remains in the thickly wooded ranges of Jarrah (*Eucalyptus marginata*) and Karri (*Eucalyptus diversicolor*) in the extreme southwest of Western Australia. Outside the breeding season it forages more widely

northwards and eastwards as far as the Darling and Stirling ranges. The staple diet appears to be the seeds of the marri (*Eucalyptus calophylla*) but it will also take a wide range of other seeds and vegetation as well as various insect food (particularly the grubs of wood-boring insects). The voice consists of various whistles and screeches.

Captive Care: Rarely available as a pet; perhaps more suitable for the breeding aviary. Will feed on a range of seeds and nuts, etc. May take mealworms and high protein, softbill food.

Breeding: In the wild, it nests in a large hollow high up in a Karri or Jarrah tree. The female enters the nest hole tail first. The nest floor may be lined with chips of wood from the sides of the nest hollow. Usually two, white eggs are laid and these are incubated by the female for about four weeks. The young leave the nest at about 10 weeks.

Yellow-tailed Black Cockatoo—*Calyptorhynchus funereus*

Length: 55-65 cm (22-26 in)

Description: The male's body plumage is dusky black; the feathers are edged with yellow, giving a scalloped effect. There is a small yellow cheek patch

and a broad, brown speckled, yellow band near the end of the tail. The two central tail feathers are black. The eye is dark brown and the bare eye-ring is pink. The bill is dark gray, the feet gray-brown. The female is similar to the male but the cheek patch is larger and brighter yellow; the bare eye-ring is gray and the feet are buff-colored. Immature birds are similar to hens but young males have a smaller, duller colored cheek patch.

Range: Tasmania and coastal ranges of mainland Australia from eastern South Australia to southeastern Queensland.

Habitat and Habits: Occurs mainly in forests and open woodland,

The courtship of the White-tailed Black Cockatoo, *C.f. baudinii*, is simple. The male only raises his crest and spreads his tail to a female, then nesting begins.

Greater Sulphur Crested Cockatoo, *Cacatua galerita*. Cockatoos have such comical personalities and are so intelligent that they are often taught to perform tricks such as riding a bike or roller skating for shows.

including cultivated pine forests. Assembles in large flocks which wander over large areas in search of food. Groups of birds are often seen flying slowly over the trees, uttering their loud wailing cries. Feeds on the seeds of *Eucalyptus* species as well as those of cultivated pines. Some birds will also feed on the larvae of wood-boring insects.

Breeding: They nest in a hollow high up in a tree. Two white eggs are laid and these are incubated by the hen for about four weeks. The young fledge at about 12 weeks. A few instances of captive breeding have been recorded.

Glossy Black Cockatoo—

Calyptorhynchus lathami

Length: 46-50 cm (18-20 in)

Description: The male is dusky brown with the underside of the tail brown-black. There is a broad, bright red band near the end of the tail but the two central feathers are black. The iris is dark brown and the naked eye-ring dark gray. The bill and feet are steely gray. The female is similar to the male but has yellow patches on the head and neck. The red tail marking is washed with yellow and has black barring. Immature specimens are similar to the females.

Range: Coastal forests of eastern Australia.

Moluccan Cockatoo, *Cacatua moluccensis.* All cockatoos enjoy eating a variety of foods. All table food that is good for humans to eat can be fed to cockatoos in addition to their regular diet.

Habitat and Habits: Occurs in the eucalypt forests of eastern Australia, feeding largely on the seeds of the casuarina tree. Unlike other black cockatoos, this species does not appear to assemble in large flocks and spends most of its time in groups of two or three, quietly feeding in the trees. The voice is a relatively soft, drawn out wheezing to a louder alarm call.

Captive Care: This species is notoriously difficult to keep in captivity due to its specialized feeding habits. Its beak is adapted for opening the cones and extracting the seeds of the Casuarina tree and, if not given cones, the beak will soon become overgrown. In Australia, a mixture of Casuarina cones and sunflower seeds has been a successful diet.

Breeding: In the wild, this species usually nests high up in a tree hollow, often in a dead limb. A single, white egg is laid and this is incubated by the female for about 29 days. The young fledge in about 10 weeks. Successful captive breeding is a rare occurrence and presents a challenge.

Long-tailed Black Cockatoo—*Calyptorhynchus latirostris*

Length: 55-60 cm (22-24 in)

Description: The male is dusky black, the feathers edged with off-white giving a scalloped appearance. There is a broad, plain white band near the end of the tail but the two central feathers are black. There is a small patch of dull white on the cheeks. The eyes are dark brown and the bare eye-ring is pink. The bill is dark gray and the feet dark gray-brown. The female is similar to the male but the cheek patch is larger and whiter. The bare eye-ring is dark gray and the feet flesh-buff. Juveniles are similar to the adult female.

Range: Southwestern Australia.

Habitat and Habits: Found chiefly in dry eucalypt woodlands but are sometimes seen foraging in gardens in Perth, Western Australia. Outside the breeding season, the seemingly slow-flying birds make for the coastal plains and assemble in large flocks. They feed on the seeds of various trees and also forage on the ground. The call consists of a drawn out whistle. The alarm call is a harsh screech. This species and *C. baudinii* were originally thought to be two races of the same species and only recently have they been separated.

Captive Care: As described for *C. funereus.*

Breeding: Nests in a hollow limb from 2-20 meters (6-65 ft) above the ground. Two white eggs are laid and incubated by the female for about four weeks. The young fledge in 10-11 weeks. No reports of

For their size, the Rose-breasted Cockatoo, *Eolophus roseicapillus* is a fairly expensive bird, but well worth the money. They have very agreeable personalities and are very quiet when compared to other cockatoo species.

captive breeding have been found.

Gang-gang Cockatoo—
Callocephalon fimbriatum

Length: 36 cm (14 in)

Description: There is only a single species in the genus *Callocephalon*. The male is generally gray with lighter edging to the feathers. On the wings, the feathers are washed with dull green. The head and crest are bright red. The eyes are dark brown. The bill is horn-colored and the feet gray. The female lacks the red on the head, this being replaced with gray. The underside feathers are edged with orange and greenish yellow. Immature specimens are similar to adult females but with the underside of the tail heavily barred with gray or off-white. Young males develop red on the head by one year of age.

Range: From the coast to the higher inland ranges of extreme southeastern Australia.

Habitat and Habits: This species lives in heavily wooded areas feeding on the seeds of native trees and shrubs. It is noted for its remarkable "tameness" in the wild, allowing one to approach almost to touching distance before it becomes alarmed. Outside the breeding

Moluccan Cockatoo, *Cacatua moluccensis*, six weeks old. Cockatoo chicks grow very quickly. In another six weeks this chick will be ready to leave the nest, and will have almost attained full size!

season, birds may assemble in flocks of up to 100, especially where there is a bountiful food supply. The voice is a series of guttural croaks and growls.

Captive Care: The Gang-gang usually thrives well in captivity and will learn to say a few words. It may be fed on the usual seed mixture, only with fruit and berries. It is especially fond of hawthorn berries which can be given when in season.

Breeding: Chooses a nest hole usually high in a tree. The two or three white eggs are incubated by both sexes for about 30 days. The young fledge in about seven weeks and are fed by the parents for a further four to five weeks. The species is occasionally bred in captivity.

The Umbrella Cockatoo, *Cacatua alba*, has the most agreeable and affectionate personality of all the cockatoo species. They most often prefer to cuddle with their owner rather than be rough-housed.

Umbrella Cockatoo— *Cacatua alba*

Length: 45 cm (18 in)

Description: This species is similar in size and form to the Moluccan Cockatoo, *C. moluccensis* but lacks the additional pink coloration. The male is all white, tinged with yellow on the underside of the wings and the tail. The crest is broad and rounded and, when erected, appears somewhat like an umbrella which gives the bird its common name. The naked eye-ring is grayish blue and the bill and legs are black. The iris is black. The female is very similar to the male except that the iris is brown.

Range: The Moluccas and neighboring islands.

Habitat and Habits: Found in woodland and cultivated areas, feeding on a range of seeds, fruits, and greenfood. Can be an agricultural pest in some areas.

Captive Care: Makes a very good pet, becoming extremely tame and trusting. However, its powers of mimicry are not very great and it has a harsh scream. It should be given a fair amount of greenfood in its diet. Natives remove wild chicks

Umbrella Cockatoo, *Cacatua alba*. A characteristic common in all cockatoo species, and present upon hatching, is a bald spot directly behind the crest.

from nests and hand-rear them for export. Such hand-reared chicks are ideal as single pets.

Breeding: This species has been bred in captivity several times. Usually only one, rarely two chicks are reared. Requires a very large hollow log or barrel in which to nest. The two or three eggs are incubated by both sexes for about 26 days and the young leave the nest in about 11 weeks.

Ducorps's Cockatoo—*Cacatua ducorpsii*

Length: 40 cm (16 in)

Description: The male is white with an orange base to the crest. The cheeks, underwings and tail are yellow. The bare eye-ring is blue and the eyes are black. The female is similar to the male but may have a narrower bill.

Range: Solomon Islands and neighboring islands.

Habitat and Habits: Inhabits both woodland and cultivated areas.

Captive Care: This species is very rarely available as a pet, but its care is similar to that of other white cockatoo species.

Breeding: No records of captive breeding have been found.

Greater Sulphur-crested Cockatoo—*Cacatua galerita*

Length: 50 cm (20 in)

Description: Perhaps the best known of all cockatoo species, the Greater Sulphur-crested cockatoo makes an ideal pet. Both sexes are very similar and it is a hard job to distinguish males from females. However, it is said that the female's iris is dark brown as opposed to black; even so, this does not make visual sexing much easier. The basic color is white-washed in greater or lesser areas with yellow. The crest is bright yellow. The undersides of the wings and tail feathers are also yellow. The naked eye-ring is white or bluish; the bill and feet, dark gray.

Range: Northern and eastern Australia, south to Tasmania, New Guinea, New Britain, and Aru Islands. Introduced to Perth area, western Australia.

Habitat and Habits: Widely distributed and common in its range, especially in open, timbered country. Outside the breeding season, it assembles in flocks, ranging from half a dozen to a hundred or more individuals. The birds have a "sentinel warning system"; while the main flock is feeding on the ground, a few birds perch high up on a suitable vantage point, ready to screech a warning, should danger approach, at which the entire flock will take to the air, screeching and wheeling until the danger is past.

Captive Care: Young, hand-reared specimens make the best pets and they become very tame and affectionate, learning to repeat many words and perform simple tricks. Suitable for cage, stand, or aviary, they may be fed on a diet of mixed seed, a little fruit, and greens and other occasional treats.

Breeding: In the wild, this species nests in a hollow, high up in a tree, usually not far from water. In some areas, it is known to nest in cliff holes. Both sexes share in the incubation of the two or three white eggs, which hatch in about 30 days. The chicks leave the nest in about six weeks. The species has been bred fairly frequently in captivity. It requires a large nesting barrel or log, and a spacious, quiet aviary, with little disturbance. During the rearing of the chicks, the birds should be given ample soaked seed and soaked stale bread from which the excess moisture has been squeezed.

Goffin's Cockatoo—
Cacatua goffini

Length: 36 cm (14 in)

Description: Goffin's Cockatoo is sometimes regarded as a subspecies of *C. sanguinea*, in which case it is scientifically described as *C. sanguinea goffini*. It is very similar to *C. sanguinea* except that it is usually smaller in size, lacks the reddish coloration on the forehead, and possesses yellow coloration on the underside of the crest. Sexes are similar.

Range: The Tanimbar Islands of Indonesia.

Habitat and Habits: As described for *C. sanguinea* but inhabits thicker woodland.

Captive Care: As described for *C. sanguinea*.

Breeding: As described for *C. sanguinea*.

Red-vented Cockatoo—*Cacatua haematuropygia*.

Length: 36 cm (14 in).

Description: The male is white with a suffusion of yellow and vermilion. The

The smaller size of the Lesser Sulphur-crested Cockatoo, *Cacatua sulphurea*, is an advantage over the more desirable, but much bigger Greater Sulphur-crested, *Cacatua galerita*. The apartment or condominium dweller will find the Lesser much easier to house than the larger species.

Leadbeater Cockatoo, *Cacatua leadbeateri*. If you are fortunate to have a cockatoo that mimics words, note the sweet innocent voice it possesses — and compare it to the "wild call" that it will occasionally emit.

underside of the tail is bright red. The crest is small and broad. The bare eye-ring is white, the bill and feet grayish blue. The female is similar to the male, but may have a narrower bill.

Range: The Philippines and Palawan.

Captive Care: Very rarely available in the pet trade. Said to be very quiet and docile, lacking the nervousness of some of its relatives.

Breeding: No records of captive breeding are available.

Leadbeater Cockatoo— *Cacatua leadbeateri*

Length: 36 cm (14 in)

Description: This must surely be the most beautiful and attractive of all the cockatoos. The male is light salmon pink with the wings and top of the crest white. The remainder of the crest is bright scarlet, divided with a band of sulphur yellow. The eyes are dark brown, the bill bone-colored and the feet light gray. The female is similar to the male except that the iris is light brown. Immature specimens are similar to the adults excepting the eyes are dull brown.

Range: Distributed sporadically throughout the arid and semi-arid interior of Australia.

Habitat and Habits: Not as common as they used to be, these cockatoos seem less able to adapt to the cultivation of their habitat than other species. They usually occur in pairs or small groups, often in the company of Rose-breasted or Little Corellas. They feed just as much on the ground as in the trees, eating a wide range of seeds, nuts, fruits, and roots. The voice consists of a variety of screeches.

Captive Care: In spite of its attractive coloration, this species is not often

kept as a pet; probably due to its rarity, coupled with the export ban of all Australian native birds and the fact that the species does not so readily adapt to captivity as do some of the more popular species. Its diet is as described for the Greater Sulphur-crested Cockatoo.

Breeding: Nests in a suitable hollow limb, lined with chewed up wood chippings. The two to four (usually three) white eggs are incubated by both sexes for about 28 days. The young fledge in about six weeks.

Moluccan Cockatoo—*Cacatua moluccensis*
Length: 50 cm (20 in)
Description: The largest of the "white" cockatoos. The male is white suffused with pink, especially on the breast. The underside of the wings and tail are yellowish salmon. Its broad crest is white, the longest feathers, salmon red. The beak is black and the feet dark gray. The naked, eye-ring is light, blue-gray. The female is similar to the male except that the iris is red-brown rather than dark brown.

Range: The Moluccan

The call of the Moluccan Cockatoo, *Cacatua moluccensis*, consists of different whistles with low and high pitches. They also emit a piercing scream when alarmed.

In choosing a cockatoo as a pet, consider its disposition toward any other birds in your home.

Islands of Ceram, Saparua, and Haruku.

Habitat and Habits: Found in both wooded and cultivated areas. Feeds on a variety of seeds, fruits, and greenery. Said to cause a large amount of damage to cultivated crops. Voice consists of loud screeches.

Captive Care: A hand-reared Moluccan Cockatoo makes one of the finest pets, soon becoming tame and affectionate to its owner and acquiring a considerable vocabulary. In its native habitat, wild youngsters are collected from nests and hand-reared for export.

Breeding: Nests in a hollow tree limb. The two or three white eggs are incubated by both sexes for about 25 days. The young fledge in about 12 weeks. In captivity, the birds should be supplied with a large, sturdy, nesting barrel or a hollow length of tree trunk. When rearing chicks, soaked seed and a mixture of squeezed, milk-soaked, stale bread should be given.

Rosebreasted or Galah— *Eolophus roseicapillus*

Length: 35 cm (14 in)

Description: The head, nape, and underparts are rich pink, much lighter on the short crest and forehead. The back, wings, and tail are light gray. The naked eye-ring may be red or crusty white, respectively in the eastern or western races. The beak is horn-colored and the feet, gray. The sexes are similar except that the eyes of the male are brown while the female's are red. Immature specimens have a pinkish gray breast.

Range: Almost the whole of Australia.

Habitat and Habits: The most common and widespread of cockatoos often seen in flocks of over

1,000 birds. Found in a variety of habitats, ranging from the dry, semi-desert of the interior to the grassland, woodland and coastal plains. Frequently inhabits gardens and parks in urban areas. It is a serious pest in agricultural areas and a large flock can soon decimate crops. Culling is carried out on a large scale but, in spite of this, Australia does not relax its policy of not exporting live birds, even pest species. Galahs are primarily seedeaters, gathering most of their food from the ground. The voice consists of a series of harsh screeches.

Captive Care: A very common cage bird in Australia and probably the most frequently bred of all cockatoos in other parts of the world. The Galah makes a very entertaining pet, but its powers of mimicry are relatively limited; however, it may learn to repeat a few words. It is one of the least offensive of the pet cockatoos with regard to screaming. It will do very well on a proprietary parrot mixture with the addition of fresh greens and supplements.

Breeding: The only cockatoo which collects nesting material from outside of the nest-hole, the Rose-breasted lines its nest with leaves and twigs from eucalypt trees. The two to six white eggs are brooded by both sexes for about 30 days. The young leave the nest in about six to eight weeks. In captivity, a pair

The Rose-breasted Cockatoo, *Eolophus roseicapillus*, is an avid chewer and can destroy a large tree branch in a short period of time.

The Rose-breasted Cockatoo, *Eolophus roseicapillus*, is the most popular species of cockatoo in Australia. They are very prolific birds, and there have been many successful breedings in captivity.

should be provided with a suitably sized nest box or log and a regular supply of leafy twigs when nesting.

Little Corella—*Cacatua sanguinea*

Length: 35-42 cm (14-17 in)

Description: The sexes are alike. The plumage is generally white with a strong yellow tinge under the wings and tail. The feathering between the eyes and bill is dull red. The naked eye-ring is blue-gray to whitish. The eyes are dark brown but may be redder in the female. The beak is bone-colored and

the feet are medium gray. Immature birds are similar to the adults.

Range: Wide areas of central and western interior of Australia.

Habitat and Habits: Noisy and gregarious, Little Corellas assemble in flocks of several thousands outside the breeding season and often roost in trees along water courses, stripping the leaves, and leaving them bare. In the early morning, they fly off to feeding areas on the ground and feed for several hours, eating seed grasses and digging up roots with

Citron-crested Cockatoos, *C.s. citrinocristata.* Cockatoos pair for life, but during breeding a male sometimes becomes so aggressive towards the female that an accidental death may occur.

their strong bills, before returning to the roosting sites around midday. Towards evening, they again feed for a couple of hours before returning to the roosting trees for the night.

Captive Care: Like the Rosebreasted, the Little Corella is a common cage bird in its native Australia and is occasionally available elsewhere. It is very hardy and makes a charming and affectionate pet, many specimens quickly learn to repeat a large vocabulary. May be fed on the usual seed mixture, supplemented with nuts, greenfood, and other occasional treats.

Breeding: In the wild, it nests in a hollow limb, the cavity lined with chips from the interior. The nest hollow may be used over several seasons by the same pair and may be eventually destroyed by the birds' gnawing activities. The two or three white eggs are incubated for about 28 days, probably by both sexes.

Lesser Sulphur-crested Cockatoo—*Cacatua sulphurea*

Length: 32 cm (13 in)

Seven week old Umbrella Cockatoo, *Cacatua alba*.

Description: Similar to the Greater Sulphur-crested Cockatoo but smaller. Ear coverts are deeper yellow. The sexes are similar but the iris of the male is black, compared to brown in the female.

Range: Celebes and adjoining islands. Six races, including one with an orange crest (Citron-crested Cockatoo, *C. s. citrinocristata.*

Habitat and Habits: Found in woodland and cultivated areas: Assembles in small flocks outside the breeding season. Classified as a pest in agricultural areas.

Captive Care: Very popular as a cage bird and often available; becomes very tame and affectionate and learns to repeat a few words and phrases. May be fed on the usual seed mixture, fruit, and greenstuff.

Breeding: Nests in a tree hollow. The two or three white eggs are incubated by both sexes for about four weeks. The young fledge in about 12 months. The birds keep the nest spotlessly clean and the young emerge in perfect condition.

Long-billed Corella— *Cacatua tenuirostris*
Length: 37 cm (15 in)
Description: The sexes are similar; the general color is white, with a faint yellow tinge under the wings and tail. The forehead is red with the color extending around the eye; a further band of red extends across the throat. The wide, naked eye-ring is light blue. The eyes are dark brown, the bill, bone-colored and the feet, gray. Immature birds are similar to adults but the upper mandible is shorter.

Range: Southeastern Australia, from southwestern South Australia and through Victoria to the central border region of New South Wales.

Habitat and Habits: Open forest, woodland, and grassland. Assemble in flocks of 50 or more birds outside the breeding season. They roost in trees but feed mainly on the ground digging up roots with their long, pointed upper mandibles. Like the Greater Sulphur-crested Cockatoos, these birds have a "sentinel warning system," some individuals keeping watch in trees while the others feed on the ground.

Captive Care: Said to be the best talker of all the Australian cockatoos. Although not particularly attractive in appearance, its ability to talk and its bizarreness make it extremely popular. May be fed on the usual seed mixture, supplemented with a range of vegetables, particularly root vegetables.

Breeding: Nests in a tree hollow. Lays usually two white eggs which are incubated by both sexes for about 24 days. The young leave the nest in seven to eight weeks.

Cockatiel—*Nymphicus hollandicus*

Length: 30 cm (12 in)

Description: It is only recently that the Cockatiel has been definitely classed as a cockatoo. In previous classifications, it has been designated as a parakeet or even classed in a subfamily (Nymphicinae) of its own. However, its cockatoo characteristics outweigh others and it is now classed in the subfamily Cacatuinae. It is the smallest and slimmest of the cockatoos. The male is predominantly slate-gray, with a bright yellow head, merging into gray on the pointed crest. The cheek patches are orange and there is a white stripe along the outer wing. The female is altogether duller in color, with the outer tail feathers yellow, barred with brown.

Range: Most of Australia's interior in suitable areas.

Habitat and Habits: Common in open and lightly wooded country; nomadic, moving seasonably to favorable feeding and breeding areas. They congregate in groups of several hundreds and roost communally. They feed primarily on smaller seeds and, as such, their diet differs appreciably from that of the larger cockatoos. Also, unlike cockatoos, the voice is a rather pleasant whistle.

Captive Care: The Cockatiel is kept and bred more extensively than any other cockatoo species and, as such, is in a class of its own with many color varieties. Persons interested in Cockatiels should refer to one or more of the excellent reference books available on the subject.

Breeding: In the wild, the Cockatiel nests in tree hollows. The two to eight white eggs are incubated for about 20 days by both sexes. The young fledge in about five weeks. Cockatiels breed readily in captivity if provided with a suitably sized nesting box or log. Cockatiels are much less destructive and aggressive than most other cockatoos.

Breeding

In many parts of the world, cockatoos are not as readily available now as they were in the past. This is probably due to the fact that most countries are now strongly concerned with the conservation of wildlife, and the export of native species is either banned or severely restricted. In 1973, the Convention on International Trade in Endangered Species of Flora and Fauna (CITES), which is sometimes referred to as the "Washington Convention," heralded a new era in the field of protective legislation. Most countries have ratified the convention or incorporated it partially or wholly with national legislation. This means that wildlife is monitored both at its ports of departure and destination, making it extremely difficult for the illegal trade of many species. On the whole, the

Umbrella Cockatoo, *Cacatua alba*. Truly, the greatest reward of owning birds is raising your own young. Although not very attractive upon hatching, there is nothing better than a hand-raised bird.

Greater Sulphur-crested Cockatoo, *Cacatua galerita*. Large, galvanized trash cans are often used as nesting sites for cockatoos because of their destructive nature.

legislation is good but some aviculturists maintain that the nonavailability of some species makes it impossible to continue captive breeding projects and that these are important if the species is to be saved for future generations.

At the time when many cockatoo species were easily available, few people went out of their way to attempt to breed them and it is only in the last two or three decades that a reasonable number of birds are being bred in captivity and, perhaps surprisingly, these are mostly outside the bird's native Australia. The Australian government's policy on the export of native wildlife is well-known; even species classified as agricultural pests, which may be culled in great numbers in the field, are not allowed to be exported live for the pet trade. This means, of course, that unscrupulous and cruel methods of smuggling have arisen and the birds demand very high prices in their countries of destination. It is therefore imperative that anyone lucky enough to have or to obtain a pair of cockatoos (of any species) should make every effort to breed his charges, thus increasing the availability of stock for other fanciers.

Cockatoo breeding has always been fraught with difficulties. Birds which have been hand-reared as pets rarely make good breeders as they have become fixated on their human foster parents and may not recognize the potential delights of a cockatoo mate when introduced to one. Another problem is the difficulty in externally determining the sexes of many species. New methods of surgical and hormone sexing have alleviated this problem somewhat and your veterinarian should be able to do this, or put you in touch with someone who can.

The first requirement for breeding cockatoos is to have a true pair and hope that they are compatible. Birds which have hitherto not met should be introduced with great care. A new bird should never be introduced into a cage or aviary which has been occupied for some time by another bird. It is best to place both birds into a completely different breeding aviary so that they are both initially occupied with exploring and getting used to the new "territory" rather than being aggressive to each other. A pair introduced in this way will soon become the best of friends and, hopefully, mates.

The minimum sized breeding aviary for a pair of cockatoos should be 3 m long by 1.5 m wide by 2 m high (10 ft x 5 ft x 6.5 ft). The aviary should be sited in a quiet area, and not one which receives many visitors. In fact, the best successes have been achieved by very "secretive" aviculturists, who allow nobody other than their immediate family to go anywhere near a pair of potential breeders. The aviary is best partially screened off from the rest of the garden with hedging or fencing so that the birds are not put off by the activities of the family.

Under normal conditions, many cockatoos breed in the spring and summer months in the southern hemisphere, that is September through January, and it may take several seasons for them to

Little Corellas, *Cacatua sanguinea*. In the wild, cockatoos often take shelter from the hot sun by resting within the shade of a nest entrance.

Baby Umbrella Cockatoos, *Cacatua alba*. Brooders can be purchased to accommodate the specific needs of cockatoo chicks. Inquire at your local pet store as to where such devices can be obtained.

reverse their seasons to those of the northern hemisphere. Most species are surprisingly hardy and some have even been successfully bred outside in a northern winter although one should try to ensure that this occurs in the warmer months whenever possible.

The breeding pair should be provided with a nesting log, barrel, or very large nest box. The size of the nesting container will, of course, be influenced by the size of the birds, but they seem to prefer a "minimum" size rather than a "maximum" one. The entrance hole should be of a size that the birds can comfortably squeeze through. Remembering the destructive powers of the beaks of most cockatoos, one should protect the entrance holes with sheet metal, fixed in such a way that no potentially dangerous, jagged edges are left exposed. The floor of the nest box can be lined with a thin layer of wood shavings and these may be added to by the cockatoos as they "rearrange" the inside of the cavity to their liking.

Prior to and during breeding, you should

Umbrella Cockatoo, *Cacatua alba*. Because captive breeding is becoming more popular, it is important to keep detailed records. The weight of a newly hatched chick should be monitored and recorded up until a few weeks after weaning.

ensure that the birds have an adequate diet, paying particular attention to grit and calcium (cuttlefish bone, crushed shells, etc.). Soaked seed and soaked stale bread, with the addition of a little milk, can also be given from the onset of breeding and particularly while chicks are being reared. These items in the diet will ensure that the parent birds can quickly produce a "soup" in their crops, to be regurgitated for feeding the young.

The number of eggs laid varies from species to species and, in some species, both sexes incubate while in others only the hen incubates (the black cockatoos). During the incubation period, the birds should be disturbed as little as possible and the nest should be inspected only on rare occasions—for example if you suspect something is wrong. Do not be discouraged if your cockatoos are not successful in breeding the first time or so. By trial and error, you will soon be able to provide the conditions your birds require to breed successfully.

Health and Hygiene

Hygiene and health go hand in hand. Cockatoos are generally healthy birds and greatly resistant to disease and, provided they receive a balanced diet, are kept in clean conditions and protected from drafts and dampness, they are unlikely to fall victim to disease. Hygiene must be emphasized and the importance of regular cleaning and disinfecting of accommodations and feed and water containers must not be underestimated.

Quarantine:

If you wish to keep and breed several cockatoos, any new stock must be kept separately from existing stock for a period of three weeks, in case the

Toenail clipping should be done professionally. If you insist on doing it yourself, use the utmost of caution not to cut the vein. It may be best to only file the tips off until you can have them professionally done.

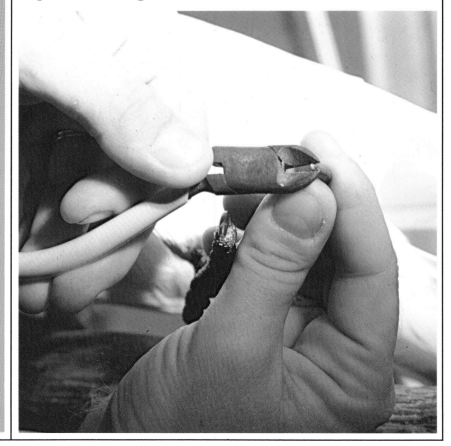

bird is suffering from a disease which you obviously would not want your other birds to catch. If no symptoms appear in the three week period, you can safely assume the bird is free of disease and the introduction can take place.

Signs of sickness depend to some extent on the type of disease but, in general, a sick cockatoo will appear dull and lethargic, lose its appetite and sit moping with its feathers fluffed out. When showing these signs, an individual should be moved to a warm place, preferably a hospital cage, and kept at about 30°C (85°F). A hospital cage is usually enclosed on all sides except the front (which may also be partially covered) and is usually heated with a bulb. Needless to say, food and water should be available at all times, even if the bird is not apparently feeding. As most cockatoos are extremely valuable birds, veterinary advice should be sought without delay.

In cases of infection by pathogenic organisms, antibiotic treatment will usually prove successful, providing this starts in the early stages of the disease. After an outbreak of disease, however small, all cages, aviaries, and accessories should be cleaned and disinfected without delay. A 10% solution of household bleach is an excellent disinfectant which can be used safely in most situations providing it is well rinsed away with clean water and dried out before the birds are permitted to return.

Wounds:

Wounds are unlikely to occur if correct husbandry is carried out. Wounds usually occur through fighting or by the birds' injuring themselves through panic. Open wounds should be bathed in an antiseptic solution and then dried. In cases of excessive bleeding, a veterinarian should be consulted as soon as possible.

Overgrown Nails and Beaks:

Under normal circumstances cockatoos keep their nails and beaks in shape through exercise and gnawing. The birds should be provided with frequently changed, natural perches of nonpoisonous wood. If the perches are of varying thicknesses, the birds' nails will be kept worn to the correct size. Also, by gnawing at twigs and branches, the bird's beak will be kept in shape.

As the feathers of a bird grow in, the shaft is filled with blood. If this is cut, it will bleed like an open vein. Never cut within the pinkish area, but always beyond.

If toenails should become overgrown, for whatever reason, they must be cut to size using a sharp pair of nail scissors or clippers. Great care must be taken not to cut into the blood supply (the quick) or profuse bleeding will occur. If you are unsure what to do, your veterinarian or your avicultural supplier may be able to help. The same rules apply for an overgrown beak, which must be trimmed; otherwise the bird will be unable to feed properly and could starve.

Egg Binding:
This occasionally occurs in gravid hens when an egg becomes lodged in part of the reproductive tract. Possible causes include a shortage of calcium, cold surroundings and immaturity of the bird concerned. The offending egg may have a soft, rubbery shell that complicates the issue as, if it breaks in the bird's body, peritonitis is likely to develop. By removing the bird to a warm hospital cage, the egg is often passed within an hour or

so. Stubborn cases should not be bred until the following season and husbandary should be rectified where possible.

Enteritis:

This may be caused by a number of different infections of the digestive tract. Apart from the usual "sick bird" symptoms, the bird may have watery diarrhea. Any bird with diarrhea should have adequate drinking water available as diarrhea can cause rapid dehydration, a condition that, in itself, can be fatal. A sick bird should be moved to a hospital cage, a veterinarian should be consulted as soon as possible, and laboratory testing of fecal samples will verify the nature of the disease. Most enteric infections in cockatoos can be satisfactorily treated with the appropriate drugs.

Respiratory Infections:

The symptoms of respiratory infections include labored breathing, wheezing, blocked nostrils, coughing and nasal discharges. Again, there are

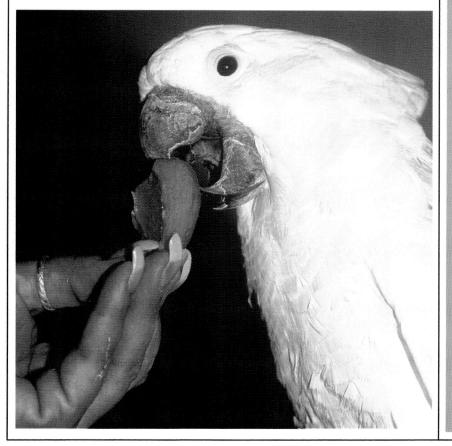

Fresh fruits and vegetables can be used as rewards when training.

Umbrella Cockatoo, *Cacatua alba*. It is not advised to allow your pet cockatoo and cat to play together. If a fight were to occur, both animals could be seriously injured.

a number of causative organisms, ranging from bacteria and viruses to fungi (notably Aspergillosis). Sick birds should be immediately isolated in warm conditions. Recent research has found cures for most psittacine respiratory infections and a veterinarian will be able to help you.

Ectoparasites:

These are bloodsucking insects or arachnids which attack the bird's skin and take blood. Some ectoparasites can build up to such large numbers that the birds become anemic through loss of blood and also become stressed from the irritation of the bites. Red mite is one such parasite that lives in nooks and crannies in the bird's housing, coming out at night to feed on the bird. Bird lice that live in the feathers can also be a problem. Ectoparasites are often transferred to aviaries by wild birds and will build up especially in unhygienic conditions. All mites and lice are easily exterminated by using one of the safe avicultural aerosol sprays available from your supplier. At the end of the breeding season, nest boxes should be removed and thoroughly washed and disinfected before the next season.

Endoparasites:

These are organisms which live inside the body.

The most important kinds of endoparasites are various intestinal worms. These worms live in the intestinal tract and feed on the bird's partially digested food. The worms lay eggs which are passed out in the feces and can continually reinfect the bird or other birds. They can be brought to your aviary by wild birds defecating through the cage wire. Concrete floors to flights are the surest way of keeping infestations down, as the floors can be scrubbed and hosed at regular intervals to remove the eggs. Signs of worm infestations are usually not noticeable unless the bird is heavily infected. Regular examination of fecal samples in a veterinary laboratory will verify the presence of worm eggs in your stock and the vet will provide the appropriate medication.

Index

Page numbers in **boldface** *refer to illustrations.*

COACHING CHILDREN IN SPORT

EDITED BY IAN STAFFORD

Routledge
Taylor & Francis Group

LONDON AND NEW YORK

First published 2011 by Routledge
2 Park Square, Milton Park, Abingdon, Oxon, OX14 4RN

Simultaneously published in the USA and Canada
by Routledge
711 Third Avenue, New York, NY 10017

Routledge is an imprint of the Taylor & Francis Group, an informa business

British Library Cataloguing in Publication Data
A catalogue record for this book is available from the British Library

Library of Congress Cataloging-in-Publication Data
Coaching children in sport / edited by Ian Stafford.
p. cm.
1. Sports for children–Coaching. I. Stafford, Ian.
GV709.24.C63 2011
796.083–dc22
2010046671

ISBN: 978–0–415–49390–1 hbk
ISBN: 978–0–415–49391–8 pbk
ISBN: 978–0–203–85068–8 ebook

Typeset in Zapf Humanist and Eras by
Keystroke, Station Road, Codsall, Wolverhampton

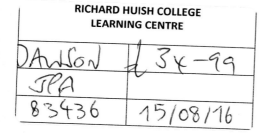

MIX
Paper from
responsible sources
FSC
www.fsc.org   FSC® C004839

Printed and bound in Great Britain by
TJ International Ltd, Padstow, Cornwall

This book is dedicated to all those coaches who give their time freely and willingly to work with children and who believe that their coaching has value beyond that of producing good sports performers. To all coaches who appreciate that coaching children in sport is about developing young people through sport as well as in sport; you are a valuable asset and your good work will be recognised and accorded the importance it deserves – it's just a matter of time.

Because time is such a valuable and limited commodity, I would also like to dedicate this book to my own family: Kate, Helen and Rachel. This is by way of thanking them for not complaining too much about all the time I spent coaching, rather than being at home playing my primary roles of annoying husband and dad. I promise to be more attentive now that the coaching and this writing have stopped.

CONTENTS

ILLUSTRATIONS

FIGURES

TABLES

X

illustrations

CONTRIBUTORS

Ian Stafford is now a consultant and writer in education, sport and coaching; his previous work having been in teaching, coaching, lecturing in universities and coach development. His recent work has included a book, *Coaching for Long-Term Athlete Development* (Coachwise, 2005), and the production of coaching children and mentoring resources. He has presented papers at various international conferences, written a number of articles and facilitated a wide variety of training programmes.

Andy Abraham is a Principal Lecturer in Sport Coaching at Leeds Metropolitan University, England. His teaching and research both centre on understanding and developing coaching expertise. More specifically, he is interested in how coaches make good decisions in order to achieve their long-, medium- and short-term goals. He has recently been involved with the UK Centre for Coaching Excellence, examining formal coach development opportunities for high-performing coaches.

Richard Bailey is a writer and researcher in the areas of education and sport. His recent work focuses on talent development, learning and expertise, and he has explored these topics in sport, dance and other domains. He is the author of numerous articles and books.

Di Bass lectures at Loughborough University, England, specialising in pedagogy with an emphasis on coaching. Her interests include youth sport and sport for people with a disability. Di has coached swimming for over 40 years and was coach to the British swimming team at the 2000 Sydney Paralympics. She currently coaches one of the swimming squads at Loughborough University.

Ken Black has spent a lifetime of work as a practitioner in the field of inclusive physical activity and disability sport, as teacher, coach and development officer, among other roles. He has developed, advised and provided training on inclusive and disability sport programmes for numerous organisations, agencies, sports governing bodies, government departments and higher education institutions including the Youth Sport Trust in the UK, the Australian Sports Commission, UK Sport, the British Council, Loughborough University, England and the British Heart Foundation National Centre on Physical Activity and Health. He has developed training and practical educational resources, book and journal material and delivered practical interactive workshops and presentations on every continent. Recent projects have included coordinating the development of educational training and practical tools for those training or working with older disabled people in physical activity programmes as part of THENAPA 2, a European-wide adapted physical activity network.

Celia Brackenridge is Director of the Centre for Youth Sport and Athlete Welfare at Brunel University, West London. She trained as a physical education teacher and was also a national coach, athlete and coach educator for sports coach UK for many years. Her specialist areas of research are gender equity and child protection in sport.

Clive Brewer is Head of Human Performance for the Rugby Football League in England, having previously led the national programme for athlete development for sportscotland. An accredited strength and conditioning coach (UKSCA, BOA, NSCA) and interdisciplinary sports scientist (BASES), Clive has also been a director of the UK Strength and Conditioning Association for six years. He has 15 years of experience working with elite and developmental performers from a range of team and individual sports, and has supported a number of governing bodies in coach education. A recognised international speaker, Clive has written two books on conditioning for sports coaches, and a number of articles in related fields.

Dr Mark Bruner is an Assistant Professor in the School of Physical and Health Education at Nipissing University in North Bay, Canada. His program of research focuses on understanding how social processes in group-based activity (sport and exercise) settings influence adolescent psycho-social development and physical activity adherence.

Dave Collins is Professor of Coaching and Performance at the University of Central Lancashire, England, and Director of Grey Matters Consultants. Previously, as Performance Director of UK Athletics, Dave directed the programme that improved the team from 24th to 5th (World, then Olympic), 21st to 3rd (World Indoors) and 12th to 1st (European Team). He has also coached martial arts and rugby to national level. Dave has over 90 peer-reviewed publications and 25 books or book chapters published. He has worked with over 50 World or Olympic medallists plus professional sports teams, dancers, musicians, and executives in business and public service. Current research interests include performer and coach development, cognitive expertise, and the promotion of peak performance across different challenge environments.

Michael Collins is Visiting Professor in the Faculty of Sport, Health and Social Care, University of Gloucestershire, Cheltenham, England. Mike was a geographer and then a town and traffic planner, publishing *Transport in a Great City* (Allen & Unwin, 1970). From 1972 to 1989, he was head of research, strategy and town planning at The Sports Council in England, where he managed 500 research projects, including the Training of Young Athletes and the National Fitness Survey, and produced two national sport strategies. Since moving to Loughborough, he has researched, among other things, social capital and social exclusion.

Dr Jean Côté is professor and Director in the School of Kinesiology and Health Studies at Queen's University in Kingston, Canada. His research interests are in the areas of children in sport, sport expertise, and coaching. Dr Côté holds a cross appointment as a visiting professor

in the School of Human Movement Studies at the University of Queensland in Australia. In 2009, Dr Côté was the recipient of the 4th EW Barker Professorship from the Physical Education and Sport Science deparment at the National Institute of Education in Singapore.

Chris Cushion is a Senior Lecturer and Programme Leader for the MSc in Sports Coaching at Loughborough University, England. He has a wide interest in coaching, being involved in the development of the UK Coaching Certificate and a range of coaching-related research projects. Chris is actively involved in coaching practice as a UEFA-qualified soccer coach and has a range of research and teaching interests around coaching. These include understanding the coaching process, coach education, learning and professional development, coach behaviour and learning environments. Chris is an editorial board member and reviewer for a range of peer-reviewed national and international journals.

Joan L. Duda is Professor of Sports Psychology in the School of Sport and Exercise Sciences, University of Birmingham, England. She has over 200 scientific publications concerning motivational processes in physical activity settings and is the editor of the book *Advances in Sport and Exercise Psychology Measurement* (Fitness Information Technology, 1998). Joan has been an executive board member of a number of professional organisations, including serving as President of the Association for Applied Sport Psychology. In 2008, she was awarded an honorary doctoral degree from the Norwegian School of Sport Sciences for her scholarly and applied contributions to the field.

Patrick (Pat) Duffy is Professor of Sport Coaching at Leeds Metropolitan University, England. Prior to this appointment, he was the Group Chief Executive of sports coach UK for a four-year term. During his tenure, sports coach UK successfully led the development of the UK Coaching Framework, which has set out a clear vision and action plan for coaching in the United Kingdom up to 2016. Prior to leading sports coach UK, Pat was the Director of Ireland's National Coaching and Training Centre (NCTC) for an 11-year term. During this time, the NCTC pioneered the establishment of the National Coaching Development Programme with the involvement of 35 governing bodies of sport on an all-island basis. Pat has also been heavily involved with the creation of a European framework for the recognition of coaching competence and qualifications and has been Chair of the European Coaching Council since 2003. He is also Vice-President for Europe of the International Council for Coach Education. Pat has published on this work in a number of European Union-related publications and has also been a lead author on key policy publications in Ireland and the United Kingdom, as well as leading policy and strategy publications in coaching at European and global levels.

Paul Ford is a Senior Lecturer in Exercise Physiology at the University of East London. He is a British Association of Sport and Exercise Sciences-accredited Physiologist (Scientific Support) who has worked with numerous amateur and professional athletes and sports teams within the United Kingdom, including West Ham United FC, Brighton and Hove Albion FC, Leyton Orient FC, Essex CCC and London Wasps RFU. Paul's research is in paediatric physiology, principally the effects of growth and maturation upon athletic performance development. Paul has written peer-reviewed journal articles and book chapters, and has presented papers at national and international conferences. Currently, Paul is working with several National Olympic and Paralympic Committees, including the United States Olympic Committee, on the creation and maintenance of world-class pre-games and games-time training camps for the London 2012 Olympic Games.

Nicholas L. Holt is an Associate Professor in the Faculty of Physical Education and Recreation at the University of Alberta, Canada, where he directs the Child and Adolescent Sport and Activity research lab. His research examines psycho-social aspects of youth involvement in sport and physical activity in three main areas: positive youth development through sport, neighbourhood physical activity and clinical programmes for paediatric weight management. He is the Associate Editor of *Sport Psychologist* and recently edited *Positive Youth Development through Sport* (Routledge).

Ruth Jeanes is currently working as Research Fellow at the University of Central Lancashire, Preston, England. Her research focuses on youth sport policy, gender and sport and the impact of youth sport policy on young people. Overarching this is a methodological interest in innovative ways to engage young people in the research process. In the past four years, Ruth has also been involved in a research partnership with other English universities working in Lusaka, Zambia, with a range of non-governmental organisations delivering HIV/AIDS education through sport. Ruth has examined the experiences of young people taking part in these programmes. Ruth has published several book chapters and journal articles from her PhD study, 'Tackling gender: girls, football and gender identity construction'. Prior to taking up her current post, Ruth was a research associate at the Institute of Youth Sport at Loughborough University, England.

Tess Kay is Professor of Sport and Social Sciences at Brunel University, England and Director of the Brunel Centre for Sport, Health and Wellbeing. She has an extensive background in youth sport research and a special interest in the role of sport in family life. Tess undertakes a wide range of research into sport, inclusion and diversity and is currently researching the use of sport in international development contexts. She is the editor of the international research collection, *Fathering through sport and leisure* (Routledge 2009) and author of *Understanding Sport in International Development*, published by Routledge in 2011.

John Lyle has recently returned to a role as a full-time research consultant, collaborating with a number of universities and national sports agencies. He is Adjunct Professor at the University of Queensland, Australia, and has been Professor of Sports Coaching at Leeds Metropolitan University, England. This appointment followed a long and successful career in higher education, first in physical education and thereafter specialising in sports coaching studies. He established the first professional diploma in sports coaching and the first Master's degree in coaching studies in the United Kingdom. He has played a significant role in the development of sports coaching as an academic field of study, and is the author of the influential textbook *Sports Coaching Concepts* (Routledge, 2002). John's academic experience is complemented by a considerable personal experience as a coach, and engagement in the delivery of coach education and development.

Áine Macnamara is a Lecturer in Sport Psychology in the Department of Physical Education and Sport Sciences at the University of Limerick, Ireland. Áine's current research interest is talent development processes across performance domains, with particular focus on the role that psychological characteristics play in the realisation of potential. Áine is also involved in sport psychology consultation and support work with national- and international-level athletes, accredited by the Irish Institute of Sport.

Robert M. Malina is Professor Emeritus in the Department of Kinesiology and Health Education at the University of Texas at Austin, and a Research Professor in the Department of Health and Physical Education at Tarleton State University, Stephenville, Texas. He has earned doctoral degrees in physical education (University of Wisconsin, Madison, 1963) and anthropology (University of Pennsylvania, Philadelphia, 1968), and honorary degrees from the Catholic University of Leuven, Belgium (1989), the Academy of Physical Education, Kraków, Poland (2001), the University School of Physical Education, Wroclaw, Poland (2006), and the University of Coimbra, Portugal (2008). One of his primary areas of interest is the biological growth and maturation of children and adolescents with a major focus on young athletes and the influence of training for sport. He has worked extensively in the area of children's growth in a number of sports, including swimming, diving, gymnastics, track and field, American football, basketball and soccer among others.

Andy Miles is the Director of Enterprise for the Cardiff School of Sport, Wales. His main area of focus is coach education and he is currently a National Trainer for sports coach UK. He has trained and assessed over 100 coach educators and tutors as well as personally delivering in excess of 500 coach education workshops in areas such as child protection, fitness, coaching methods and mentoring. Andy's research interests are associated with the development and education of practitioners in sport, with a particular interest in the role of reflective practice and mentoring in professional development. He has published several research articles and reports on reflective practice and mentoring.

Gareth Morgan is a Senior Lecturer and Course Leader of BSc (Hons.) Sports Coaching in the Carnegie Faculty of Sport and Education at Leeds Metropolitan University, England. He also acts as a consultant to the UK Centre for Coaching Excellence, working with several national governing bodies of sport to scope and develop a UK Coaching Certificate Level 4 Talent Development coaching programme. Having completed a PhD in youth football academy coaches' behaviour and its impact on players' motivation and learning at Loughborough University, England, Gareth is currently interested in researching coaches' planning and talent development. As a UEFA 'B' licensed football coach, Gareth has also worked part-time in Academy football as a coach and sport psychologist for most of the past ten years. Further, he also works as a coach educator for the Football Association, delivering on its Age-Appropriate Youth Awards and Psychology for Football courses.

David Morley has taught Physical Education (PE) in a number of secondary schools and has been a Director of a football academy. He recently held the position of Senior Lecturer in Physical Education and Sport Pedagogy at Leeds Metropolitan University, England. In his time at Leeds, he led a talent development in PE research unit, inclusive PE and multi-skills modules within teacher and coach education, and was project director across a range of research areas. David was the Director of the national 'Talent Development in PE and Sport' project for four years and he continues to act as a consultant, adviser and project director for PE, sports and educational agencies on projects ranging from multi-skills delivery to talent development in PE and sport. His most recent educational development activity has involved designing the PE curriculum for trail-blazing Egyptian schools located around the Nile. He advises national governing bodies of sport and professional sports clubs on establishing developmentally appropriate talent progression pathways. He has published extensively in these areas and presented his work at national and international conferences. His latest involvement in nurturing movement competences is in developing multi-skills within the playground and he heads an exciting, multifaceted international initiative with Education and Special Project in a bid to make a difference to every child's involvement in PE, sport and physical activity.

Bob Muir is a Senior Lecturer in the Carnegie Faculty of Sport and Education at Leeds Metropolitan University, England. He also acts as a consultant to the UK Centre for Coaching Excellence, working with several national governing bodies of sport to scope and develop their United Kingdom Coaching Certificate Level 4 programmes across different coaching domains. A practising basketball coach for over 14 years, across participation and performance pathways, he currently coaches a men's National League Division 1 team. Bob is also undertaking a PhD, investigating effective coaching practice across the participant development pathway – essentially, considering what works for coach and participant in different contexts and why. Before entering higher education, Bob spent six years developing and managing a sport and social inclusion project.

Gemma Pearce is a postgraduate student in the School of Sport and Exercise Sciences at the University of Birmingham, England. Her areas of research focus around life transitions, health and body image. She previously worked as a research methods specialist at Roehampton University, England. Recent publications and presentations focus on children's perceptions of health and play; research methods and literature reviews; body image concerns; elite athletes' attitudes towards doping; gifted and talented education; and player pathways in sport.

Eleanor Quested is a Research Fellow in the School of Sport and Exercise Sciences at the University of Birmingham, England. Her doctoral research focused on motivational processes and well- and ill-being among young elite dancers. Eleanor's work as a Research Fellow centres upon the social-environmental and motivational processes associated with adaptive and health-conducive physical activity participation among children and adolescents. Eleanor has lectured in sport, exercise and dance psychology at undergraduate and Master's level.

Anthony Rossi is a Senior Lecturer in the School of Human Movement Studies at the University of Queensland, Australia. He writes widely in the broad area of human movement studies. Currently, his main research concerns at the moment are workplace learning in related fields (including physical education teaching, exercise physiology, coaching and sports psychology) sports programmes in Aboriginal and Torres Strait Islander communities (specifically surfing), and health literacies. His work is mostly funded through national or international funding agencies.

Dr Leisha Strachan is an Assistant Professor in the Faculty of Kinesiology and Recreation Management at the University of Manitoba in Winnipeg, Canada. As a coach and judge in the sport of baton twirling, she has a keen interest in the growth of children and youth in highly competitive sport contexts. With help from the Social Sciences and Humanities Research Council (SSHRC) and in collaborations with Dr Jean Côté and Dr Janice Deakin, she has examined outcomes and experiences in youth sport programs. She plans to further examine recreational and elite sport programs for children and youth and delve more deeply into their experiences.

Hamish Telfer was a Senior Lecturer at the University of Cumbria, England. His area of specialism is in coaching practice, reflective practice and applied practice ethics. He has been a Great Britain team coach in three sports but has particular experience in endurance events in track and field athletics. He has acted as the Vice-Convenor of the Coaches Commission of Scottish Athletics and led the postgraduate provision in coaching at University of Cumbria. He is a Senior Tutor and Tutor Mentor for sports coach UK and has co-authored a number of its coaching resources.

Richard Tinning is Professor of Pedagogy and Physical Education in the School of Human Movement Studies at the University of Queensland, Australia, and Adjunct Professor of Physical Education in the School of Critical Studies in Education at the University of Auckland, New Zealand. As a teacher educator, he has been involved in major Australian curriculum development projects for physical education, has worked on large-scale professional development programmes for teachers and has acted as a consultant to both schools and universities. Richard was one of the early advocates of critical pedagogy within physical education and has written extensively on physical education and teacher education. His most recent book, *Pedagogy and Human Movement: Theory, Practice, Research* (Routledge, 2010), develops an analysis of the pedagogical work done on physical activity, the body and health within the field of kinesiology and human movement studies.

Martin Toms is currently Director of Education in the School of Education at the University of Birmingham, England, where he lectures in sports coaching. He was formerly a professional coach, but his work is now focused on participant development, talent development and the influence of the family in the youth sports coaching experience. His focus is on grassroots sports and he is currently working with the Professional Golf Association of Great Britain and Ireland on education and development, participant and talent development models and profiling the 'social' aspect of the bio-psycho-social approach to sports participation. He is currently a member of sports coach UK's Higher Education Advisory Group.

Julia Walsh is Director of Sports Studies and Physical Education at University College Cork in Ireland. Her research and recreational interests are coaching focused. Her research is in the area of coach expertise and education. Her particular interests are in the development of novice coaches, how they learn, and what mentoring structures support their learning. Julia has also investigated the communication process between athletes and coaching staff. She is an active coach with over 30 years of coaching experience at all levels of competition. In Cork, she is actively involved in coach education in the community and at the university.

Karl Wharton is a Senior Lecturer and Programme Leader for BSc and MSc Sport Coaching within the School of Life Sciences; Department of Sport Management, Development and Coaching at Northumbria University, England. Previously, he worked as National Coach for British Gymnastics for eight years. Prior to entering into a career in full-time coaching and higher education, Karl was a teacher of physical education for 15 years and held a position as a head of department for a 12-year period. He is a highly experienced coach and coach educator and has been involved with British Gymnastics for over 25 years as a national coach, tutor, tutor trainer, assessor and technical writer. He has coached at international level with the British Gymnastics Association and has produced more than 50 world and European medallists, including three world and three European champions. Karl has also served as a consultant to the International Federation of Gymnastics, British Gymnastics, English Gymnastics, the English Institute of Sport and the United Kingdom's Department of Culture, Media and Sport.

FOREWORD

The nurture, safety and dignity of children should be at the heart of adult and societal responsibility across the globe. Children, as well as providing joy and happiness to their parents, families and friends, are the adult citizens of the future. The socialisation of children to play a positive, fulfilling and productive part in society is one of the most important roles played by their older and seemingly wiser parents, teachers, carers and mentors. The desire among children to play and to have fun through physical activity prevails in every corner of the globe. From the moment they are born, children experience the world through movement. As they begin to make sense of their world, young children soon realise that, while they have to crawl before they can walk or run, movement is fun. Our bodies provide the channel through which we extend the boundaries of our personal worlds and through which we explore the potential that is the essence our very being.

Thankfully, the rights of children have been assigned a high priority in most societies, with their care, education and development being informed by ethical and child-centred policies and practices. Yet for all this, far too many children endure appalling circumstances in which their daily existence, safety and dignity are at risk. Tragically, many children die or suffer unspeakable abuse at the hands of adults, while many others face an abject future that is visited upon them through poverty, lack of education and grinding living conditions.

Despite this grim reality, it is evident that the safety, education and development of children in and through movement are an important focus for families and education systems across the world. Within this more positive context, significant challenges remain in providing children with the skills, knowledge and attitudes that underpin a healthy appreciation and love of their own bodies, as well as the capability to take part in physical activity that is sufficiently frequent and challenging to meet their needs. Within an increasing number of societies, sport is a powerful and motivating force for children to go out and play. The influence of the media and the process of globalisation have increased the visibility of sport. Sporting terms, icons and teams have become almost ubiquitous. To add spice to the mixture, the nature of sport varies significantly from nation to nation, enriched by local, community and indigenous flavours.

This powerful force for good also has the characteristics of a double-edged sword. For all its capacity to engage, challenge and excite, the world of sport for children can exclude, degrade and demotivate. This can be evident when adults try to relive their past sporting lives (or unsuccessful or non-sporting lives) through their children, or in situations where the well-meaning efforts of adults to engage children in sport are misdirected through inappropriate approaches to play, practice and competition. Most adults mean well when they lead and support children's sport. The provision of accessible, up-to-date and evidence-based guidance for coaches, parents and teachers is vital if we wish to maximise the extraordinary power of sport to light up the lives of children. Well-informed and capable coaches guide the improvement of children in sport in line with their needs, capabilities and stage of development. Through their work, coaches help develop the skills, confidence and competence that empower lives and strengthen the fabric of communities and wider society.

Within this context, the first publication of *Coaching Children in Sport* in 1993 was a pioneering piece of work. In recognising the need for a child-centred approach to the provision of sporting experiences, Martin Lee edited the contributions of a range of authors that have helped to shape modern-day thinking on children's sport. The initiative by Ian Stafford to revisit and update the publication with new topics and authors could not be timelier, as the focus on the ethical and inclusive involvement of children in sport sharpens. The chapter themes and the range of authors provide the basis for a comprehensive treatment of the core issues associated with the healthy and positive involvement of children in sport.

This systematic approach to the development of the knowledge and capability of children's coaches will also play a ground-breaking role. Within the United Kingdom and the wider European Union, there has been formal recognition of the significance of children's coaches, reflected in an emerging model of coach development. This new departure recognises that the engagement, recruitment, education and development of coaches should be more strongly informed by the needs of the participant. Currently, four coaching domains have been identified: Children's Coach, Participation Coach, Performer Development (Talent) Coach and High-Performance Coach. It is evident from this emerging landscape within the coaching profession that children's coaches are increasingly recognised for their efforts and for the foundational role they play in laying the base for future sports participation.

This publication provides an informed, balanced and educational resource that will be invaluable to those involved in coaching children, in the development of children's coaches and in the creation of environments and systems where children's sport takes place. This is true for both volunteer and paid children's coaches, with a strong recognition within this text that much of children's sport takes place in community-based contexts where parents and neighbours work together to shape the sporting experience for young people. While the publication cannot address all of the ills that the world imposes upon many young and fragile souls, it provides an important set of tools to set children and their coaches free to experience and benefit from the beautiful medium of sport and physical activity.

Patrick Duffy
Professor of Sport Coaching,
Leeds Metropolitan University, United Kingdom

foreword

ACKNOWLEDGEMENTS

First, I would like to acknowledge the immense contribution of Richard Bailey, student turned teacher, trusted adviser and friend, although he'll never admit to this in public. He had an idea for an updated book on coaching children in sport and this is the result. His work and support were central to ensuring that this book was published.He is one of the most intelligent and truly learned men I have ever met, who has helped shape thinking on physical education and sport through his research, writings and thought-provoking presentations.

Pat Duffy was the first choice to write the Foreword to this book. He is an inspiring advocate for coaching and for the importance and value of coaching children. His work in guiding and shaping the UK Coaching Framework was influential in recognising the important role that children's coaches play in sport and in wider society. He will continue to be influential in ensuring that this belief permeates coaching on a European and global basis.

Thanks to all the authors who worked tirelessly to respond to queries and deadlines, despite their own heavy workloads. Your efforts were really appreciated and I hope you are pleased with the fruits of your labours.

Finally, the efforts of all the staff who worked on this book at Routledge must be acknowledged. Their cooperation and patience were valued, as were their constant prompts and reminders that ensured the production of the book kept moving.

INTRODUCTION

IAN STAFFORD

When Martin Lee edited the first edition of *Coaching Children in Sport* in 1993, it was a timely acknowledgement for all those involved in sports coaching that children were not simply 'mini adults'. It highlighted that coaches needed to understand fully the key factors relating to child development in order to produce appropriate and effective coaching programmes for children.

In the intervening period between the publication of Martin's book, there has been a considerable increase in the amount and quality of research underpinning children's sport. In many countries, we have witnessed the ongoing development of agencies that promote and safeguard children's participation in sport. Also, governments across the world have put initiatives in place that see participation in sport being promoted not only for sport's sake but also to address wider social issues relating to health, antisocial behaviour and community relationships.

With these developments in mind, it seemed that the time was right to revisit some of the central themes of the first book, update the content and take a fresh look at key principles and issues. The finished product looks quite different from Martin Lee's collection, and that was to be expected. Sport and science move on, and so should coaches and coach developers.

The book is divided into three parts: On coaching, On children and On sport. There is a deliberate mixture of chapters that adopt a more theoretical approach, examining under-pinning principles, concepts and processes, sitting alongside chapters that are more focused on coaching and coach education practice. A clear central message is that coach education and development needs to integrate theory and practice more effectively in the future.

Children are the future of sport – *your* sport and sport in general. If we do not work to ensure the continued participation of the future generation of athletes, swimmers, gymnasts and games players in sufficient numbers, then sport will undoubtedly not have such a bright future. If children are the future of our communities, cultures and societies, and teachers are the key to instilling a love of learning and key educational standards, then coaches are central in instilling a love of sport to ensure that children develop active lifestyles and drive up standards of both behaviour and performance in sport as they develop towards adulthood.

Put simply, children must continue to take up sport and participate safely in large numbers, with a sense of fun and enthusiasm, in order for sport to have a healthy life in the future. Without committed, effective children's coaches, the chances of young participants developing a real love for sport and fulfilling their own dreams and potentials will undoubtedly be diminished. If we return to the point made earlier about governments across the world using sport to address key health and social issues, then the role of the children's coach takes on even greater significance. Let us not forget the important role that sport can play in developing happier, healthier communities, if it is structured appropriately to meet needs and interests.

Such importance can create a sense of pride and value in what we do as children's coaches, but it can also be quite daunting through the attendant responsibilities that the role brings. Children's coaches could easily be put off coaching children through the increased demands that are being made of them. We must have due regard to the fact that the vast majority of children's coaches are unpaid volunteers. Just like the children they coach, these coaches need support and encouragement.

I hope that this book not only encourages you to continue coaching children but also provides support in enhancing your knowledge and thinking about coaching children. Ultimately, this enhanced understanding needs to be reflected in your actual coaching or coach education practice, with developmentally appropriate learning and sport environments provided for all children starting out on what we all would like to be their valuable and enjoyable, lifelong sport experience.

2

PART I

ON COACHING

CHAPTER ONE

WHAT IS A COACH AND WHAT IS COACHING?

JOHN LYLE

CHAPTER OUTLINE

- How have the boundaries been drawn to date?
- The social space of coaching
- Distinctive domains
- Adopting a position: a summary
- Learning more

INTRODUCTION

Despite the self-evident significance of the question in the title of this chapter, it is a surprisingly difficult question to answer. We could simply adopt a position that accepts a sports coach as an individual who occupies a coaching role – but that would not resolve the issue of whether the role itself could be understood as 'coaching'. Definitions rarely do more than identify the core function of the activity or role. On the other hand, the concept of coaching and understanding the 'boundaries' that are implied in our use of the term have implications that go far beyond a mere definition. This is why what may seem like a rather 'dry' or boring question will take us into the realms of coach education, professionalisation, expectations about the coach's role, coach–athlete relationships, and the expectations of athletes.

Although there is a danger of reprising the arguments that will be developed throughout the chapter, it will be obvious that the professionalisation of sport coaching (Taylor and Garratt, 2010; sports coach UK, 2008) depends on being able to identify what the occupation consists of (what do coaches do that others cannot do?) and who should be included and excluded (how can we tell whether a 'coach' qualifies for the profession?). As the writers on professions express it, there will be a body of knowledge and skills that is particular to sports coaching. The expertise that this confers is what coaches 'profess', and for which they can be held accountable. Much of the debate may be focused on relatively narrow, arcane matters about threshold levels of expertise and distinctive role functions, but coaches occupy a social 'space' (by this I mean that they inhabit real roles that we can see and understand), and issues of esteem, career development and reward will be impacted by the boundaries that we choose to draw around coaching.

The title of this book is *Coaching Children in Sport*. Why did the editor use the term 'coaching' and not 'teaching' or 'instructing'? Did he mean the use of the term to imply a particular purpose, approach, set of behaviours or set of values? Did it mean that he included some topics and excluded others because of this? Perhaps it was a combination of these criteria, or perhaps there were assumptions built into the term that were simply not questioned. I am sure that he was well aware of these issues, but the reason I raise the questions is to highlight the objectives for the chapter. Having considered the propositions in the chapter, you should feel able to evaluate critically, and with reasoned argument, others' use of the terms 'coach' and 'coaching'.

HOW HAVE THE BOUNDARIES BEEN DRAWN TO DATE?

It is very tempting to begin by saying, 'not very well' and 'most people don't bother'. Indeed, it may seem an unnecessary exercise, because you feel that the use of the term 'coach' is obvious, non-contentious or taken for granted. However, we should examine carefully anything that appears to be taken for granted. The most useful starting point is the variety of ways in which the term 'coach' has been understood to date. The following examples illustrate a number of different approaches, with some implications attached.

The most common approach is to apply the term 'coach' in association with the generic purpose of improving sporting performance (performance when used in this context refers to any level or stage of sporting ability), or exerting any leadership role associated with a team or athlete. This is difficult to illustrate because of its ubiquity, but the lack of precision means that this generic usage is not helpful. Perhaps understandably, another approach is 'assumption by named role'. In other words, if an individual has the title 'coach', they must be coaching. Examples would be coaches in schools and colleges in North America, 'community coaches' in the United Kingdom and coaches associated with representative teams or squads. This is not unreasonable but has its dangers. No presumption can be made about the coach's practice, and there are no threshold criteria. Coaches often exercise a multiplicity of roles, and there is some prestige in 'badging' oneself as a coach.

An obvious mechanism for identifying coaches is to check whether they are 'certificated' – that is, have a coach education qualification recognised by a national agency. The issue is that these qualifications range from the minimal (two or three days) to the fairly extensive. Expertise is minimally assured by these qualifications, and, of course, no assumptions can be made about the coaches' subsequent practice. A lack of certification would not disqualify a person from being considered a coach, but it does convey a measure of quality assurance, and may impact on professional recognition. On the other hand, it may seem surprising to identify 'self-designation' – I think I'm a coach, therefore I am! In a survey of coaches in the United Kingdom (MORI, 2004), the guidance provided to survey respondents was 'an individual that is involved in providing coaching'. Whether or not an individual is to be 'counted' as a coach was left to the respondent's interpretation of the term 'coaching'. In the elaboration (ibid.: 2), the survey intends that 'those who might coach their friends on a casual basis' should be included. Readers may feel that this suggests a threshold for occupying the social space that is not sufficiently related to expertise, certification or practice.

There have been some attempts to argue that the coaching process itself should be identified as a means to circumscribe the use of the term 'coach'. The most comprehensive of these is that by Lyle (2002), who identifies a number of 'boundary criteria' that can be applied to an individual's practice, including stability, frequency of contact, intensity of engagement, goal orientation and planned progression. It is important to note that these are a means of differentiating between coaching roles, not a prescription for practice.

These different approaches confuse role, expertise, experience, purpose or function, and context. A useful mechanism to illustrate the potential implications of this variation is the sample populations used by researchers. The student who reads a series of papers on coaching may be forgiven for assuming that 'coaching' or 'coach' could be assumed to convey a consensual meaning. However, nothing could be further from the truth. A useful exercise to illustrate this is to review a series of research papers and examine the coach population samples used. In passing, you might note that research papers most often identify the coaches and their characteristics rather than their coaching practices, which would be far more valuable.

REFLECTION

No criticism is intended of the sample populations used for any individual paper. However, you are invited to read those identified and other similar papers and to consider two issues: (1) the extent to which such a range of populations and circumstances can be expected to generate findings that translate well to coaching more widely; and (2) the extent to which authors contextualise their findings.

Suggested papers: Côté and Sedgwick (2003), Erickson et al. (2007), Gilbert and Trudel (2001), Trudel et al. (2007) and Vergeer and Hogg (1999).

Your review will identify a wide range of characteristics: number of coaches, employment status, gender balance, experience, role, sports coached, and athletes' stage of performance development. One might be critical of the extent to which generalisations from findings in such papers are sufficiently limited to the populations being used. The range of ages, experience, coach education, role deployment, and performance level and motives of athletes coached is very broad and reinforces my arguments about the 'family of distinctive coaching roles'.

7

It is important to acknowledge that an extensive range of perspectives or 'lenses' can be adopted to portray sports coaching. There is no space to elaborate on these, but one should recognise a sociological lens (Jones 2000), humanistic lens (Kidman 2005), performance lens (Johns and Johns, 2000), pedagogical lens (Armour, 2004) and functional lens (Lyle, 2002). Bush (2007) has described four approaches: psychological, modelling, sociological, and pedagogical. When Jones states that 'at the heart of coaching lies the teaching and learning interface' (2006: 3), he is illustrating the use of a particular perspective. A similar argument is the advocacy of a 'holistic' approach to coaching (Cassidy *et al.*, 2009). A useful exchange of ideas can be viewed in papers in the *International Journal of Sports Science & Coaching* (Cushion, 2007a, b; Lyle, 2007). This provides a flavour of the argument about the balance of emphasis between the relative complexity and untidiness of much of sports coaching, with a dependence on an intervention management practice that requires continual adjustment, and the stability of a core process of planned intervention.

Côté and Gilbert (2009) review conceptual models of coaching and identify a number of perspectives from which these have been generated: leadership, expertise, coach–athlete relationships, motivation and education. They make a convincing case for three ubiquitous components in these models: coach's knowledge, athletes' outcomes and coaching contexts. However, the question raised is whether, given the extensive variation and interrelationship of these generic components, they can be anything other than useful descriptors of coaches' practice; they do not help us to delineate common purpose or practice within the family of sports coaching roles. In the component 'athletes' outcomes', they argue a case for four desirable outcomes; these are the 4 Cs, described elsewhere (see the 5 Cs described in Chapter 17 and Côté *et al.*, 2010): competence, confidence, connection and character/caring. The authors state that 'effective coaching should result in positive change' (Côté and Gilbert, 2009: 313) in these outcomes. We may well agree with this position, at least in youth sport. Nevertheless, we need to ask whether it describes an essential feature of coaching, or whether it is a value position. For example, in operationalising the concepts, the authors identify the adoption of 'an inclusive focus as opposed to an exclusive selection policy based on performance' (ibid.: 317) as a potential criterion. Once again, this may characterise desirable practice in one or more coaching domains, but it cannot be an essential characteristic of coaching practice. I do not cease to be a coach if I operate a contrary policy.

REFLECTION

These different perspectives on coaching may be more about changes in priorities, applications in context, and intended outcomes, rather than substantive disagreements about the role of the coach. Nevertheless, I urge you to read any research papers or book chapters with a critical interpretation of the lens being used, and recognise the level of

THE SOCIAL SPACE OF COACHING

We have been content to think of coaches as 'occupying a social space' with taken-for-granted cultural assumptions about the coaching role. For example, the lack of precision with which the terms 'coaching' and 'managing' are used in professional soccer in the United Kingdom feeds a public perception that the role is one of leadership, but that relatively little training or formal education may be required. Knowledge is perceived to be esoteric and relatively superficial. Part of the reason for this is that soccer managers receive considerable publicity, unlike the majority of coaches of non-televised (particularly non-team) sports. Sports coaching might be described as a 'hidden profession'. On the other hand, we can contrast this with the 'coach' of young people. This role may be interpreted in many ways, but it is widespread and commands a measure of acceptance of its 'place' in sport.

We can probably agree that the assumption about coaches in the 'social space' is that they offer some form of technical leadership role in sport. This may be at all stages of participation, with no limits of athlete engagement, quality of practice or expertise – unless we choose to set limits as to what we 'accept' as sports coaching. We have made it difficult to comprehend the 'social space' of sports coaching by accepting a multiplicity of divergent roles and assuming a strong relationship between them. In addition, we have conflated the person and the role. Therefore, we will need to define the process and practice of sports coaching. Coaches can occupy many different roles, and it would be helpful to be specific about what is implied. If someone says to you, 'What do you do?', and you reply, 'I'm a coach', what can be read into that? Is it a sufficient description to convey what you do, how you do it or the context in which you do it? Does it imply that you are qualified, that you are experienced or that you have a current set of responsibilities?

It is likely that when we describe ourselves as a coach, we mean that we are certificated, or that we have occupied that role in the past. We are asserting that we have the capacity to exercise a version of the role and 'qualify for that social space'. Of course, as coaches we will all have different qualities, and perhaps a significant variety of interpretations of how we think coaching should be approached. Any set of personal qualities or values (even if they are non-mainstream) does not disqualify us from being described as coaches. We ought, therefore, to focus on the role and the function, rather than the person, and be aware when we insert value-laden assumptions into our definitions. A specific instance that is often raised is the interpretation

9

to be placed on inappropriate or unethical behaviour; would we continue to accept someone as a coach if they breached a code of conduct (similar to a doctor who is 'struck off')? This can become a very complex argument. Coaches or doctors in such circumstances remain 'qualified' but have their right to practise withdrawn. This suggests a threshold of inappropriate behaviour that goes beyond mere expressions of personal preferences or values about the coaching role (methods, styles, approaches, technical preferences, and so on).

DISTINCTIVE DOMAINS

The aggregation of behaviours and practice that characterise coaching in different sporting environments can be labelled coaching domains. A coaching domain is a distinctive context in which the environmental demands lead to an identifiable community of coaching practice, with attendant demands on the coaches' expertise and practice. It will be obvious why the question 'what is coaching?' would need to account for such domain diversity. We can argue that the intensity of the attachment, the complexity of the intervention programme, demands on the coaches' expertise and interpersonal skills, the emphasis on competition, and value systems will differ. I have argued for a simple categorisation of three domains: participation, development and performance (Lyle, 2002). Trudel and Gilbert (2006) settle on recreational sport, developmental sport and elite sport as their classification. Recent attempts by sports coach UK to 'chart' the landscape of coaching roles and domains have highlighted the potentially very distinctive contexts in which coaches might operate (see North, 2009).

A recent exercise to scope coaching domains carried out by the UK Centre for Coaching Excellence (sports coach UK, 2009) charted distinctive territories for children's, developmental, talent development, adult recreation, adult participation and high performance domains. The study concluded that these domains differed in the demands that the participants made on coaching roles and expertise. In particular, the short-term, non-competition and technique characteristics of the 'instructor' were emphasised. In the United Kingdom, coach education pathways in gymnastics and swimming distinguish between the coaching role and the teaching or instructing role. In addition, the instructor's role was often recognised in 'individual' sports such as skiing, golf, tennis and martial arts. This lends weight to the argument that sports coaching can be described as a family of roles, but the coaching role is a distinctive one, and is usefully differentiated from teaching and instructing.

The professionalisation imperative may require an interpretation of sports coaching that is sufficiently all-embracing to create a justifiable scale of occupations. Nevertheless, I will argue that sports coaching cannot be treated as a synonym for all forms of sports leadership: teaching, instructing, coaching, training, and leading.

There are considerable differences between sports, differences that help to 'shape' coaching practice (Lyle, 2002: 144). Elsewhere, it has been argued that the range of 'coaching roles' is simply too large for a similar set of processes to be inferred (Lyle and Cushion, 2010). The roles identified were the primary school teacher working in extra-curricular classes, the local authority summer programme coach, the community centre leader, the golf club professional (instructor), the national league team sport club coach, and the national representative squad coach; it may seem obvious that these roles have fewer commonalities than they have differences.

REFLECTION

As you read through these comments on roles, I suspect that you will begin to construct your own matrix of roles and distinctive features. In other words, you will begin to distinguish between the roles on the basis of characteristics such as the frequency of the coaching, the motives and level of commitment of the participants, the balance of preparation and play, the place of competition, the technical development involved, and so on.

Formalise your thoughts by constructing a table. Identify six to ten different coaching roles (in context) in the left-hand column and create further columns using the distinctive features suggested above as a starter. Complete each row/role. (This would be a very useful group exercise.)

From a coach education certification perspective, it is difficult to argue that a two-day course and a postgraduate-equivalent programme over two years form part of a meaningful continuum. Would we argue that a three-day first aid course is an appropriate starting point for medical training? There would be substantial merit in researchers focusing on the 'spaces between certificates'. What rewards, recognition, or requirements to practise act as barriers or enablers to further certification? What might be the characteristics of those who take advanced qualifications?

A necessary response to the question 'what is coaching?' is to describe the coach's practice. What does the coach actually do? You will appreciate that this is inevitably an extended treatment or a brief overview. I have approached this by describing the view of coaching competences adopted in a document that offers guidance to designers of coach education programmes (sports coach UK, 2010):

- reflect continuously on coaching practice and challenge personal assumptions and beliefs to improve future performance;
- seek out, synthesise and apply relevant concepts, theories and principles;
- make and critically reflect on decisions in complex and unpredictable situations;
- recognise and resolve problematic and atypical coaching issues through the generation of innovative strategies and solutions;
- build and maintain effective coach–athlete relationships;

11

- design and implement an optimal learning environment to impact on athletes' performance needs;
- adapt interpersonal, teaching and instructing behaviours to the needs of the athlete(s) and context;
- develop athletes to be autonomous decision makers;
- design, implement, monitor, evaluate and regulate advanced training and competition programmes;
- design and implement a planned and strategic approach to performance improvement;
- develop and manage appropriate support structures to facilitate improved performance;
- manage change in the context of the wider sporting, legal, political and socio-economic landscape.

This list of competences is intended to describe high-performing coaches in situations of intensive, high-quality coaching. Nevertheless, the question to ask is 'How far away from this practice does the individual need to be before it is no longer considered to be sports coaching?' Does this image of the 'ideal' coaching process help to differentiate some roles from others? The competences are not value free, and they reflect what might be termed 'higher-order' competences that would be expected of the incumbent of a profession. However, they also narrow considerably the coaching roles in which these competences could be demonstrated.

ADOPTING A POSITION: A SUMMARY

Here we come to the nub of the argument. The following propositions are presented as a series of statements intended to stimulate your critical thinking.

We need to appreciate the 'coaching process' as the descriptor of a coach (rather than individual characteristics). However, it is necessary to understand sports coaching as a 'field of endeavour' that has social meaning – even if that meaning is somewhat obscure. We need to conceptualise sports coaching as a family of roles, rather than an activity or an individual's behaviour.

Sports coaching has a core purpose: to improve sport performance. This is important in relation to other assumed purposes. For example, sport activity may be used instrumentally to encourage social cohesion, and the athletes' personal development may be an underlying driver for individual coaches or for sports policy. Nevertheless, these are applications rather than core purposes.

Taking part in sport involves taking part in sport competition, since this is intrinsic to the activity. There are also many other sport-related forms of activity (e.g. physical education or recreational exercise), many forms of competition, and a range of preparatory forms of sport activity (training). This is a debating point that creates division, but note that the excesses of competition practice do not impact on the definition of the coaching role. I propose that we need to distinguish between preparation for organised forms of competition activity (coaching) and introducing and developing basic techniques and skills outside the competition programme (teaching or instructing). Yes, there are 'grey areas', but we need to adopt a position that has the power to differentiate in the majority of cases.

Sports coaching involves 'preparation with a purpose' – and the purpose is sports participation within identifiable competition. The process attached to this purpose implies a coordination of capacities (individual and team), and therefore attention to the component parts of performance (technical, tactical, psychological, physical, equipment, and so on), and the planning and delivery of the intervention programme necessary to achieve this. If an individual does not direct an intervention programme but offers advice during competition – would this be considered coaching? The answer comes from being willing to adopt a position of applying thresholds, and also from having a more sophisticated classification of sports coaching roles. The individual in question would not satisfy coaching criteria because of the absence of preparation and an intervention programme, but the 'performance management' role might fall into the broad family of sports coaching roles (perhaps also subject to a threshold judgement). We must try not to fall into the trap of offering a critical interpretation of the situation without suggesting alternative definitions.

A coach is defined in two ways:

1 By his or her relationship to the sporting intentions of a particular athlete, squad or team. The coach occupies a technical leadership role in a context in which an improvement in performance is intended, and that sporting performance is to be expressed in organised sport competition. (This is subject to a 'threshold' or set of criteria within the social space that is acknowledged as coaching. If the sport performance is a by-product of activity, or not expressed in organised sport competition, the role occupied by the 'coach figure' might better be described as leader or teacher – although it still falls within the overall family of sports coaching roles.)
2 By a demonstrable capacity – that is, a level of developed expertise. This is likely to be evidenced by certification or prior experience. This does not imply any specific behaviour or practice, and is not related to a current or specific attachment, but merely means that the individual has a capacity to exercise the coaching role.

'To coach' has been interpreted as implying a set of behaviours, processes, even style. This all-embracing shorthand is not sufficient for academic study. It would be more helpful if the term described a relationship – in other words, defined an 'attachment' (level and nature) between the coach and the individual(s) being coached. It does not imply anything about how, why or with what purpose the attachment might be operationalised. Another reason for not using the term to describe practice is that it has come to be used for the behaviours associated solely with the delivery (court-side, pool-side, track-side) aspects of the role.

Sports coaching is defined as:

1 A field of activity with a multiplicity of possible roles. We can conceptualise this as a family term for these roles. Yes, there is a complex matrix of levels of expertise, levels of

athlete and team performance, role responsibilities, social status, personal characteristics, career pathways and coaching domains. One of the marks of our conceptual maturity as a field of study will be when we can bring clarity and understanding to this matrix.

2   An aggregation of behaviour and practice intended to result in improved sport performance. It is marked by the design and delivery of a comprehensive intervention programme (preparation and competition), which is monitored and regulated. This process is subject to threshold judgements, but not easily quantified. The intensity, reach and sophistication of the intervention in different domains need further research. The association of intensity, athlete commitment and motives with the 'quality' of coaching means that coaching is most often associated with performance athletes.

It is very tempting to conclude a discussion of 'what is coaching?' by saying, 'Well, that depends.' It is to be hoped that the arguments presented in this chapter will have persuaded you that nothing should be taken for granted, and the question is more significant than it would first seem to be. What can you do?

- Separate out core function and value-laden prescriptions.
- Appreciate the social space and the impact of deployment circumstances on coaching practices.
- Acknowledge that the use of the term 'to coach' delineates an 'attachment' between coach and athletes, but that this role has very many variations.
- Consider the proposition that each of the coaching roles within the family of sports coaching has its place in the panoply of sports provision, but that the professionalisation of sports coaching depends on the acceptance of a threshold level of engagement, purpose, complexity, expertise and context.

LEARNING MORE

It is common practice at the end of a chapter to suggest how you might further develop your insights into the subject matter of the chapter. Certainly the references will help you. However, this chapter is different from many others in that (1) it is 'conceptual'; (2) its purpose is to stimulate – to raise questions and not necessarily answer all of them; and (3) it is demanding because it requires substantial reading and immersion in the literature. Therefore, this is a 'starter' chapter; it should have stimulated your thinking about coaching and led you to question some common assumptions. You should continue to read as widely as possible. In doing so – if you accompany your reading with discussion, debate and reflection – you will begin to develop a mature perspective on key concepts in sports coaching.

14

The inevitable conclusion is that there are layers of complexity and context, multiple lenses, and a very wide-ranging social space for coaching; don't be taken in by the apparent simplicity of the initial questions.

REFERENCES

Armour, K. (2004) Coaching pedagogy. In R.L. Jones, K.M. Armour and P. Potrac (eds), *Sports coaching cultures: from practice to theory*. London: Routledge.

Bush, A. (2007) What is coaching? In J. Denison (ed.), *Coaching knowledges: understanding the dynamics of sport performance*. London: A & C Black.

Cassidy, T., Jones, R.L. and Potrac, P. (2009) Introduction. In T. Cassidy, R.L. Jones and P. Potrac (eds), *Understanding sport coaching* (2nd ed.). London: Routledge.

Côté, J. and Gilbert, W.D. (2009) An integrative definition of coaching effectiveness and expertise. *International Journal of Sports Science & Coaching* 4(3): 307–323.

Côté, J. and Sedgwick, W.A. (2003) Effective behaviors of expert rowing coaches: a quantitative investigation of Canadian athletes and coaches. *International Sports Journal* 7(1): 62–77.

Côté, J., Bruner, M., Erickson, K., Strachan, L. and Fraser-Thomas, J. (2010) Athlete development and coaching. In J. Lyle and C. Cushion (eds), *Sports coaching: professionalisation and practice*. Edinburgh: Churchill Livingstone.

Cushion, C.J. (2007a) Modelling the complexity of the coaching process. *International Journal of Sport Science and Coaching* 2(4): 395–401.

Cushion, C.J. (2007b) Modelling the complexity of the coaching process: a response to commentaries. *International Journal of Sport Science and Coaching* 2(4): 427–433.

Erickson, K., Côté, J. and Fraser-Thomas, J. (2007) Sport experiences, milestones, and educational activities associated with high-performance coaches' development. *Sport Psychologist* 21: 302–316.

Gilbert, W.D. and Trudel, P. (2001) Learning to coach through experience: reflection in model youth sport coaches. *Journal of Teaching in Physical Education* 21: 16–34.

Johns, D.P. and Johns, J. (2000) Surveillance, subjectivism and technologies of power: an analysis of the discursive practice of high-performance sport. *International Review for the Sociology of Sport* 35: 219–234.

Jones, R.L. (2000) Towards a sociology of coaching. In R.L. Jones and K.M. Armour (eds), *The sociology of sport: theory and practice*. London: Addison Wesley Longman.

Jones, R.L. (2006) How can educational concepts inform sports coaching? In R.L. Jones (ed.), *The sports coach as educator: re-conceptualising sports coaching*. London: Routledge.

Kidman, L. (2005) *Athlete-centred coaching: developing inspired and inspiring people*. Christchurch, NZ: Innovative Communications.

Lyle, J. (2002) *Sports coaching concepts: a framework for coaches' behaviour*. London: Routledge.

Lyle, J. (2007) Modelling the complexity of the coaching process: a commentary. *International Journal of Sports Science & Coaching* 2(4): 407–409.

Lyle, J. and Cushion, C. (2010) Narrowing the field: some key questions about sports coaching. In J. Lyle and C. Cushion (eds), *Sports coaching: professionalisation and practice*. Edinburgh: Churchill Livingstone.

MORI (2004) *Sports coaching in the UK*. Leeds: sports coach UK.

North, J. (2009) *The coaching workforce 2009–2016*. Leeds: National Coaching Foundation.

sports coach UK (2008) *UK coaching framework*. Leeds: sports coach UK.

sports coach UK (2009) UKCC Level 4 participation coaching: scoping exercise. Internal paper, May 2009. Leeds: sports coach UK.

sports coach UK (2010) UKCC Level 4 guidance document. Internal paper. Leeds: sports coach UK.

Taylor, W. and Garratt, D. (2010) The professionalisation of sports coaching: definitions, challenges and critique. In J. Lyle and C. Cushion (eds), *Sports coaching: professionalisation and practice*. Edinburgh: Churchill Livingstone.

Trudel, P. and Gilbert, W.D. (2006) Coaching and coach education. In D. Kirk, M. O'Sullivan and D. McDonald (eds), *Handbook of research in physical education*. London: Sage.

Trudel, P., Lemyre, F., Werthner, P. and Camiré, M. (2007) Characteristic development in youth sport: the perspectives of ice hockey and baseball coaches. *International Journal of Coaching Science* 1(2): 21–35.

Vergeer, I. and Hogg, J.M. (1999) Coaches' decision policies and the participation of injured athletes in competition. *Sport Psychologist* 13: 42–56.

16

CHAPTER TWO

DEVELOPMENTALLY APPROPRIATE APPROACHES TO COACHING CHILDREN

BOB MUIR, GARETH MORGAN, ANDY ABRAHAM
AND DAVID MORLEY

CHAPTER OUTLINE

- Child development principles: to specialise early or not?
- The coach decision-making model
- Theory into practice
- Learning more

INTRODUCTION

There are two typical approaches to coaching children prevalent in the United Kingdom today, neither of which is likely to support the long-term developmental needs of children. Worryingly, within the domain of children's coaching it is the more dominant cultural influence of performance sport that has strongly contributed to 'modified' adult sport-specific practices becoming the accepted norm. Many coaches equate their effectiveness to win–loss records, aspiring to emulate the behaviours of 'high-performance' coaches. Common features of such practice include episodic planning and delivery (i.e. responding to performances as opposed to working towards long-term goals), blocked practices that work on specific techniques, a focus on tidy practice that discourages mistakes (mistakes are often a key marker of children trying new things), communication methods focused on coach-led problem solving, and selecting children on the basis of current performance. Indeed, studies of elite athlete development in sport suggest an ongoing current trend towards early specialisation, identification and selection (Ford *et al.*, 2009).

There are those who recognise the problems with this approach (or are simply not aware of it) and try to offer a more developmentally appropriate sporting environment for children. This form of 'coaching', often delivered by parents and other volunteers, typically leads to less formalised, unstructured environments focused on keeping children 'active and busy'. While these practices may be underpinned with some thought to 'development through experimentation and play', they probably lack sufficient structure and direction to ensure that learning occurs for everyone.

Consequently, lots of children are at risk of being exposed either to demanding physical programmes that promote high volumes of competition and pressure to win, often resulting in a lack of playing time, or to practices that are so free that development is due to chance and therefore only the naturally gifted develop. Both approaches can contribute to drop-out in youth sport settings (Weiss and Williams, 2004). To interrogate these trends effectively, the question 'who are we coaching and for what purpose?' arises.

The purpose of this chapter, therefore, is to offer alternative approaches to coaching children in order to stimulate 'ideas' for your own coaching practice that are grounded in an 'understanding' of the needs of children as opposed to meeting the ego or babysitting needs of adult coaches.

CHILD DEVELOPMENT PRINCIPLES: TO SPECIALISE EARLY OR NOT?

We made reference earlier to an increasing trend for early specialisation, identification and selection in sport. This is probably reflective of human desire to see and reward children who display desirable adult characteristics, such as sport skill. Indeed, the media are very quick to report and hype child prodigies in a broad range of domains such as academia, music and sport. Examples in sport include Tiger Woods in golf, Theo Walcott in football and, more recently, Tom Daly in diving; but are these examples of early specialisation successes really enough to direct a fundamental approach to coaching? The obvious answer to this question should be no. Indeed, there are now a number of participant development models from a broad range of authors that should lead coaches to question the usefulness of early specialisation and selection (Côté et al., 2010). However, a recent review by Baker et al. (2009) suggests that inadequate evidence exists to resolve this matter.

In principle, early specialisation is reliant on identifying talent early in a child's life against some set, normally performance-related, criteria (Abbott and Collins, 2004), and predicting that they will respond to prolonged and specific training in a single sport thus becoming elite performers. Indeed, there is some evidence to support the idea that elite footballers in the United Kingdom have come through such a process. In reality, research identifies that such approaches have a very low success rate in predicting future elite success, and elite coaches working with talented performers agree that the approach is flawed (Martindale et al., 2005). Furthermore, the approach is potentially psychologically and biologically damaging to many of the children involved in early specialisation approaches.

Consequently, research in participant development argues for coaches to take a long-term developmental approach to coaching children, one that matches both curriculum and teaching approach to the needs of the child, not to the needs of the coach. Children's coaches must therefore pay attention to the biological, psychological and social (bio-psycho-social) develop-

18

ment needs of each individual child in order to provide a platform for future engagement in sport and physical activity. Importantly, coaches must look beyond 'here and now' markers of physical skill and maturation and consider factors that 'distinguish between potential and the ability to translate that potential into performance' (Bailey *et al.*, 2010: 57). Such distinctions in bio-psycho-social developmental and personal goals of individual children reveal much about the complexity of coaching children. In the next section, we offer a model of coach decision making as a framework to help coaches of children guide their planning in order to deliver practice to meet the needs of their participants.

DIRECTED TASK

Think about a coaching session that you have recently delivered. What were your goals for the session? Where did these goals come from and whose needs were they aimed at fulfilling? What impact did these goals have on one another? What goal was your priority? Why was that goal your priority? How did the focus on these goals build on previous sessions and help prepare for future development?

THE COACH DECISION-MAKING MODEL

Coaching is often portrayed as being about doing, but what is it that good (i.e. high-performing) coaches spend their time doing? Evidence from a number of authors suggests that they are thinking about how to solve the problem of improving their participants' development and performance. In short, high-performing coaches are continually making decisions, which are then put into action in order to stimulate, challenge and facilitate the meaningful development of their participants towards identified goals. A coach's practice often involves a constant internal dialogue that compares their predetermined plans, set learning tasks and accompanying teaching strategies with the reality of their participants' progress towards the set goals within a session. This constant shift in practice requires the coach to make decisions about whether to change the plan on the basis of observations, evaluation and reactions to 'goings on' (Jones and Wallace, 2006) in order to make appropriate adjustments that deviate from predetermined plans (Saury and Durand, 1998). Consequently, Abraham and Collins's (2010) conclusion that coaching practice is a goal-led decision-making process would seem to be a fair one.

In order to demonstrate this process, we offer a model (Figure 2.1) of coach decision making drawn from our work with high-performing coaches. The model displays how high-performing coaches can develop ideas, based on an excellent understanding of:

- the child they coach (in terms of their biological, psychological and social development);
- the sport (in terms of developmentally appropriate movement, technical and tactical skills);
- teaching and learning (in terms of learning tasks and associated instructional behaviours).

This breadth and depth of knowledge and practical skill enables high-performing coaches to explicitly plan for and implement coaching that is developmentally appropriate, builds on where the child has come from and helps prepare them for where they wish to go.

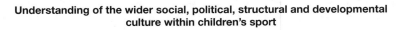

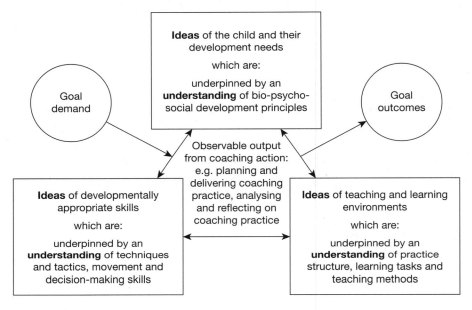

Figure 2.1 Summary of the coach decision-making process.

Source: Adapted from Abraham and Collins (2011).

DIRECTED TASK

Think about a coaching session that you have recently delivered. What bodies of knowledge did you draw on to make decisions during the planning and delivery of the coaching session?

After reflecting on this question and noting down your thoughts, consider the balance of knowledge related to the child, the sport and teaching and learning that informed your thinking. Does this highlight any opportunities for further development of your coaching knowledge and practice?

KEY CONCEPT: IDEAS AND UNDERSTANDING – A CLARIFICATION

We have already used the terms 'ideas' and 'understanding'; however, we suggest that spending a little time considering the meaning of these words can clarify why both are important in coaching. Simplistically, ideas are often about things that we can do, but where do ideas come from? They can come from other people, they can come from guesswork or they can come about through understanding.

Distinguishing where ideas come from in this manner is important because it can lead to more critical thought about why we do what we do. Anderson (1982) suggested that knowledge can be split into two broad domains: declarative knowledge and procedural knowledge. Declarative knowledge can be defined as the 'why' knowledge, or the knowledge of 'understanding', while procedural knowledge is 'doing' knowledge, or 'ideas' concerning how to do something (see Abraham and Collins, 1998, for a more in-depth discussion of this topic within the coaching environment). This separation is important since it explains how it is possible to have one without the other – that is, the coach who does something (procedural) based on 'ideas' without sufficient understanding of knowing why (declarative). It also displays how if we spend more time understanding why things happen, new ideas are more likely to develop.

Working through the process from a coach's perspective

In essence, we are suggesting that the practice of a high performing children's coach (i.e. the observable output) entails the constant integration and constructive alignment (Biggs, 2003) of declarative and procedural knowledge relating to the child, developmentally appropriate skills, and teaching and learning in order to guide the progress of their participants towards short-, medium- and long-term goals using the process shown in Figure 2.1.

KEY CONCEPT: CONSTRUCTIVE ALIGNMENT

The 'constructive' aspect acknowledges that children construct their own meaning through the learning activities; learning is not something that is transmitted from coach to child but is something that children create for themselves. Therefore, coaching is the catalyst for learning. The coach's primary task is to facilitate children's engagement in learning activities that provide a scaffold to achieve their desired goals. Remember, what the child does is actually more important in determining what is learned than what the

21

coach does. The 'alignment' aspect refers to the coach establishing a learning environment that connects the developmentally appropriate skills, learning tasks (i.e. focus on
single or multiple skills; opposed or unopposed practice; blocked, random or serial
practice; drill, modified game or game, etc.), coaching behaviour (i.e. timing and type
of feedback; open or closed questioning; demonstrations; reinforcement behaviours,
etc.) and assessment (i.e. meaningful, authentic assessment that provides feedback
against the learning for both child and coach) to the child's personal and sport-specific
goals.

Ideas

So, for example, a coach of a group of mixed-ability 8-year-old children working in an after-
school programme at a local primary school may be focusing in the short term on developing
their fundamental movement skills and associated personal characteristics in order to build
their perceived and actual competence, while working towards a medium-term goal of
developing transitional movement skills to provide a platform for lifelong participation and the
achievement of personally referenced excellence in sport and physical activity (Bailey et al.,
2010). In order to achieve these goals, the coach will require ideas about the developmentally
appropriate skills the children need to develop (i.e. fundamental and transitional movement
patterns; increased awareness of space, time and possession, etc.). Equally, the coach will have
ideas about the personal characteristics development needs of the children (i.e. grouping
participants by physical maturation, focused on increasing perception of competence and
confidence; promoting positive social interaction through team games, etc.); and, finally, the
coach will have ideas about the types of teaching and learning environments that they need
to create (i.e. modifying the space, task, equipment, people and speed, etc.) in order to enable
the children to realise their potential and make unrestricted participation choices across their
lifespan (Bailey et al., 2010).

Conversely, a coach of a talented 14-year-old basketball player may agree a medium-term
goal of supporting the player's progress towards being selected for an under-16 national league
team, while keeping in mind the player's potential for progressing to professional senior
teams. In order to achieve this goal, the coach will draw on ideas about the developmentally
appropriate skills that the player needs to develop (i.e. individual position-specific skill
development such as improving their shooting and/or tactical skill development such as
improving their decision making in zone defence, etc.). Equally, the coach will have ideas
about the personal characteristics that need to be developed by the player (i.e. emphasis on
physical, mental and social development, etc.). Finally, the coach will have ideas about the
types of teaching and learning environments that they need to create in order to enable the
player to achieve their personal and sport-specific goals (i.e. blocked, single-skill unopposed
drill progressions versus variable, multiple-skill opposed modified practice, etc.).

22

Understanding

Building on this, we would argue that the ideas outlined above should be underpinned by an understanding of the biological, psychological and social (bio-psycho-social) development needs of the child; techniques, tactics, movement and decision-making principles; and practice structure, learning tasks and teaching methods. This can only be achieved through the coach developing a breadth and depth of knowledge in each of the areas.

Understanding of the child

So, deeper understanding of a child will come from developing a sound knowledge of some key principles:

- All human development is facilitated and constrained by an interactive dynamic of biological, psychological, and sociological factors that change as children grow chronologically (Bailey *et al.*, 2010).
- Children's skeletal, muscular and nervous systems develop at different rates throughout childhood, and the variance associated with these different rates has significant implications for each individual child's physical development and, consequently, their sporting performance and improvement.
- Further, this biological development will have most obvious connotations for children's psycho-motor development. That is, each child's capacity to demonstrate the movement skills fundamental to sports participation (e.g. balancing, travelling, controlling objects) will vary according to (the maturity of) their physical make-up. Hence, as developing these psycho-motor behaviours is critical to all children, whether they progress to elite-level sport or to lifelong participation, coaches should be considerate of each child's individual needs.
- Children have been found to possess a variety of reasons for participating in sport, but these essentially comprise a mixture of desiring skill development, physical development and social interaction (Bailey *et al.*, 2010).
- These motives, however, will most likely change over time, with younger children seeking excitement and pleasure while older children strive for achievement and satisfaction (Bailey *et al.*, 2010).
- Evidence suggests that key correlating indicators of learning and development include participants' self-regulatory and meta-cognitive skills (e.g. goal setting and performance evaluating), and that these appear to begin developing around the age of 9–11 (Freeman, 2000). These psychological skills are particularly important for enhancing motivation, optimising focus and, ultimately, leading to improved learning.
- Côté *et al.*'s (2010) 4 Cs perspective on positive youth development offers a useful framework from a psycho-social perspective, with key messages for coaches relating to *competence* (individualise competence information that is positive but also realistic in relation to what participants can observe through peer comparison), *confidence* (enable competence to be evaluated by participants according to self-referenced improvement

and effort), *connection* (promote positive participant–peer, participant–parent and participant–coach interaction and the demonstration of pro-social behaviours by encouraging cooperation and recognition of the needs and abilities of others) and *character* or *caring* (promote moral reasoning and provide opportunities to demonstrate character and caring), which is important for coaches attempting to understand their athletes.

- Childhood includes certain critical social development periods, with the initial interactions experienced with adults and other children in early school years and the transition that occurs as they move from primary to secondary school being regarded as significant milestones that can influence children's longer-term social competence.

Understanding of skills

Equally, a greater understanding of developmentally appropriate sport-specific skills will come from developing a sound knowledge of the following principles:

- A fundamental basis for the development of both performance excellence and lifelong participation requires the incorporation of a wide variety of cognitive, perceptual and motor skills into the development programmes of all children.
- Children aged 0–6 require informal learning opportunities in the home and pre-school environments aimed at developing rudimentary movement skills (e.g. pushing, kicking, reaching) and a love or enjoyment of physical activity.
- From the age of approximately 5 or 6 to 8 or 9, children benefit from a broad range of fundamental skills (e.g. hopping, skipping, jumping, sending, receiving and pivoting) in a playful context, with these contributing to participation in sport and developing more advanced skills in later years.
- Then, from the age of 8 to 12, appropriate opportunities should be provided for participants to learn a wide range of transferable sport skills (e.g. creating space for self and others).
- As athletes progress in training age and skill, fundamental skills should assume proportionately less of the practice time, with sport-specific and decision-making skills emphasised in order to underpin the development of future successful performance and involvement in more specialised activities.

Understanding of teaching and learning

Finally, a greater understanding of teaching and learning will come from developing a sound knowledge of the following principles:

- Coaches influence the learning climate and participants' learning through behaviours and practices such as the manner of their interactions with participants, the way tasks are structured and managed, and how performance is judged and acknowledged.
- Careful planning is required if learning is to be strategically facilitated across the long- (e.g. seasonally) to short-term (e.g. individual session) continuum. To achieve this, bio-

24

B. Muir *et al.*

psycho-social and sport-specific targets must be established and worked towards through consideration of the overall management of sessions (i.e. use of space, time and equipment), selection of learning tasks and cues, and identification of learning assessment methods.

- Certain coaching behaviours, when used appropriately, can greatly facilitate learning (see below for some elaboration on this, and Williams and Ford, 2009, for a more comprehensive review).
- For instance, demonstrations can be very effective for learning (especially with new skills; Horn and Williams, 2004), but not so effective at other times (e.g. refining already learned skills, or introducing complex new skills; Horn and Williams, 2004), and even ineffective or harmful on certain occasions (i.e. situations in which one specific technique is not necessarily required to achieve an outcome; Wulf, 2007). Hence, coaches need to think about how they use this behaviour with their children.
- Coaches should also consider what type of feedback (i.e. informational, behavioural, correctional, reinforcing, motivational, positive or negative, etc.) they should be providing, when, and how often. While younger children trying to master new tasks may benefit from more (amount) immediate (timing) feedback to encourage quick improvements, less (amount) delayed (timing) instructional feedback may prove most beneficial for retention, transfer and learning (Wulf and Shea, 2004). Too much feedback may overload the child and create coach dependence.
- Instead of telling children how well they did, they should ask them relevant and challenging questions that provoke children's curiosity, improve understanding of skills, focus attention, increase confidence and develop decision-making and problem-solving skills. However, coaches must also pay attention to avoid inappropriate excessive questioning, which can create anxiety and defensiveness within children, who feel as though they are being tested (Morgan, 2006).
- The type of practice tasks that coaches devise for their children can affect children's learning. This can also be linked to the overall structure of the learning programme within which children participate.
- In terms of the practice type, while blocked and constant practice of a skill leads to improved short-term performance, random and variable practice is associated with better learning in the medium to long term (see Williams and Ford, 2009, for a review). Hence, coaches need to consider the associated trade-off between short-term feelings of competence and longer-term retention within their coaching when selecting practice tasks for their children.
- The larger-scale programme structure within which children participate and progress through can be adapted to most effectively promote long-term participant development towards excellence and/or lifelong physical activity.
- During the early stages (sampling years, i.e. 6–12) of participation, with an emphasis on playful activities (i.e. deliberate play), the coach's role is mainly to act as a 'resource person' (Macdonald et al., 2005: 4) who can modify the environment or supply directive feedback and instructions in order to quickly correct errors. (Note: this approach does

need to be balanced with the need to develop self-regulatory skills in the older end of this age group.)

- As children get a little older (specialising years, i.e. 13–15), coaches should shift the emphasis of their practice structure in order to retain the sense of (deliberate) play that perhaps made initial participation so appealing, but now also introduce a more intensive direction towards learning and improvement (i.e. deliberate practice).

- With a further maturing of age, children will either become more intensely involved in development (investment years, i.e. 16-plus) or seek to participate for other reasons (recreational years, i.e. 13-plus). For the latter, coaches should carry on the role they performed during the specialising years. To assist participants' ongoing development, however, the coaches' technical and tactical instruction should become more focused, with an increasingly 'serious' (Macdonald et al., 2005: 5) approach to athletes' practice involvement.

- Ongoing throughout childhood is the necessity for coaches to make formative and, sometimes, summative assessments of their participants' development. These judgements, which in certain contexts (e.g. youth academies) dictate participants' retention within development programmes, occur to some extent in every context. For instance, at the beginning of all coach–athlete relationships, coaches will make an appraisal of their participants' attributes, which will then inform the types of goals they deem to be appropriate. Furthermore, coaches are then required to make ongoing decisions regarding the type of challenges they regard as being pertinent for each participant, and then increase or decrease (depending on what is appropriate for each individual) the demands of the tasks they create so as to facilitate their participants' progression towards 'improved performance' (with 'performance' referring to the holistic sense of child development here).

Given the breadth and depth of factors that the coach has to cope with and the knowledge required to do this, the really innovative skill that high-performing coaches exhibit is the synthesis of ideas from these three interdependent areas to inform their actions, decisions and behaviours during the planning, delivery and reflective process (i.e. the observable output). Indeed, coaches who spend time considering these three areas while planning prior to their session are more likely to be attentive to the child's needs, to be clearer with learning task instructions and to be able to provide specific, congruent feedback more frequently. In addition, coaches who reflect in (during the coaching session) and on (after the coaching session – see Chapter 8 for a more thorough discussion on reflection) the constructive alignment between the developmental objectives, the selected learning tasks and the associated teaching behaviours are more likely to enhance the learning experience of the child and subsequent progress towards specified goals – interestingly, a goal of planning!

THEORY INTO PRACTICE: IMPLEMENTING THE COACH DECISION-MAKING MODEL

To conclude this chapter, we illustrate the application of the decision-making model within a children's coaching context. Obviously, this is pretty difficult to achieve within a book chapter! Therefore, picking up from the previously stated viewpoint that planning is integral to the facilitation of learning, we shall draw upon appropriate 'child', 'sport' and 'teaching and learning' considerations to apply some of the associated principles that have been overviewed within a vignette and associated session plan for a specific situation.

In order to try to make this exemplar as accessible to readers as possible, we present a practice session involving 11-year-old boys. Hence, those readers who work with children of a younger or older age should consider how they would adapt the principles referred to in order to reflect the needs of their participants. Further, rather than focusing on an individual athlete (which would obviously make the ethos of individualisation much more attainable for us as authors), this exemplar will be for a group of 16–20 children, a number that is perhaps much more realistic to you, the reader. The following vignette and accompanying plan illustrates how Martin, a children's football coach, uses the coaching decision-making model (Figure 2.1) to inform his planning for coaching practice.

physical, psychological and social skills that will provide a platform for lifelong participation in sport.

Martin is in his third year of coaching this particular group of boys, and during this time he has changed the emphasis within practice time from fundamental movement skills to transitional sport and decision-making skills. Over the course of the past three seasons, Martin has emphasised the development of fundamental movement and technical sport skills by drawing on a range of blocked, random and variable practices. In addition to focusing on these skills, Martin has also worked on the hidden curriculum of developing the boys' psychological skills, to develop better and more independent learners. While he has always used deliberate play and various forms of modified games to apply these skills in sport-specific contexts, the emphasis of his teaching behaviour has not been on developing concepts of team play and tactical understanding.

Moving into the fourth year, he is keen to harness the previously learned fundamental and transitional movement skills (with particular focus on short, sharp acceleration, stopping, changing direction and body positional change in response to movement of the ball, team-mates and opponents) in an integrated fashion to focus on the development of tactical principles that apply across invasion sports. In preparation for the forthcoming season, Martin wants to create practices that emphasise defending territory, regaining possession of the ball, retaining possession of the ball, and creating space to attack and exploit. With these goals in mind, Martin has decided he wants to focus tonight's practice on:

- movement off the ball to create space for self and others;
- identifying team-mates in space and sending effective passes;
- appreciating the risk–reward associated with a penetrative pass versus a lateral routine pass.

As with all of Martin's sessions, in addition to his desire to develop his participants' technical and tactical skills, of equal importance to him is that every child leaves the session with a sense of personal achievement and enjoyment.

Building on his own experiences as a football player, he prefers to design games-based practices that develop skills which combine movement and sport-specific techniques, perception and decision making. In doing so, he sometimes encourages free play and experimentation, during which times he sees his role as one of facilitating the organisation of their games, while at other times he uses adaptations and game conditions to guide his participants towards specific goals. During these more structured games, Martin likes to draw on a range of divergent questions that encourage children to take responsibility for their own learning and develop their understanding of techniques and tactics. On other occasions, he uses a combination of teaching behaviours, including positive reinforcement, demonstrations, and corrective feedback to guide their learning.

Drawing on these principles, Martin has decided to construct a variety of deliberate play scenarios (with increasingly demanding game conditions) in working towards the goals of tonight's practice. In order to reduce the technical complexity of the task and allow greater focus and attention on tactical decisions (i.e. goals 1, 2 and 3, above) Martin has decided to use a throw–catch game. During the planning process, Martin considered the factors that impact his participants' capacity to meet the demands of the learning tasks and their subsequent feelings of competence. Therefore, to make the tasks appropriately challenging while also still providing a realistic opportunity to experience success, Martin decided to split the groups according to their ability and physical maturation. In addition, Martin recognised that by running two games simultaneously he would provide greater opportunities for practice while enabling him to observe and help children at their own level. Martin intends to use rotations as an opportunity to speak individually with children and provide differentiated, personalised feedback away from their peers and to engage them in observational learning by directing their attention to specific technical and tactical cues.

Martin has particular concerns that some of his participants are not as forthcoming as they used to be and are tending to operate on the periphery of the session. He is conscious that his participants are at an age where they are beginning to recognise that other children can do things more easily than they can. Consequently, he planned the structure and rules of the game scenarios to include unopposed wide support positions, thereby enabling these children to play a central role within the game but without the pressure of opposition. He also wants to use the game-based scenarios to promote positive participant–peer interaction by encouraging cooperation and recognition of the needs and abilities of each participant.

While Martin's plan has the potential to shape his coaching practice and serve as a guide for delivery, he cannot completely predict his participants' behaviour or the accompanying practice adjustments he will need to make. Consequently, once practice begins, his effective interactive decision making and ability to respond to the differing needs of each of his participants become very important. Martin's practice is therefore likely to involve a constant interplay between his intentions within the plan, selected learning tasks and associated teaching behaviours, and how he adapts to the situation as it unfolds, on the basis of his previous experience and knowledge of his participants.

General Details:

Date: 26-01-2011   Time: 16:30–18:00   Venue: Sports Hall

Session Objectives:	1. Movement off the ball to create space for self and others
	2. Identifying team-mates in space and sending effective passes
	3. Appreciating the risk–reward associated with a penetrative pass versus a lateral routine pass

No of Players: 18–20 players   Age: 10–11yrs

Participant Considerations:

Physical:
Generally good level of agility and coordination among the group; some participants' object control, speed, strength and power more advanced than others.

Psychological:
All participants are measuring themselves against each other; most are able to combine basic skills efficiently; some participants are strong at being able to scan and take decisions based on information, whereas others need additional support – time and space. Make use of *scaffolding questions and demonstrations.*

Social:
Strong feelings of connectivity and teamwork within the group – remind those with greater confidence and ability to be sensitive and supportive of their peers.

Technical:
Some participants are modifying basic skills to create their own sequences in response to the game constraints; some are still refining basic movement skills and need support in applying them to bigger games.

Tactical:
Some participants are demonstrating excellent understanding of time, space and selection of appropriate technique – others need support to progress from 2v2/3v3 to 5v5 scenarios.

Specific individual points to consider:
Mike and James – recent growth spurt; lacking confidence on ball when under pressure.
Richard, Ben, Ian and Sam – strong, physical, technical and tactical ability.
Speak with Max and parents – check on injury status.

Content Considerations:

Technical:
Bounce pass and overhead pass – NB. focus on body position and movement today.

Figure 2.2 Coaching plan.

30

Tactical:	Spatial awareness – check for scanning skills – work in triangles – pass selection and decision making.
Movement skills:	Emphasise change of pace and direction – signalling with body positioning, communication – hand–arm signals.

Teaching and Learning Considerations:

Learning tasks:	Use blocked and variable practices for warm-up progressions.
	Modified throw–catch invasion game scenarios to reduce the technical complexity.
	Use wide support players to provide overload conditions and encourage penetrative passes.
	Increase game complexity using conditions and zones.
	Start with small 4v4 game – split group into four teams working on two pitches simultaneously – progress to 8v8 – revert back to 4v4 if necessary.
Teaching methods:	Use participants within demonstrations to organise and explain activities.
	Use specific positive reinforcement to emphasise cooperative behaviours and achievement of objectives.
	Focus on divergent questioning – use convergent questioning and corrective feedback where necessary to guide learners.
	Use rotations to provide differentiated, personalised feedback and direct observational learning to specific tactical cues.
Specific individual points to consider:	Ensure that Mike and James have an opportunity to play the role of unopposed wide support players. Assign leadership responsibilities to Richard, Ben, Ian and Sam. Encourage them to use a range of verbal cues and movement to create time and space for their team-mates to receive the ball.

Figure 2.2 Continued

31

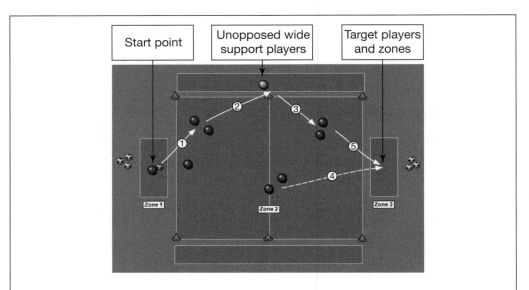

Start point | Unopposed wide support players | Target players and zones

Organisation and game objectives – 4v4 with 1 unopposed wide sender-receiver:

- Ball starts in zone 1 with the blue player. The ball is transferred into zone 2 to a team-mate using hands.
- Objective for the blue team is to work as a team and move the ball into the opponents' (red team) target zone 3. 1pt for a successful catch by a blue player in target zone 3. Upon scoring, the ball will start with a red player in zone 3 and they will attack through zone 2 towards zone 1.

Game conditions:

- The ball must remain in the air and players can't travel with the ball.
- When in possession of the ball, both teams are able to use the unopposed wide support player (yellow player) but they can only operate in their designated area.

Game progression:

- The ball can either be passed aerially or through a bounce pass.
- Once the ball enters into zone 2 then the ball must go wide to the designated unopposed wide player (yellow).
- The designated unopposed wide player (yellow) may enter zone 2 after they have received and sent a pass – in this instance another player from the team in possession must take the place of the yellow player in the wide channel.

Figure 2.3 Game scenario 1.

B. Muir *et al.*

Teaching strategy | Sample questions:

- Question 1: On winning possession of the ball, what strategy do we need to use in order to transition quickly?
  Answer: Provide good width and depth to the field through positive and intelligent movement away from the player in possession of the ball.
- Question 2: If a defender is tight to your team-mate, to what side in relation to defensive pressure should we pass the ball?
  Answer: The opposite side to pressure.
- Question 3: What is essential in relation to attacking team shape when the ball is played into the wide support players?
  Answer: We don't all get attracted to the ball and look to maintain width and depth.
- Question 4: If the defensive player is screening the line of the ball into the target players, what other passing techniques can we use to effectively transfer the ball?
  Answer: Look to either play the ball with a more 'looped' technique or quickly change the point of attack to prevent the defender cutting the line of the pass off.

Figure 2.3 Continued

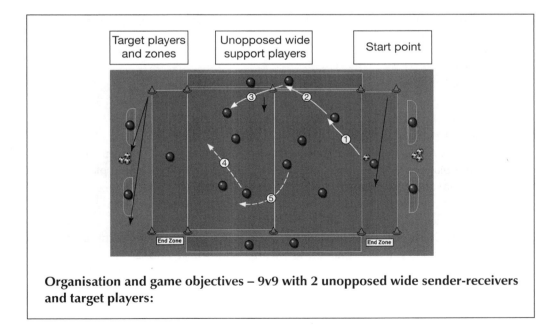

Organisation and game objectives – 9v9 with 2 unopposed wide sender-receivers and target players:

Figure 2.4 Game scenario 2.

- Ball starts in end zone with the blue player. The ball is transferred into the first of the two middle zones.
- The team in possession can overload each zone by one player. The players on the side can operate up and down unchallenged and support as additional overload mechanisms.
- The ball can either be passed aerially or through a bounce pass.
- If the reds win the ball, then they will operate in the opposite direction. If blues score, then the ball will start with the reds in their end zone.
- Any spare players will work with the coach, analysing performance to then help support and feed back to team-mates.

Game conditions:

- The ball can only be transferred one zone at a time with the objective of getting the ball into the target players.

Teaching strategy | Sample questions:

- Question 1: When defending as a team, what type of principles will be important if we want to prevent the forward pass into the target player?
  Answer: Team need to quickly become compact on the side of play and force play backwards or across the field.
- Question 2: If we have the opportunity to overload each zone by one player, how will we utilise this overload?
  Answer: By maximising zone space and supporting quickly – create good angles of support.
- Question 3: If the attacking team can overload the zone they occupy, is the danger with the player in possession or their team-mates advanced of the ball?
  Answer: Players advanced of the ball.
- Question 4: So what should we do about this?
  Answer: We need to mark the player advanced of the ball. Immediately put pressure on the player in possession to make distribution predictable (force play in one direction) and difficult.
- Question 5: If the defensive team cut off the forward pass between the two middle zones, what strategy could we implement?
  Answer: Utilise the unopposed wide support players to adjust the point of attack. (These players must be encouraged to operate quickly along the side of the field.)

Figure 2.4 Continued

> **Player rotation notes:**
>
> - Each player must spend one game of the five being a target player.
> - Each player must spend one of the five games as a wide support player.
> - Any resting players will analyse the game using the following questions:
>
> Question 1: How well is your team using the opportunity to overload the zones when attacking?
>
> Question 2: What would you do differently to gain more success?

Figure 2.4 Continued

SUMMARY

Our aim at the beginning of this chapter was to discuss and highlight different procedural 'ideas' in association with declarative explanations in order to develop an 'understanding' of the coaching of children. In doing so, we offered a framework for coach decision making to display how having and applying a knowledge of the child, developmentally appropriate skills and teaching and learning can lead to a more comprehensive approach to delivering coaching practice for children. We have illustrated that effective coaching practice rests on the coach's ability to draw on knowledge from several linked domains to develop optimal learning environments; it involves a continuous process of decision making about when and how to intervene in order to maintain momentum and progression towards the achievement of specified goals relative to the child's age and stage of development.

LEARNING MORE

Baker *et al.* (2009) present an interesting review on early specialisation and the specific issues related to training the child athlete – as of course do the other chapters in this book. An excellent overview of coaches' roles in the development of athletes at different ages and competitive levels in sport is provided by Côté *et al.* (2010); as in this chapter, a strong case is made for a more participant-centred definition of coaching excellence. Other useful sources of information on the application of skill acquisition and the implications for structuring coaching practice are presented by Abraham and Collins (2011), Ford *et al.* (2009) and Williams and Ford (2009). In addition, Morley *et al.* (2011) present a fascinating account of a context in which talent development, the inter-dependency of participation and performance, and the use of developmentally appropriate practices became real-life issues for a national governing body of sport.

REFERENCES

Abbott, A. and Collins, D. (2004) Eliminating the dichotomy between theory and practice in talent identification and development: considering the role of psychology. *Journal of Sport Sciences* 22: 395–408.

Abraham, A. and Collins, D. (1998) Examining and extending research in coach development. *Quest* 50: 59–79.

Abraham, A. and Collins, D. (2011) Effective skill development: how should athletes' skills be developed? In D. Collins, H. Richards and A. Button (eds), *Performance psychology for physical environments: a guide for the practitioner*. Oxford: Elsevier.

Anderson, J.R. (1982) Acquisition of a cognitive skill. *Psychological Review* 89(4): 369–406.

Bailey, R.P., Collins, D., Ford, P., Macnamara, A., Toms, M. and Pearce, G. (2010) *Participant development in sport: an academic review*. Leeds: sports coach UK.

Baker, J., Cobley, S. and Fraser-Thomas, J. (2009) What do we know about early sport specialization? Not much! *High Ability Studies* 20(1): 77–89.

Biggs, J.B. (2003) *Teaching for quality learning at university* (2nd ed.). Buckingham, UK: Open University Press.

Côté, J., Bruner, M., Strachan, L., Erickson, K. and Fraser-Thomas, J. (2010) Athlete development and coaching. In J. Lyle and C. Cushion (eds), *Sports coaching: professionalisation and practice*. Oxford: Elsevier.

Ford, P.R., Ward, P., Hodges, N.J. and Williams, M.A. (2009) The role of deliberate practice and play in career progression in sport: the early engagement hypothesis. *High Ability Studies* 20(1): 65–75.

Freeman, J. (2000) Teaching for talent: lessons from the research. In C.F.M. van Lieshout and P.G. Heymans (eds), *Developing talent across the life span*. Hove, UK: Psychology Press.

Horn, R.R. and Williams, A.M. (2004) Observational learning: is it time we took another look? In A.M. Williams and N.J. Hodges (eds), *Skill acquisition in sport: research, theory and practice*. London: Routledge.

Jones, R. and Wallace, M. (2006) The coach as 'orchestrator': more realistically managing the complex coaching context. In R. Jones (ed.), *The sports coach as educator: re-conceptualising sports coaching*. London: Routledge.

Macdonald, D., Côté, J. and Kirk, D. (2005) Physical activity pedagogy for junior sport. *Junior Sport Briefing Papers*. Canberra: Australian Sports Commission.

Martindale, R., Collins, D. and Daubney, J. (2005) Talent development: a guide for practice and research within sport. *Quest* 57: 353–375.

Morgan, G. (2006) Coaching behaviours and players' motivation in elite youth football. Unpublished PhD thesis, Loughborough University, Loughborough, UK.

Morley, D., Webb, V., Muir, B. and Morgan, G. (2011) A 'fit for purpose' approach within the Rugby Football League. In A. Navin (ed.), *Sports coaching: a reference guide for students, coaches and competitors*. Marlborough, UK: Crowood Press.

Saury, J. and Durand, M. (1998) Practical knowledge in expert coaches: on-site study of coaching in sailing. *Research Quarterly for Exercise and Sport* 69: 254–266.

Weiss, M.R. and Williams, L. (2004) The why of youth sport involvement: a developmental perspective on motivational processes. In M.R. Weiss (eds), *Developmental sport and exercise psychology: a lifespan perspective*. Morgantown, WV: Fitness Information Technology.

Williams, A.M. and Ford, P.R. (2009) Promoting a skills-based agenda in Olympic sports: the role of skill-acquisition specialists. *Journal of Sports Sciences* 27: 1381–1392.

Wulf, G. (2007) *Attention and motor skill learning*. Champaign, IL: Human Kinetics.

Wulf, G. and Shea, C.H. (2004) Understanding the role of augmented feedback: the good, the bad, and the ugly. In A.M. Williams and N.J. Hodges (eds), *Skill acquisition in sport: research, theory and practice*. London: Routledge.

CHAPTER THREE

MODELS OF YOUNG PLAYER DEVELOPMENT IN SPORT

RICHARD BAILEY, MARTIN TOMS, DAVE COLLINS,
PAUL FORD, ÁINE MACNAMARA AND GEMMA PEARCE

CHAPTER OUTLINE

- ▪ **Why models?**
- ▪ **The 'traditional' model of player development**
- ▪ **Formal models of player development**
- ▪ **Making sense of models**
- ▪ **Learning more**
- ▪ **Theory into practice**

INTRODUCTION

There are many reasons why young people might play sport. There are also many reasons why they might stop playing. Models of player development are attempts to understand the complex patterns of engagement, development and drop-out from sport. Successful models can assist coaches and policy makers to present sport in ways that will help young people realise their ambitions, whether those be competitive success, enjoyable recreation or healthy physical activity. Poor models can promote strategies that actually turn young people off sport, waste their talent and disillusion all involved.

This chapter discusses some of the most influential models of player development. It unpicks their assumptions and scientific bases, and highlights some of the tensions that exist between different ideas of the purposes and processes of youth sport development.

WHY MODELS?

Model building is an increasingly common approach in research and policy development. Models can help makes sense of the varied factors that might impact on particular events or situations, and their possible interrelationships. Most national sports development and sports performance strategies are presented in the form of models, which provide a concise statement of the key factors that have been judged to be especially significant in the evolving national approach to coaching and participation.

It is not the case, though, that all models aim to prescribe best practice. Perhaps the simplest way of characterising models in sports development is to distinguish between descriptive and prescriptive accounts: the former type attempt to provide an accurate description of an event and its variables; the latter focus on the values or principles that ought to characterise the event. An example of a descriptive model comes from the Canadian psychologist Jean Côté (1999), who interviewed players and parents to depict the processes through which young people become socialised into sports participation. In contrast, Kirk *et al*. are clear about where their interests lie: 'The model prescribes the process in terms of setting out clear guidelines for how junior sport participation should proceed' (2005: 2). In the real world of youth sport, it can be difficult to make a clean division between these two types of models. However, generally speaking, prescriptive models rely on indirect evidence to justify them whereas descriptive accounts move from actual portrayals of successful experiences to recommendations to others regarding the replicating of such success.

DIRECTED TASK

Consider how models of young player development have evolved in your own country or sport. Which approach is taken (descriptive or prescriptive), and what method is used to evaluate how successful it is?

THE 'TRADITIONAL' MODEL OF PLAYER DEVELOPMENT

There is always a danger of using the concept of a 'traditional', or 'standard', or 'conventional' model simply as a straw man to knock down, rather than as a genuine stance. However, there do seem to be certain presumptions or working principles that have historically characterised discussions about sports development, and these are often accepted as self-evident truths. For the purposes of this chapter, these assumptions are interesting, too, because the academic models that are discussed later were partly provoked by the perceived weaknesses of older accounts. So, the intention here is simply to make explicit some of the themes that have characterised the 'traditional' model.

Pyramid thinking

Simply put, the pyramid model shares the following characteristics: a broad base of foundation skills participation, with increasingly higher levels of performance, engaged in by fewer and fewer people (see Figure 3.1). Fisher and Borms report that 'the pyramidal system of development [is] favoured by most countries' (1990: 15), and Kirk *et al.* argue that its influence can be seen in numerous international sports participation models and that 'the assumptions underpinning the pyramid model continue to have a powerful residual influence on thinking about junior sport participation and sport development in sport policy' (2005: 2).

Despite its popularity, there have been numerous criticisms levelled at the pyramid approach. One line of attack has been the moral one: built into the pyramid's design is the systematic exclusion of players, no matter how good they are, as fewer and fewer players can play at each level. Another difficulty raised by critics is that the logic of the model means that the quality of performers at the higher levels is dependent on the experiences and resources offered to those at the lowest levels: a poor foundation undermines the whole system. Finally, the pyramid model takes no account of individual choice, and presumes that players compete up to the level of their abilities. In other words, it leaves no room for players who do not aspire to competitive success.

Bailey (2005) has suggested three further problems with pyramid thinking:

The problem of prediction

The pyramid model presumes that successful progression from one level to the next is indicative of later ability, while in most cases this is not accurate. Abbott *et al.* (2002) present a wide range of evidence that effectively undermines confidence in the notion of 'talent spotting', especially during childhood.

Figure 3.1 The pyramid model of sports development.

Source: Adapted from Tinning *et al.* (1993).

The problem of participation

The pyramid model presumes that selection for progressively higher levels within the system is based on merit, while in practice participation is mediated by a host of psycho-social and environmental factors, such as the ability to take part in the first place. This seems to be the case in all contexts of player development. Consider, for example, the role of the family in high-level sports performance. Research by Bailey and Morley (2006) suggests that certain types of family background can strongly support engagement in youth sport:

- The child's parents achieved high standards in the domain.
- The child's parents are of relatively high socio-economic status.
- The child's parents have the ability and willingness to financially support participation and provide specialist support.
- The parents have the ability and willingness to invest large amounts of time to support the child's engagement in the activity.
- The parents are car owners.
- The family size is relatively small.
- The child is from a two-parent family.
- The child attends an independent school.

Alongside the family we might also add factors such as availability and quality of coaching, availability and quality of facilities, access to funding and choice of sport. Since young players can hardly be held responsible for the type of their families, schools, cities, etc., it seems fair to say that, to some extent, their sporting achievement (or simply engagement) is mediated by pure luck, irrespective of their ability in a sport.

The problem of potential

These models take it for granted that current performance in a domain represents a player's ability, but there are numerous reasons to doubt that this is, in fact, the case. Some have highlighted the subjective nature of talent assessment procedures, whereby players find themselves removed from a system for rather arbitrary reasons. A striking example of such arbitrariness is the effect of relative age on performance. Numerous studies have shown that players born early within a selection year have a considerable advantage over those born later. This seems to be partly because of the relative physical size and strength and further matured coordination of players who can be up to one year older than their peers (Helsen *et al.*, 2000). Those with the benefit of extra months of development are more likely to be identified as talented and progress to the next level of the pyramid, where they would be expected to receive better coaching, play with a higher standard of team-mates and opposition, and compete and train more frequently.

Player development as talent development

Closely related to the pyramid model is the equation of player development with talent development. Indeed, it is interesting how little attention has been paid in the past to approaches to sports development that do not focus on elite sport. Balyi's Long-Term Athlete Development (LTAD) model certainly does not follow the consensus in representing development in pyramidal form. However, its focus on a progression towards performance and winning implies that its primary concern is elite performance, rather than mass sports participation.

Following Siedentop, we might think about sports participation in terms of three primary goals:

- *elite performance goal* – 'to allow the most talented and interested young athletes to pursue excellence' (2002: 395);
- *educative goal* – 'supported primarily for the educational and developmental benefits. . . . If the educative goal was to dominate . . . it would be as inclusive as possible' (ibid.: 394);
- *public health goal* – 'to contribute to the public health of a nation . . . it would emphasise playful activity above all and would specifically target for inclusion those . . . who are most at risk' (ibid.: 394–395).

Siedentop argued that there was an inevitable tension between these goals:

> One can legitimately question the degree to which elite-development goals of a junior sport system can be served as part of a comprehensive system and still direct sufficient resources to achieve the educative and public health goals that are more fundamental to the system as a whole.
>
> (ibid.: 396)

Siedentop's framework seems to be a useful way of splitting up the types of interests people have when they enter a pathway in sport. However, things are rarely so clear-cut when human interests are involved. For example, it is entirely possible, even likely, that individuals will be attracted to different objectives at different points of their engagement with sport; they may also have different objectives in mind at the same time, when playing different sports (a player may be a competitive golfer and a recreational swimmer, while learning martial arts). Also, Siedentop's objectives are not mutually exclusive; achievement in one area can be accompanied by achievement in the others, although, as Siedentop makes clear, in policy terms one tends to dominate.

42

Unitary development

According to traditional ways of thinking, ability in sport is seen in quite narrow terms: people are 'good' at specific sports. However, as we have already seen, players are relatively good and bad at different aspects of an activity. For example, a footballer can have highly developed movement skills but suffer from poor communication skills, tactical awareness or self-confidence. If any of these problems is present, then the likelihood of that player achieving success is severely limited. Just to add to this complication, it seems that different skills may be important at different stages as the player progresses, or even at elite level (Abbott and Collins, 2002).

Potential and performance

One of the most common versions of the traditional model of development in sport occurs when the assessment of ability in an area is reduced to levels of current performance. Abbott and her colleagues (2002: 26) argue that 'there is a need to distinguish between determinants of performance and determinants of potential/skill acquisition'. It seems more plausible that individual development is the result of an interaction between inherited abilities and social learning, and it is this interaction that undermines simplistic correlations of ability and performance.

Researchers of ability in sport can be positioned along a simple continuum between those who think that expertise is almost entirely the result of genetic gifts and those who think it is the result of experience and environment. A third group, the interactionists, think that ability cannot be understood without taking account of both genes and experience. Almost every scientist today is an interactionist. In other words, almost everyone who studies the development of expertise in sport thinks that it is vital to consider both nature and nurture. Many interactionists adopt a 'complex systems' view. This means that development is the result of numerous factors that interact with each other: development is more than the sum of the individual parts. A simple way of thinking about this in sport is in terms of three types of factors: biological factors (e.g. innate speed; physique; natural endurance), psychological factors (e.g. mental skills and attitude; motivation; resilience) and sociological factors (e.g. family; social class and income; peer groups; geographical location). As can be seen from Figure 3.2, it makes no sense to talk about 'the most important' factors: all are important.

The complex systems approach helps explain engagement at every level of sport, from young children sampling for the first time to elite adults. It also illustrates why current performance in an activity is a poor indicator of ability, since it is affected by so many influences. Successful negotiation of these factors can lead to high levels of performance and/or enjoyment, while unsuccessful negotiation can lead to burn-out and/or drop-out.

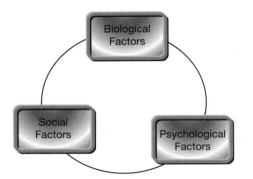

Figure 3.2 The complex system of sports performance.

Source: Adapted from Bailey *et al*. (2010).

Development as a continuum

Traditional models (such as the pyramid) present sports development as a relatively simple and direct progression along a continuum, from childhood to retirement. Many theorists suggest that developmental pathways in sport are not like this and that players pass through a set of stages as they develop from novice to expert. The influence of Bloom's (1985) studies of expert sportspeople, musicians and academics can be seen today in the increasing frequency of stage-based models of development. Bloom was led to distinguish three stages in the careers of 120 talented individuals:

- the 'early years' (the first stage, or initiation), when the individual is drawn into the area;
- the 'middle years' (the second stage, or development), when the individual becomes committed to the area;
- the 'later years' (the third stage, or mastery), when the individual makes the domain the centre of his or her life.

The hypothesised existence of stages of development suggests that individuals need to learn to deal with the distinctive challenges inherent within each stage. It also means that they need to be able to make and deal with the changes required to transfer between stages, which can be significant events in their lives. Therefore, alongside the obvious challenges of participation in a sport, the player also needs to negotiate the transitions encountered during his or her sporting career, and every participant's pathway is unique to that participant.

FORMAL MODELS OF PLAYER DEVELOPMENT

The discussion now turns to four models that have been particularly influential in recent discussions of youth sports participation and development, especially in the United Kingdom:

R. Bailey *et al*.

1   Istvan Balyi's Long-Term Athlete Development;
2   Jean Côté's Developmental Model of Sport Participation;
3   Abbott *et al*.'s Psychological Characteristics of Developing Excellence;
4   Bailey and Morley's Model of Talent Development in Physical Education.

Balyi's Long-Term Athlete Development

Long-Term Athlete Development (LTAD), associated with the ideas and theories of Istvan Balyi, has probably been the most influential model of participant development in the United Kingdom in recent years. All of the main national governing bodies for sport have been required to adopt and adapt a version of LTAD and to promote it among their members, which is in itself an interesting example of the influence of models over practice. Though this type of model is not original, it combines the training ethos employed within East European countries alongside a scientific basis of biological maturation. It attempts to use physiological measures related to growth and maturation to facilitate athletic capabilities through appropriate training load prescription. Stafford acknowledges that the model's primary aim is to produce greater numbers of performers who are capable of achieving at the highest level, but also claims that it provides a platform for coaches and participants at every level 'to fulfil their potential and remain involved in sport' (2005: 1).

Balyi, like almost everyone who writes about developing excellence, quotes Herbert Simon – 'It takes ten years of extensive training to excel in anything' (quoted in Balyi, 1998: 8) – as a way of introducing and justifying his model. Long-term development, he argues, is the basis for realising and optimising potential, and focuses upon the idea that training design should account for pubertal changes during childhood, particularly based around the 's-shaped' modified-developmental growth curve (Malina and Bouchard, 1991). This development is conceptualised in terms of a series of stages through which players pass.

The precise timing and nature of these stages is determined by the type of sport in question. Balyi distinguishes between 'early'- and 'late'-specialisation sports. Early-specialisation sports include gymnastics, diving, figure skating and table tennis – in other words, those sports that conventionally require their players to begin to specialise and seriously train from a relatively early age. Late-specialisation sports comprise almost all other sports, and Balyi's model prescribes a more generalised approach, including an emphasis in the early stages on fundamental movement skills.

Table 3.1 outlines LTAD's stages and progressions for early- and late-specialisation sports.

Since our concern here is with children, we will limit our discussion to those stages related to young players:

- *Phase 1: FUNdamental.* This phase is appropriate for boys aged 6–9 years and girls aged 5–8 years. The main objective should be the overall development of the child's physical

Table 3.1 Long-Term Athlete Development stages

Early specialisation	Late specialisation
FUNdamental	FUNdamental
Training to train	Learning to train
Training to compete	Training to train
Training to win	Training to compete
Retaining	Training to win
	Retaining

Source: Based on Stafford (2005).

capacities and fundamental movement skills. The key points of this phase include participation in as many sports as possible and the development of basic skills and competences using enjoyable games.

■ *Phase 2: Learning to train.* This phase is appropriate for boys aged 9–12 years and girls aged 8–11 years. The main objective should be for them to learn fundamental sports skills. The key points of this phase include the further development of fundamental movement skills, strength, endurance, learning general sports skills, and a relatively small amount of competition.

■ *Phase 3: Training to train.* This phase is appropriate for boys aged 12–16 years and girls aged 11–15 years. The main objective should be the overall development of the child's physical capacities (focus on aerobic conditioning) and fundamental movement skills.

■ *Phase 4: Training to compete.* This phase is appropriate for boys aged 16–18 years and girls aged 15–17 years. The main objective should be to optimise fitness preparation, sport- or event-specific skills and performance.

A prominent component of Balyi's LTAD model is the concept of critical opportunities to accelerate and enhance physical athletic development using appropriate training stimuli linked to the natural growth and maturation processes. If these 'windows of opportunity' are not acted on during childhood and adolescence, then optimal performance will never be achieved during adulthood.

In short, the types of sources Balyi cites suggest that LTAD has its origins in biological or physiological scientific literature. LTAD can reasonably be described as a physiologically orientated development model. However, Balyi and Hamilton (2004) claim that their work is based on 'empirical observations', which means that it needs to be assessed in terms of its scientific validity. At the moment, the scientific basis of LTAD is questionable, and various researchers have suggested that its foundations are not strong (see Bailey *et al.*, 2010, for a critical review of LTAD).

R. Bailey *et al.*

Côté's Developmental Model of Sport Participation (DMSP)

If Balyi's LTAD model can be described as a biologically or physiologically orientated frame-work, then Jean Côté's DMSP model is a psychological one. It extends Bloom's earlier work with talented individuals through interviews with elite Canadian and Australian gymnasts, basketball players, netball players, hockey players, rowers and tennis players. Like Bloom, Côté identified stages of development, in his case three of them:

1   the *sampling phase* (6–12 years) – when children are given the opportunity to sample a range of sports, develop a foundation of fundamental movement skills, and experience sport as a source of fun and excitement;
2   the *specialising phase* (13–15 years) – when the child begins to focus on a smaller number of sports and, while fun and enjoyment are still vital, sport specificity emerges as an important characteristic of sport engagement;
3   the *investment phase* (16-plus years) – when the child becomes committed to achieving a high level of performance in a specific sport, and the strategic, competitive and skill development elements of sport emerge as the most important.

Progression from the sampling phase (Figure 3.3) can take one of three forms: children can become involved more seriously in one or two sports in the specialising phase; they can choose to stay involved in sport as a recreational activity; or they can drop out of sport. Likewise, at the specialising phase, players have three options available to them: recreation; drop-out; or progress to the investment phase, when they aspire to a high level of performance in one sport. Those players who have reached the investment years can subsequently either progress to recreational sport or simply drop out.

The DMSP places great importance on sustained engagement in an activity if expertise is going to be achieved. However, it is not the case that practice makes perfect! Ericsson *et al.* (1993) concluded their comprehensive review of the literature into skill acquisition and expert performance with the finding that the most effective learning occurs through participation in what they called 'deliberate practice'. This form of practice requires effort, is not inherently

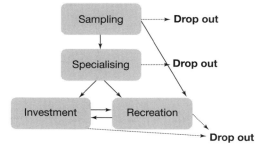

Figure 3.3 Côté's Developmental Model of Sport Participation.

enjoyable and is specifically designed to improve performance. Like Simon, Ericsson and their colleagues claimed that expert performance is the result of at least ten years of deliberate practice. Subsequently, sports researchers have supported aspects of this view, but with some qualification. Côté (1999) introduced the term 'deliberate play' to describe sporting activities that are intrinsically motivating and involve modified version of standard rules. Deliberate play requires minimal equipment, flexible contexts and challenges, and allows children the freedom to experiment with different movements and tactics.

Figure 3.4 shows Côté's view of the relationship between deliberate practice and deliberate play at different stages of participant development.

Abbott *et al.*'s Psychological Characteristics of Developing Excellence (PCDE)

On the basis of the descriptions offered earlier, the work of Abbott and her colleagues should be described as a prescriptive model. Their work does not offer a comprehensive description of all facets of participant development, as a model should arguably aspire to do. What it does offer, however, is a well-evidenced case for the role of psychology as arguably the most influential factor in the development process (Abbott and Collins, 2004). Their approach questions the pre-eminence of physical and performance measures as 'snapshot' identification tools, stressing the complex pathway to elite success while also trying to prescribe those characteristics that both predict and support the pathway to success. They call these characteristics the Psychological Characteristics of Developing Excellence (PCDEs).

Another crucial element of this work is its emphasis on the successful negotiation of transitions between stages as the major factor in progression along the performance pathway, as opposed to the focus on stages that characterises many of the other models.

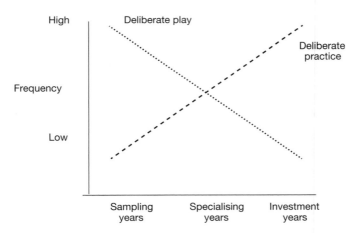

Figure 3.4 The relationship between deliberate play and deliberate practice and Côté's three levels of sport participation.

R. Bailey *et al.*

More crucial for the concerns of this chapter was the development of an intervention based on the principles of PCDEs and the promotion or movement ability. Based on a taught intervention with primary-age children, this project (Developing the Potential of Young People through Sport, DPYPS; Abbott *et al.*, 2007) demonstrated significant changes in attitude towards, and actual participation rates in, a broad range of physical activities. Abbott and colleagues saw changes in key psychological constructs such as perceived ability and self-determination as the mechanisms through which the combined impact affected behaviour.

Perhaps the PCDE account might be better described as a philosophy or approach rather than a model. It does not offer a clear framework of structures and processes that can be used as the basis of youth sport development. However, it does highlight some of the core psychological principles that underpin successful engagement in sport. Also, implicit within the approach is an emphasis on the importance of the multi-agency collaboration that ought to characterise any effective player development work.

Bailey and Morley's Model of Talent Development

The fourth formal model of participant development was based on substantial empirical research into the processes of talent development in school physical education. Bailey and Morley sought to understand the perceptions of teachers, students and policy makers and the strategies they used to identify and provide for the most able young people. From the findings from these studies, they progressed to develop guidance for teachers and coaches. So, rather as with Côté's approach, this group began with a descriptive presentation of processes of strategies and then moved to a prescriptive account of effective practice.

The model highlights a set of main hypotheses that, it is maintained, are crucial for an adequate talent development system. The first hypothesis is a differentiation between potential and performance. Following Abbott *et al.* (2002), it is argued that the common reduction of talent identification procedures to levels of current performance is flawed. As has already been discussed, individual development is the result of an interaction between inherited abilities and social learning, so it is an error to assume a direct relationship between ability and performance.

The second hypothesis is that development is multidimensional. Bailey and Morley distinguish between the expression of abilities and the progressive emergence of these abilities into certain outcomes, such as elite success, recreational play and healthy physical activity. These abilities are developed within certain domains that are (sometimes) refined, combined and elaborated into particular behaviours, such as sporting success. These abilities are as follows:

- psychomotor ability (which is revealed through movement and the physical performance of skills);
- interpersonal ability (which is exhibited in social contexts and is the basis of leadership, teamwork and similar concepts);
- intrapersonal ability (which underpins an individual's capacity for self-control, self-efficacy and emotional intelligence);

- cognitive ability (which is shown in tactical settings, as well as knowledge and understanding of central physical educational concepts);
- creative ability (which is evidenced when learners respond to challenges and tasks with fluency, originality and sensitivity to problems).

Underlying this multidimensional framework is a claim that success in physical education (and youth sport in general) needs to be understood in terms of the emergence of a wide range of abilities rather than simply physical prowess, which has tended to dominate talent development practices.

The third major hypothesis is that practice is of vital importance in the realisation of talent. In this respect, Bailey and Morley share an assumption of each of the models presented in this chapter: that the development of competence and even expertise requires the investment of great amounts of time and effort on the part of players and their support systems, especially coaches and parents.

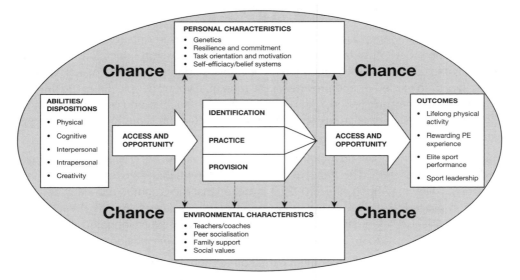

Figure 3.5 Bailey and Morley's model of talent development in physical education.

DIRECTED ACTIVITY

From your perspective as a reader, coach, policy maker or athlete, consider how each of the models shown in Table 3.2 has been (or can be) applied to your own sporting activities. Additionally, using the key academic sources highlighted, reflect upon how they can best be applied to the development of young athletes.

Table 3.2 Comparing the models of player development

	Balyi's Long-Term Athlete Development	Côté's Developmental Model of Sport Participation	Abbott et al.'s Psychological Characteristics of Developing Excellence	Bailey and Morley's Model of Talent Development
Aim	To present 'an all-embracing coaching philosophy that puts the needs of participants/ athletes at the centre of decision-making about sports system development' (Balyi and Ross, forthcoming)	'[T]o understand different pathways of sport involvement from childhood to adults' (Côté, pers. comm., 23 September 2009)	'[T]o explore prerequisites to success in sport, and the comparative efficacy of employing these prerequisites within talent identification schemes' (Abbot and Collins, 2004)	'[T]o make explicit theorising about the nature, content and character of the talent development process in physical education' (Bailey and Morley, 2006)
Primary disciplinary background	Exercise physiology Anatomy (esp. biological maturation)	Social psychology Developmental psychology	Performance psychology	Education Philosophy
Research methods	Analysis of literature Empirical observations of practice	Retrospective recall with elite performers, recreational participants, and drop-outs from sports Analysis of literature	Analysis of literature Retrospective recall with elite performers in various performance domains Sliding populations tracking with developing elites in various performance domains Pilot interventions in schools	Qualitative research with teachers and young people Quantitative research with schools Analysis of literature School-based case studies
Key sources	Mainly Eastern European sources: physiology and training methods	Bloom's stages Ericsson's research on deliberate practice	Orlick and others' work on characteristics of excellence A 'complex systems' perspective on determinants of performance, learning and development Cross-domain studies on meta-cognitive skills	Abbott et al.'s critique Ericsson's research on deliberate practice

Table 3.2 Continued

	Balyi's Long-Term Athlete Development	Côté's Developmental Model of Sport Participation	Abbott et al.'s Psychological Characteristics of Developing	Bailey and Morley's Model of Talent Development
Main theoretical framework	Non-linear biological maturation	Expertise theory Developmental theories	Psychological concomitants/precursors of effective development	Munich model of giftedness and talent
Core constructs	Stages of development (FUNdamental, Learning to Train, Training to Train, Training to Compete, Training to Win, Retaining) Critical periods	Stages and trajectories towards elite performance, continued participation and personal development in sport Sampling Deliberate play Deliberate Practice	Psychological Characteristics of Developing Excellence (PCDEs) Effective Talent Development Environments (TDEs) Systematic development of PCDEs to address challenge in the pathway, particularly transition Talent identification – stressing development over identification	Multi-abilities Personal and environmental influencers Deliberate practice
Practical applications	Use of biological maturation measurements to inform individual training and competition loading rather than chronological age classifications	Broad foundation of sampling sports and involvement in deliberate play during childhood Progressive involvement in deliberate practice from childhood to adult Developmentally appropriate training patterns and psycho-social influences Holistic approach to sport participation	Teaching 'characteristics of excellence' as cross-domain facilitators Developing and refining optimum TDEs Acknowledging and catering for the non-linear and dynamic pathway to excellence Recognition that these applications also impact on participation – a continuum approach	Strategies for talent identification Strategies for talent provision Multi-skills practices

MAKING SENSE OF MODELS

Traditional models have tended to portray player development as a relatively simple affair in which participants' entry into and engagement in sport are almost exclusively determined by their interests, while their success is the result of their ability and effort. Clearly, such factors are of vital importance, but so too are a host of mediating elements, such as physical maturity, the provision of skills within an effective development environment, socialisation and the opportunity to practise. This is why it is vital that all of those involved in youth sport understand the range of factors that influence youth sport.

Different theories emphasise different aspects of player development. It is interesting that the four models discussed in this chapter grew from four distinct academic fields: exercise physiology (Balyi), social psychology (Côté), cognitive psychology (Abbott et al.) and education (Bailey and Morley). We all look at the world through conceptual lenses that are heavily influenced by our background experiences and training, so it is not surprising that academics tend to look at sport in ways that reflect their disciplinary biases. However, this is not helpful for coaches, who are less interested in the narrowly focused research of academics than in practical ways of supporting and challenging their young players. So, models of development can be useful ways of representing research into certain aspects of sport, but none of the models could claim to be comprehensive. Instead, they seek to highlight what their creators believe are the most important factors influencing participant development. Consider, for example, Abbott and Collins's (2004) explicit emphasis on the central role of psychology in the development of performance and participation. There are some similarities between the four models presented in this chapter: the most apparent point of connection is in the emphasis on the central importance of practice in player development. But there are differences, too. For example, do young players progress through discrete stages? Bailey and Morley make no mention of stages at all in their model. Balyi and Côté think they do, although their accounts differ with regard to when and why these stages occur. Abbott et al. also implicitly accept that stages exist, but not in the universal sense presumed by most theorists. For them, the stages a player experiences during a sporting career are idiosyncratic, and so what matters most is that players develop the skills needed to negotiate their own, highly individualistic pathways.

What can the coach conclude from this? Since the authors of the models have all drawn on a considerable body of research, it would be unhelpful to reject the models out of hand. Instead, what is needed is a healthy dose of critical thinking. Scientific knowledge is constantly evolving, so it is extremely unlikely that anyone will find the 'correct' model. There will always be room for error or incompleteness. For this reason, coaches need to be critical consumers of the information and ideas produced by academics and model makers.

SUMMARY

Models can be useful means of capturing a wide range of evidence related to a topic. But the value of these models is significantly determined by the quality of the evidence being re-presented and inevitable interpretations of that evidence by the model-builders. This chapter has discussed the value and limitations of models in sports participation research and introduced four influential models. Ultimately, models ought to be selected or deselected on the basis of their usefulness. For this to happen, coaches need to test the assumptions and ideas of models in the real world of coaching youth sport.

LEARNING MORE

By far the most comprehensive discussion of models of player development is provided by Bailey et al. (2010) in their sports coach UK report. Other useful surveys of specific aspects of development are provided by Régnier et al. (1993) and Abbott et al. (2002). There are many useful sources of information on young people's engagement in sport, and these should be read as background to the debate on models. Readily available sources include Smoll and Smith (1996), Côté (2002), Côté and Hay (2002), David (2005) and Houlihan and White (2002), and, of course, the other chapters in this book.

THEORY INTO PRACTICE

So, what are the practical implications of this chapter for coaches? Initially, the concept of developing a model needs some consideration: within your own sport, who should develop it and what practical evidence should it be based upon? More than this, as a coach, how are you involved in this process and how can you apply these models to your practice?

This chapter highlights the need to understand young athletes in a more holistic fashion – not just their sporting ability, biological age, physical stature and maturity, but also their background and influences, and the social environment that they inhabit and in which you coach. Clearly, there are implications for what the coach can do to influence young player development in sport. While many of the issues here highlight the general over-reliance on factors that could be argued to be genetic (such as biological factors), there are other factors (such as the coaching environment) that can be influenced by the coach's style and approach style. In short, the coach can make a difference.

The development of these participation models can be interrogated more fully from a coaching perspective. The assumptions and appropriateness of these models need to be explored and tested in a 'real world' sense by coaches. In this way, we need to ensure that the usefulness of the models and ideas can provide the driver behind their ongoing development, and, rather than just academics providing theoretically based strategies, we need the involvement of those in the field to support this work.

ACKNOWLEDGEMENTS

The material for this chapter has been taken from a research project funded by sports coach UK.

REFERENCES

Abbott, A. and Collins, D. (2002) A theoretical and empirical analysis of a 'state of the art' talent identification model. *High Ability Studies* 13: 157–178.

Abbott, A. and Collins, D. (2004) Eliminating the dichotomy between theory and practice in talent identification and development. *Journal of Sports Sciences* 22: 395–408.

Abbott, A., Collins, D., Martindale, R. and Sowerby, K. (2002) *Talent identification and development: an academic review*. Edinburgh: sportscotland.

Abbott, A., Collins, D., Sowerby, K. and Martindale, R. (2007) *Developing the potential of young people in sport*. Edinburgh: sportscotland.

Bailey, R.P. (2005) The many and the few: solving the problem of talent development in sport. *British Journal of Teaching Physical Education* 36: 23–26.

Bailey, R. and Morley, D. (2006) Towards a model of talent development in physical education. *Sport, Education and Society* 11: 211–230.

Bailey, R., Collins, D., Ford, P., Macnamara, A., Toms, M. and Pearce, G. (2010) *Participant development in sport: an academic review*. Leeds: sports coach UK.

Balyi, I. (1998) Long-term planning of athlete development: the training to train phase. *FHS, The UK's Quarterly Coaching Magazine*, no. 1: 8–11.

Balyi, I. and Hamilton, A. (2004) *Long-term athlete development: trainability in childhood and adolescence. Windows of opportunity. Optimal trainability*. Victoria, BC: National Coaching Institute British Columbia and Advanced Training and Performance.

Balyi, I. and Ross, G. (forthcoming) Participant development in sport. In N. Holt and R.P. Bailey (eds), *Lifelong engagement in sport and physical activity*. London: Routledge.

Bloom, B.S. (ed.) (1985) *Developing talent in young people*. New York: Ballantine Books.

Côté, J. (1999) The influence of the family in the development of talent in sport. *Sport Psychologist* 13: 395–417.

Côté, J. (2002) Coach and peer influence on children's development through sport. In J. Silva and D. Stevens (eds), *Psychological foundations of sport*. Boston, MA: Allyn & Bacon.

Côté, J. and Hay, J. (2002) Children's involvement in sport. In J. Silva and D. Stevens (eds), *Psychological foundations of sport*. Boston, MA: Allyn & Bacon.

David, P. (2005) *Human rights in youth sport*. London: Routledge.

Ericsson, K., Krampe, R. and Tesch-Römer, C. (1993) The role of deliberate practice in the acquisition of expert performance. *Psychological Review* 100: 363–406.

Fisher, R. and Borms, J. (1990) *The search for sporting excellence*. Berlin: International Council of Sport Science and Physical Education.

Helsen, W., Hodges, N., Van Winckel, J. and Starkes, J. (2000) The roles of talent, physical precocity and practice in the development of soccer expertise. *Journal of Sports Sciences* 18: 727–736.

Houlihan, B. and White, A. (2002) *The politics of sports development*. London: Routledge.

Kirk, D., Brettschneider, W.-D. and Auld, C. (2005) Junior sport models representing best practice nationally and internationally. *Junior Sport Briefing Papers*. Canberra: Australian Sports Commission.

Malina, R. and Bouchard, C. (1991) *Growth, maturation and physical activity*. Champaign, IL: Human Kinetics.

Régnier, G., Salmela, J. and Russell, S. (1993) Talent detection and development in sport. In R. Singer, M. Murphey and L.K. Tennant (eds), *Handbook of research in sport psychology*. New York: Macmillan.

Siedentop, D. (2002) Junior sport and the evolution of sport cultures. *Journal of Teaching in Physical Education*, 21: 392–401.

Smoll, F. and Smith, R. (1996) *Children and youth in sport: a biopsychosocial perspective*. Dubuque, IA: Brown & Benchmark.

Stafford, I. (2005) *Coaching for long-term athlete development*. Leeds: sports coach UK.

Tinning, R., Kirk, D. and Evans, J. (1993) *Learning to teach physical education*. Sydney: Prentice-Hall.

CHAPTER FOUR

COACHES' LEARNING AND DEVELOPMENT

CHRIS CUSHION

CHAPTER OUTLINE

- ▓ **Learning theory: an overview**
- ▓ **Coaches' informal learning**
- ▓ **Coaches' formal learning**
- ▓ **Learning styles and expertise**
- ▓ **Optimal mix of learning experiences?**
- ▓ **Theory into practice**
- ▓ **Learning more**

INTRODUCTION

The coaching environment has traditionally been viewed as a place where athletes learn. More recently, however, this context has also begun to be thought of as a place in which coaches' professional learning and development takes place (Cushion, 2006). 'Learning' is an important term, as it places the emphasis on the person in whom change is expected to occur or has occurred, and is therefore described as an 'act or process by which behavioural change, knowledge, skills, and attitudes are acquired' (Jarvis, 2004: 100–101). Learning, therefore, can happen through a number of means, for example through experience, reflection, study or instruction. In this sense, learning can embrace all of the mechanisms through which coaches acquire the knowledge that informs their professional practice. This chapter will demonstrate that coach learning occurs not only inside but outside of educational settings (Cushion et al., 2010). Consequently, while the coach learner is the essential element in the learning process, the coach educator is not, as learning often occurs without teaching.

The idea of coach learning has only recently been presented as a wider term that encapsulates research into, and understanding about, the broader learning of coaches. As has been suggested already, the recognition and use of coach learning as a term enables a view of the development of coaches that 'extends far beyond any formal training program' (Côté, 2006: 221). Yet within the literature there remains a 'lack of concern about how coaches learn' (Nelson and Cushion, 2006: 174). In addition, Lyle (2007) argues that coach educators are often unaware of frameworks that could underpin and guide their practice. With this in mind, learning is the central focus of the chapter, as it better encapsulates the means through which coaches develop an understanding of their working knowledge and skills. This process, as the chapter will illustrate, involves a considerable number of approaches to learning, a range of learning activities and a variety of sources. The purpose of this chapter, then, is to address the central theme of coach learning. The aim is to draw conclusions that can suggest how learning can be promoted and developed inside and outside of coach development structures and interventions.

REFLECTION

- What are the assumptions about coaching that inform coach learning?
- What are the intended outcomes of coach learning?
- What kind of learning should be promoted?

It is important to consider these questions in order to identify a framework or 'lens' through which coach learning can be understood and developed. Coaches should be transparent and recognise the assumptions about coaching practice and coach learning that may inform their beliefs. Indeed, these assumptions need to be set out at the outset of any learning.

LEARNING THEORY: AN OVERVIEW

What is learning? There are significantly different ways of understanding learning (Hodkinson et al., 2008). Any understanding relates to how the person is perceived, the nature of reality and the nature of knowledge; in other words, there exists an underlying philosophy that informs that understanding. It is this underlying philosophy that frames theories and theoretical models, so every approach to learning has a set of values and beliefs that affect practice (Light, 2008; Brockbank and McGill, 2007). Importantly, theory is not value free, and theory cannot be divorced from the wider world of ideology and belief (Jarvis, 2004). All theories of learning are based on assumptions concerning the individual, the world and the relationship between the two.

Learning, therefore, is a broad and complex field. It is a contested construct informed by a range of theories drawn from three main approaches: behaviourism, cognitivism and social constructivism. Behaviourists focus on the outcomes of stimuli, and reinforce desired behaviour

C. Cushion

without necessarily attending to social meaning (Brockbank and McGill, 2007). Unlike behaviourism, cognitive approaches tend to scrutinise internal cognitive structures and see learning as transforming those structures (ibid.). Cognitivists relate their theories to the subject matter, and these theories are primarily about acquiring knowledge (Jarvis, 2004). Constructivism is not strictly a theory but rather an epistemology, or philosophical explanation about the nature of learning (Simpson, 2002; Schunk, 2009). Constructivist approaches are concerned with how learners build their own mental structures through interaction with their environment, and often with these theories, learning has an historical and cultural aspect with respect to individual experience (Brockbank and McGill, 2007). With constructivism, understanding and experience are in constant interaction, which means that through participation (doing coaching), persons, action and the world are connected in all knowing and learning (Lave and Wenger, 1996). Several constructivist theories exist, but the common thread running through them suggests that learning is most effective when new knowledge and skills are used and individuals construct meanings for themselves within the context of interaction with others (Kerka, 1998).

Principles and theories of adult learning, which are increasingly common in sport governing bodies' coaching awards, tend to draw on constructivist assumptions, which are that learning principles per se do not exist, but rather learners create their own learning and are situated in physical and social contexts (Schunk, 2009). Common approaches in adult learning include problem-based learning, reflection and experiential learning, all of which will be discussed in this chapter.

Views about learning are present and influential in any approach to learning, and these underlying views can be explicit or implicit. The approaches to learning that are briefly described here demonstrate the complexity of learning (Tusting and Barton, 2006). Indeed, there is no right or wrong way to approach learning, but the core concepts are paradigmatically different and largely incompatible (Alexander, 2007). Therefore, a given philosophical approach to understanding the nature of knowledge, the person and social world will carry with it an implicit model of learning. Despite having assumptions about learning with views of how people learn built in, approaches to coach learning remain largely uninformed explicitly by learning theory. Most learning is undertaken within a cluster of ideas or experiences, or the result of the 'default' view for the particular programme.

COACHES' INFORMAL LEARNING

Learning in informal situations has been identified as 'the lifelong process by which every person acquires and accumulates knowledge, skills, attitudes and insights from daily experiences and exposure to the environment' (Coombs and Ahmed, 1974: 8). Thus, learning takes place in a wide variety of contexts, the majority of which occur in an informal setting beyond dedicated formal learning institutions (Brookfield, 1986; Merriam and Caffarella, 1999). Research into coach learning has consistently demonstrated that practitioners learn through various informal avenues, including previous experiences as an athlete, informal mentoring, practical coaching experiences and ongoing interactions with peer coaches and athletes.

Self-directed learning is a term that is often used interchangeably with informal learning (Merriam and Caffarella, 1999), although the former implies an instrumental sense of purpose that may not apply to some 'experiential' learning. In addition, coaches will use a range of sources in their informal or self-directed learning, such as the internet, coaching manuals, books, journal articles, magazines, videos, footage of coaching sessions and recordings of the performance of their and other coaches' athletes (for a complete review, see Cushion et al., 2010).

Informal learning through coaching experience and engaging with other coaches is consistently reported as the dominant mode of learning. This could suggest a swing towards informal methods to develop coach learning; however, the use of such approaches may be as much a commentary on the efficacy of other learning provision as on the effectiveness of learning informally. Indeed, the dominance of informal and self-directed learning is, arguably, due largely to the limitations and low impact of current formal provision (Cushion et al., 2010). Moreover, coach education has lacked any coherent or overarching structure, which has meant that coaches have been left to 'go it alone'. This has often resulted in coaches having an ad hoc, negotiated and individual learning curriculum.

While learning occurs (intentionally and unintentionally) when one is practising as a coach, evidence also suggests that learning to become a coach often starts when the coach is him- or herself an athlete. The usefulness of knowledge developed during this period, however, has to be subject to greater scrutiny and cannot be simply accepted as positive. Informal learning occurs without a prescribed curriculum and is often facilitated by an 'other'. Importantly, this learning ignores power relations in which the 'other' dominates the process, and particular ideological interpretations of high-status knowledge are enforced (Cushion et al., 2010).

Lastly, experiential learning can be defined as being intentional and can be mediated or unmediated. It is different from learning from experience, which is largely unintentional. Therefore, experiential learning is more than just doing, and coaches must become competent at setting problems and then developing and evaluating their strategies for solving the problems they have identified (Trudel and Gilbert, 2006). Without a form of reflective process, coaches simply accrue experience without learning from it (see Chapter 8, 'The reflective coach').

DIRECTED TASK

Calculate the number of hours you have spent being coached or actively coaching. Compare this to the number of hours spent in formal coach education. What mechanisms do you engage with to learn from your experiences? Are you learning and accruing years of meaningful experience, or repeating the same year's experience over and over and not learning?

C. Cushion

Reflection

The theory of reflection appears to offer a great deal to the understanding of coaches' informal experiential learning. Several theoretical and conceptual approaches argue that reflection is a valuable tool for understanding and impacting informal learning in coaching. However, as Gilbert and Trudel (2006) suggest, experience and interaction with others are inevitable phenomena in coaching; this type of learning deals with knowing, not knowledge (Sfard, 1998), and control of the learning content is therefore impossible. The implication of this is that these experiences and interactions should be facilitated in some way. However, there remain concerns about the relationship between reflection and effective coaching behaviour and practice. Related to this is what Moon (2004) describes as an increasing awareness of a 'depth dimension' to reflection, and a recognition that superficial reflection may not be effective as a means of learning. Often, there is a struggle to get learners to reflect, but this can be overcome. However, reflection can often be undertaken in a superficial way, which in fact might be little different from simply recounting events in a form of descriptive writing. Indeed, a number of authors have commented on the inadequacy of much activity performed in the name of reflection because it is in fact largely non-critical and non-reflective (e.g. Kim, 1999; Moon, 2004). This suggests, therefore, that reflection has a range of application, with a continuum from shallow description at one end to deep critical reflection at the other. The key to this process is learning the skill of reflection and allowing enough time for the skill to be developed and supported.

REFLECTION

How useful are coaching 'logbooks'? Very often, writing these is a chore for coaches, and they are even 'made up' to fulfil the requirements of a course. Perhaps this exercise could be more useful if coaches were asked specifically to consider critical incidents from sessions (accepting that there may be none in some sessions), or if more challenging and critical thinking by coaches were encouraged by asking them to justify what they have done in a session.

Mentoring

Mentoring has been identified as offering both structured and unstructured support for coach learning. Mentoring is widely advocated in a range of domains, including coaching, with a significant outcome being increased reflection for both mentor and mentee. The literature highlights the importance of formal mentoring, suggesting that this will influence learning. However, the success of learning will be dependent upon the quality of the relationship between mentor and mentee (Dymock, 1999; Cushion, 2006). Indeed, there are some common issues identified as negatively affecting mentoring that are worthy of consideration. These include lack of time and training, personal or professional incompatibility, undesirable attitudes or behaviours, and increased workloads that went unnoticed. Mentees were concerned with a lack of mentor interest and training, and problematic behaviours (overly critical, defensive, controlling). In addition, Jones *et al.* (2009) highlight the possibilities of 'toxic mentoring', with asymmetric power relationships shaping both the mentoring experience and the learning that takes place. Ehrich *et al.* state that 'mentoring is a highly complex dynamic and interpersonal relationship that requires at the very least, time interest and commitment of mentors and mentees and strong support from educational or organisational leaders responsible for overseeing programmes' (2004: 533).

Situated learning

Situated learning and communities of practice have been identified in coaching and other domains as useful concepts to structure and understand learning. Participation in social (communities of) practice will, by definition, involve learning (Cushion, 2006). The process of becoming a member of a community allows learning to take place; thus, the processes, relationships and experiences that constitute a participant's sense of belonging underpin the subsequent learning (Fuller *et al.*, 2005). Lave and Wenger characterise this notion as 'legitimate peripheral participation' providing 'a way to speak about the relations between newcomers and old-timers, and about activities, identities, artefacts and communities of knowledge and practice. It concerns the process by which newcomers become part of a community of practice' (1991: 29).

Learners progress from less important tasks towards crucial 'core' tasks, thus moving from peripheral to full or central participation. As this occurs, understanding unfolds, with the learner developing a view of what the activity entails. This process ensures that learning itself is an improvised practice where the 'curriculum' unfolds in opportunities for engaging in practice (Fuller *et al.*, 2005). The individual is located within the community of practice and facilitates learning through mutual engagement in an activity that is defined by negotiations of meaning both inside and outside the community (ibid.). As communities are social structures, they involve power relations, and the way power is exercised can make legitimate peripheral participation empowering or disempowering, thus affecting learning (Lave and Wenger, 1991; Fuller *et al.*, 2005).

COACHES' FORMAL LEARNING

To date, only one study has considered the influence of formal learning (education and courses) on the development of coaches' knowledge and understanding, and their practice, or considered whether coaching programmes have matched the expectations of the learner. However, research highlighting coaches' experiences and perceptions of formal provision has

C. Cushion

been highly critical: courses often give little more than a basic understanding; coaches already know about and put into practice much of what is covered; some of the theoretical material covered is considered too abstract, too removed from everyday practice to be worthwhile; courses can be guilty of trying to cram too much information into a relatively short period of time; and coaches, later in their careers, have come to question much of the information acquired during initial courses (Cushion *et al.*, 2010). As a result of such experiences, some coaches have admitted to attending later awards only because they are compulsory.

In addition, there is a body of research criticising formal learning for taking an atheoretical approach and not aligning delivery with a view of how people learn (Cushion *et al.*, 2010; Trudel and Gilbert, 2006). Furthermore, this literature has questioned the conceptual boundaries of coaching, the definitions of what a coach is, and the lack of alignment between these and formal learning provision.

The many critiques of formal coach education call into question the 'education' within coach education. Importantly, such questioning is largely based on the key assumption that provision of this nature has been conceived of as an educational endeavour. Despite this, courses could, perhaps even should, be more appropriately labelled 'coach training' (Nelson and Cushion, 2006). Education and training have a number of significant conceptual differences. Training is more job orientated, because it focuses on the acquisition of knowledge, behaviours and skills specific to a profession. Training, therefore, 'tends to be a more mechanistic process which emphasises uniform and predictable responses to standard guidance and instruction reinforced by practice and repetition' (Buckley and Caple, 2002: 2). Education, on the other hand, is viewed as being more person-orientated, focusing on providing 'more theoretical and conceptual frameworks designed to stimulate an individual's analytical and critical abilities' (ibid.: 2). While training promotes uniformity of knowledge and practices, education attempts to increase variability, by emphasising and explicating individual differences.

The research critiquing formal provision for coaches would seem to locate it as training rather than education. The literature suggests that coaches are often subjected to a standardised curriculum that privileges a 'technocratic rationality' through a 'toolbox' of professional knowledge and a 'gold standard' of coaching. This approach is aimed at developing coaches to have the requisite standardised knowledge and a battery of strategies to overcome what are perceived as typical coaching dilemmas in their domain. This would suggest that much of formal learning provision could in fact be labelled coach training. When viewed in this light, coach training is arguably effective in achieving its desired learning objectives. The gaining of certification offers support to this notion, as it demonstrates that many practitioners have satisfied the governing bodies' criteria by achieving the outcomes or competences set.

Some formal learning provision could perhaps even be described as indoctrination, which can be defined as 'activities that set out to convince us that there is a "right" way of thinking and feeling and behaving' (Rogers, 2002: 53). In this respect, indoctrination denies learners choice and instead exposes them to a single set of values and attitudes that they are expected to acquire and abide by. Examples of this might include indoctrinating a prescribed method of delivery, feedback sequence, coaching philosophy, and tactical and technical approach. Currently, formal coach learning defines what knowledge is necessary for coaches to practise and how that knowledge can 'best' be transmitted. Certification often requires coaches to structure sessions, deliver information to athletes and provide feedback in a prescribed manner.

Perceptions of formal learning are changed by a given perspective of coaching: how it is defined, and what that then requires the coach to do. If one believes that coaching is stable, consistent, and identical across and between contexts, the generation of best-practice models that are taught through training becomes a logical proposition. Likewise, for those who believe that coaching is individual, with its own contextual make-up, and that it is itself in constant flux, then educating coaches to become aware of this inherent complexity and diversity, and assisting them in becoming capable of adapting to these contextual demands, would be an appropriate way to develop learning.

In response to criticisms of formal learning, alternative approaches have been proposed that draw on principles from adult learning. These include reflection and mentoring, and approaches such as problem-based learning (PBL). Adult learning principles have tremendous intuitive appeal, but unfortunately they have often not undergone rigorous analysis. Few studies have been performed assessing the basic tenets of adult learning principles, and the theories underlying these principles are not rigorously derived from scientific theory that, in turn, has been shown to be evidence based (Cushion et al., 2010).

Despite this, it would seem that adult learning principles, specifically PBL and reflection, are tools to draw on and provide useful insight into understanding learning more broadly. In their review of coaching and coach education literature, Trudel and Gilbert (2006) note that, as in other domains, the structuring of coach learning with adult learning principles is supported, but, with the exception of one initial study (Jones and Turner, 2006), there is no empirical research in coaching that shows whether PBL will be more or less effective than any other method.

Moreover, a key issue raised by Trudel and Gilbert (2006), which limits the potential of any new approach, is that coaching courses tend to be condensed. A problem-based learning approach requires time for participants to define the nature of the problem and how they can deal with it using a variety of resources (Jarvis et al., 1998). If participants are encouraged to work in small groups, it is important to give them time to develop trust and rapport (Trudel and Gilbert, 2006). The limited amount of time that coaches have to invest in their preparation has been noted (Abraham and Collins, 1998), and the appropriateness of 'weekend education programmes' is questionable if we want to facilitate coach learning and development by taking experience into account (Trudel and Gilbert, 2006). These reservations notwithstanding, PBL, like any learning method, needs clear tutor/facilitator training and support, and a well-planned curriculum with clear learning objectives.

While problem-based learning can be viewed as participation learning (Sfard, 1998), Trudel and Gilbert (2006) point out that the participation metaphor involves the focus on the actual practice of coaching in real time. In actual coaching practice, (1) problems are not simply presented but have to be recognised and defined; (2) problems have their origins in events that have happened weeks, months or even years before (Gilbert and Trudel, 2001); (3) the process of creating solutions includes interactions with other participants in the sports environment (ibid.); and (4) there is no appointed facilitator to stimulate the reflective process (Trudel and Gilbert 2006). Trudel and Gilbert (ibid.) suggest that instead, and because of time constraints, coaches are provided with what is called a 'common coaching problem' that they usually discuss in sub-groups. They then have to compare what they have said with what was an 'appropriate solution' (ibid.). They argue that 'in most problem-solving approaches, coaches will only "practise" addressing the kinds of issue they might encounter in the field' (ibid.: 520). They cite Barab and Duffy (2000: 34) from education, who note that

> the practices that the learner engages in are still school [or coaching] tasks abstracted from the community, and this has important implications for the meaning and type of practices being learned, as well as for the individuals relations to those meaning and practices.

LEARNING STYLES AND EXPERTISE

Although popular in many coach development programmes, the large-scale reviews of the existing literature, and research in a number of domains, suggest that the evidence base for learning styles can be considered fragile and often contested (Cushion et al., 2010). There seems a need to evaluate the theoretical robustness of the research findings and the applicability of these to a coach learning agenda. Indeed, it is important that the assumptions about learning styles should not become axiomatic, but rather remain an element of learning to be scrutinised as social constructions in an area of developing work. An approach of balance and variety seems warranted, with learning styles a tool to open up a dialogue about personal development, rather than one of pedagogical impact. As a result, there is currently insufficient evidence to warrant learning styles being a key tenet of coach learning.

Like the broader expertise literature, the majority of studies considering coaching have centred on the general properties and characteristics of expertise and knowledge, and there is less of a focus on the detail of acquisition, development and/or construction of expertise. Consequently, it is difficult to extrapolate meaningful guidance for coach learning. The learning process identified in developing expertise does, however, suggest practical experience and mentoring as mediating factors, and a need to master the relevant knowledge and skills of the domain. The research also suggests the domain specificity of superior performance. The interesting challenge for coaching is the question of whether coaching domains are defined clearly enough to identify the relevant knowledge and requisite skills. This is not currently evident in the coaching literature. The expertise literature suggests that there is a need in coaching for more robust definitions of domains, so that knowledge and skills can clearly be identified as informing curricula. The findings from the coach learning literature cannot realistically be stretched to fit across all domains and points in coach development.

65

OPTIMAL MIX OF LEARNING EXPERIENCES?

As the chapter has suggested, coach learning is influenced by an often complex mix of formal, non-formal, informal directed and self-directed learning experiences. However, the developmental 'mix' for coaches is largely individualised and ad hoc. While the literature suggests that the balance tends to be towards informal learning, the optimal mix of learning experiences needs to be addressed. In this respect, the research available on coach learning is limited by a tendency to focus on 'expert' or 'elite' coaching practitioners. This group of coaches has been shown to favour self-directed learning and therefore engage in activities to match. Indeed, the research into coach learning currently gives us little appreciation of the teaching and learning preferences, and needs, of coaches across coaching domains and within the developmental spectrum.

THEORY INTO PRACTICE

- There are significantly different ways of understanding learning.
- There is a relative absence of empirically informed research into coach learning.
- A mixture of theories is preferable to 'the only' (perfect) way. But coach learning needs to be explicit about the assumptions informing it, and how these relate to an understanding of how people learn, and align with the objectives of a programme.
- The research currently gives us little appreciation of the teaching and learning preferences, and needs of coaches across coaching domains and within the developmental spectrum.
- Reflection, mentoring and situated learning can structure learning, but each of these is not without its own issues. They require time and effort to develop, and become embedded into coach learning. They need research evidence linking them to changes in coaching practice.
- It is unclear to what degree coach experiential learning is intentional or unintentional, and a clearer understanding would inform the choice of experiences to be incorporated into planned learning episodes.
- Coaching needs to engage critically with the central tenets behind the theories and alternative approaches to learning to specifically develop 'coach learning' theory. As with a number of domains, there is a tendency to look at 'second-order' research that has taken ideas from 'first-order research'. Uncritically recycling theory and learning approaches into coaching runs the risk of compounding limited thinking.
- Coach learning should provide a learning environment that encourages practitioners who think creatively about alternative ways of coaching that are capable of pushing back the boundaries of coaching theory and practice, and as a result are better prepared to deal with the associated realities of their professional work (Cassidy et al., 2009). Indeed, current thinking about coaching practice and the coaching process suggests that coaches should be equipped to deal with the unique, uncertain and dynamic social demands of their position. This interpretation of coach learning is founded on the assumption that the

coach will also have a solid base of applied knowledge and experience relevant to sports performance, learning, the technical aspects of the sport, understanding individuals and appreciating the consequences of his or her own behaviours. Such an approach to coach development and learning should help avoid what Jones and Turner (2006) describe as the 'reality shock' of assuming an actual coaching position within a given coaching context and being unprepared for the specific demands this entails.

LEARNING MORE

Detailed reviews of coach education and learning are available (e.g. Cushion *et al.*, 2010; Trudel and Gilbert, 2006). Further reading around coaching practice and coach education is also available (e.g. Cassidy *et al.*, 2009; Jones, 2006, Lyle and Cushion, 2010).

ACKNOWLEDGEMENTS

The material for this chapter has been taken from a research project funded by sports coach UK.

REFERENCES

Abraham, A. and Collins, D. (1998) Examining and extending research in coach development. *Quest* 50: 59–79.

Alexander, P.A. (2007) Bridging cognition and socioculturalism within conceptual change research: unnecessary foray or achievable feat? *Educational Psychologist* 41(1): 67–73.

Barab, S.A. and Duffy, T.M. (2000) From practice fields to communities of practice. In D.H. Jonassen and S.M. Land (eds), *Theoretical foundations of learning environments*. Mahwah, NJ: Lawrence Erlbaum.

Brockbank, A. and McGill, I. (2007) *Facilitating reflective learning in higher education* (2nd ed.). Maidenhead, UK: Open University Press.

Brookfield, S.D. (1986) *Understanding and facilitating adult learning*. Milton Keynes, UK: Open University Press.

Buckley, R. and Caple, J. (2002) *The theory and practice of training* (4th ed.). London: Kogan Page.

Cassidy, T., Jones, R. and Potrac, P. (2009) *Understanding sports coaching: the social, cultural and pedagogical foundations of sports practice* (2nd ed.). London: Routledge.

Coombs, P.H. and Ahmed, M. (1974) *Attacking rural poverty: how non-formal education can help*. Baltimore: Johns Hopkins University Press.

Côté, J. (2006) The development of coaching knowledge. *International Journal of Sports Science & Coaching* 1(3): 217–222.

Cushion, C.J. (2006) Mentoring: harnessing the power of experience. In R.L. Jones (ed.), *The sports coach as educator: re-conceptualising sports coaching*. London: Routledge.

Cushion, C.J., Nelson, L., Armour, K., Lyle, J., Jones, R.L., Sandford, R. and O'Callaghan, C. (2010) *Coach learning and development: a review of literature*. Leeds: sports coach UK.

Dymock, D. (1999) Blind date: a case study of mentoring as workplace learning. *Journal of Workplace Learning* 11(8): 312–317.

Ehrich, L., Hansford, B. and Tennent, L. (2004) Formal mentoring programs in education and other professions: a review of the literature. *Educational Administration Quarterly* 40(4): 518–540.

Fuller, A., Hodkinson, H., Hodkinson, P. and Unwin, L. (2005) Learning as peripheral participation in communities of practice: a reassessment of key concepts in workplace learning. *British Educational Research Journal* 31(1): 49–68.

Gilbert, W.D. and Trudel, P. (2001) Learning to coach through experience: reflection in model youth sport coaches. *Journal of Teaching in Physical Education* 21: 16–34.

Gilbert, W. and Trudel, P. (2006) The coach as a reflective practitioner. In R.L. Jones (ed.), *The sports coach as educator: re-conceptualising sports coaching*. London: Routledge.

Hodkinson, P., Biesta, G. and James, D. (2008) Understanding learning culturally: overcoming the dualism between social and individual views of learning. *Vocations and Learning* 1: 27–47.

Jarvis, P. (2004) *Adult education and lifelong learning: theory and practice* (3rd ed.). London: Routledge.

Jarvis, P., Holford, J. and Griffin, C. (1998) The Theory and Practice of Learning London: Kogan Page.Jones, R.L. (ed.) (2006) *The sports coach as educator: re-conceptualising sports coaching*. London: Routledge.

Jones, R.L. and Turner, P. (2006) Teaching coaches to coach holistically: can problem-based learning (PBL) help? *Physical Education and Sport Pedagogy* 11(2): 181–202.

Jones, R.L., Harris, R.A. and Miles, A. (2009) Mentoring in sports coaching: a review of the literature. *Physical Education and Sport Pedagogy* 14(3): 267–284.

Kerka, S. (1998) New perspectives on mentoring. *ERIC Digest*, no. 194. Columbus, OH: ERIC Clearinghouse on Adult, Career, and Vocational Education (ED-99-CO-0013).

Kim, H.S. (1999) Critical reflective inquiry for knowledge development in nursing practice. *Journal of Advanced Nursing* 29(5): 1205–1212.

Lave, J. and Wenger, E. (1991) *Situated learning: legitimate peripheral participation*. Cambridge: Cambridge University Press.

Lave, J. and Wenger, E. (1996) Practice, person, social world. In H. Daniels (ed.), *An introduction to Vygotsky*. London: Routledge.

Light, R. (2008) 'Complex' learning theory in physical education: An examination of its epistemology and assumptions about how we learn, Journal of Teaching in Physical Education, 27(1), 21-37.

Lyle, J. (2007) A review of the research evidence for the impact of coach education. *International Journal of Coaching Science* 1(1): 17–34.

Lyle, J. and Cushion, C.J. (eds) (2010) *Sports coaching: professionalisation and practice*. Oxford: Elsevier.

Merriam, S.B. and Caffarella, R.S. (1999) *Learning in adulthood* (2nd ed.). San Francisco: Jossey-Bass.

Moon, J.A. (2004) *A handbook of reflection and experiential learning: theory and practice*. London: Kogan Page.

Nelson, L.J. and Cushion, C.J. (2006) Reflection in coach education: the case of the national governing body coaching certificate. *Sport Psychologist* 20: 174–183.

Rogers, A. (2002) *Teaching adults*, 3rd ed. Buckingham: Open University Press.

Schunk, D.H. (2009) *Learning theories: an educational perspective* (international edition, 5th ed.). Upper Saddle River, NJ: Pearson Prentice Hall.

Sfard, A. (1998) On two metaphors for learning and the dangers of choosing just one. *Educational Researcher* 27: 4–13.

Simpson, T.L. (2002) Dare I oppose constructivist theory? *Educational Forum* 66: 347–354.

Trudel, P. and Gilbert, W. (2006) Coaching and coach education. In D. Kirk, D. Macdonald and M. O'Sullivan (eds) *The handbook of physical education*. London: Sage.

Tusting, K. and Barton, D. (2006) *Models of adult learning: a literature review*. Leicester: NIACE.

CHAPTER FIVE

THE ESSENTIAL SKILLS OF A COACH

IAN STAFFORD

CHAPTER OUTLINE

- **The skills of a coach and effective coaching**
- **Wider perspectives on coaching**
- **Theory into practice**
- **Learning more**

INTRODUCTION

Much has been written describing, comparing and contrasting what could be summed up as 'the art and the science' of coaching. The 'science' of coaching is viewed as those aspects which, for example, can be acquired through sound learning programmes in physiology or biomechanics or developed through less formal experiential learning from mentors or more experienced coaches. Examples of these 'scientific' aspects include the knowledge required to set out training programmes and the skills required to undertake a performance analysis or plan and organise a coaching session effectively. The 'art' of coaching covers those aspects of a coach's practice and behaviour that are more dependent on the coach's individual personality traits and how these are manifested in the coach's interaction with their participants and others. Examples of such components of coaching practice include the sensitivity that a coach exhibits or the degree to which they are able to use humour to good effect.

How does this introductory reference to the 'art and science' of coaching relate to an examination of the essential skills of a coach? It is acknowledged that skills relate to capabilities that are learned and developed through practice, rather than solely reliant on rather more innate and stable abilities (Knapp, 1967; Schmidt and Wrisberg, 2000). So, although a coach needs not only relevant and well-developed skills to be effective and successful, but also key personal qualities or attributes, the emphasis within this chapter will be on skills that can be improved through practice and learning rather than on the underpinning knowledge and relevant personal qualities. However, at the end of this chapter we will revisit the relationship between skills and personal attributes in coaching, particularly as this relates to coaching children, and suggest that it might not be quite as simple or as useful a distinction as has been claimed.

REFLECTION

Make a table that is divided into three columns headed 'Knowledge', 'Skills' and 'Personal Attributes'. Make up *your own* list of what you would put in each of the three columns in relation to being 'essential' for a coach to *know, be able to do* (skills) and *be like* (personal attributes).

Before we explore the essential skills of a coach, it is useful to recap on what a coach is and what coaches do (see Chapter 1). In the United Kingdom, the term 'coach' is used to cover a group of people whose roles may differ significantly from one another. In the United Kingdom, a 'coach' just starting out on their coaching career who holds a UK Coaching Certificate Level 1 would fulfil the function of a 'coaching assistant', normally working under the direct supervision of a more qualified coach (sports coach UK, 2004). Within the coaching spectrum, there are also coaches operating at the 'expert' level, whose role could involve not only working to improve performers but also directing and managing the work of other coaches. In addition to the variation within coaching roles and skills related to stages of development and expertise, coaches also operate in many different environments and contexts, from recreation to high-performance sport. At the community club level in the United Kingdom, coaches have to fulfil wide and varied roles. In other countries, however, such as the United States or some East European countries, the role of the coach is more focused on the development of techniques, skills, tactics and strategies within their performers. In such systems, the coach would not necessarily be expected to acquire and develop the same breadth of skills.

In short, the roles that a coach has to fulfil will dictate what skills are deemed 'essential'. Having acknowledged this, how do we then go about trying to set out a list of essential coaching skills that would cover all conceivable systems, environments and specific contexts that exist in our current sporting world? The simple answer is that such a task is impossible. The only practical approach is to attempt to identify those essential or 'core' skills that are common to the *coaching process* and thus the vast majority of coaching situations, regardless of where they take place, the level of the coach or the nature of the performers.

Following this introduction, literature on 'the skills of a coach' and 'effective coaching' will be examined. Throughout this section, the skills that appear to be most relevant for coaches of children and young people will be highlighted.

As sport is only one, albeit highly important and popular, context in which 'coaching' occurs, the literature from business and life coaching will be reviewed to ascertain whether some common 'coaching skills' can be identified, regardless of the general context in which that coaching takes place. An interesting 'skill sets' approach adopted by Downey (2003) will be examined and the potential relevance for the coaches of children and young people identified.

THE SKILLS OF A COACH AND EFFECTIVE COACHING

Before we examine the literature, it is useful to consider one recurring issue that is not only examined in the literature but also discussed and argued about by those involved in sport and coaching. To what extent does a coach in a specific sport have to possess well-developed performance skills in that sport in order to be able to coach it effectively? Does a tennis coach have to be able to serve, drive and volley well? Does a football or hockey coach have to be able to control the ball, pass and shoot well? One answer that may be offered to such questions is that it depends on the nature of the sport and the level at which the coach is operating. For example, in racket sports, where one-on-one practice requires the coach to feed or maintain a rally, the quality of the practice will very much depend not only on the coach's ability to diagnose key areas to work on and their decision-making skills about how much pressure to put on the player, but also the coach's ability to hit with precision to the desired points on the court. Although this situation can be addressed by employing a machine or another competent player to feed or rally, it does make many coaches' work somewhat easier if they are able to work one-on-one on court and feed or rally effectively with players.

When examining the situation in high-level, competitive or professional sport, Lyle (2002) claims that many coaches in professional sport are 'recruited almost exclusively from a performer base'. He expands by stating that '[h]igh value is placed on lengthy experience, sport-specific skills and technical insight, to the exclusion of other knowledge and skills' (ibid.: 245). Although this claim is acknowledged to be drawn from anecdotal accounts, it does appear to be a sound summary of the situation that exists – and not only in the professional arena. In coaching, previous experience of participating in the sport and developing per-formance skills is associated with acquiring a high level of technical expertise and knowledge. Cassidy et al. (2004) claim that it is not only the people selecting coaches who value such technical knowledge and expertise, but the coaches themselves, when working at the highest levels. However, do we need to consider 'playing skills' on the part of the coach to be essen-tial, or is it rather the development of an in-depth technical knowledge that can be gleaned from performing in the sport that is more important? A former international rugby union coach, Bob Dwyer of Australia, definitely thinks so: 'I certainly don't think you need to have good rugby ability physically, but I think you need good rugby ability mentally' (Jones et al., 2004: 45). Whereas credibility gained from a successful career as a performer may be a significant factor when coaching at the highest levels in adult sport, is this the case when coaching children?

Look at the three columns list you have compiled from the first reflection task. Is there any reference to playing or performance experience or skills? In the 'personal attributes' column (or elsewhere), is there any mention of the credibility that may emanate from a successful performance career and well-developed playing or performance skills?

Now, consider the following two coaching contexts and, focusing on just the 'skill' column, rate how important you consider each skill in relation to these contexts:

- coaching elite performers in top-class competitive sport;
- coaching children in a community club.

Use a 1–3 rating system where 1 is least important and 3 is most important. An example could be that you have identified strategic/tactical skills in your list and you rate these as most important for a coach working with elite performers in your sport, thus noting 3E ('E' for elite) beside it. You also decide that this skill would be much less important than others in your list for a community coach working with children, so note 1C ('C' for children) beside it.

To conclude this brief examination of the importance of playing or performance skills in coaching, we should consider the work of Cassidy et al. (2004) who contend that emphasising sport-specific, technical 'playing' experience over other skills and attributes is not useful in promoting sports coaching as a profession. As the UK Coaching Framework (sports coach UK, 2008) identifies an aim of developing coaching into a professionally regulated vocation, an aim that many other countries share, other coaching skills would be identified as far more relevant and essential than performance skills within the sport being coached, particularly for a coach working with children.

Coaches will come into coaching from a variety of backgrounds. They will possess a range of different personal attributes and experiences that will influence the development of their coaching skills and style. Despite these individual variations, Crisfield et al. (1999) claim that it is possible to identify certain skills that underpin effective coaching. They state that all coaches need to be able to:

- *Communicate effectively* with participants to identify their needs, interests and goals and to provide information and feedback. Communication is a two-way process, with listening being as important as, if not more important than, talking, particularly when coaches are exploring their participants' motives, needs and ambitions. Coaches are often good at telling and explaining, but sometimes not as good at listening, especially when working with children.

- *Plan and organise sessions and programmes* to meet the needs of participants and guide development. These skills are fundamental in providing appropriate and effective coaching programmes. Planning in a systematic manner is key to ensuring that participants achieve and develop within their sport. When appropriate goals are set and sound activities progressed, the chances of participants achieving are greater, and this sense of achievement should lead to an enhanced self-confidence, which is particularly important when dealing with children and young people (see the 5 Cs approach explained in Chapter 17). Children will quickly become bored and lose interest when presented with badly structured sessions and programmes.
- *Analyse and evaluate performance* (their own coaching practice and behaviour as well as the performance of their participants) to assess achievement and direct progress. Coaches need to demonstrate good analytical skills in relation to technical and tactical aspects of performance, the physical and psychological state of their participant(s), achievement and progress, and their own coaching practice and behaviour. A significant part of this will be coaches reflecting *in* action, while they are coaching, and *on* action, before and after sessions. It is only by reflecting *in* action that coaches will make any necessary adjustments to their planning during sessions and, for example, either increase or reduce the degree of difficulty inherent in the tasks presented. Reflection will be revisited in the concluding section of this chapter, and greater detail can be found in Chapter 8.

It is interesting to note that such 'basic skills' are highlighted even by coaches who work at the highest levels of competitive sport. Graham Taylor, the former head coach to the England football team, refers to the importance of focusing on 'the basics' of planning and organisation, even when working with elite players. He also identifies the importance of instruction and feedback skills in ensuring that key messages are as understandable and meaningful for the individual as possible (Jones *et al.*, 2004). The messages here for coaches of children and young people are self-evident (see Chapter 6 for more detail on communicating with young players).

Throughout this chapter, while focusing on 'essential skills', we will reinforce the point that quality coaching is not just about developing skills. A useful example of this is in building good relationships with participants, parents, administrators, other coaches and officials. Whereas communication and interpersonal skills are of fundamental importance in building harmonious relationships, this process also involves trust, integrity and respect, none of which can be achieved by someone with well-developed coaching skills alone.

As was explained earlier, coaching covers a variety of contexts, levels and environments, and because of this it will be no surprise that no one single objective measure of coaching effectiveness has been identified as appropriate in all situations. Lyle (1998, in Cross and Lyle, 1999: 51) offers the following definition:

> Effective coaching performance is a measure of output over input and can only be understood in relation to 'external factors' – material context, goals and performer

74

capabilities. Like successful coaching performance, it is bounded by time and circumstances. The effective coach is one whose capacity for effective coaching has been demonstrated over time and circumstance.

For the purposes of this chapter, the key question that arises from this definition is: what generic skills do we consider central to a coach's 'capacity for effective coaching'? If we focus on coaching as a process, this should help identify those skills that may be deemed more 'transferable' across different coaching situations. The most basic model of the coaching process identifies three central aspects: planning, coaching and reviewing. Every coach, regardless of the context in which they are coaching, will:

- involve themselves in some sort of planning;
- actively coach in a face-to-face situation with participants;
- review their own practice and that of their participants to inform future planning and coaching.

Lyle (2002: 50, figure 3.4) has produced the following diagram of 'coaching process skills' (Figure 5.1), identifying the three characteristic elements of this process as *planning*, *delivery* and *management*. The subdivisions set out in relation to the three central elements shed more light on what skills need to be developed as central or essential to the coaching process.

When examining the findings from observations of effective coaches, Douge and Hastie (1993) identified the following characteristics:

- frequent provision of feedback and incorporation of numerous prompts and hustles;
- provision of high levels of correction and re-instruction;
- use of high levels of questioning and clarifying;
- predominantly being engaged in instruction;
- management of training environment to achieve considerable order.

These characteristics reinforce the importance of coaches needing to develop interpersonal and communication skills, such as explanation or instruction and questioning skills, observation, analysis and feedback skills, and organisation and management skills in order to be effective.

It is acknowledged that this bullet point list is not an exhaustive or definitive one, but it does serve to highlight key skills to be developed by coaches. To this list, we need to add the coach's skill in synthesising all relevant information, modifying their coaching to fit the needs of the situation and the performers, and reflecting on the coaching programme and sessions. This point is highlighted by Douge and Hastie (1993) and Lyle (2002) when they state that observable coaching behaviours and skills, the so-called delivery skills, while of fundamental importance, are not the only components of effective coaching. This reinforces the value of considering the coaching process in terms of planning, managing, monitoring and reviewing, and not just focusing on the practical coaching delivery.

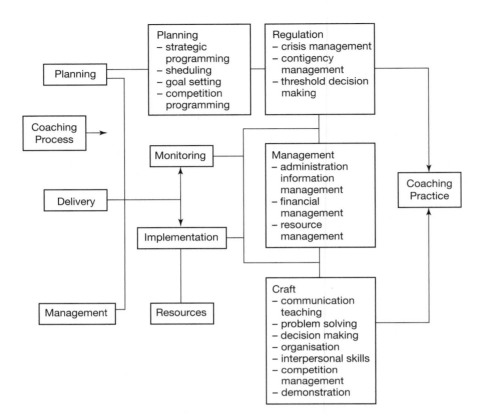

Figure 5.1 Coaching process skills.

Source: Lyle (2002).

To summarise so far, we have identified that the coach requires skills relating to:

- planning;
- organising;
- building rapport and relationships;
- providing instruction and explanation;
- questioning;
- observing and analysing;
- providing feedback;
- evaluating and reflecting.

In all of the skills areas identified in this list, the issue of safety is paramount, particularly when working with children. For coaches to provide a safe environment for young participants, they must be able to assess the risk of what they are planning or coaching. This includes examining

I. Stafford

the area, equipment and participants before starting the session, continuing to assess risks throughout the session, and ensuring that participants are kept on task and are following correct procedures.

There is an argument, rehearsed earlier in the chapter, about the coach needing to possess good performance skills and being able to demonstrate. In lists of coaching skills available from popular coaching websites, demonstration skills often appear. Whereas for some sports this may still be a prerequisite, and a very useful tool in the coach's 'skill box', the value of coach demonstrations and the need for coaches to be able to demonstrate has become less of an issue. Bailey (2001) provides a balanced summary of the 'pros and cons' of teachers providing demonstrations in explaining that although there are some benefits from teacher demonstrations, there are also some issues with this, especially when too much of an emphasis is placed on teacher/coach demonstrations as opposed to participant demonstration. He also cites interesting research on imperfect demonstrations being used to good effect (Rink 1999) and the value of watching someone, such as a peer, who is not expert, but rather learning and receiving feedback (Pollock and Lee 1992).

WIDER PERSPECTIVES ON COACHING

In the foreword to Downey's (2003) book *Effective Coaching*, Timothy Gallwey, whose 'inner game' approach has been employed in sports coaching, states:

> We are witnessing the emergence of a new profession called 'coaching in business and in life'. Though coaching in sports has a long heritage, executive coaching, manager as coach, and life coaching are new means by which people are helping other people professionally. Ironically, the business coaching profession has learned much from sports coaching and is, in turn, exploring approaches which could come full circle and end up transforming traditional sports coaching.

Indeed, Downey does bring a different perspective to what coaches, students and academics in sport would recognise as key skills in coaching. He attempts to bring together all the skills that he feels are essential to become an effective coach in order that both the breadth and depth of what is involved in coaching can really be appreciated. He presents a diagram that identifies key *skill sets*, explains the *intent* of each skill set and provides examples of *specific skills* related to each skill set (2003: 55, diagram 5). Skill sets are defined by a common intent, with some skills appearing in more than one set. In this context, 'intent' defines the use and application of each of the skills. Within the diagram, reproduced here as Table 5.1, there are some skills, such as questioning and listening, that we have already highlighted, but there are others, such as hypothesising and creating a contract, that are not apparent within the sports coaching literature.

It is clear that Downey's view of what constitutes a skill is not shared by those of us who study and practise coaching in sport. In explaining the notion of 'intent', and using Gallwey's 'inner

Table 5.1 Coaching skills and intents

Skill sets	Intent	Specific skills
Generating understanding/ raising awareness	To help the player understand themself/their situation more fully so that they can make better decisions	Listening in order to understand Repetition, paraphrasing and summarising Using silence Asking questions that follow interest Asking questions to clarify Grouping
Proposing	To make available to the player the coach's observations, knowledge, experience, intelligence, insight, intuition and wisdom	Giving feedback Making suggestions Giving advice Challenging Evoking creativity and innovation Giving instruction
Managing self	To ensure that the impact of the coach's needs and preconceptions on the player is minimised To maximise one's own performance as coach	Self-awareness Boundary awareness Transparency Clarifying intent Entering 'flow'/Self Two
Structuring	To ensure that the player achieves meaningful results from the coaching	Following interest Using the GROW model and the Model T Setting goals
Building relationship	To create an environment in which the player feels safe and unjudged	Generating understanding (as above) Creating a contract
Understanding the organisational context	To ensure that the coaching engagement meets the client's needs	Generating understanding (as above) Hypothesising/testing hypotheses

Source: Adapted from Downey (2005: 55).

game' terminology, he explains that '[s]kills are the stuff of the "outer game" as are behaviours and competencies. They can be described and measured and you get a sense of what is to be done' (2003: 56). He introduces the issue of competences beginning to pervade the workplace and states that 'the notion of competencies is insufficient to our task. This is because it gives you no idea of when or why to deploy the skill or behaviour, or critically, to what effect' (ibid.: 56). In skill acquisition and sport literature, this preceding explanation is akin to the difference between technique and skill. In sport, we view skill as being the application of the technique to the specific situation; thus, skill is the way the technique is effectively and efficiently deployed within any given situation. However, there is agreement between Downey's view and the sport-specific definition of skill in terms of the importance of intent. We would not term coaching *effective* or *successful* if a coach produced 'accidental champions' – performers who succeeded despite receiving misguided coaching directions and activities.

I. Stafford

Downey alludes to another key issue that is of prime concern for sports coaches: the difference between coaching individuals and coaching teams. The key difference may appear obvious: in coaching teams or squads, there are more people to consider, and the aim is to blend individual performances into effective team performance. But what impact does this have on the coaching skills required? The following reflection task asks you to consider the difference between coaching squads or teams and coaching individuals.

REFLECTION

▪ If you coach *on an individual, one-to-one basis*, what skill demands do you believe are placed on you to a greater extent than the coach working with a squad or team?
▪ If you coach a *squad or team*, what skill demands do you believe are placed on you to a greater extent than on a coach who works more on an individual one-to-one basis?
▪ If you coach a *children's team*, do you think you need different skills as compared with a coach of an adult team or do you think that the skills are largely the same and it is just the application of those skills that may differ?

In examining literature on life coaching, a recent publication by Dunbar (2009) identifies the following essential skills:

▪ relationship-building skills;
▪ listening and questioning skills;
▪ intuitive skills;
▪ challenging skills;
▪ motivating skills.

These are mostly self-explanatory and similar to the skills we have identified previously, apart from 'intuitive skills'. At first, the two terms 'intuitive' and 'skills' may present as a contradiction. The generally accepted definition of intuition that Dunbar presents is 'the ability to understand or know something immediately, without conscious reasoning' (2009: 115). Although the general interpretation of this is perhaps that it involves thoughts and ideas simply 'popping into your head from nowhere' (as opposed to skills, which require practice and need to be learned), there has been some recent research (Hodgkinson *et al.*, 2008) which proposes that this process is a product of the way the brain stores, processes and retrieves information on a level that we might term 'non-conscious'. Dunbar argues that some coaches have an 'uncanny knack' of picking up on what is happening with the individuals they are coaching and therefore where to focus the attention of their coaching and how to deploy their skills. The issue is whether this 'gut instinct' or 'feeling' can be improved; is it a skill that can be enhanced greatly through practice and reflection or is it more an inherent ability that cannot really be improved to any major extent? If it can be improved, how do we go about developing this important skill in our coaching? 'Sensory acuity' is a term familiar to those who study or practise Neuro-Linguistic Programming (NLP), and involves enhancing observational skills to identify subtle changes that alert the sensitive coach to key aspects of, and changes in, an individual's behaviour, attitude or mood. McDermott and Jago (2001: 76) explain the term as follows:

> 'Sensory acuity' involves paying greater attention to the information you get through your senses. The more you pay attention, the greater your discriminating ability, the finer detail you can gather, and the more you can make comparisons between different sorts and degrees of information.

For the children's coach, this would involve listening intently to their young participants, while taking in key information about body language, in order to assess their motivation and mood and decide on how to approach a session and present activities. Gladwell (2005) referred to this as 'the power of thinking without thinking' and he cites many examples of the value of intuition, where individuals have been able to arrive at an instant impression of something that has later proved to be quite accurate. So, to return to the question posed previously, can we think of our intuition as a skill that can be improved through practice and reflection? Dunbar (2009) certainly thinks so, and provides examples of exercises designed to improve this capability.

In sport, we should be familiar with the three phases of learning: cognitive, associative and autonomous (Fitts and Posner, 1967, in Schmidt and Lee 1999), in which the autonomous stage of skill learning is characterised by the 'mechanical' aspects of the skill, such as dribbling a ball, being so well ingrained that they can be performed without much conscious attention being paid to them – 'thinking without thinking'. This then allows the player to focus more on 'higher-order' aspects such as where to pass. If we extend this analogy to coaching, once the coach has mastered the initial skills of management and organisation and acquired a good knowledge of the sport, the participants and a bank of appropriate activities, they can focus on the elements for which 'sensory acuity' and 'intuition skills' are needed, such as developing good relationships and responding sensitively to their participants' needs and moods. It could be argued that children change so much during their development years in sport that coaches really need to be even more sensitive to and 'in tune' with their young participants during this period than when working with adults, where greater emotional stability results in behaviour being more consistent and predictable.

In introducing her examination of skills required to be an outstanding life coach, Dunbar (2009: 55) states that 'skills alone won't make you a great coach'. She proposes that the coach's knowledge and 'attitude', which she defines as 'the emotional framework through which we perceive everything' (ibid.: 55) underpins these skills. Furthermore, she identifies the coach's values and beliefs as being fundamental to this underpinning.

SUMMARY

Essential skills have been identified and examined from perspectives within sport, business and life coaching. Whereas the importance of developing such skills cannot be overestimated, coaches will need more than just well-developed skills if they are to do the best job possible when working with children. This is where we return to the 'science' and the 'art' issue set out in the introduction to this chapter. Coaches are not simply 'blank canvases' upon which skills can be imposed. Each coach will come with a unique set of personal attributes that will impact on how readily and to what extent different 'essential' skills can be developed. Some coaches may find themselves much more able to identify with their young participants or reflect critically on their own coaching than others. So, perhaps the simplistic distinction between the science and the art of coaching is not quite as accurate a reflection of the situation or as useful as it may first appear.

THEORY INTO PRACTICE

In a chapter highlighting the importance of children's coaches developing 'essential skills', it may seem odd to conclude that whereas skills are fundamental to coaching, they are not the only key consideration. Developing a sound philosophy of coaching and adopting an appropriately sensitive and empathetic approach is fundamental when working with children and young people. How skills are used will be largely determined by a coach's philosophy and approach – by what she or he thinks coaching is all about. So, the first task is for coaches to examine how sound their own philosophy and approach are and how well they are reflected in their coaching practice. How coaching skills are developed and used will be influenced by the coach's own motivations as well as by any outcomes that are externally set for the coaching programme. While it is true that coaching skills should always be viewed in a wider context, they are the essential 'tools of the trade', and in order to be most effective, skills need to be understood and well developed. So, as a coach you need to commit to your own professional development, and as a children's coach there is certainly much to learn and many important skills to master.

In addition to the often-cited coaching process skills relating to planning, delivery, monitoring and reviewing, coaches need to develop their skills in relation to reflection and synthesis. Cushion, in Chapter 4, clearly thinks that reflection is a skill and that '[t]he key to this process is learning the skill of reflection and allowing enough time for the skill to be developed and supported' (p. 61). The question, posed previously, is whether some coaches, because of their particular personal attributes, are more open to reflecting and therefore able to develop the skill more readily or to a higher level. The key implication for coach development is summed up by Miles in Chapter 8 (p. 113) where he states:

> For reflective practice to be fully and effectively adopted within a sports coaching context, there is a need for coach educators to offer coaches practical training in

reflective practice skills in order that the experiential learning they are encouraged to undertake can be effectively utilised to create and extend their knowledge. If the appropriate skills are not developed, then the suggested benefits of experiential learning will not be harnessed and coaching practice will not be advanced.

With the fundamental coaching requirement of providing developmentally appropriate experiences for children in sport, coaches have to be able to synthesise – to consider information from many sources (e.g. developmental psychology, anatomy and physiology), see relationships and integrate information into the big picture of what constitutes the most beneficial coaching programme for their young participants. This skill is one of the six key senses identified by Pink (2006). He refers to this as 'symphony' and highlights its importance by stating that '[w]hat's in greatest demand today isn't analysis but synthesis – seeing the big picture, crossing boundaries and being able to combine disparate pieces into an arresting new whole' (ibid.: 66).

Many of the essential skills listed previously can be acquired relatively easily, but unless coaches are able to 'bring all the pieces together' for children and reflect critically, their coaching will always be limited.

LEARNING MORE

Useful lists and explanations of essential skills and effective coaching in sport are set out in the texts cited in the reference lists of Crisfield et al. (1999), Cross and Lyle (1999) and Lyle (2002). For wider perspectives on essential coaching skills from business and life coaching, see Downey (2003), Bavister and Vickers (2003) and Dunbar (2009). Finally, the book by Pink (2006) is recommended not only as a 'good read' in terms of representing a different view of our dynamically changing world, and what we'll need to be successful in it, but also as having some very pertinent messages for children's coaching, particularly within the topics of empathy, symphony and play.

REFERENCES

Bailey, R.P. (2001) *Teaching physical education: a handbook for primary and secondary school teachers*. London: Kogan Page.

Bavister, S. and Vickers, A. (2003) *Coach: be your best and beyond*. London: Hodder Headline.

Cassidy, C., Jones, R. and Potrac, P. (2004) *Understanding sports coaching: the social, cultural and pedagogical foundations of coaching practice*. London: Routledge.

Crisfield, P., Cabral, P. and Carpenter, F. (1999) *The successful coach: guidelines for coaching practice*. Leeds: Coachwise.

I. Stafford

Cross, N. and Lyle, J. (1999) *The coaching process: principles and practice for sport*. Oxford: Butterworth-Heinemann.

Douge, B. and Hastie, P. (1993) Coaching effectiveness. *Sport Science Review* 2(2): 14–19.

Downey, M. (2003) *Effective coaching*. New York: Texere.

Dunbar, A. (2009) *Essential life coaching skills*. London: Routledge.

Gladwell, M. (2005) *Blink: the power of thinking without thinking*. Boston, MA: Little, Brown.

Hodgkinson, G.P., Langan-Fox J. and Sadler-Smith, E. (2008) Intuition: a fundamental bridging construct in the behavioural sciences. *British Journal of Psychology* 99: 1–27.

Jones, R., Armour, K. and Potrac, P. (2004) *Sports coaching cultures: from practice to theory*. London: Routledge

Knapp, B. (1967) *Skill in sport*. London: Routledge & Kegan Paul.

Lee, M. (1993) *Coaching children in sport*. London: E & FN Spon.

Lyle, J. (2002) *Sports coaching concepts: a framework for coaches' behaviour*. London: Routledge.

McDermott, I. and Jago, W. (2001) *The NLP coach*. London: Judy Piatkus.

Pink, D.H. (2006) *A whole new mind: why right-brainers will rule the future*. New York: Penguin.

Pollock, B.J. and Lee, T.D. (1992) Effects of model skill level on observational motor learning. *Research Quarterly for Exercise and Sport* 63(1): 2–29.

Rink, J.E. (1999) Instruction from a learning perspective. In C. Hardy and M. Mawer (eds), *Learning and teaching in physical education*. London: Falmer Press.

Schmidt, R.A. and Lee, T.D. (1999) *Motor control and learning*. Champaign, IL: Human Kinetics.

Schmidt, R.A. and Wrisberg, C. (2000) *Motor learning and performance*. Champaign, IL: Human Kinetics.

sports coach UK (2004) United Kingdom Coaching Certificate Qualification Guidance (Levels 1–3).

sports coach UK (2008) *The UK Coaching Framework*. Leeds: Coachwise.

CHAPTER SIX

COMMUNICATION WITH YOUNG PLAYERS

JULIA WALSH

CHAPTER OUTLINE

- **The role of communication**
- **The science of communication**
- **Communication delivery**
- **Coach communication guidelines**
- **Theory into practice**
- **Learning more**

INTRODUCTION

> *Communication. Communication has got to be No 1. You have to be able to get on with that person. If you don't you are pushing uphill.*
>
> *(Coach 13, Walsh, 2004: 154)*

Coaches and athletes highlight the importance of communication in creating an environment that builds athlete competence, confidence, connection, character, cooperation and sense of community (Lynch, 2001). However, communication has attracted little interest in the research community. The general guidelines that explain the communication process have been borrowed from other disciplines and applied to the sports setting (Martins, 1987; Weinberg and Gould, 2007). It is only recently that the relational aspects of coach–athlete communication have been explored (LaVoi, 2007), and connections made explicit between learning theory and communication (Fleming *et al.*, 2008).

This chapter moves beyond transmission of communication where people are treated as empty vessels who simply respond and react to sensory input, and explores the complex nature of interactions that occur between the coach and young child in a sport or physical activity context. Children are unique; their growth and development are ongoing; they process information differently and use learning strategies different from those used by adults. Even the most experienced coach will find communication with children a challenge. This chapter explores the role communication plays in human interaction, the science of communication, communication delivery, and guidelines for coaches working with young children in a sport or physical activity context. The challenge facing coaches is to develop capabilities in children through expanding, and continually seeking and testing out, communication strategies that build relationships and provide a learning environment where everyone is encouraged to develop.

This chapter makes explicit a number of processes involved in communication and provides guidelines for communicating relational and sports-specific information to young children.

THE ROLE OF COMMUNICATION

The purpose of communication is multifaceted and moves beyond teaching children how to play and participate in sport and physical activities:

- The coach uses communication to deliver information and knowledge that enables children to learn, build confidence, competence and capacity, and problem-solve in a dynamic sport and physical activity environment (Côté, 2008). To achieve this result, the coach must understand the participants and the context and weave this information with her knowledge of the sport and pedagogy to create an appropriate learning environment.
- Communication is used to motivate, persuade, and provide reason for engagement in a behaviour or activity (Weinberg and Gould, 2007). For example, consider a child competing in the national championships in distance running for the first time. The coach starts encouraging the child by asking her to think about her past achievements and encourages her to compete to achieve a personal best. If the child is hesitant, the coach may resort to persuasion, particularly if it requires further training commitment, to achieve this. He uses reason to justify the extra effort.
- Coaching is a relational job and communication is the mechanism used to develop positive relationships with young children. Interpersonal communication is developmental and changes as the relationship evolves. The coach and the child interact together to build mutual trust, warmth and understanding in their relationship (LaVoi, 2007).
- The coach has the potential, through effective communication, to influence the child's psychological development, learning strategies, cultural conventions, as well as their sport competence. When adults collaborate and communicate with children on a problem-solving task, it helps children develop individual thinking skills that lead to control and regulation of their own performance (Vygotsky, 1978; Wood, 1998).

In summary, communication between the coach and young participant creates an environment where children can develop as individuals and team members, build competence and confidence in physical activity, and know that there is mutual support and understanding for all involved in the process.

REFLECTION

From your personal experience, what strategies have worked best in establishing an environment where communication was open and everyone was valued?

Create a session plan where one of the objectives is to introduce a new skill and incorporate it into game practice. Think about how you would communicate this skill as a problem-solving task where the solution requires collaboration from you and the young athlete.

The young participant requires some motivation and persuasion to engage in the problem-solving task. What strategies might be useful in persuading him or her to engage in action?

THE SCIENCE OF COMMUNICATION

Humans are social animals; we congregate in groups, and use several forms of language to communicate. The diversity of communication forms and the relational aspects of how we live and work together make us unique. The ability of humans to coordinate actions is due in part to effective communication (Traber, 1999). Sport at all levels of competition and across different contexts is a very human activity, involving high levels of engagement among participants, and is dependent on all forms of communication.

Sport takes place in a social environment; people work together and rely on communication both on and off the field to achieve goals. The coach plays a significant role in this process through the establishment of communication conventions and use of delivery channels. Coaching is complex and requires the combination of delivering technical and game skills, and, equally important, the building of strong relationships that relays trust, care, concern and respect for both parties (LaVoi, 2007). Unfortunately, communication is a taken-for-granted skill. Because it is second nature to humans, there has been little investment in educating people about how best to communicate, particularly in a sporting environment.

The mechanics of the communication process: encoding and decoding

Communication is inescapable; coaches and participants are continually sending and receiving messages and information through a variety of communication channels (social, physical or other). At its most basic level, communication involves the coach coming up with an idea or message and a strategy for delivering it (encoding). The athlete receives the message through sensory input, interprets the message (decoding) and responds.

In this simplistic description of communication, the message is like a parcel being delivered to a destination. On receiving the parcel, the person has a clear picture of what the message represents. The description assumes that the information transmitted was correctly interpreted and acted upon. An extensive study investigating youth coach behaviours (Smith *et al.*, 1978) found that this was not always the case. The players' evaluative reactions to the coach communication were mediated by the players' perceptions and recall of those behaviours. For example, the coach communicates information to the athlete, the athlete perceives and recalls this behaviour and, on the basis of the perception and recall, the athlete evaluates and responds. It is the meaning attributed to the communication that evokes the response, not the actual communication. Hence, the athlete can either correctly interpret the message – a positive outcome for the sender and receiver – or totally misinterpret the message, in which case the coach then reacts to the athlete's response and a total breakdown in communication can take place.

Figure 6.1 Successful communication.

Figure 6.2 Unsuccessful communication.

Communicating messages explicitly and implicitly sends other pieces of information, for example the power relationships between the coach and participant, cultural conventions, attitudes, values, belief systems, biases, identity issues, relationships, and ways of belonging (Giles and Wienman, 1987; LaVoi, 2007). The coach may unintentionally communicate information to the participants through non-verbal communication. The language, whether verbal or non-verbal, and channels (social, physical or other) are versatile and serve many different kinds of functions, which can also make interpretation difficult. Every step of the communication process is complex and requires attention giving, registering, coding (encoding or decoding), and *interpretation*.

> I have had it happen a couple of times during my coaching career where the player doesn't think I believe in them. They probably are right so subconsciously I must have done things. Whether it was the way I communicated with them, the feedback I'd given them, the playing time they got or whatever else that shows that, so I'm pretty careful now to make sure they know exactly where I'm coming from.
>
> (Coach 2, Walsh, 2004: 141)

This coach makes the point that participants gather information from many sources and decide for themselves what the message contains. The coach must be an avid observer of their communication and be conscious of the participants' response to that communication. With practice, the coach can develop sensitivity to misinterpretation of information and correct it before it becomes a problem.

J. Walsh

COMMUNICATION DELIVERY

Communication can be divided into two categories: intrapersonal communication and interpersonal communication.

- Intrapersonal communication is self-talk. It is the communication we have with ourselves and it serves several purposes. Self-talk during a task helps people problem-solve; it also influences how people think about themselves and predicts how they will perform (Vygotsky, 1978; Weinberg and Gould, 2007). Coaches can teach players how to use positive self-talk to enhance performance and reduce opportunity for negative thoughts during performance (Rushall, 2002).
- Interpersonal communication takes place between two people in a dynamic environment. It is premised by three principles. The first principle is that communication is all-pervading; it governs human behaviour. The coach and athlete are always communicating with each other, whether explicitly or implicitly. Second, once communication happens, the process cannot be reversed. If a coach rolls her eyes, or makes a comment, she cannot take it back. The third principle is that communication is complex. It is not a direct transmission process; for those involved, there are multiple factors, such as identity and relationships, that influence the communication (LaVoi, 2007).

Communication channels

Communication channels are versatile and provide an opportunity to send messages in a number or in a combination of ways (Weinberg and Gould, 2007). Combining communication channels can reinforce a message, such as when a coach calls out 'well done' to a player (verbal) and claps her hands (physical). On the other hand, it can provide a mixed message, for example when the coach tells a substituted player coming off the court that she played well but the coach's body language, with no eye contact and turning away from the player (non-verbal), indicates that this is not the case.

Verbal and non-verbal communications are the most common channels used for sending messages and information.

Verbal communication is the channel that people rely on most to send a message to another. People use words to try to convey meaning to others. Verbal communication requires language, and this language is represented in words presented in a variety of ways, such as voice, writing, email and sign language. Verbal communication is an important channel for sending messages when the words clearly convey a meaningful message for the participant. It is a learned skill that takes practice and rehearsal for it to be effective.

Non-verbal communication, otherwise known as body language, can be used to send an explicit message, to reinforce a verbal message, or to tell the observer that all is not what it seems when the verbal and non-verbal communication are in contradiction. It has been suggested that the spoken word, voice tone and facial expression contribute 7 per cent, 38 per cent and 55 per cent respectively to the total meaning of the message (Mehrabian and Ferris, 1967; Mehrabian and Wiener, 1967). This suggestion has been contested on the grounds of experimental design. It is difficult to control non-verbal behaviour, and this behaviour can provide cues for the receiver. For example, the coach might invite questions from team members, but his arms are crossed and his feet are facing away from the group, suggesting he is closed to any new ideas and is anxious to leave. Physical touching is a powerful form of non-verbal communication. The media provide many examples of coaches and athletes hugging or receiving a pat on the back for achieving success or experiencing failure. Although this is a powerful gesture, caution must be exercised in using such forms of com-munication, particularly in the child and youth sport context. The trust relationship between a child and adult has at times been abused, hence child protection courses and literature are now available for clubs, coaches and parents that clarify appropriate behaviour in this context.

Communication beyond words: paralanguage

Paralanguage is an extension of verbal and non-verbal communication. It can be used to modify meaning and convey emotion. It can be expressed consciously or unconsciously and includes the tone, pitch, rhythm, timbre, loudness and inflection of voice. It has the potential to be used very effectively as a tool in children's sport. Paralanguage can be used to paint a picture, place emphasis on skill components, and teach rhythm. For example, if the coach is asking an athlete to bend their knees and take a low position, voice *pitch* can be altered to exaggerate the information presented. When coaching children to perform skills with a temporal component, augment instruction with rhythmic support (Hodges and Franks, 2004). For example, creating a rhythmic beat with numbers (1, 2, 1, 2) or phrases (swing, hit, as in golf), or by clapping hands, assists participants to establish tempo.

Receiving information

Receiving information is the other significant component of communication. Seventy per cent of people's activity is spent in verbal communication: reading, writing, speaking and listening. Of that time, up to 45 per cent is spent receiving information (Sathre et al., 1973), and the untrained listener can miss up to 80 per cent of that communication. Yet seldom are coaches or participants educated about how to listen. Listening is a very different skill from hearing. Hearing is receiving messages, but it does not guarantee the message has been interpreted and given consideration. The mere fact that the coach or participant receives information does not mean that they understand the message or the emotion attached (Fleming et al., 2008; Weinberg and Gould, 2007).

Making time and listening to players makes them feel valued and builds a belief that the coach has a real interest in them beyond their athletic abilities. It takes a concerted effort to listen but there are many benefits: it enhances the relationship between the coach and participant and conveys the message that the coach understands the participant.

One technique available to coaches and participants is *active listening*. This teaches people to focus on the main ideas of the sender, support the ideas, acknowledge and respond, provide appropriate feedback and pay attention to the verbal and non-verbal communication. To engage in active listening requires the establishment of a certain mindset and rehearsal of verbal and non-verbal communication. The following information provides guidelines for engaging in active listening.

The mindset

- Make yourself available to participants by creating a receptive and welcoming environment.
- Focus on the immediate thoughts and feelings of the child.
- Describe the behaviour rather than trying to evaluate it for a counter-attack.
- Remain open to new ideas, and be flexible, as different situations require different responses.
- Respect the rights of children to share their views with you.

Communication: verbal and non-verbal

- Maintain an open posture and ensure that the child knows they are receiving focused attention.
- Communicate confirming behaviour (you are listening!) by the use of verbal and non-verbal language. Use supportive communication, head-nodding or verbal language such as 'I see' or 'uh huh'.
- Avoid interrupting the participant when they are speaking; give them undivided attention and search for the real message.
- Continue to ask yourself, 'What is the athlete feeling at this moment?'

The coach also needs to know whether the athlete is listening. Asking questions may only result in the athlete repeating the information, not necessarily listening and making meaning of the message. When teaching a new skill, or providing game information, ask the participants to explain their understanding to other team members or have them teach each other and provide feedback on the skill. This will provide the coach with a quick assessment of participant understanding.

REFLECTION

- Self-talk helps young children to problem-solve. Design a drill that requires the participants to use self-talk as they participate in the skills. For example, in a basketball right-hand basketball lay-up, have the players say 'left', 'right', 'up', or in a set shot, 'bend and extend'; in soccer dribbling, participants recite 'inside, outside' (foot).
- Think of a skill specific to your sport that has a temporal component. What communication strategies could you use to assist children develop their rhythm?
- Practise your listening skills. In groups of three, perform a role-play where one person is the participant with an issue to discuss with the coach, the second person is the coach whose job it is to actively listen, and the third person observes and provides feedback at the conclusion of the coach–participant discussion. Rotate through these roles and discuss your learning at the conclusion of the role-plays.

COACH COMMUNICATION GUIDELINES

The novice coach has 20 children arriving for training in 30 minutes. Their chronological age ranges between 8 and 10 years, and their anatomical, biological and neurological development ranges between 6 and 12 years of age. The coach is faced with a complex task: to communicate successfully with these participants requires understanding of each individual, their growth and development, and the context.

In brief, children differ from adolescents and adults in their cognitive and physiological capacity. Children may be hearing the message but, at their developmental stage, are unable to make meaning of the message or perform the task unless the information is adapted to meet their needs.

Children's cognitive capacity

Young children have limited experience, storage processes and frames of reference to be able to understand or perform skills perfectly during the early stages of learning; it requires a

J. Walsh

gradual adaption to achieve performance increases. Experienced athletes are able to make connections to knowledge stored in their long-term memory, but young children are at a disadvantage as they have limited experience and their storage and organisation of knowledge are in the early stages of development (Ericsson and Delaney, 1999). This has implications for how coaches communicate with young children. For example, it is difficult for the young athlete to *feel the difference* if they do not have a frame of reference. The following coaching guidelines are designed to help young children develop a frame of reference and encode information:

- Use questions to find out what experience the young participants have had previously.
- Do they have a frame of reference? Ask participants demonstrate and/or verbalise the action.
- If appropriate, help participants make connections to other skills they have learned so that they can embed the information in long-term memory.
- Explain the relevance of the action so that the participant can make meaning of the information (help them to encode it).
- Have participants perform the task several times in multiple contexts.

Cognitive capacity, if overloaded, limits the participant's ability to problem-solve in context. Communication strategies that paint pictures through the use of analogies have potential to free up space for problem solving (Masters and Maxwell, 2004). An analogy used in badminton is throwing a Frisbee to describe the backhand drive; or skimming a stone across the water could create the picture for the forehand drive.

Experienced coaches continually look for ways of painting pictures that athletes can understand. With children, the pictures or analogies must be relevant to their experiences and context.

Learning styles

The identification of learning styles has influenced the way teachers and coaches have engaged children in learning. Learning styles refers to the participants' preferred way of gathering and storing information. Young children learn in a variety of ways. For example, some children may have a preference for visual, aural, read/write or kinaesthetic instruction, while others use a combination of these learning styles. However, coaches often make the mistake of coaching in a style that suits them rather than the child (Fleming *et al.*, 2008).

Tapping into each individual's learning preference can be challenging, particularly if the coach is working with a large team. The coach should aim to strike a balance and use a variety of learning styles within the training programme and throughout the season. One training session might be based on children shadowing a skill that is explained using verbal communication, whereas at another session, instruction is based on written charts and film clips. Of course, this is much easier if you have a small number of athletes whom you can ask about their preference and coach accordingly.

Building individual relationships and teams through communication

Relationship building relies on more than knowing the child's athletic profile. The coach needs to take an interest in the child's life and find out about what interests them, for example information about their family and school life. Communication often breaks down on the sports field, and coaches need to look for ways of keeping communication channels open. Having other topics to talk about (family, school, other interests) helps to maintain the coach–athlete relationship during these difficult times. For the child, it also reinforces that the communication breakdown on the sports field is not personal and the coach still values them.

There are many ways coaches can use communication to build team cohesion and identity. Coaches should encourage teams to establish an image they wish to communicate. For example, the team wear their full uniform to games and events, they walk in and warm up together and communicate to all who are watching that they are unified as a team. Before and after the match, they shake hands with the opposition team, or other participants in individual events, and thank the officials and host at the conclusion of the event. These types of behaviours communicate an image of connection, character, cooperation and sense of community.

Create a shared language to use with participants that is specific to the activity and context. Create *buzzwords* that the team can identify and use in their training and competition context. Initially, it will be necessary to use an elaborated code that spells everything out so that all participants can understand what the buzzword represents. When everyone has a thorough understanding, use a restricted code. This shared team knowledge is economical and rich and conveys a vast amount of meaning with few words or no words (non-verbal communication). Each buzzword is made up of a complex set of information and acts like an index, pointing the receiver to a lot more information that remains unsaid.

REFLECTION

As coach with a new team, design a strategy that enables you to source information about your participants that you can use to build the coach–athlete relationship.

Create a lexicon of buzzwords relevant to your sport to use with participants. Develop definitions for all buzzwords as a reference guide for current members and to assist new members of the club.

Design a selection process for your team that communicates to participants and significant others the following information:

- selection objectives;
- selection strategy;
- feedback delivery for all participants at the conclusion of selection.

THEORY INTO PRACTICE

Good communication requires practice and reflection. It starts with understanding your own communication practice ('self-awareness'), and viewing communication as a skill requiring constant attention and investment in learning. Understanding the young child, their potential and stage of development is central to this process. Your planning should include a communication strategy covering not only what you plan to teach but how you plan to communicate the message. As a coach, ask yourself, 'How do I plan through communication to engage the young child so that they develop competence, confidence, capability and a sense of community in a sport or physical activity context?'

LEARNING MORE

Communication is a multidisciplinary field and there is limited research that applies directly to the sport context. For information on the relational aspects of communication, Jowett and Lavallee (2007) on social psychology provide the most current information. The VARK website (www.aboutus.org/Vark-learn.com) provides information on learning styles and provides testing facilities. The website www.center-for-nonverbal-studies.org/1501.html provides extensive information on non-verbal communication.

REFERENCES

Ericsson, K.A. and Delaney, P. (1999) Long-term working memory as an alternative to capacity models of working memory in everyday skilled performance. In A. Miyake and P. Shah (eds), *Models of working memory: mechanisms of active maintenance and executive control*. New York: Cambridge University Press.

Côté, J. (2008) Coaching expertise defined by meeting athlete needs. In *sports coach UK coaching summit research forum*. Stirling, UK: Stirling University.

Fleming, N., Robson, G. and Smith, R. (2008) *Sports coaching and learning* (4th ed.). Christchurch, New Zealand: Fleming, Robson & Smith.

Giles, H. and Wienman, J. (1987) Language, social comparison, and power. In C.R. Berger and S.H. Chaffee (eds), *Handbook of communication science*. London: Sage.

Hodges, N.J. and Franks, I.M. (2004) Instruction, demonstrations and the learning process: creating and constraining movement options. In A.M. Williams and N.J. Hodges (eds), *Skill acquisition in sport: research, theory and practice*. London: Routledge.

Jowett, S. and Lavallee, D. (eds) (2007) *Social psychology in sport*. Champaign, IL: Human Kinetics.

LaVoi, N.M. (2007) Interpersonal communication and conflict in the coach–athlete relationship. In S. Jowett and D. Lavallee (eds), *Social psychology in sport*. Champaign, IL: Human Kinetics.

Lynch, J. (2001) *Creative coaching: new ways to maximize athlete and team potential in all sports*. Champaign, IL: Human Kinetics.

Martins, R. (1987) *Coaches' guide to sport psychology*. Champaign, IL: Human Kinetics.

Masters, R.S. and Maxwell, J.P. (2004) Implicit motor learning reinvestment and movement disruption: what you don't know won't hurt you? In A.M. Williams and N.J. Hodges (eds), *Skill acquisition in sport: research theory and practice*. London: Routledge.

Mehrabian, A. and Ferris, S. (1967) Inference of attitudes and nonverbal communication in two channels. *Journal of Consulting Psychology* 31: 248–252.

Mehrabian, A. and Wiener, M. (1967) Decoding and inconsistent communications. *Journal of Personality and Social Psychology* 6: 109–114.

Rushall, B. (2002) *Mental skills training for sports: a manual for athletes, coaches, and sport psychologists* (3rd ed.). Spring Valley, CA: Sports Science Associates.

Sathre, S., Olson, R.W. and Whitney, C.I. (1973) *Let's talk*. Glenview, IL: Scott, Foresman.

Smith, R.E., Smoll, F.L. and Curtis, B. (1978) Coaching behaviors in little league baseball. In F.L. Smoll and R.E. Smith (eds), *Psychological perspectives in youth sport*. Washington, DC: Hemisphere.

Traber, M. (1999) Communication is inscribed in human nature. Available at: http://archive.waccglobal.org/wacc/content/pdf/1089 (accessed 1 August 2009).

Vygotsky, L.S. (1978) *Mind in society: the development of higher psychological processes*, ed. M. Cole, V. John-Steiner, S. Scriber and E.E. Souberman. Cambridge, MA: Harvard University Press.

Walsh, J. (2004) Development and application of expertise in elite-level coaches. Unpublished doctoral dissertation, Victoria University, Melbourne, Australia.

Weinberg, R.S. and Gould, D. (2007) *Foundations of sport and exercise psychology*, 4th ed. Champaign, IL: Human Kinetics.

Wood, D. (1998) *How children think and learn* (2nd ed.). Oxford: Blackwell.

CHAPTER SEVEN

PROFESSIONAL RESPONSIBILITIES OF CHILDREN'S COACHES

HAMISH TELFER AND CELIA BRACKENRIDGE

CHAPTER OUTLINE

- Development of coaching standards
- Safeguarding and coaching practice
- Professional engagement and responsibilities
- Coaching in different contexts
- Theory into practice
- Learning more

INTRODUCTION

UK Vision for Coaching stated that by 2012, 'the practice of coaching in the UK will be elevated to a profession acknowledged as central to the development of sport and the fulfilment of individual potential' (UK Sport, 2001: 5). Inherent within this statement is the notion that all those who participate in sport, particularly children and young people, will be coached in a way that is responsive to their needs. The coaching should be based on clear principles of practice that are grounded in relevant bodies of knowledge and accepted ethical principles and values. Moreover, this approach should be subject to a process of scrutiny, review and feedback that informs improvements in practice.

This chapter explores the challenges to coaches and coaching of embedding principles of safeguarding (formerly called child protection) into professional practice to provide purposeful, safe and enjoyable experiences. In recent years, the development of structures and processes for safeguarding children and young people has become a major priority in the training and education of coaches, teachers and sports leaders. Coaches' education and practice should thus accommodate increasing expectations of professional accountability. This should not alarm coaches, who are, and will remain, largely volunteers acting in an unpaid capacity:

rather, it should be seen as an opportunity to develop practice and respond to changing societal demands and expectations.

In cooperation with other European nations, the United Kingdom has implemented new coaching structures and harmonised qualification levels (sports coach UK, 2009a). These new structures, minimum operating standards (MOS) and new legal obligations with regard to children and young people now provide the foundations for good coaching practice (sports coach UK, 2009b). The principle of athlete welfare has also become a key factor in shaping good coaching practice (Brackenridge et al., 2007).

Alongside technical knowledge, communication and an understanding of relevant methods combine to define competent professional practice. Professional responsibilities with regard to safeguarding should therefore be embedded in practice and capable of being 'evidenced'. Indeed, evidence-based practice is the hallmark of any good practitioner who claims to be operating competently. What determines competence are standards that have been developed, understood and accepted by coaches and the coaching profession. This chapter sets out the basic parameters and requirements of professional practice with particular reference to safeguarding and athlete welfare, and embeds these standards within the everyday practice of coaches.

DEVELOPMENT OF COACHING STANDARDS

The development of sets of standards in sport, particularly for safeguarding, is intended to provide guidance and support to those working with young people (NSPCC, 2006). However, important as standards are in giving guidance and setting minimum requirements, they cannot serve completely to regulate coaching practice. Only coaches with a robust sense of judgement can be expected to marry the interpretation of minimum standards to their practice. In this sense, standards serve to define the *minimum* obligations of sport practitioners. Since coaching practice is nuanced, fluid and highly situational, there is an increasing reliance on all practitioners to be able to assess, interpret and integrate the requirements of coaching standards into meaningful and responsive practice.

Coaching standards have been developed in response to Europe-wide initiatives designed to share and develop information that enhances coaching practice (European Coaching Council, 2007). The development of standards, particularly those related to safeguarding, has also occurred in response both to changes in law and to cases of proven negligent or abusive practice. Guidance on safeguarding has been matched with that on race, gender and disability equity and with the development of a coaching code of practice (sports coach UK, 2005). Together, these inform the National Occupational Standards for Coaching, Teaching and Instructing (NOS for CTI) (SkillsActive, 2004).

Standards are designed to give guidance and strengthen practice. In particular, they attempt to define and confirm relevant competences required of sports practitioners. These

98

competences range from the identification of *tasks* relevant to coaching to the issue of *capacity* in coaches. This is an important distinction, since sports practice is as much about *how* practitioners work as what they *do*.

REFLECTION

- Have you considered what your strengths and weaknesses are in relation to your coaching? How valid are these views?
- Are your strengths and weaknesses more to do with your methods of coaching than with your knowledge base?
- Have you ever considered how you 'come across'?

See Cross and Lyle (2002) and Lyle (2002) for more information about coaching practice and coaching behaviours.

Working with children and young people spans the performance spectrum from club beginner to high performance; thus, coaching environments and coaches' skill-sets, both technical and behavioural, need to accommodate this variation. It is sometimes difficult for coaches to move along the behavioural continuum as they adjust from what feels most comfortable dispositionally to what is demanded situationally. The ability of the coach to adapt their practice situationally is a key factor in safeguarding performers; it also helps to avoid practices that place inappropriate demands on young people, whether in terms of technical skills, physical loadings or emotional coercion.

While all sports practitioners are educated about the ethical basis of their practice, especially with regard to working with children, the law has intervened and placed obligations upon those working with children and young people. Professional responsibilities therefore encompass both what *ought* to be done and what is *required* to be done in order to ensure compliance with minimum standards.

REFLECTION

- Are you able to evaluate whether your practice feels or seems more 'comfortable' and 'successful' with certain groups or in certain situations? For example, are you better at coaching technical skills rather than physical conditioning? Better at working with males or females, large rather than small groups?

■ What impact does this have on embedding safeguarding principles into your practice?

See sports coach UK's *Safeguarding and Protecting Children* resource guide (2009c), particularly pp. 20–36, for examples of good practice.

Underpinning sports practice is the notion of 'duty of care'. This has to be understood in the context of developmental age, competitive 'readiness' and the power relationship that exists between coach and performer. This is of particular importance as the performer makes the transition from recreational sport and learning to train, to performance sport, where they are training to compete and win. Duty of care is most commonly understood in the context of ensuring that practice is not negligent and that practitioners must understand not only what they do (acts of commission) but also what they do *not* do (acts of omission). In this respect, the United Kingdom, in common with most other countries, gives guidance about populations that may be particularly vulnerable in terms of sport opportunities and experiences. The most obvious groups here are children and young people. However, women and girls, participants with a disability, and ethnic groups are, among others, identified as requiring particular consideration in relation to their coaching needs (UK Sport, 2003). These have sometimes been referred to as 'target groups' (a term now out of favour) or 'hard to reach', since they tend to be under-represented within sports participation generally. Coaching environments therefore need to reflect the various and diverse needs of all those taking part in coaching sessions.

With regard to coaching children, specific training courses are available about 'safeguarding'. These complement equity courses, disability awareness courses and specialised first aid courses; some are sport-specific (sports coach UK, 2009c, d). With the addition of codes of practice and codes of conduct, a National Governing Body of Sport coaching award and Criminal Records Bureau check, these courses form the basis of Minimum Operating Standards (MOS) for coaches (in England), particularly with regard to the Active Sport programmes (sports coach UK, 2009b). These standards are a response to the processes of professionalisation and legal regulation of the coaching workforce (UK Sport, 2004). The United Kingdom's Coaching Code of Practice, in particular, reinforces the professional expectations placed on coaches.

What is often problematic for sports practitioners is how all of these various and at times seemingly disparate standards affect their day-to-day coaching. The next section offers guidance as to how safeguarding standards impact upon coaching responsibilities.

100

SAFEGUARDING AND COACHING PRACTICE

While competition is often seen by adults as the essence of sporting engagement, it is appropriate to remember that for children and young people, enjoyment, fun and physical competence (being able to 'do things') are of most importance (sports coach UK, 2006). Creating the right conditions for engagement in sport is a primary quality of sports practitioners who specialise in working with children and young people. (What is meant by coaching relative to this age group is an essential question, covered in other chapters.) It is clear that if sport is to be a safe, happy and productive place for young people, coaches need to be able to translate their understanding of duties and obligations into tangible and relevant practice. In this short section, the focus is on making safeguarding 'come alive'.

Safeguarding children and young people is grounded on the five key principles enshrined within the United Kingdom's Every Child Matters (ECM) guidance (to be healthy, be safe, enjoy and achieve, make a positive contribution and be able to enjoy a degree of economic well-being) (HMSO, 2004). Coaching practice should be based on these principles. Thus, coaches should consider the design of each coaching session in terms of content relevant to the learners, the creation of an environment that fosters achievement, a positive rapport, effective communication and a range of techniques that promote active engagement.

It is undoubtedly the case that the majority of experiences within sport for young people are positive and fulfilling. Nonetheless, coaches are obliged to be aware that, for some young people, the experiences that they bring to sport can be, or have been, abusive, often caused by people whom they should be able to trust. Sport itself is a potential site for abuse if coaches behave or act inappropriately, whether wittingly or unwittingly. Sports practitioners therefore have a significant opportunity to provide a safe and fulfilling environment for young people through practice that is competent, knowledgeable and reflective. In this regard, practitioners should consider themselves as role models with regard to their attitudes, values and modes of expression.

In the context of safeguarding, coaches must evidence their practice against the main categories of abuse (neglect, physical abuse, sexual abuse, emotional abuse and bullying) in order to identify potential breaches of good practice. Evidence-based practice should be one of the primary auditing and reflective skills of a competent practitioner. The following examples illustrate how coaching practice can be connected to safeguarding principles through reflecting on the focus, content and behaviours within the coaching session.

It is generally accepted that good coaching is situational – that is, it adapts so as to suit different situations. This adaptation is achieved through the use of a range of behavioural 'styles'. The repertoire of styles should include ways of hearing the 'voice' of the young performer, where the coach uses more 'reciprocal' techniques rather than simply 'telling'. The skilful use of questioning not only gives ownership of learning to the learner but also encourages self-confidence and allows opinions to be expressed, which in turn helps to tell the coach how the learner is thinking. In this way, children's opinions and views are heard, not neglected, and a more equal balance of power between coach and learner is achieved. Simple shifts of techniques at appropriate moments are sometimes all that is required.

One of the most controversial topics for coaches is the nature of 'appropriate' physical loadings in training. The connection between physical abuse and inappropriate physical demands is clear. This becomes all the more problematic in relation to the Principle of Overload, since, by its very nature, there is no adaptation without overloading the system. This raises the question 'How much is too much?' The answer is that 'it depends' – which can be singularly unhelpful! Key questions here relate to maturational level and whether the session has been appropriately subdivided into ability groups (also known as 'differentiation') relative to the varying degrees of learner level and competence. Coaching sessions should only contain the number of performers that a coach can manage safely, being able to attend to the skill and conditioning needs of all concerned. Keeping the numbers to this level will enable the practitioner to attend adequately to the level of physical demands required of each and every performer.

DIRECTED TASK

Write down how you attend to individual needs in your coaching sessions.

- Do you subdivide groups (differentiate) into ability or different learning sets often enough?
- Do you ever get distracted by one group or individual at the expense of others?
- Do you ever work on a one-to-one basis?
- What safeguarding issues may potentially arise from physical contact in a demonstration or in correcting technique?

See sports coach UK's *Safeguarding and Protecting Children* (2009c) resource guide and its resource *Equity in Your Coaching* (2009d) for examples of good practice.

The issue of inappropriate touching in sport is also of concern to coaches, not only in contact sports but also in technical correction and safety (handling) work. This is related both to the varying degrees of physical development of young people and to issues of perceived intimacy. Chronological age groupings do not necessarily match individual differences in physical development, so coaches need to be reflexive in situations where chronologically the child may 'fit' but developmentally they do not. It is possible to maintain safety and avoid accusations of intimacy by small adjustments in coaching technique and by good communication (such as asking prior permission to touch, keeping in clear view of others, commentating during handling, and so on). It should go without saying, of course, that the use of physical activity as chastisement has no place in a professionally run session.

H. Telfer and C. Brackenridge

Competitive pressure on young athletes is an area of increasing concern within coaching. It is important to remember that winning (an outcome) is ranked relatively low by children and young performers themselves compared with simply having fun (a process). Nevertheless, competition is also an indicator of achievement that should be celebrated (sports coach UK, 2006). Coaches should be aware of the various forms that competition can take and use these as a 'scaffolding' (support) mechanism in working gradually towards the adult model of competition. Part of the coach's role in counselling young performers is differentiating between reasonable and unreasonable levels of expectation on individuals and teams. All too often, coaches are judged as successful or not on the basis of the achievements (outcomes) of their performers. They must therefore help both athletes and parents or carers to understand that improvements in processes (such as teamwork or communication) and incremental out-comes (keeping an opponent from scoring for 10 minutes, 15 minutes, etc.) can also be rewarding. Children's sport is often emotionally laden, leading to unreasonable demands, rapid disillusionment and drop-out. The coach therefore must play a key role in ensuring that parents or carers have realistic expectations of their children.

Selection and playing time also feature strongly in judgements about whether a coach is fair and equitable. This can prompt self-examination in the coach, who might be drawn to the more talented at the expense of the less talented. Language and contact (the latter both in time and in the physical sense) can give unwitting evidence as to a coach's moral compass. The ability to self-audit coaching behaviours and the use of behavioural 'styles' can be a helpful tool for ensuring more effective inclusion.

REFLECTION

- If someone were to describe you and the way you coached, what words do you think they would use?
- How do you think you 'come across'? (As fun, disciplined, organised, structured, a good communicator, motivator, fair?)
- What words do you use that could be open to misinterpretation? How would you 'benchmark' your practice with young people in order to be sure that it integrates safeguarding principles?

See Cassidy et al. (2009) for an overview of the social, cultural and pedagogical aspects of coaching, which will help establish a clear view of the foundations of good coaching practice.

All of the above connect to safeguarding obligations in sport. Professional responsibilities require coaches to be able to audit potentially abusive behaviours in their own practice as well as identifying children in their coaching sessions who may show signs of being abused or troubled outside sport.

PROFESSIONAL ENGAGEMENT AND RESPONSIBILITIES

'Looking out' for children is one of the key principles and obligations for all who work with children and young people. Knowing what to 'look out' for and what to do about it is now considered a key skill for the coach of young performers. Two key sets of principles govern professional practice. First, there is what the law requires, and second, there are moral and ethical considerations. The two combine to inform minimum standards or thresholds for practice. McNamee (1998: 149) adopted Koehn's seven conditions in determining the moral and professional authority of practitioners. It is worth reprising these here:

1   The professional must aim at the client's good (whose desires do not simply define that good).
2   The professional must exhibit a willingness to work towards this aim.
3   Such willingness to act thus must continue for as long as is necessary to reach a determination.
4   The professional must be competent (in the appropriate knowledge and skills).
5   The professional must be able to demand from the client (specific appropriate knowledge and performances).
6   The professional must be free to serve the client with discretion (which, as with (1) above, need not be consistent with their desires).
7   The professional must have a highly internalised sense of responsibility.

Implicit in these conditions is the trust relationship at the heart of professional practice. It is the trust relationship and the higher 'duty of care' required when working with legal minors that guides much of what is considered good practice. The principle of long-term athlete welfare should be at the core of long-term athlete development. Sport systems theorists such as Côté (Fraser-Thomas et al., 2005) advocate for a greater focus on the child as the centre of the coaching process, an approach that causes us to redefine the coaching skills and systems required to develop the child. The skills of the coach as a 'technician' must be combined with an understanding of the developmental assets and welfare needs of the child. Jones et al. (2004) underpin this principle, highlighting the various roles that coaches are often required to play in the lives of young people and the sensitivities associated with these roles.

The notion of the practitioner as offering a 'service' helps us to balance the outcome orientation of sport with the process of guiding young people to enjoy and achieve in sport. A service orientation reinforces the idea that the individual, rather than merely the competition result, is at the heart of the process. In this sense, the coach is a buffer between the developmental needs of the performer and the demands sometimes imposed by the culture of the sport; this is a key safeguarding issue.

104

Accountability is a standard tenet of professional practice (Taylor and Garratt, 2008). Inherent within the idea of accountability is working to and within a level of competence. Competence, in this sense, can best be described as the coach's abilities to synthesise their knowledge and experience and to offer experiences that are relevant to the child's age and level of performance. This is sometimes referred to as the 'craft' of coaching (Knowles et al., 2005). Coaches should work within their qualification level and experience since this will be what determines their competence. However, they should also endeavour to improve and progress their professional capacities for the benefit of those they coach. Engaging in continuous professional development (CPD) is, in itself, a key principle of professional obligation and a requirement of most governing bodies of sport. Determining one's competence level is not easy, but operating at, and not beyond, one's level of competence helps to ensure that the duty of care is properly observed.

Codes of practice are increasingly used to give guidance to practitioners working with young people. They are reinforced by entry-level education and training for coaches that places a strong emphasis on safeguarding. Accountability in coaching is further demonstrated through the use of interviews and selection procedures when coaches work for agencies other than sports clubs (such as youth groups and local authority schemes). There is therefore an expectation that coaches should be able to examine their practice across a range of coaching situations that involve children and young people. Reflective practice is a particularly useful method for determining a practitioner's accountability and sense of competence.

COACHING IN DIFFERENT CONTEXTS

Coaches are increasingly required to work with young people through a multi-agency approach, since the boundaries between sport, physical activity and physical education are becoming more and more blurred and contested. Because of this eclectic approach, coaches often encounter young people with, for example, specific learning needs, behavioural problems or social inclusion challenges. Being able to work with and within other agency settings and still deliver high-quality experiences to children and young people requires greater understanding by coaches of their role and function as one of a team of professionals in such settings. School physical education specialists, for example, are increasingly using coaches as part of a school's provision, especially in the extended curriculum. Youth agencies and community groups are also engaging in physical activity agendas and using sport as a means of reaching out to young people. So, the ability of coaches to embrace and understand the demands of inter-agency working is of increasing importance.

In a number of these agencies, such as education and the youth service, there is already a strong and well-developed sense of professional practice. An important function of inter-agency provision is to reach specific groups in society who are marginalised for some reason. Sport can help to develop social capital in such settings. Coaching children and young people can therefore take place in some challenging and diverse environments.

Fundamental to working with young people across all coaching environments are child protection and safeguarding policies and practices. These include recruitment procedures and criminal record checking. 'Designated lead persons' (often called child protection, safeguarding or welfare officers) support those working with young people and implement systems of reporting and referral that enable issues to be dealt with swiftly and appropriately. These policies and practices are underpinned by specific legislation such as (in the United Kingdom) the Children Act 2004 and the associated guidance document *Working Together to Safeguard Children* (HMSO, 2006). The guidance document is of particular importance to all agencies providing services to children.

Coaches working with children and young people will increasingly become drawn in to work with children's services, local safeguarding children boards, police and other agencies in the statutory and voluntary sectors. Many of these coaches now fulfil roles, such as that of club welfare officer, that extend their own work with children. Recruitment, training, monitoring and reporting are more likely to become part of the weekly work of such coaches, and developing an understanding of the various discourses associated with such activities will become the next challenge for sports coaches.

DIRECTED TASK

Can you describe what you would do and whom you would seek advice from with regard to a concern you had about a young person you coached?

See sports coach UK's *Safeguarding and Protecting Children* (2009c) resource guide, pp. 87–113, for guidance.

THEORY INTO PRACTICE

Safeguarding principles should be part of a strong and robust coaching session. Engaging young people in sport through an approach that accounts for individual difference and that is fun, yet challenging, is good practice. Extending the range of coaching skills – through improved and more appropriate use of ability groupings, varied communication styles, age-appropriate language and empowerment strategies – is essential in professional practice. One of the greatest challenges, however, is to match the developmental needs of the young performer to relevant technical and competitive demands – in other words, to balance the sporting outcome of achievement through winning with that of achievement of mastery (process).

H. Telfer and C. Brackenridge

LEARNING MORE

For further information on safeguarding standards in sport relating to children and young people, consult the relevant children's services or organisations: in the United Kingdom this would be the National Society for the Prevention of Cruelty to Children (NSPCC). All national governing bodies of sport in the United Kingdom and in most other countries have links to statutory agencies. To help embed safeguarding within your coaching practice, see sports coach UK's *Safeguarding and Protecting Children* resource guide (2009c), particularly pp. 20–36 for examples of good practice.

To learn more about the principles underpinning an understanding of coaching behaviours, see Cross and Lyle (2002) and Lyle (2002).

Cassidy *et al.* (2009) provide a clear overview of the social, cultural and pedagogical aspects of coaching, which will help establish clear principles of the foundations of good coaching practice.

REFERENCES

Brackenridge, C., Pitchford, A., Russell, K. and Nutt, G. (2007) *Child welfare in football*. London: Routledge.

Cassidy, T., Jones, R. and Potrac, P. (2009) *Understanding sports coaching: the social, cultural and pedagogical foundations of sports practice*. London: Routledge.

Cross, N. and Lyle, J. (2002) *The coaching process: principles and practice for sport*. Oxford: Butterworth-Heinemann.

European Coaching Council (2007) Proposed convention on the recognition of coaching competence and qualifications [online]. European Network of Sports Science, Education and Employment, available at: www.enssee.de (accessed 9 July 2009).

Fraser-Thomas, J.L., Côté, J. and Deakin, J. (2005) Youth sport programmes: an overview to foster positive youth development. *Physical Education and Sport Pedagogy* 10(1): 19–40.

HMSO (2004) *Every child matters: change for children*. Office of Public Sector Information, HM Government, London.

HMSO (2006) *Working together to safeguard children*. Office of Public Sector Information, HM Government, London.

Jones, R., Armour, K. and Potrac, P. (eds) (2004) *Sports coaching cultures*. London: Routledge.

Knowles, Z., Borrie, A. and Telfer, H. (2005) Towards the reflective sports coach: issues of context, education and application. *Ergonomics* 28(11–14): 1711–1720.

Lyle, J. (2002) *Sports coaching concepts: a framework for coaches' behaviour*. London: Routledge.

Lyle, J. (2008) Sports development and sports coaching. In K. Hylton and P. Bramham (eds), *Sports development: policy, process and practice*. London: Routledge.

McNamee, M. (1998) Celebrating trust: virtues and rules in the ethical conduct of sports coaches. In M. McNamee and J. Parry (eds), *Ethics and sport*. London: E&FN Spon.

NSPCC Child Protection in Sport Unit (revised 2006) *Standards for safeguarding and protecting children in sport*. Leicester: National Society for the Prevention of Cruelty to Children.

SkillsActive (2004) *National occupational standards for coaching, teaching and instructing*. London: SkillsActive.

sports coach UK (revised 2005) *Code of practice for sports coaches*. Leeds: sports coach UK.

sports coach UK (2006) *UK action planning for coaching consultation*. Leeds: sports coach UK.

sports coach UK (2009a) United Kingdom coaching certificate [online]. Leeds: sports coach UK, available at: www.sportscoachuk.org (accessed 9 July 2009).

sports coach UK (2009b) Minimum Operating Standards (MOS) for coaches Consultation [online]. Leeds: sports coach UK, available at: www.sportscoachuk.org/index.php?Page ID=4&sc=41&uid=171 (accessed 9 July 2009).

sports coach UK (2009c) *Safeguarding and protecting children*. Leeds: sports coach UK.

sports coach UK (2009d) *Equity in your coaching* (2nd ed.). Leeds: sports coach UK.

Taylor, W. and Garratt, D. (2008) *The professionalisation of sports coaching in the UK: issues and conceptualisation*. Leeds: sports coach UK.

UK Sport (2001) *The UK vision for coaching*. London: UK Sport.

UK Sport (2003) *The UK strategy framework for women and sport*. London: UK Sport.

UK Sport (2004) *The equality standard: a framework for sport*. London: UK Sport.

H. Telfer and C. Brackenridge

CHAPTER EIGHT

THE REFLECTIVE COACH

ANDY MILES

CHAPTER OUTLINE

- The origins of reflective practice
- Defining reflective practice
- Making the case for reflective practice in sports coaching
- Reflective practice: practical issues for sports coaches
- Theory into practice
- Learning more

INTRODUCTION

This chapter will explore both the theoretical origins and practical applications of reflective practice. It will start by identifying, through reference to literature in the teaching and nursing professions, that reflective practice is an established procedure used in various professional domains as a means of facilitating learning from professional experience. Having identified the origins of reflective practice, the chapter will define the concept and outline how and why reflective practice has been adopted within sports coaching.

The chapter will continue by examining some of the practical issues associated with reflective practice and will offer some guidance as to what coaches should be reflecting on, and how and when they should go about conducting reflective practice. This will include the introduction and critique of some models of reflective practice and a discussion of their suitability for use by sports coaches.

THE ORIGINS OF REFLECTIVE PRACTICE

Understanding how people acquire and develop knowledge is fundamental to effective education, with educators facing the challenge of finding appropriate ways for learners to engage in the learning process. One line of thinking is that learning is most effective when it begins with experience – specifically, a problematic experience (Osterman and Kottkamp, 1993). This so-called experiential learning theory was developed by Dewey (1933) and holds that learning is most effective when a person is actively engaged in the learning process and that when they are exposed to a problematic situation, resolving the situation can lead to learning.

The concept of experiential learning was first introduced into a professional practice context by Schön (1983) when he sought to identify how practitioners from a range of professional domains acquired their professional knowledge. From his work, he maintained that professional knowledge is grounded in professional experience and that its development occurs when one reflects on a problem or dilemma that occurs within the professional setting. The work of Schön (1983) became very influential in the nursing literature (Teekman, 2000), and the concept of experiential learning is well embedded in nurse practitioner training.

In nursing, the ability to make correct decisions and carry out appropriate interventions is dependent on practitioners' ability to apply their knowledge and skills effectively within an ever-changing environment. Nurses, according to Bowman, operate within 'complex systems of human interaction whose organisation and successful management demand specialist knowledge and skills, in addition to those acquired in basic nursing curricula' (1986: 234); thus, it is not possible for all the skills and knowledge required by a nurse to do their job to be acquired through standard theoretical knowledge delivery mechanisms such as textbooks and classroom-based delivery. Such methods are considered insufficient, and therefore trainee nurses require 'on-the-job' learning. It is advocated that the best way for nurses to develop the required complex clinical decision-making and management skills is for them to encounter real-life problems and challenges. This is consistent with Schön's (1983) theory, and thus a key feature of nurse practitioner training is the requirement for a period of placement-based learning to acquire the necessary 'on-the-job' skills that cannot be taught through standard curriculum delivery methods. Currently, half of a nurse's three-year training programme in the United Kingdom is spent on placement.

This approach is mirrored in initial teacher education, where trainee teachers also operate in a dynamic environment. They need to acquire not only the necessary subject knowledge but also the appropriate pedagogical and classroom management skills, which may not be deliverable through standard theoretical knowledge delivery processes. Thus, 'on-the-job' learning is a necessary element of teacher training, and hence teaching practice in schools is an essential component of the teacher training process.

It would be wrong to assume that simple exposure to a professional experience will bring about learning. The development of expertise is not a passive process. To become better,

A. Miles

novice practitioners must do something with their experiences in order to develop knowledge and expertise. Schön (1983) introduced the term 'reflective practice' to reinforce the principle that practitioners need to undertake 'reflective thinking' regarding their professional experience in order to develop their professional knowledge and subsequent understanding.

The term 'reflective thinking' was first used by Dewey (1933) to describe the type of human thinking that transforms obscurity and doubt into clarity and coherence. He argued that it was a controlled and focused pattern of thinking that helped humans find material to resolve doubt and that past experiences were important as they often provided the source of the solutions. This philosophy has been extended to consider how an individual actually constructs knowledge from previous experiences. The main premise is that knowledge construction occurs as a result of reflecting on problems or dilemmas that are encountered within an activity (Gilbert and Trudel, 1999) and that learning results from puzzling situations or uncertainty followed by the act of deliberate inquiry to resolve the troubling situation (ibid.). The process of acquiring knowledge through experience is therefore seen as an active process. Exposure to an experience cannot, on its own, bring about learning. Simply contemplating an experience or event is not always purposeful and does not necessarily lead to new ways of thinking or behaving in practice, and thus is not considered to be reflection. Individuals need to put into place a process of deliberate inquiry in order to evaluate the experience and give the experience some meaning. It is this act of deliberate inquiry to bring about learning that is 'reflective practice'.

In teacher training, reflective practice has been seen as a critical dimension of the professional development of teachers (Leitch and Day, 2000), while the nursing literature regarding reflective practice is so influential that it has been identified as a prerequisite competence for beginning nurse practitioners, and professional bodies have advocated the development of 'reflective nurse practitioners' (Teekman, 2000). Hence, within teaching and nursing, reflective practice is seen as an integral tool that helps convert professional experiences into new or altered knowledge and behaviours.

DEFINING REFLECTIVE PRACTICE

Many authors have sought to define reflective practice concisely, but, as Ghaye and Lillyman (2000) have suggested, because it impacts on thoughts, feelings and emotions as well as knowledge and skills, a simple definition is elusive. However, some authors have tried to capture the essence of reflective practice by seeing it as a staged process. For example, Reid defines reflective practice as 'a process of reviewing an experience of practice in order to describe, analyse and evaluate and so inform learning from practice' (1993: 305). Boyd and Fales define it as '[t]he process of internally examining and exploring an issue of concern, triggered by an experience, which creates and clarifies meaning in terms of self and results in a changed conceptual perspective (1983: 100). Both these definitions suggest that there are three key elements to reflective practice: first, the process is initiated when an individual becomes aware of an important issue arising from an experience; second, the individual undergoes a deliberate process of evaluation (reflection) in order to try to make sense of the issue; and finally, a noticeable resultant change in behaviour or knowledge (learning) occurs as a result of the process. Reflective practice is an active process and is therefore seen as a deliberate act of inquiry brought about by the awareness of an issue arising from an experience, the result of which is an improved awareness, an increased level of knowledge or an altered state or behaviour.

MAKING THE CASE FOR REFLECTIVE PRACTICE IN SPORTS COACHING

Children's coaches fulfil a wide variety of roles and need to manage the coaching environment as well as address the unique demands associated with working with children. Traditionally, the education of sports coaches has been based around the development of theoretical knowledge, with the provision of formal learning materials (e.g. coach education workshops, textbooks and manuals) being the basis of most structured coach education programmes. However, the process by which children's coaches are prepared to meet the demands of their coaching environment does not mirror the multidimensional nature of the role, and hence coaches may find themselves lacking in certain skills and knowledge. The delivery of this so-called theoretical knowledge does not necessarily allow the learner coach to be effectively introduced to all the aspects of the diverse and multifaceted role that they are seeking to fulfil.

In preference to the somewhat simplistic concept that coaches only learn through the delivery of theoretical knowledge, there have been many calls for coach educators to adopt elements of Schön's (1983) conception that an individual constructs knowledge best through direct experience. This has led to many authors (Gilbert and Trudel, 1999; Knowles et al., 2001) advocating experiential learning as a key factor in the development of a coach's knowledge, as they argue that the development of 'experiential' or 'professional' knowledge through coaching practice and interaction with other coaches is an important contributor to coaching expertise. It is also argued that a coach's main source of coaching knowledge is direct coaching experience (Gilbert and Trudel, 1999) and it is immersion in the coaching role, and the specific context that it creates, that best promotes coach learning. Research has indicated that coaches' effectiveness is rarely enhanced by formal coach education courses (Haslem, 1990) and is not based solely on theoretical knowledge but is also dependent on how well they can use their experiential knowledge. Current thinking therefore suggests that effective coaching practice results from building and using appropriate knowledge bases (Knowles et al., 2005), with these knowledge bases being built through practical coaching experiences and then used as the platform for skill development and behaviour change.

Given that sports coaching, like teaching and nursing, takes place within a complex system of human interaction, one that demands specialist knowledge and skills that cannot be taught within the standard curriculum time, this argument that 'on-the-job' learning is the best format in which coaches can learn the necessary knowledge and skills is a sound one. As a result,

A. Miles

recent developments in coach education have sought to capture the 'real-world' experiences of active coaches so that they can become an integral part of the formal education provided by coaching qualifications. With these developments comes the necessity for reflective practice, and thus the adoption of reflective practice as a tool for enhancing coach learning is a natural progression. Nelson and Cushion (2006) have suggested that the process of reflection can act as a bridge that links the knowledge that a coach gains from professional experience and observations, with coaching theory. Indeed, Knowles *et al.* (2001) argue that a study of trainee coaches undertaking a degree course in sports coaching, in which six of the eight coaches studied were found to have developed their reflective practice skills after a period of instruction, is evidence to suggest the potential effectiveness of reflective practice in coach education. Therefore, reflective practice is increasingly seen as a means by which individuals can learn from their coaching experiences, hence both experience and reflection have been identified as essential elements of coach education (Cushion *et al.*, 2006).

The theoretical rationale for the adoption of reflective practice into coach education systems is strong, and many authors are now strongly advocating it. Indeed, numerous studies have begun to explore how coach educators and national governing bodies of sport in the United Kingdom can integrate reflective practice into their coaching qualifications (Knowles *et al.*, 2005; Nelson and Cushion, 2006).

Reflective practice within sports coaching is still relatively in its infancy, and little instructional guidance is offered to coaches about how to engage in reflective practice. Also, as Knowles *et al.* (2005) suggest, there are limited structures or processes within national governing body qualifications to teach coaches how to undertake reflective practice. Reflective practice is seen as a higher-order cognitive skill that requires practice and training, and practitioners cannot simply be left to develop the skills on their own. For reflective practice to be fully and effectively adopted within a sports coaching context, there is a need for coach educators to offer coaches practical training in reflective practice skills in order that the experiential learning they are encouraged to undertake can be effectively utilised to create and extend their knowledge. If the appropriate skills are not developed, then the suggested benefits of experiential learning will not be harnessed and coaching practice will not be advanced.

REFLECTIVE PRACTICE: PRACTICAL ISSUES FOR SPORTS COACHES

As a step towards beginning to develop the necessary reflective practice skills, sports coaches need first to come to terms with some of the practical issues associated with reflective practice. Aside from the complex issue of trying to fully understand the theory behind reflective practice, there is a need to consider:

- what exactly they should be reflecting on;
- how they might go about undertaking reflective practice;
- when is the best time for reflective practice.

What to reflect on

Sports coaches are typically very good at observing and analysing the participants they work with, and accordingly are able to identify and correct errors in order to improve performance. However, reflective practice is essentially about self-evaluation and the analysis of one's own actions, something that many sports coaches are less comfortable with. To be effective reflective practitioners, coaches need to turn their observational and analytical skills on themselves and be able to identify and critique their own actions and behaviours. This will help sports coaches develop an increased self-awareness and thus aid them in the development of new knowledge and perhaps open up new ways of doing things.

When considering what to reflect on, a sport coach must be realistic. The role of the children's coach is multifaceted, and to try to develop expertise in all the different components at the same time is both unrealistic and unachievable. Hence, sports coaches embarking on reflective practice may first wish to categorise the knowledge, skills and behaviours they feel are necessary for effective coaching. Having done this, the coach may try to identify strengths and weaknesses within each area and then focus on areas that may be in need of development. A coach may, for example, choose to focus on their ability to give feedback and, after a coaching session, reflect on how well they delivered feedback in the context of that specific session as well as analysing the factors involved.

DIRECTED TASK

Make a list of the different things that you think you need to know and be able to do as a coach. Try to group them together under the following headings:

- *technical* (sport-specific) – related to the techniques and skills performers require to perform effectively, sometimes referred to as the 'what to coach' elements of coaching;
- *scientific* – related to how the body and mind work during sport and how they respond to training and growth;
- *pedagogical* – related to the coaching methods that coaches use to deliver sessions, sometimes referred to as the 'how to coach' elements of coaching;
- *personal and interpersonal* – related to the way in which coaches conduct themselves and interact with others.

Reflective practice is not just about reflecting on one's knowledge, skills and behaviours; coaches may also wish to consider how and why they do things and how their coaching values may inform the way in which they coach. For example, a children's coach may strongly believe that coaching children is about skill and character development and that it is participation and involvement that are important. Accordingly, they may choose to reflect on whether this philosophy is evident within their coaching practices and behaviours. Mature reflective practitioners are also able to engage with their feelings as well as their actions and values and are thus able to reflect on how they felt at specific points in time during their practice. If, for example, a particular coaching drill did not work effectively, during reflection a coach may recall feeling angry when they first noticed that the drill was unsuccessful. Understanding why they felt angry may help them resolve the issue. Was the anger directed at the children because they were not doing the drill correctly? Or was the anger directed at themselves because they had not set the drill up correctly? An appreciation of what caused the anger can lead to a more effective drill in the future.

There is a natural assumption that reflective practice has to focus on the negative aspects of coaching – the bits that did not go as well as expected. Coaches assume that if they address the things that went wrong, they will be able to improve. In essence, this is true, but to constantly identify and reflect on the negative aspects of one's coaching can be demoralising and can make reflection a constant process of self-criticism. It can be of immense value to reflect on those aspects of coaching that went well within a specific session and those things that are consistently done well within a coaching programme. Understanding why things went well can help reinforce good practice and will help coaches associate their actions with positive outcomes. Coaches who consistently create a fun environment in which children enjoy learning need to understand what it is that they do that creates that environment, so that they can recreate it in the future. Being successful without knowing what it was that made you successful is highly unsatisfactory. Reflective practice that focuses on positive outcomes can help coaches understand why they do certain things well and thus reinforce positive actions and behaviours.

How to reflect

Reflective practice is a complex skill, and coaches should not expect to become proficient reflective practitioners right from the outset. Knowles *et al.* (2001) produced evidence to suggest that a period of structured instruction can enhance coaches' reflective practice skills, but as yet no formal instructional programme exists for coaches to develop their reflective practice skills.

A number of authors, principally in education (Gibbs, 1988) and nursing (Johns, 1994), have sought to offer novice reflective practitioners some structured guidance to aid the reflective process. This guidance typically comes in the form of questions that practitioners should ask themselves to help kick-start the reflective process. Gibbs (1988) presented his model as a six-stage cyclical model (Figure 8.1) in which the reflective practitioner follows a cycle of questioning that builds on an initial description of an experience and explores the thoughts and feelings encountered in order to try to make sense of the situation. From this, alternative

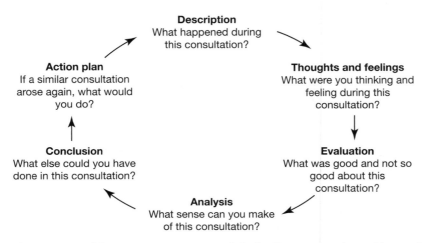

Description
What happened during this consultation?

Thoughts and feelings
What were you thinking and feeling during this consultation?

Action plan
If a similar consultation arose again, what would you do?

Evaluation
What was good and not so good about this consultation?

Conclusion
What else could you have done in this consultation?

Analysis
What sense can you make of this consultation?

Figure 8.1 Gibbs' (1988) six-stage model of reflection as adapted by Anderson *et al.* (2004)

courses of action are explored and an action plan set out. Such a model is designed to offer prompts to the practitioner as they begin to reflect on an experience. One criticism of this model is that it only offers the practitioner prompts and that it does not allow them to produce a more in-depth reflection on an experience. Hence, it has been suggested that Gibbs's (1988) model is best used by practitioners who have some experience of reflective practice and are already some way down the path of developing reflective practice skills.

In contrast, Johns (1994) reaffirmed the difficulties associated with reflective practice and suggested that practitioners require more detailed guidance and support to undertake reflective practice effectively. As a result, he offered a series of questions to guide the novice reflective practitioner through an analysis of their actions and to help them understand their thoughts and feelings as a means of better understanding their practice. In addition, the questions encourage the consideration of the consequences of actions and the identification of possible alternative actions. This step-by-step approach, while a valuable guide to novice reflective practitioners, can be problematic if the reflective practitioner blindly follows the structure every time. Johns (ibid.) himself warned against this and suggested that the guide be adapted and developed to meet different contexts. In response to this, Anderson (1999) revised the questions to suit a sports psychology context, and it is this sport-specific adaptation that is presented in Table 8.1. Further adjustment may be needed to make it fully contextual to the sports coaching domain, but sports coaches should be able to use this guide as a first step to undertaking reflective practice.

Sports coaches aiming to start the process of reflective practice should first explore the use of Anderson's (1999) structured guide as a basis for initial reflections and perhaps, as they become more adept at reflective practice, subsequently move away from the structured approach to the less rigid framework offered by Gibbs (1988).

116

Table 8.1 Structured reflection procedures

Core question: What information do I need access to in order to learn through this consulting experience?

Cue questions:

1.0 Description of the consulting experience
1.1: Phenomenon: Describe the 'here and now' of the experience (where, when and what)
1.2: Causal: What essential factors contributed to the experience? (why)
1.3: Context: Who are the significant background actors in this experience? (who)
1.4: Clarifying: Put it back together and establish what the key issues are in this experience that I need to pay attention to.

2.0 Reflection
2.1: What was I trying to achieve?
2.2: Why did I intervene as I did?
2.3: What internal factors influenced my actions? (thoughts, feelings, previous experience)
2.4: What external factors influence my actions? (other people, organisational factors, time)
2.5: What sources of knowledge did/should have influenced my decision making?

3.0 Consequences of actions
3.1: What were the consequences of my actions for (what did I learn/realise – cognitive component):
     Myself?
     The athlete?
     The people I work with?
3.2: How did I feel about this experience when it was happening (affective)?
3.3: How did the athlete feel?
3.4: How did I know what the athlete felt like?

4.0 Alternative tactics
4.1: Could I have dealt better with the situation?
4.2: What other choices did I have?
4.3: What would be the consequences of these choices?

5.0 Learning
5.1: How do I now feel about this experience?
5.2: How have I made sense of this experience in light of past experiences and future practice?
5.3: Action: Write down the key lessons in your notebook.

Source: Johns (1994), as revised by Anderson (1999) and presented by Anderson *et al.* (2004).

CASE STUDY

An experienced football coach was coming to the end of a six-week block of coaching with a group of young 5- to 9-year-olds and felt that things had gone well in the sessions and the players had picked up many of the basic skills. However, he sensed that some of the younger children were not totally happy. He noticed that they enjoyed the skill practices, but when they came to small-sided games at the end, the older players dominated the games and the younger ones hardly ever got to touch the ball and put into practice the skills they had learned. The coach had heard about reflective practice in a recent coaching course and tried to work through Johns' (1994) series of questions to reflect on his observations and to consider how he could address the concerns. Consideration of the issues and consequences of his actions helped him identify alternative tactics, and in the next six-week block he arranged the teams so that all the 5- and 6-year-olds were in two teams on one pitch and the 7- to 9-year-olds were on another pitch. Immediately he noticed a difference in the way the younger players engaged in the matches and that they were able to practise some of the skills and score some goals to get some positive rewards.

REFLECTIVE TASK

With reference to the above example, can you identify what issues and consequences you think were key to the reflection undertaken by the coach?

When to reflect

The timing of reflection is important, and logic would suggest that in order to reflect on an experience, one needs to wait until the experience has been completed. However, Schön (1983) argued that reflection could take place both during an experience (reflection-in-action) and after an experience (reflection-on-action). Each of these approaches has clear advantages and disadvantages. Reflection-in-action has the advantage that it can lead to decision making that may influence the outcome of an experience and thus has immediate impact on practice. Schön (ibid.) argued that this is central to the process by which professionals handle and resolve their difficulties and concerns about their practice. The obvious disadvantage is that reflection-in-action requires rapid processing and gives the practitioner only limited time to reflect on events, thus increasing the opportunities for error, or misinterpretation of information. Such an approach to reflection is naturally best suited to experienced reflective practitioners.

Reflection-on-action allows for a longer period of reflection with limited urgency for an outcome and hence offers a 'safer' environment for reflective practice. Although having the disadvantage that the outcomes come too late to influence an event, there is still scope for reflection-on-action to affect future actions, and having time to gather more information regarding the thoughts and feelings associated with an experience in order to make a more considered evaluation of an incident increases the potential for improved performance. However, leaving too long a period between an experience and undertaking the associated reflection is not advisable, as the accuracy of recollection of events, thoughts and feelings will decrease with time.

Inevitably, a combination of reflection-in-action and reflection-on-action may be the best solution. Indeed, Knowles *et al.* (2001) suggest that a 'dual-staged reflection', a combination of immediate and delayed reflection, may be the best approach to adopt. Immediate problems can be resolved *in situ* while future learning can be developed post-event.

THEORY INTO PRACTICE

Reflective practice is a complex skill that can serve to support a coach as they try to learn from their practical coaching experiences. In practical terms, coaches cannot be expected to reflect on all aspects of their coaching practice at any given time. They may choose to reflect on how well they apply a particular piece of knowledge, how well they can perform a certain skill or on how their coaching style reflects their beliefs and values. As they become more skilled at reflective practice, they may begin to focus on their thoughts and feelings in response to certain incidents. Remembering to reflect on positive aspects will also help a coach understand why they do certain things well and make reflective practice a less negative or self-critical activity. Many models exist to help practitioners develop reflective practice skills, although none is specific to the sports coaching context. Coaches can, however, draw on some of the structured models that offer progressive questioning to help identify and reflect on issues. Post-experience reflection (reflection-on-action) is recommended, as this allows the coach time to consider events yet also offers opportunity to make changes in the future.

LEARNING MORE

As is indicated within the text, there is limited guidance on reflective practice specifically for sports coaches. However, the work of Anderson *et al.* (2004), while essentially about reflective practice in sport psychology, gives a good overview of reflective practice and how it could be applied in a sporting context. In addition, coach educators interested in issues related to how reflective practice could be integrated into governing body qualifications should read Nelson and Cushion (2006) and Knowles *et al.* (2005).

REFERENCES

Anderson, A.G. (1999) The development of a model to evaluate the effectiveness of applied sports psychology practice. Unpublished doctoral dissertation, University of Coventry, UK.

Anderson, A.G., Knowles, Z. and Gilbourne, D. (2004) Reflective practice for sports psychologists: concept, models, practical implications, and thoughts on dissemination. *Sport Psychologist* 18: 188–203.

Bowman, M.P. (1986) *Nursing management and education: a conceptual approach to change*. London: Routledge.

Boyd, E. and Fales, A. (1983) Reflective learning: key to learning from experience. *Journal of Humanistic Psychology* 23: 99–117.

Cushion, C.J., Armour, K.M. and Jones, R.L. (2006) Locating the coaching process in practice: models 'for' and 'of' coaching. *Physical Education and Sport Pedagogy* 11(1): 83–99.

Dewey, J. (1933) *How we think: a restatement of the relation of reflective thinking to the educative process*. Boston, MA: D.C. Heath.

Ghaye, T. and Lillyman, S. (2000) *Reflection: principles and practice for healthcare professionals*. Salisbury, UK: Mark Allen.

Gibbs, G. (1988) *Learning by doing: a guide to teaching and learning methods*. Oxford: Oxford Brookes University Further Education Unit.

Gilbert, W. and Trudel, P. (1999) Framing the construction of coaching knowledge in experiential learning theory. *Sociology of Sport Online* 2(1). Available at: http://physed. otago.ac.nz/sosol/v2i1/v2i1.htm.

Haslem, I.R. (1990) Expert assessment of the National Coaching Certification Programme (NCPP) theory component. *Canadian Journal of Sport Sciences* 15: 201–212.

Johns, C. (1994) Guided reflection. In A. Palmer, S. Burns and C. Bulman (eds), *Reflective practice in nursing*. Oxford: Blackwell Science.

Knowles, Z., Gilbourne, D., Borrie, A. and Nevill, A. (2001) Developing the reflective sports coach: a study exploring the processes of reflective practice within a higher education coaching programme. *Reflective Practice* 2: 185–207.

Knowles, Z., Borrie, A. and Telfer, H. (2005) Towards the reflective sports coach: issues of context, education and application. *Ergonomics* 48: 1711–1720.

Leitch, R. and Day, C. (2000) Action research and reflective practice: towards a holistic view. *Educational Action Research* 8(1): 179–193.

Nelson, L.J. and Cushion, C.J. (2006) Reflection in coach education: the case of the national governing body coaching certificate. *Sport Psychologist* 20(2).

Osterman, K.F. and Kottkamp, R.B. (1993) *Reflective practice for educators*. Newbury, CA: Corwin Press.

Reid, B. (1993) 'But we're doing it already!' Exploring a response to the concept of reflective practice in order to improve its facilitation. *Nurse Education Today* 13: 305–309.

Schön, D.A. (1983) *The reflective practitioner: how professionals think in action*. New York: Basic Books.

Teekman, B. (2000) Exploring reflective thinking in nursing practice. *Journal of Advanced Nursing* 31(5): 1125–1135.

PART II

ON CHILDREN

CHAPTER NINE

ENHANCING CHILDREN'S POSITIVE SPORT EXPERIENCES AND PERSONAL DEVELOPMENT

A MOTIVATIONAL PERSPECTIVE

ELEANOR QUESTED AND JOAN L. DUDA

CHAPTER OUTLINE

- The nature of motivation
- Self-determination theory (SDT)
- Achievement goal theory (AGT)
- Motivational climate
- Rewards and feedback
- Need satisfaction, autonomous motivation and quality sport experiences: the research evidence
- Theory into practice
- Learning more

INTRODUCTION

As you read this page, parks, playgrounds and pitches all over the world are populated with millions of children – playing sport. The physical advantages of sport participation have long been recognised. Importantly, sport also holds the propensity to contribute towards a child's emotional and social well-being (Gagné and Blanchard, 2007). While exposure to sport is a commonality of childhood, the quantity and quality of this experience are less consistent. Alarmingly, the greatest rates of drop-out from sport occur in 12- to 15-year-olds (Sarrazin et al., 2007). As a consequence, a considerable number of Westerners are sedentary by adulthood. According to recent statistics, 22 million children under the age of 5 are reported to be overweight (WHO, 2007). In an era coloured by fears of the snowballing global obesity crisis, such statistics are troubling. Moreover, with 10 per cent of children in Britain estimated to be suffering from an emotional or other mental disorder (Green et al., 2005), the importance of promoting optimal and long-term sport engagement has never been more apparent.

Motivation is an important determinant of participation in sport as well as drop-out from sport. For over three decades, theories of motivation have been applied as frameworks through which to explore antecedents of sustained, healthful and sporting engagement. In this chapter, we explore the role of motivation as a central determinant of the *quality* and longevity of a child's sport experiences.

We begin by examining contemporary interpretations of 'motivation'. Next, the determinants and consequences of motivation are considered from the perspective of two major theories. The self-determination theory (SDT; Deci and Ryan, 1985, 2000) evaluates the determinants and benefits of 'self-determined motivation', an important prerequisite for optimal sport engagement. The way in which competence is judged is a major focus of achievement goal theory (AGT; Ames, 1992; Nicholls, 1989). This perspective considers the health- and performance-related implications of self-referenced as opposed to normative (i.e. 'other-referenced') interpretations of ability. Collectively, these theories have delineated the motivational antecedents and consequences of 'quality' sport engagement. Accordingly, we present some classic and contemporary research that has examined children's involvement in sport contexts through the theoretical lenses of SDT and AGT. Drawing from these perspectives and, more specifically, the TARGET framework (Epstein, 1989), we close the chapter with some practical recommendations for sports teachers and coaches.

THE NATURE OF MOTIVATION

Despite the prevalence of its common usage, 'motivation' remains one of the most vague and inadequately understood constructs in both colloquial and academic dialogue (Roberts, 2001a). Typically, motivation is considered as a quantitative entity, discernible in the degree of effort a child may expend in a sporting activity or the level of performance at that moment in time. In this view, a child might be considered 'low' in motivation or highly motivated. This 'high to low' perspective of motivation does not capture the meaning and value of engagement in sport for the child concerned. In other words, the reasons *why* the child participates in sport or attends training are ignored. In recent years, sport psychologists have begun to focus on the *type* of motivation undergirding sport engagement. This perspective evaluates motivation in terms of quantity *and* quality, encompassing the cognitive processes that may instigate actions, as well as interpretations of these reasons to act (Ames and Ames, 1984).

Children play sport for a variety of reasons. For some, sport participation is driven by 'love for the game' and the authentic enjoyment that can be realised through playing sport. Other young athletes may not enjoy sport, but continue to play to please a pushy parent or coach. Alternatively, the opportunity to receive some reward (e.g. a trophy) or a desire to meet healthy or socially defined body ideals might motivate some adolescents to engage in sport. These differing reasons for participation are termed 'motivation regulations' and are a central feature of self-determination theory (Deci and Ryan, 2000).

E. Quested and J.L. Duda

SELF-DETERMINATION THEORY (SDT)

Why play sport? A motivation continuum of behaviour regulations

Early theorists categorised motivation regulations in a bipolar fashion (Deci, 1971). 'Intrinsic motivation' was understood to capture internal reasons for participating in sport, such as enjoyment, pleasure or intrinsic fulfilment. Extrinsic reasons were associated with something or someone else, such as pressure from a coach or desire to win a medal. With the recognition that this conceptualisation did not adequately capture or differentiate between the potential range of regulations, a motivational continuum for sport motivation was developed (Vallerand and Losier, 1999). The continuum (Figure 9.1) reflects the varying degree of autonomy captured in reasons to play sport and recognises that reasons to engage in athletic activities cannot easily be categorised as purely intrinsic or extrinsic (Deci and Ryan, 2000).

According to the continuum, intrinsic motivation is the most autonomous (or self-determined) regulation. Intrinsically motivated children participate in sport for inherent reasons such as enjoyment, interest and satisfaction. Identified regulation also reflects autonomous motives to play sport. However, identified reasons are primarily linked to the potential value of participation, such as personal fitness or skill gains. Participation in the activity is considered to be a means to an end; however, the 'end' is personally endorsed. Introjection lies next on the continuum and reflects engagement in activities that have been internalised but are

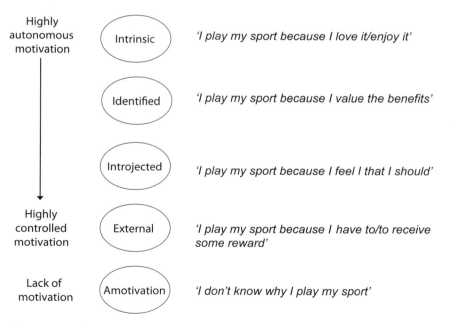

Figure 9.1 The continuum of motivation regulations.

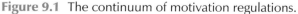

underpinned by self-imposed contingencies, sanctions and pressures. Participation in sport in order to avoid feelings of guilt or the demonstration of failure is a common example of intro-jected regulation. For example, a child may train because he or she feels that one 'should' do so. External regulations are derived from a source external to the athlete and are con-sidered the least self-determined of the behaviour regulations. When externally regulated, a child's sport participation is controlled by motivators such as praise, prizes and punishment avoidance. Sometimes children cannot identify why they play sports at all, and cannot see any point to their participation. This state describes amotivation, which lies at the far end of the continuum.

Over the past 20 years, this continuum has provided an underlying framework for numerous studies concerned with understanding variability in the quality of sport engagement. Collectively, these studies have shown that the degree of self-determination undergirding sport participation is a central determinant of athletes' cognitive, behavioural and emotional responses both in and outside of the sport setting (Ryan and Deci, 2007). In other words, research suggests that the extent to which a child's reasons to participate in sport are self-determined will impact upon the quality of the sporting experience.

REFLECTION

Just about all actions that we perform are underpinned by motivation regulations. Write down three activities that you have engaged in this week (e.g. studying, spending time with family and friends, training for your sport, cleaning your teeth). For each activity, consider the reasons why you performed the behaviour. Which motivation regulation(s) do you think were the central determinants of your engagement in these behaviours? You may find it helpful to refer to Figure 9.1 as you complete this task.

Enhancing intrinsic motivation for sport

Self-determination theory (Deci and Ryan, 1985, 2000) focuses on the determinants and consequences of differential motivation regulations (i.e. reasons to play) for participation in activities such as sport. Figure 9.2 presents the major components of the theory.

Where one falls along the continuum of motivation regulations is a function of satisfaction versus thwarting of the three basic psychological needs of autonomy, competence and relatedness. The need for competence is satisfied when one feels capable and proficient at one's sport; the individual feels that he or she can meet the sport-related demands. Relatedness infers feeling cared for, respected and connected with one's coach, team and/or squad. When actions are self-endorsed and undertaken with a sense of volition and choice, one's need for autonomy is satisfied.

E. Quested and J.L. Duda

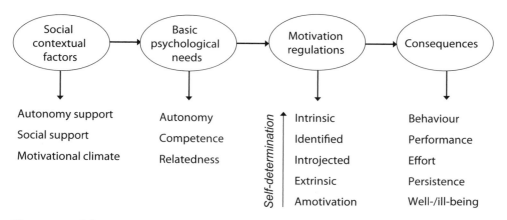

Figure 9.2 Schematic representation of the self-determination theory.

According to SDT, when a child's basic psychological needs are fostered, the child is more likely to participate in sport for intrinsic reasons, and optimal psychological development and well-being are the expected consequences (Deci and Ryan, 2000). Social agents (such as teachers and coaches) are in a prime position to foster the three basic psychological needs. Later in the chapter, we will consider specific coaching behaviours (i.e. the extent to which the climate is autonomy supportive, socially supportive and task- and/or ego-involving) that may help to foster young athletes' basic need satisfaction and ensuing self-determination.

ACHIEVEMENT GOAL THEORY (AGT)

'Am I any good?' The importance of competence construal

Achievement goal theory (Ames, 1992; Nicholls, 1989) posits that children's sport experiences are shaped by the way in which success is defined and one's personal competence is judged. The two dominant approaches to judging competence are termed 'task' and 'ego' (Nicholls, 1989). Highly task-orientated children tend to judge their level of competence in a self-referenced manner. When task-involved, children focus on self-referenced criteria, judging their success by evaluating levels of personal improvement, effort and/or task mastery (Ames, 1992). For the task-orientated child, success will always be possible, as long as effort is exerted. Consequently, task-orientated children are likely to try hard, feel good about their game and feel good about themselves, regardless of whether they think they are able or not so able. A tendency to focus on normative indicators of success (i.e. comparisons with others) and the demonstration of superiority is termed 'ego orientation'. A strongly ego-orientated child will feel competent only when he or she performs better than team-mates or opponents. Outperforming others with equal or, especially, less effort will engender a sense of high competence and personal success when an ego-involved perspective prevails (see the

Table 9.1 Task and ego goal perspectives in sport

Task-orientated	Ego-orientated
▪ Competence judgments are self-referenced ▪ Success is based on personal performance, mastery, effort ▪ Perceived competence is robust and enduring ▪ The young athlete is likely to feel good about him/herself regardless of the standard of teammates and/or opponents ▪ Positive achievement behaviours and outcomes are likely to ensue	▪ Competence judgements are other-referenced ▪ Success entails outdoing others, showing superiority ▪ Perceptions of competence are vulnerable, as criteria for success outside of the young athlete's control ▪ The young athlete will only feel good about him/herself when team-mates and/or opponents are of a lower standard than him or her ▪ Undesirable achievement behaviours and outcomes are likely to ensue

summary in Table 9.1). Thus, for the ego-orientated child, competence will always be fragile, as the 'yardstick' against which success is judged is out of their control (Duda, 2001). It is difficult always to be the best.

According to Nicholls (1989), very young children are innately 'task orientated', meaning that they naturally focus on their own effort and improvement. This is clearly apparent when watching very young children play. Their attention is solely on their own attainment in the task at hand. With maturity comes awareness that success can also be experienced on account of luck, by selecting easier challenges or simply by being better than others. By age 12, most children are cognitively capable of being more or less task-involved (focusing on personal improvement and effort) or ego-involved (a normative focus) in sport (Fry, 2001). However, the dominance of an ego orientation upon reaching adolescence is not inevitable. Coaches (and other significant others such as parents and peers) play a central role in determining the young athletes' interpretation of their sporting achievements (Ames, 1992; Nicholls, 1989).

Over the years, a strong case has been made for the advantages of more task-involved sport participation (Duda and Balaguer, 2007). A range of positive health, social and performance-related outcomes has been linked with task-involvement (Duda, 2001). However, less desirable responses are discernible among strongly ego-involved sports performers, particularly when their task orientation is low and/or they have doubts about their competence. Thus, understanding how task involvement can be nurtured is an important consideration for youth sport coaches.

The role of the coach

A shared characteristic among successful coaches is the capacity to create an optimal motivational atmosphere for their players (Duda and Balaguer, 2007). The coach can influence

E. Quested and J.L. Duda

the extent to which a child is more or less task- and ego-involved in sport (Ames, 1992) as well as his or her degree of self-determination (Amorose, 2007). In the next section, we will examine characteristics of the coach-created social environment that have been recognised to enhance the quality of children's motivation for, and responses to, their sport engagement.

MOTIVATIONAL CLIMATE

Research suggests that motivational, behavioural and health-related responses to sport are shaped by the coaches' emphasis on task- and/or ego-involving cues (Duda, 2001). Two types of motivational climate have been identified. Task-involving climates encourage self-referenced judgements of competence, focus on individual effort and improvement, and emphasise personal development and cooperative learning. On the contrary, in ego-involving climates children are encouraged to assess their competence by comparing their performance with that of others and to focus on demonstrating supremacy. Rivalry between players, low tolerance for mistakes and favouritism are emphasised in ego-involving settings (Duda, 2001).

Research suggests that task-involving motivational climates are likely to promote children's well-being and enjoyment of sport. However, when ego-involving cues are prevailing, children are more susceptible to low self-esteem, anxiety and health risks such as engagement in unhealthy eating practices (Duda, 2001). Sport drop-out is also more likely in ego-involving climates (Duda and Balaguer, 2007).

Recent investigations have indicated that basic need satisfaction may be the psychological mechanism accounting for the relationships between perceptions of the motivational climate and young athletes' cognitive, emotional and behavioural responses (Gagné and Blanchard, 2007). Studies undertaken with young adult athletes (Reinboth and Duda, 2006) and young dancers (Quested and Duda, 2010) as well as physical education (PE) students (Standage et al., 2003) have found that when coaches or teachers are perceived to create a task-involving climate, feelings of self-determination, belongingness and efficacy (i.e. need satisfaction) are more likely to ensue. Need thwarting is the expected consequence of engagement in a com-petitive and comparative (i.e. an ego-involving) climate. However, this latter hypothesis has received less empirical support. To date, research examining the associations between perceptions of the motivational climate and need satisfaction has primarily targeted older adolescent or young adult sport participants. This topic warrants further research attention to determine whether the observed patterns of findings are replicated in studies involving children in sport.

REWARDS AND FEEDBACK

Motivating children while simultaneously maintaining acceptable standards of behaviour is no mean feat. For this reason, many coaches use reward systems and praise to condition desired performances and behaviours. Experiments undertaken in the 1970s and 1980s challenged this popular application of incentives and verbal feedback (Deci, 1971). As one might expect, the studies found that reinforcement cues (such as praise and rewards) enhance children's competence and promote intrinsic motivation for the activity in question. However, in some instances rewards had a detrimental impact upon self-determined motivation. When rewards are conditional on performance, task engagement or task completion, the participants' intrinsic motivation can be undermined. Thus, in such circumstances the reward (rather than intrinsic interest) becomes the reason for participation, and engagement in the activity becomes conditional on the incentive. For example, children who begin swimming for the fun and enjoyment of swimming may experience a reduction in their intrinsic motivation if they are encouraged to participate in order to collect certificates or medals. The potential for reward becomes the overriding drive to swim.

Since the early work of Deci and colleagues, numerous studies have supported the need for careful consideration when applying rewards in achievement settings (Deci *et al.*, 1999). Nevertheless, praise and feedback have the propensity to foster desirable motivational consequences. This is most likely when rewards are given in such a way that they are informational (i.e. informing the child that he or she did well and, preferably, *why*) rather than controlling. In the context of a PE class, a recent study found that the children's intrinsic motivation for a shuttle-run task was enhanced, and amotivation tempered, when positive competence feedback was provided (Mouratidis *et al.*, 2008).

CASE STUDY

You are a coach working with a team of lively, mixed-ability 11-year-old hockey players. One of your fellow coaches has suggested the implementation of a reward system. The proposed system would recognise good behaviour, as well as efficient and satisfactory completion of the drills set in training. How would you respond to your colleague's suggestions? On the basis of the findings of past research, what might be the positive and negative consequences of such an initiative for the intrinsically motivated young players?

Autonomy support and social support

The extent to which coaches consider the perspective of the athlete, provide choice and encourage the use of initiative and self-regulation is termed 'autonomy support'. Research has indicated that autonomy support fosters athletes' need satisfaction and promotes autonomous motivation for sport engagement (Pelletier *et al.*, 2001). In contrast, controlling coaches tend to adopt an authoritarian style and employ specific agendas to control the athletes' actions. When coaches impose rules with no explanation or input, or use rewards, punishments or

E. Quested and J.L. Duda

other strategies to coerce behaviour, young athletes' self-determined reasons for engaging in sport are likely to be undermined (Amorose, 2007).

Showing that you care about their welfare and treating athletes with respect is inferred by the term 'social support' (Amorose, 2007). In studies involving team sport athletes, socially supportive coaching was positively related to the feelings of relatedness reported by the players (Reinboth et al., 2004). However, the expected positive association between perceptions of social support and athletes' autonomous sport motivation is less well supported (Amorose and Horn, 2000). When studied in a longitudinal manner, socially supportive coaching has been found to undermine athletes' intrinsic motivation (Amorose and Horn, 2001). It is possible that young athletes would want to please a coach who exhibits care and concern. This might create a sense of internal pressure, overriding previously intrinsic reasons for sport involvement (Amorose, 2007). It is possible that a combination of high social support coupled with low autonomy support may be problematic. Thus, children's adaptive sport-related motivational patterns may be dependent on the provision of social support *alongside* autonomy-supportive coaching behaviours.

Enhancing the social environment in youth sport settings: what can coaches do?

In the light of the research findings presented in this chapter, it appears important for coaches to consider the nature of the support they provide for young athletes. The extent to which support is controlling, hinges on contingencies and is meaningful seems to hold implications for the motivational responses of young children.

Coaches can apply the TARGET framework (Epstein, 1989) as a guide for promoting sustained, constructive and healthful sport engagement. The acronym represents specific components of the coach-orientated context via which the coach interacts with his or her athletes: **T**ask, **A**uthority, **R**ecognition, **G**rouping, **E**valuation and **T**iming. Coaches can apply strategies within these dimensions to enhance the extent to which their coaching is autonomy supportive, socially supportive and task-involving, and temper their controlling and ego-involving behaviours. As a consequence, athletes may be more likely to experience greater need satisfaction and adopt more autonomous behaviour regulations for sport. It is worth noting that these dimensions of the coach-created climate are interrelated. Thus, it is also likely that coach behaviours and strategies may affect (positively or negatively) more than one basic need. Later in the chapter, we will explore in more detail how the TARGET framework can be applied to foster need satisfaction and adaptive motivational patterns among young athletes.

NEED SATISFACTION, AUTONOMOUS MOTIVATION AND QUALITY SPORT EXPERIENCES: THE RESEARCH EVIDENCE

So far in this chapter, we have alluded to the potential benefits of children's self-determined sport engagement. In this section, we will specifically review and evaluate the research that has considered the behavioural and health-related consequences of need satisfaction and more or less autonomous sport engagement.

Predicting adherence and persistence

Longitudinal research involving young swimmers (Pelletier *et al.*, 2001) suggested that more self-determined young athletes were less likely to drop out of sport. By contrast, more controlling behaviour regulations were common characteristics among those swimmers who ultimately ceased participation. The results of this study also showed that the characteristics of the coaching climate played an important role in this process. Pelletier and colleagues identified that externally motivated or amotivated swimmers were more likely to perceive their coaches as controlling. Self-determined reasons to swim were positively associated with the swimmers' perceptions of autonomy supportive coaching.

Research by Sarrazin and colleagues (2002) found that the extent to which the motivational climate is perceived as task- and/or ego-involving may also influence sustainable sport participation. Basic need satisfaction and the longevity of handball players' participation over a 21-month period were positively predicted by the young athletes' perceptions of a task-involving coaching climate. Moreover, the results indicated that the players who dropped out were lower in basic need satisfaction and intrinsic motivation, and reported higher amotivation, than persistent players. Collectively, these findings support the utility of the SDT framework in understanding social-psychological predictors of sustained youth sport participation.

Need satisfaction and well- and ill-being

Sport can provide a forum for enhancing the psychological well-being of children and adolescents. However, taking part in sport can sometimes diminish the well-being of young participants. The quality of sport participation and the degree of well- and ill-being an athlete experiences may depend upon the extent to which sport engagement fosters the child's needs for autonomy, competence and relatedness (Gagné and Blanchard, 2007). For example, in an investigation involving young Spanish soccer players, basic need satisfaction positively related to the degree of enjoyment experienced by the players and was negatively associated with the players' reported boredom (Álvarez *et al.*, 2009). Basic need satisfaction has also been found to positively predict the positive affective states experienced by dancers (Quested and Duda, 2010), as well as young gymnasts' daily experiences of vitality (i.e. feeling alive and energised) and positive affect (Gagné *et al.*, 2003). Worryingly, low basic need satisfaction has been linked with undesirable consequences. The degree of physical symptoms (i.e. sore throat,

132

runny nose), emotional and physical exhaustion (Reinboth and Duda, 2006; Reinboth et al., 2004) and burn-out symptoms (Perreault et al., 2007) reported by athletes, as well as the negative affective states experienced by dancers (Quested and Duda, 2010), have been associated with reduced or diminished need satisfaction.

Research indicates that, over time, coaches and teachers can impact upon the basic need satisfaction and well- and ill-being of young performers. Longitudinal studies have found increases in basic need satisfaction to account for young athletes' (Reinboth and Duda, 2006) and dancers' (Quested and Duda, 2009) lower susceptibility to negative emotional states and increased experiences of positive affect. In line with the premise of self-determination theory, these changes were attributable to increases in the athletes' and dancers' perceptions of task-involving strategies employed by their coaches or teachers.

Autonomous motivation and young athletes' welfare

The assumed positive association between self-determined motivation and well-being is a central feature of self-determination theory (Deci and Ryan, 2000). In their study involving young gymnasts, Gagné and colleagues found that the young athletes' autonomous motivation positively predicted their degree of reported positive affect, self-esteem and vitality. In line with SDT, negative emotional states were negatively predicted by autonomous reasons for engaging in gymnastics (Gagné et al., 2003). Similar findings have been found in studies involving PE students (Standage et al., 2005).

Motivation regulations are also predictive of young performers' appraisals of their physique. In our recent work with vocational student dancers (Quested and Duda, 2011), feeling amotivated about one's dance participation was associated with low self-esteem and more pronounced reports of body dissatisfaction and social physique anxiety. More controlling regulations were related to higher physique-related anxiety. These self-evaluation tendencies have been associated with disordered eating, a behaviour that is most prevalent among young performers in aesthetic sports (Smolak et al., 2000).

Collectively, these studies highlight the importance of coaches and teachers nurturing more self-determined motivation among young athletes. It is noteworthy that these investigations to date have involved adolescent or young adult participants. Future research is warranted to determine whether these patterns of findings are replicated in studies involving children.

DIRECTED TASK

Table 9.2 defines each aspect of the TARGET framework (introduced earlier in the chapter) and suggests strategies that can be implemented to maximise the motivational

Table 9.2 Optimising the climate in youth football settings: structures and targeted strategies based on the TARGET framework

	Structure	Strategies	Example	Your example
Task	The activities, exercises, and drills that players are asked to complete.	Provide varying, optimally challenging training exercises that are personally meaningful to players. When possible, individualise the task requirements.	Set up challenging and fun drills in a manner that enables each player to work on his/her own specific goals.	
Authority	The extent to which the player takes part in decision making.	Include players in decision making, particularly in association with their personal involvement in training activities and matches.	Each player can self-monitor using a training log and discuss his/her ideas for improvement with the coach.	
Recognition	The rewards and incentives that are used for progress and achievement.	Provide recognition that is one-on-one (wherever/when possible), based on effort, improvement, learning from mistakes. Ensure that there is quality and the potential for equality in reward provision.	Acknowledge hard work in private discussions with players after training.	
Grouping	How groups are organised during training.	Organise groups in training so as to promote peer learning, interaction and cooperation.	Plan specific times in training for small-group, mixed-ability drills. Vary the strategies used to organise groups.	
Evaluation	The nature of evaluation and appraisals.	Involve players in evaluation. Ensure that appraisals by coaches are based on progress and effort.	After matches, allow each player the opportunity to identify his/her own strengths and weaknesses. Use the players' suggestions as the impetus for further feedback.	
Timing	The time limits for meeting learning and performance outcomes or completing training tasks.	Provide flexible time allocations for drills that are adaptable to the players' own rates of skill development.	Work with players in setting different short-term goals. Vary delivery of instruction.	

climate in youth soccer settings. A soccer-specific example is provided for each structure. In a different sport setting of your choice, suggest a potential application of each TARGET dimension. Consider how your suggestion might enhance the extent to which the coaching climate is task-involving and/or autonomy and socially supportive. Which basic need(s) do you think might be fostered via each of your suggested strategies?

SUMMARY

This chapter has focused on the social-psychological predictors of optimal sport experiences among young athletes. Research indicates that when youth sport settings are marked by autonomy-supporting, socially supporting and task-involving features, young athletes are more likely to experience greater well-being and adaptive achievement-related thoughts, emotions and behaviours. More task-involved and autonomous sport engagement may also promote other desirable outcomes. For example, studies have found that task-involved, self-determined young athletes are less likely to engage in antisocial sporting behaviours, such as aggressive reactions or cheating (Vallerand and Losier, 1994). In school-based studies, autonomous motivation has been positively associated with more fulfilling learning experiences, as well as better quality learning and higher grade achievement (Guay *et al.*, 2008). Studies have also indicated that a task goal orientation may be more likely to optimise a young athletes' skill development, whereas less adaptive learning strategies tend to be displayed by ego-orientated athletes (Duda, 2001).

Coaches have the propensity to foster or thwart young athletes' sense of competence, autonomy, and connection with others, and ensuing self-determined motivation. The coach is also assumed to impact upon the goal perspectives adopted by young athletes. Coaches play a crucial role in shaping the motivational atmosphere in their team. Evidence suggests that the coach-created atmosphere has an important influence upon the *quality* of a child's sport engagement. Delineating the positive impact of specific facets of the coaching climate, as well as identifying how to realise these ideals in 'real life' situations, is an important consideration for researchers, coaches, teachers and others with a vested interest in enhancing the physical and psychological welfare of young people. The nature of sports coaching may be a principal catalyst for improving the health of young adults, via the promotion of quality sport engagement in the early years.

THEORY INTO PRACTICE

The research reviewed in this chapter points to the importance of nurturing a coaching environment that is need-supportive. That is, the social environment created is characterised by autonomy support, social support and a focus on task involvement, conducive to promoting young athletes' feelings of autonomy, competence and relatedness.

Drawing from the TARGET framework specifically, coaches may revise the extent to which the drills (i.e. Tasks) employed in training allow young athletes to self-select from a range of optimally challenging drill adaptations, enhancing autonomy need satisfaction. When considering his or her approach to evaluating athletes' progress (i.e. the Evaluation facet), the coach may try to focus on player-specific improvements and discuss progress in private, rather than in a public forum. This may promote young athletes' feelings of competence, and simultaneously reduce rivalry, enhancing feelings of relatedness among athletes in a team or squad. Coaches may target the Authority dimension by involving the athletes in aspects of leadership. For example, allowing the athletes to lead the more familiar aspects of the warm-up has the propensity to target all three needs.

LEARNING MORE

Readers can learn more about the central tenets of SDT by reading Deci and Ryan's classic paper (2000) or visiting their well-sourced website: www.psych.rochester.edu/SDT/. The application of SDT in sport settings has been given good coverage in a recent book dedicated to this subject (Hagger and Chatzisarantis, 2007). Roberts's (2001b) text reviews and integrates the dominant theories that underpin contemporary perspectives of motivation in sport and exercise settings. The chapters in both texts are authored by distinguished field leaders who present stimulating and critical reviews of their specialist area.

REFERENCES

Álvarez, M.S., Balaguer, I., Castillo, I. and Duda, J.L. (2009) Coach autonomy support and quality of sport engagement in young soccer players. *Spanish Journal of Psychology* 12(1): 138–148.

Ames, C. (1992) Achievement goals and the classroom motivational climate. In J. Meece and D. Schunk (eds), *Students' perceptions in the classroom: causes and consequences*. Hillsdale, NJ: Lawrence Erlbaum.

Ames, C. and Ames, R. (1984) Systems of student and teacher motivation: toward a qualitative definition. *Journal of Educational Psychology* 76: 535–556.

Amorose, A.J. (2007) Coaching effectiveness. In M.S. Hagger and N.L.D. Chatzisarantis (eds), *Intrinsic motivation and self-determination in exercise and sport*. Champaign, IL: Human Kinetics.

Amorose, A.J. and Horn, T.S. (2000) Intrinsic motivation: relationships with collegiate athletes' gender, scholarship status, and perceptions of their coaches' behavior. *Journal of Sport and Exercise Psychology* 22: 63–84.

Amorose, A.J. and Horn, T.S. (2001) Pre- to post-season changes in the intrinsic motivation of first year college athletes: relationships with coaching behavior and scholarship status. *Journal of Applied Psychology* 13: 355–373.

136

Deci, E.L. (1971) Effects of externally mediated rewards on intrinsic motivation. *Journal of Personality and Social Psychology* 18: 105–115.

Deci, E.L. and Ryan, R.M. (1985) *Intrinsic motivation and self-determination in human behavior*. New York: Plenum.

Deci, E.L. and Ryan, R.M. (2000) The 'what' and 'why' of goal pursuits: human needs and the self-determination of behavior. *Psychological Inquiry* 11: 227–268.

Deci, E.L., Koestner, R. and Ryan, R.M. (1999) A meta-analytic review of experiments examining the effects of extrinsic rewards on intrinsic motivation. *Psychological Bulletin* 125: 627–668.

Duda, J.L. (2001) Achievement goal research in sport: pushing the boundaries and clarifying some misunderstandings. In G.C. Roberts (ed.), *Advances in motivation in sport and exercise*. Champaign, IL: Human Kinetics.

Duda, J.L. and Balaguer, I. (2007) The coach-created motivational climate. In S. Jowett and D. Lavallee (eds), *Social psychology in sport*. Champaign, IL: Human Kinetics.

Epstein, J.L. (1989) Family structures and student motivation: a developmental perspective. In C. Ames and R. Ames (eds), *Research on motivation in education*. New York: Academic Press.

Fry, M.D. (2001) The development of motivation in children. In G.C. Roberts (ed.), *Advances in motivation in sport and exercise*. Champaign, IL: Human Kinetics.

Gagné, M. and Blanchard, C. (2007) Self-determination theory and well-being in athletes. In M.S. Hagger and N.L.D. Chatzisarantis (eds), *Intrinsic motivation and self-determination in exercise and sport*. Champaign, IL: Human Kinetics.

Gagné, M., Ryan, R.M. and Bargmann, K. (2003) Autonomy support and need satisfaction in the motivation and well-being of gymnasts. *Journal of Applied Sport Psychology* 15: 372–390.

Green, H., McGinnity, Á., Meltzer, H., Ford, T. and Goodman, R. (2005) *Mental health of children and young people in Great Britain, 2004*. London: National Statistics.

Guay, F., Ratelle, C.F. and Chanal, J. (2008) The role of self-determination in education. *Canadian Psychology* 49: 233–240.

Hagger, M.S. and Chatzisarantis, N.L.D. (2007) Advances in self-determination theory research in sport and exercise. *Psychology of Sport and Exercise* 8: 597–599.

Mouratidis, A., Vansteenkiste, M., Lens, W. and Sideridis, G. (2008) The motivating role of positive feedback in sport and physical education: evidence for a motivational model. *Journal of Sport and Exercise Psychology* 30: 240–268.

Nicholls, J.G. (1989) *The competitive ethos and democratic education*. London: Harvard University Press.

Pelletier, L.G., Fortier, M.S., Vallerand, R.J. and Briere, N.M. (2001) Associations among perceived autonomy support, forms of self-regulation, and persistence: a prospective study. *Motivation and Emotion* 25: 279–306.

Perreault, S., Gaudreau, P., Lapointe, M.C. and Lacroix, C. (2007) Does it take three to tango? Psychological need satisfaction and athlete burnout. *International Journal of Sport Psychology* 38: 437–450.

137

Quested, E. and Duda, J.L. (2009) The experience of well- and ill-being among elite dancers: a test of basic needs theory. *Journal of Sport Sciences* 26: S41.

Quested, E. and Duda, J.L. (2010) Exploring the social-environmental determinants of well- and ill-being in dancers: a test of Basic Needs Theory. *Journal of Sport and Exercise Psychology* 32: 39–60.

Quested, E. and Duda, J.L. (2011) A self-determination theory approach to understanding the antecedents of dancers' self-evaluative tendencies. *Journal of Dance Medicine and Science* 15: 3–14.

Reinboth, M. and Duda, J.L. (2006) Perceived motivational climate, need satisfaction and indices of well-being in team sports: a longitudinal perspective. *Psychology of Sport and Exercise* 7: 269–286.

Reinboth, M., Duda, J.L. and Ntoumanis, N. (2004) Dimensions of coaching behavior, need satisfaction, and the psychological and physical welfare of young athletes. *Motivation and Emotion* 28: 297–313.

Roberts, G.C. (2001a) Understanding the dynamics of motivation in physical activity. In G.C. Roberts (ed.), *Advances in motivation in sport and exercise*. Champaign, IL: Human Kinetics.

Roberts, G.C. (ed.) (2001b) *Advances in motivation in sport and exercise*. Champaign, IL: Human Kinetics.

Ryan, R.M. and Deci, E. (2007) Active human nature: self-determination theory and the promotion, and maintenance of sport, exercise and health. In M.S. Hagger and N.L.D. Chatzisarantis (eds), *Intrinsic motivation and self-determination in sport and exercise*. Champaign, IL: Human Kinetics.

Sarrazin *et al.* (2002) Motivation and dropout in female handballers: A 21-month prospective study. *European Journal of Social Psychology* 32: 395–418.

Sarrazin, P., Boiche, J.C.S. and Pelletier, L.G. (2007) A self-determination theory approach to dropout in athletes. In M.S. Hagger and N.L.D. Chatzisarantis (eds), *Intrinsic motivation and self-determination in exercise and sport*. Champaign, IL: Human Kinetics.

Smolak, L., Murnen, S.K. and Ruble, A.E. (2000) Female athletes and eating problems: a meta-analysis. *International Journal of Eating Disorders* 27: 371–380.

Standage, M., Duda, J.L. and Ntoumanis, N. (2003) A model of contextual motivation in physical education: using constructs from self-determination and achievement goal theories to predict physical activity intentions. *Journal of Educational Psychology* 95: 97–110.

Standage, M., Duda, J.L. and Ntoumanis, N. (2005) A test of self-determination theory in school physical education. *British Journal of Educational Psychology* 75: 411–433.

Vallerand, R.J. and Losier, G.F. (1994) Self-determined motivation and sportsmanship orientations: an assessment of their temporal relationship. *Journal of Sport and Exercise Psychology* 16: 229–245.

Vallerand, R.J. and Losier, G.F. (1999) An integrative analysis of intrinsic and extrinsic motivation in sport. *Journal of Applied Sport Psychology* 11: 142–169.

World Health Organization (2007) The WHO European Ministerial Conference on Counteracting Obesity conference report (see http://www.euro.who.int/__data/assets/pdf_file/0006/96459/E90143.pdf).

CHAPTER TEN

PHYSICAL AND MOVEMENT SKILL DEVELOPMENT

CLIVE BREWER

CHAPTER OUTLINE

- **Long-term design of a physical training programme**
- **A progressive approach to coaching children's physical development**
- **Theory into practice**
- **Learning more**

INTRODUCTION

In recent years, the sporting community has debated about different approaches to coaching in relation to the physical development of children. There has been significant discussion and a variety of guidance material produced about the growth and maturation of the child, and how this should be reflected in the programmes delivered by coaches and teachers.

Anecdotally, there is much evidence that athletes who, as children and youths, experience well-organised and systematic practice programmes are those who tend to achieve both successful performances and longevity in their sporting careers. Coaches who are equipped with the necessary knowledge and skills to structure and monitor training programmes appropriately, and to match the anatomical and physiological development processes of the child, will be able to maximise the potential of their athletes. Such programmes need clearly defined objectives that relate to the long-term development of the child, building strong foundations from which specific physical competences can be developed. Conversely, as children show considerable and important differences in their bodily responses to exercise, compared to adults, it is important that coaches are aware of the more important differences in order to avoid imposing undue physical stress on their young participants.

Against this background, this chapter will focus on anatomical, physiological and movement skill development aspects that must be considered when coaching children and adolescents.

Knowledge of children's anatomy, and the physiological processes underlying their exercise responses, allows coaches to become better at evaluating the physical competences, capacities and potential responses of a young athlete. This knowledge will assist in the planning and implementation of improved training programmes that link maturation with the development of physical qualities in young athletes, resulting in a higher-quality preparation of the child for a lifetime of participation in sport (Gallahue and Ozman, 2002). A successful programme will be the catalyst in promoting the development of the movement skills and sporting knowledge that will encourage children to participate in lifelong physical activity and recreational sport. Ultimately, for those with ability and desire, it can also provide the platform for elite performance (Collins *et al.*, 2007).

LONG-TERM DESIGN OF A PHYSICAL TRAINING PROGRAMME

Coaching for children's long-term development should be based upon an inclusive process that encourages and equips them to become involved in lifelong physical activity. It should connect and integrate movement physical education programmes with both recreational and elite sport preparation programmes. In its simplest form, coaching for long-term development relates the nature and structure of training to the child's developmental stage and pathways so that the young participant is doing the right things at the right time for their long-term development, rather than for immediate success or gains. Coaches' aims should be child centred, based upon adopting an individual and educational approach and founded on a desire to make a long-term difference to young participants. These objectives should be reflected in the planning, delivery and evaluation of coaching programmes.

In order to achieve such aims, coaches need to understand how children develop and the key principles involved. Coaches who account for key aspects of child development in planning, delivering and evaluating their programmes are more likely to instil a lifelong love of sport in their young participants and also produce more individuals who fulfil their true athletic potential in sport.

Training principles

A coach should guide training programmes for children's development around the training principles set out in Table 10.1 (for a more comprehensive discussion, see Brewer, 2008).

Training outcomes

The aim of any physical development programme is to improve the capacity of the child's motor (movement) system to perform work. This may mean being able to do more work

140

Table 10.1 The principles of training

Progressive overload	The overload principle states that training programmes should stress the athlete's physiological mechanisms sufficiently to effect an improvement. This means that working on the same programme for a long period of time will not cause the athlete to improve; this is because the body will adapt to the training load over time. Overload can be facilitated by training more often, or for longer (volume), or training harder (intensity). This progression has to be gradual, so as to prevent a child becoming injured by overexertion (or, in the longer term, overtraining) and possibly demotivated when participating in further training because targets are not achieved. Optimal learning/training effects are achieved by advancing from general to specific movements and from extensive (typified by high-volume, low-intensity) to intensive (low-volume, highest-intensity) workouts.
Specificity	Training programmes and sessions need to be targeted towards specific objectives. Young participants need to have good all-round athletic skills and physical 'literacy' prior to specialising in a specific sport (Collins *et al.*, 2007). As physical preparation levels improve, all training routines need to be increasingly tailored to the specific demands of the sport, the position being trained for and the individual needs of the athlete, so as to maximise the transfer of training benefits to competitive performance. This concept is often misunderstood by coaches: for example, soccer players needing to run 8 miles in a game does not mean that 8-mile runs are specific training for soccer.
Recovery/ adaptation	It is important that both the coach and player realise that training and playing merely provide a stimulus for improvement: it is only through rest that the body can actually improve. Training is a stimulus that fatigues the body; it disrupts the body's normal, balanced resting state. The human body is designed to repair itself and, given time, when damage occurs it will often repair itself to a point where it is stronger, or more efficient, than it was before (adaptation). Insufficient recovery time will ultimately lead to the body becoming overtrained. This in turn will lead to poor performance and an increased risk of injury. If the recovery period is too long, then the training effect will be lost.
Variation	The human body is self-learning and evolves to its environment. Variation in training is a key principle that is often overlooked; this is where the art of coaching becomes important. It relates to how the coach manipulates progressing from general to specific training; how much overload the player is subjected to; what methods are used and how recovery is promoted within the player, so that the learning and adaptation processes are optimised. The best training effects are realised through a planned distribution or variation in training methods and workloads (volume, intensity, frequency) on a cyclic or periodical basis.
Reversibility	Long-term physical adaptations to training programme stimuli revolve around the *use it or lose it* phenomenon. If a training load is inappropriately removed or reduced too much (e.g. the athlete becomes inactive or injured), then training gains that have been achieved will be lost. Coaches therefore need to plan and manipulate training schedules, e.g. around holidays or injury, so that a sufficient level of general activity is maintained to prevent detraining (reversibility) occurring.

141

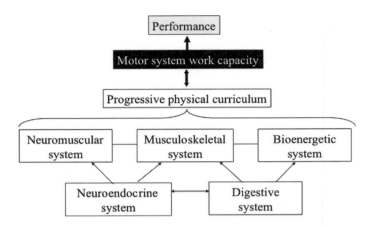

Figure 10.1 Preparing for athletic performance.

(faster, stronger, longer) or being able to work more efficiently (i.e. doing the same amount of work for less energy cost).

Nerves send signals to the muscles to cause them to contract. Therefore, skilled movement is the result of the coordinated activity of the *neuromuscular system* (Figure 10.1). Contractions of the muscles move the bones to produce movement, the bones and muscles being collectively referred to as the *musculoskeletal system*. Any practice that assists in the development of coordination can be referred to as a neuromuscular exercise, or part of neuromuscular conditioning. The circulatory and respiratory systems work together, transporting oxygen to where it is needed, and are known collectively as the *cardiorespiratory system*. This is crucial in allowing the body to produce energy (*bioenergetics*) to allow the required work to be done. The *neuroendocrine system* is the body's chemical messaging system, which is crucial in that it is the stimulus for many important events underpinning long-term maturation and shorter-term sports performance. This chapter will explore the developmental process of the growing child in sport in relation to these systems and the implications for coaching practice.

Understanding maturation in children

Coaches should recognise that more than just the chronological age of a young participant needs to be taken into consideration when planning a programme. The different ages that need to be considered are as follows:

- *Chronological age*. The number of days, months and years that have elapsed since birth.
- *Biological age*. Children within the same chronological age banding can differ by several years in their level of biological maturation. Biological age relates to the individual's stage

of development in relation to physical maturity. The integrated nature of growth is influenced by the interaction between genes, hormones (especially testosterone), nutrients and the physical environments in which an individual lives. This complex interaction regulates the child's growth patterns, neuromuscular and sexual maturation and general development during the first 20 years of life.

■ *Developmental age.* The developmental age refers to the complex interaction between the athlete's biological age and their development emotionally and socially. For example, an athlete may be biologically well developed but not have confidence in their ability, or may not have been training in an environment that offers them the opportunity to express their potential abilities.

■ *Training age.* The number of years the athlete has been in specialised training for sport.

In terms of the physical conditioning of a child, the biological age is the most important consideration, closely followed by their training age. The biological age will determine the anatomical and physiological limitations within which any coaching programme should be developed, whereas the training age may provide an indicator of the movement experiences of a child. For example, as shown in Table 10.2, a child who is an early developer may be anatomically and physiologically more able to tolerate certain training intensities, but, depending upon the programmes he or she has experienced, may have less of a movement vocabulary than a child who is less biologically mature but has more experience within a range of sports.

Table 10.2 focuses on the key physical period of development in the age-related development process: the onset of puberty. Puberty is the evolutionary process of the body maturing to make reproduction possible, and marks the transition towards adulthood. The physiological and anthropometrical changes that occur at this time are significant markers influencing coaches' practices and training routines.

Children do not mature at even rates throughout their development. Some of the changes they go through are obvious, and easy for coaches to measure. Others are less visible, and require some consideration on behalf of the coach if a child's future potential is to flourish rather than be threatened by inappropriate training volumes or intensities.

Table 10.2 The matrix of maturation in children: a hypothetical comparison of two individuals

	Child 1	Child 2
Chronological age	12	12
Biological age	11	14
Developmental age	12	11
Training age	5	3

Anatomical development

The human skeleton consists of 206 bones assembled to form a framework for the body. This provides support against gravity, a rigid lever system that muscles act upon to enable locomotion and a protective mechanism for vulnerable organs and tissue.

During childhood, the proportions of the body segments will also change in relative terms (Figure 10.2): the head will grow to twice its original size, the trunk up to three times, the arms up to four times and the legs up to five times their original proportions (Bouvier, 1989). This has implications for the child in terms of coordination. As children grow and develop, their arms and feet are not where they were relative to their head, which influences children's spatial awareness and coordination and has implications for coaching.

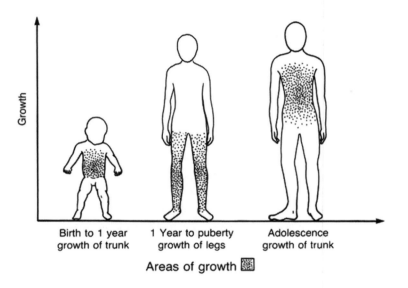

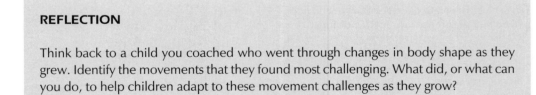

Figure 10.2 The principal areas of growth from birth to adulthood.

Source: Adapted from Thompson (2009: 41).

REFLECTION

Think back to a child you coached who went through changes in body shape as they grew. Identify the movements that they found most challenging. What did, or what can you do, to help children adapt to these movement challenges as they grow?

C. Brewer

By far the greatest of the periods of accelerated growth is the 'adolescent growth spurt', a period of time that has also come to be termed 'peak height velocity' (PHV). This occurs around puberty, and during this time children may grow up to 15 centimetres in a two-year period. The growth increase commonly starts at any age between 10 and 12 in girls, and between 12 and 14 in boys, although in both it may start even later, or occasionally earlier. Indeed, around the chronological ages of 13–16, a coach may have a group of players who are biologically anywhere between 11 and 18. This is typified by a three-year variation within a year group; for example, a coach of an under-14 team may have players who are biologically aged from 11 to 17 (see Table 10.2 above).

Longitudinal bone growth takes place at the ends of the bone, and stops with the closure of the epiphyses of the long bones. Bone mineral density, which marks the changing structure of the child's bones from cartilage to denser bone material, is also closely accelerated during PHV, as shown in the X-rays in Figure 10.3, where the cartilage epiphyseal plates (there is an example within the lighter circle) can clearly be seen in the later maturer, and the density of the bones (illustrated in the area highlighted within the dark circle) is clearly less.

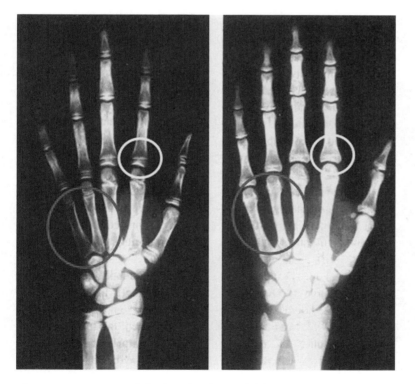

Figure 10.3 X-rays of the hands of two children with a chronological age of 14, but clearly different biological ages.

The biomechanical differences between individual's skeletal sizes at these stages contribute to differences in the energy cost of work, efficiency during exercise, and effectiveness in performance. This brings two problems, related to how we coach young performers and also how we seek to identify talent within children. Those who enter the growth spurt early often do very well in age-group sport, so become used to success without training very hard or focusing on skill mastery in their practice. In their later teens, however, when their slower-growing peers catch up and skill development and game understanding become more important, the early maturers are unused to being beaten, and often drop out of the sport. Equally, many of the children who experience the growth spurt later than their peers (and who ultimately may have the potential to be equally physically skilled) may feel hopelessly overpowered from the start, and believe simply that they are 'no good at sport'. Thus, both ends of this normal distribution need to be accounted for, with programmes that focus appropriately on skill mastery and coaches who counsel children accordingly.

If the coach is able to work closely with the parents of the child, it is important to identify when a child is approaching, entering and leaving PHV. During this time, the child's body is using energy to grow, and the neuromuscular and musculoskeletal systems are stressed more than usual. Coaches should therefore consider reducing the training volume load that the child experiences during these periods and focus on skill-based tasks that encourage the neuro-muscular system to adapt to changes in spatial patterning.

Figure 10.4 Structural differences between players who are within the same age group may cause many issues for players and coaches during the growth period.

Source: Photo courtesy of the Scottish Football Association.

C. Brewer

HOW TO IDENTIFY PHV

It is relatively easy to identify when a child is entering the adolescent growth spurt if certain data are tracked over time. This tracking can be done by recording the child's seated and standing heights on a weekly basis, and looking at the rate of change in height over a period of time.

The disparity in children's size differences is also associated with relative age effects being widely reported in youth sport, especially team sports. A relative age effect is an observed inequality in participation and performance attainment as a result of age-grouping policies (Musch and Grondin, 2001). Specifically, there is significant research evidence (e.g. Till *et al.*, 2010) to show an over-representation of players born in the first three months following an age-group cut-off (e.g. quartile 1 is January to March if calendar date is the cut-off for an age group, whereas in a 1 September dating policy, September–November would represent the first quartile).

REFLECTION

- In the group you coach, who are the children you would identify as the best performers? Are they also the most talented? How did you arrive at this decision? Is it because they are the biggest or fastest performers?
- Conduct a straw poll of the birth dates in your coaching group: are they spread throughout the year?
- What is the biological age distribution in the children you coach? How will this influence the sessions that you deliver?

Over recent years, I have had many significant discussions with people relating to the concept of mechanical loading of children's bones. Many coaches, parents, teachers, health club staff and physicians have expressed the belief that high-intensity or resistance training, in particular lifting free weights, is particularly dangerous for children (Herbert, 1991) because of the potential for damage to the growth plates. However, there is very little scientific evidence to support this theory, and in fact such misconceptions are in direct opposition to the position taken by organisations such as the UK Strength and Conditioning Association (Pierce *et al.*, 2008). Indeed, Micheli (1988) stated that there is little scientific evidence regarding the injury potential of pre-adolescents involved in resistance training, and emphasises that the potential for growth plate injury may be less in the pre-pubescent child because the growth plate is actually much stronger and more resistant to sheer stress in younger children than in adolescents. Furthermore, several studies and reviews of the literature have reported positive performance and physical and physiological adaptations in children and early and late adolescents, with no associated elevated injury potential, from weightlifting and related activities (Pierce et al., 2008) that are supervised by experienced and educated coaches. Similarly, we recognise that children who do take part in activities that stimulate bone growth (e.g. mechanically loaded activities) are less likely to have problems associated with bone mineral density in later life.

Tendons join muscles to bones, and complete fusion of tendons to their respective apophyseal (a projection on the outside of the bone) locations on bone occurs, at different ages, between 12 and 20 for different sites, potentially leading to a number of 'traction' injuries. Examples of these are Osgood-Schlatter's disease at the tibial tuberosity (12–16) in young soccer players, runners and jumpers, or Sever's disease at the calcaneum of the heel (10–13) in young swimmers, runners and/or jumpers. The iliac crest, at the top of the hip bone, is especially vulnerable to apophysitis (inflammation of the bony projection on the bone surface) between 14 and 17, especially in activities involving twisting the trunk, such as throwing, bowling, grappling and hurdling. Similar apophysites may occur in the shoulder and arm in young bowlers, swimmers and throwers. Such traction stresses, associated with 'crescendo pain' (i.e. pain above a certain threshold of activity), occur particularly through high-repetition training (Backx, 1996).

Many of these activities can be prevented by the coach ensuring that activities are programmed appropriately. Consideration needs to be given to ensuring that there is significant variation within the programme, so that repetitive, high-velocity activities are constrained in volume, and include strength work that will enable the development of the musculoskeletal system (bones, tendons and muscles) to adapt to sports-specific stressors.

Prior to the adolescent growth spurt, there is little difference between the skeletal composition of boys and girls. However, following puberty girls tend to have wider hips, and boys tend to have broader shoulders, and longer and straighter arms. This change in body shape may have implications for the coach who is working with the female athlete, whose widened hips may lead to a more steeply angled femur (thigh bone). This can result in changes to running and landing techniques (e.g. heels kicking outwards when running, knees rotating inwards when landing). Also, the resulting angle of muscular force tends to be outward, resulting in lateral tracking of the patella, causing problems to the medial and anterior cruciate ligaments and also the patella itself. For example, chondromalacia patella is an abnormal softening of the cartilage under the kneecap that can be alleviated by stretching and strengthening the quadriceps and hamstring muscle groups, especially on the medial (inside) portion.

The change in hip width and the increased trunk proportions lead to changes in the child's centre of mass. In females, this tends to lower as the hip width increases, which means that females can become more balanced and stable. In males, the centre of mass tends to rise relative to where it was prior to the growth spurt. This means that they tend to become less

C. Brewer

stable, which can cause problems for activities involving balance and stability. To accelerate in any direction, an athlete has to place his or her centre of mass outside the base of support (Brewer, 2008: chapter 6); therefore, the coach needs to help children develop strategies to do this effectively as their body proportions change.

During early childhood, boys and girls have much the same amount of body fat (normally around 16–18 per cent). Through female puberty, the release of oestrogen from the ovaries programs fat to be stored around the breasts, hips, thighs and triceps. Correspondingly, in males the increase in testosterone levels promotes a reduction in body fat stores. Thus, a normal, healthy post-pubescent range of body fat would be 22–25 per cent in females, yet only 12–16 per cent in males. This change in body composition means that girls can have a reduced strength to body weight ratio and also lowered relative endurance capabilities (aerobic power). Coakley (1996) also advises that girls of this age may well be sensitive about their changes in body fat levels, and may also be prone to eating disorders and an avoidance of some rituals associated with sports participation, such as wearing certain uniforms or changing clothes in groups. Coaches should be aware of this issue and demonstrate appropriate sensitivity in their coaching practices.

Physiological development

The physiological development of a child is one of progressive change over a number of years until the onset of puberty. At this time, the hormonal profile of the child changes considerably, with the result that significant changes occur in their endurance, strength and speed capabilities.

The gonads produce the gonadal hormones of testosterone in boys and oestrogen in girls when stimulated by increases in luteinising hormone (LH) and follicle-stimulating hormone (FSH), secreted by the anterior pituitary gland. These hormones have a number of significant influences on sexual maturity and secondary sexual characteristics, and on anatomical adaptations such as widening of the hips and redistribution of body fat. These also trigger changes in the musculoskeletal, neuromuscular and bioenergetic systems, which can significantly influence performance improvements in the child.

The triggering effect 'results from the modulating effects of hormones that initiate puberty and influence functional development and subsequent organic adaptations' (Pierce et al., 2008: 4). The idea of a 'trigger' has been inferred by some to indicate that little or no alteration in performance, physical composition or strength-based physiology is likely to occur until puberty or beyond. This misconception has often been misrepresented in popularised models that claim 'windows of opportunity' around puberty. An example of the potential trigger effects upon strength (e.g. performance outcome) is shown in Figure 10.5.

In females, menstruation normally starts during the other reproductive changes of puberty, namely mammary development, pubic hair and shape changes. There is some evidence (Hata and Aoki, 1990) that menarche, and indeed puberty itself, may be delayed in young female

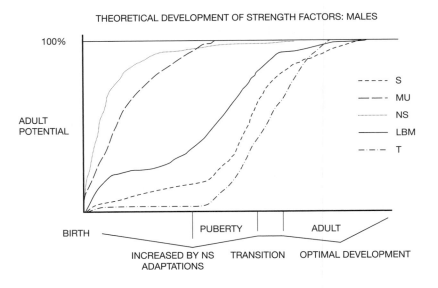

THEORETICAL DEVELOPMENT OF STRENGTH FACTORS: MALES

Figure 10.5 Theoretical alterations in male physiology with age.

Source: Pierce *et al.* (2008).
Note: S = maximum strength levels; MU = motor unit maturation; NS = nervous system maturation; LBM = alterations in lean body mass due to maturation; T = alterations in testosterone levels due to maturation.

athletes who have been involved intensively in very energetic sports from a very young age. As a rule of thumb, it has been suggested that every year of intensive training undertaken before menarche delays it by five months.

Significantly delayed menarche, or the absence of regular monthly cycles in females, has been linked to a condition called amenorrhoea, which implies low oestrogen levels that, in turn, may lead to calcium loss, giving a degree of osteoporosis (poor bone structure due to low bone mineral density). This may lead to susceptibility to stress fractures and also to skeletal problems in later life by lowering the post-menopausal fracture threshold (Rogol, 1996). So, coaches should be alert and sensitive when working, for example, with keen young female runners who have gone through puberty but who show oligomenorrhoea (irregular periods) or amenorrhoea. Medical advice should be sought.

Endurance development

Endurance capabilities in any individual rely on three major factors:

■ *Maximal aerobic power* (VO2 max.), which is the greatest rate at which an individual can process oxygen to produce energy to enable work to be done. This is either measured as an absolute value (litres per minute) or a relative value (millilitres per kilogram of body mass per minute).

■ The *lactate threshold*, which is the point at which the fatiguing by-products of anaerobic metabolism begin to accumulate in the blood, reflecting an acidic environment in the muscle cells.

■ *Movement economy*, or the energy cost of an amount of work. This is influenced by a number of factors related to:
  – size; longer limbs can cover more ground;
  – strength; stronger athletes can do the same amount of work for less energy cost;
  – technique; efficient technique is energy-sparing.

Children's endurance capacities change as they grow and develop. This is due to a number of factors relating to their anatomical and physiological (heart, lungs, blood and muscle fuel) development.

In young children, the heart is gradually increasing in size in proportion to the rest of the body. Similarly, the chest cavity is relatively small, meaning that lung volume is decreased in comparable proportion to adulthood. This means that the heart has to pump faster in order to deliver oxygen around the body and, prior to puberty, heart rates in young children can reach up to 220 beats per minute or higher when exercising, which should not worry coaches unduly.

Reduced lung volume means that children also have to breathe more rapidly, and may need up to 60 breaths per minute to achieve the ventilatory equivalent for oxygen to an adult who can achieve the same with 40 breaths per minute. This in itself is fatiguing, as breathing uses energy, and also body water is lost in exhaled breath.

Oxygen is used to break down an energy store to produce adenosine triphosphate (ATP), the body's energy source, which it uses to perform mechanical work. Adults use glycogen, the muscle store of glucose, as the preferred fuel for this process. However, children's muscle tends to use more fat as fuel, requiring approximately 10 per cent more oxygen for the same amount of energy (Casaburi et al., 1989). The younger the child is, the less they tend to use glycogen. Therefore, we can see that children are less fuel efficient than adults. This is exacerbated by the child's relative biomechanical inefficiencies, caused by the fact that, as a consequence of the anatomical growth processes, the length of a child's limbs is not completely in a kinetic balance with their muscles. Indeed, muscle makes up only 28 per cent of children's body mass (Davies, 1985) in comparison to 35–40 per cent (or more) in adolescence and early adulthood. This results in the child having to work harder, relatively speaking, than even a slow adult to perform locomotor tasks such as running or walking.

Although children are less efficient aerobically than adults, they are often referred to as 'aerobic animals'. This is for two reasons. First, young children incur less of an oxygen deficit at the beginning of exercise – that is, they get their 'second wind' quicker. As their deficit is less, they recover more quickly. Also, they have naturally higher 'anaerobic thresholds' than adults, and

151

in this, oddly enough, they resemble trained adult endurance runners. However, although the lactate threshold is higher (as a proportion of VO2 max.), a child's anaerobic energy system is not well developed prior to puberty.

Many organisations and individuals encourage the role of endurance training in children for health benefits alone (Baquet et al., 2001). The physiological benefits of this in terms of cardiovascular health cannot be disputed. There are a number of ways in which endurance training can be achieved within children, and the clever coach will incorporate activities that promote other biomotor abilities (such as skill) and decision making at the same time. Unfortunately, the traditional method of single-paced continuous training ('run around the field a few times') develops neither of these. However, modified or small-sided games, where the pitch dimensions are modified and the child has many opportunities to touch and interact with the ball, are ideal for developing endurance (Brewer, 2008). The physiological implications of changing a game situation in terms of rules, players and space available are clearly understood in adult sport (Meir et al., 2001), and the same needs to be said for children's sport.

According to current research (Fenoglio, 2003), the ability of children to make decisions in a difficult, ever-changing environment will be dictated by their developmental age, their preparation and the complexity of the situation. Professional educators and football coaches from around the world are agreed that, considering all the information, the small-sided game is the best developmental tool for under-13s. Also, the use of four- and seven-a-side games is the best means of teaching the technical and tactical parts of the game in preparation for the adult game. Small (2006) also demonstrated that, as well as these benefits, four versus four and seven versus seven games provide excellent endurance training opportunities for children. This is because the games are self-paced (that is, children can run after the ball hard when they choose to, and rest when they want to) and also involve many high-intensity speed bursts.

Speed work within children is really important. Success in many sports is determined by the ability to accelerate. This requires fast-twitch muscle fibres to be able to be activated (for an explanation of this, see Brewer, 2008: chapter 2). A child who has undertaken many activities that require high-speed or high-power movements, such as running, jumping and bounding, will have developed a neuromuscular system that can activate the fast-twitch motor units (one nerve and all the muscle fibres innervated by this nerve). Children who have been trained using predominantly steady-state activities will, over time, develop a neuromuscular profile that enables them to do just that: perform at a steady state; but this is not a profile designed to enable success in many sports. This is why intermittent activities that encourage children to run fast for four or five seconds at a time, in many directions, are an excellent means of developing biomotor abilities in children.

It is for this reason that in older pre-pubescent children, using short-interval training develops the anaerobic-alactic and aerobic systems together prior to PHV (Baquet et al., 2004; Tabata et al., 1996). Such short-interval, intermittent training has also been linked to other aspects of fitness, such as lower-limb explosive strength (Mahoney and Boreham, 1992), thought to

C. Brewer

be primarily due to developing neural activation rather than changes in muscle structure (Blimkie and Sale, 1998).

Anaerobic metabolism becomes more important as an energy source as the child gets closer to puberty. This is due to an increase in the activity of enzymes that enable anaerobic metabolic pathways to operate. Anaerobic energy production results in the accumulation of lactate in the blood, and an acidic environment within muscle cells. This acidic environment acts as a fatigue mechanism. An important physiological function of fatigue is to prevent muscle damage through excessive effort. Without this fatiguing system, children could easily be pushed in team or individual coaching situations to the point where they are overheated, dehydrated and distressed. Heat stress is a particularly important consideration for coaches, as children produce more heat than adults but their thermoregulatory system is not as well developed, and so they are not as good at dissipating this heat. This underdevelopment of the thermo-regulatory system also means that coaches need to be very careful about children quickly becoming very cold when they are outdoors, especially when they are not very active in cold and/or wet environments.

Following puberty, the adolescent needs to be trained to tolerate and develop the acidic effects of the intensity activity that characterises many sports performances. This can be done using high-intensity and longer-duration interval training methods as well as conditioning games and sport-specific practices.

REFLECTION

- Anaerobic metabolism is the predominant energy supply mechanism in high-intensity activity: How important is it for the sport that you coach?
- Think about the children you coach. What is the predominant energy system that they will utilise?
- What activities will you use to develop this and other biomotor abilities in your sessions?

One influence of the elevated levels of testosterone in the blood is an increase in the red blood cells, which carry oxygen around the body. This has led to another popular idea: that there is a potential for increased aerobic training benefits (a 'window of opportunity') associated with elevated levels of testosterone. Certainly the elevated red blood cells provide an opportunity for increased aerobic capacity training in those early-specialisation sports (e.g. swimming) where aerobic capacity is an important performance determinant. However, in most sports the ability to sprint repeatedly and being fast or powerful under fatigue is the predominant performance consideration, and this aspect should be focused upon by coaches. This means undertaking repeat-sprint-based endurance training (or using small-sided or conditioning games) to develop endurance capacities, rather than undertaking training activities that will typically target aerobic endurance capacity (high volume, continuous training). Indeed, high-intensity training (or repeat sprint work with incomplete recovery) will develop aerobic endurance capacities as a by-product.

Strength and power development in children

The question about whether children should perform resistance training was addressed earlier in the chapter. Many people, however, assume that children cannot become stronger until puberty, as the child does not have the necessary gonadal hormones to enable them to increase muscle size. Indeed, hypertrophy (size increases) in muscle cross-sectional area is one of the resultant influences of testosterone in males. However, there is significant research and anecdotal evidence to show that children can get much stronger prior to puberty.

As Figure 10.5 shows, the nervous system matures much earlier than alterations in the child's hormone profile. As the nervous system is directly associated with training-induced alterations in force production capabilities (e.g. strength), there is reason to believe that nervous system adaptations to resistance training could also effect positive performance alterations in children (Pierce et al., 2008).

The importance of the development of the nervous system for future sports performance cannot be overestimated. The ability to recruit and utilise motor units effectively is a key consideration for coaches. If skill is the forceful application of technique under pressure (Brewer, 2008), then, in general, the most powerful athlete will win. The following sub-section of this chapter will detail the importance of the child learning to execute skilled movement. This relies upon an effective and efficient neuromuscular system that will respond well to strength challenges. This also means that prior to puberty, boys and girls can be coached to develop strength in the same way.

The strength development of young athletes should be based on the established principles of basic training, aiming for a multifaceted technical and physical development. Specific strength improvement aimed at enhancing the performance level within a particular sporting context is not recommended. The development of strength must fit into the frame of the all-round training procedures and is not to be singled out for preferential attention. The aim should be for all-round muscular development to prepare for higher training loads later in life.

Following puberty, the improvements in strength levels as a result of training adaptations appear to come both from neural mechanisms and from hypertrophy of the muscle fibres. This means encouraging children to take part in a range of training modalities that will encourage the development of the neuromuscular system.

C. Brewer

Movement skill development

A motor skill is a learned sequence of movements that combine to produce a smooth, efficient action in order for the person to master a particular task (Magill, 1993). The link between central nervous system development, neuromuscular system development and movement skills is clear. The central nervous system (CNS) consists of the brain and the sensory and motor nerves. Sensory nerves relay sensory information to the brain. Motor nerves carry information to the muscles, stimulating them to contract and perform work. One motor nerve can stimulate a small number of fibres (e.g. in muscles responsible for fine motor skills) or a large number of fibres (in muscles primarily responsible for gross motor development).

The structural maturation of individual brain regions and their connecting pathways is required for the successful development of cognitive, motor and sensory functions. This maturation eventually provides for a smooth flow of neural impulses throughout the brain and the CNS.

As children develop, gradual shifts occur in their level of functioning in relation to three core classifications of movement skill (stability, locomotor and object control; see Table 10.3). Generally, large muscles develop before smaller ones, and in children, where the neural pathways to the muscles are constantly evolving, this needs to be stimulated by the coaching programme. Indeed, in pre-school and primary-aged children (aged 3–11) the neuromuscular pathways that cause muscle activation need to be stimulated. The ability to stimulate a number of muscle fibres collectively and coherently within a muscle (intramuscular coordination) and between groups of muscles (intermuscular coordination) to produce skilled movement is often referred to as physical literacy, and the importance of this in a child's future sporting participation and performance cannot be overemphasised.

The 4–11 age range is one of the most important periods of motor development. By this stage, the child is developmentally and motivationally ready to acquire the fundamental movement skills that are the cornerstones of athletic and sporting development. Indeed, developing physical literacy is crucial at this point, as children who have inadequate movement skills are often excluded from the organised and free play experiences of their peers, and subsequently spend a lifetime of physical inactivity because of their frustrations concerning early movement behaviour (Seefeldt et al., 1979). The primary, or popularly termed 'fundamental', movement skills (Balyi and Hamilton, 2001) that are associated with physical literacy are shown in Table 10.3.

By the age of 5, children can exhibit mature skill characteristics in key movement skills if they are provided with the opportunity (illustrated in Figure 10.6). Mature skills are those that, as a process of development, integrate all parts of a movement into a well-coordinated, mechanically correct and efficient act (Gallahue and Ozman, 2002). Speed-based multi-directional and games-based activities (based upon 4–5 seconds of speed movement with many opportunities for recovery) allow the neural system to be sufficiently well developed to be able to fire small muscles associated with linear, lateral, multidirectional and segmental

Table 10.3 The fundamental movement skills

Skill classification	Definition	Specific skills
Stability	The skill in sensing a change in the relationship of the body parts that alter balance, as well as the skill to adjust rapidly and accurately for these changes with appropriate compensating movements. This may be in static (stationary) or dynamic (movement) situations, where gaining or maintaining balance is essential.	Posture, Static Balance, Dynamic Balance, Falling and Landing (forwards, backwards, sideways, on feet), Rotating (forwards, backwards, sideways).
Multi-planar locomotion	*Locomotor skills* are considered to be total body movements where the body is propelled from one point to another, usually with an upright posture, in a direction which has components that are both vertical and horizontal.	Walking, Running, Vertical Jumping, Horizontal Jumping, Hopping, Galloping, Skipping.
Bilateral object control	Object control is about manipulation skills. These are large body movements where force is applied to, or absorbed (received) from, external objects. These skills are essential, not just as the basis for participating successfully in many sports, but also for allowing a child to interact purposefully with objects in their environment in a controlled manner.	Underarm Throwing, Overarm Throwing, Catching, Kicking, Bouncing, Striking Static objects, Striking Moving Objects, Trapping (Intercepting).

speed. This does not necessarily mean that they need to be coached within these skills, simply that the coach needs to provide games-based opportunities for these skills to be practised within their programme. For example, running skills can be developed through relay activities, chasing activities or movement into space activities. Coaches can also encourage children to explore how they run, by challenging them to explore running tall, small, fast, slow, without their arms, etc. and discussing with them what the differences were in their actions.

REFLECTION

'Make it fun, kids will run'; many basic movement skills can be developed through simple games-based practices (Figure 10.6).

C. Brewer

How can you modify your coaching practices to encourage more fast running (4–5 seconds in duration)?

Think about your coaching sessions; list three games that you can use to develop each of the skill classifications identified within Table 10.3.

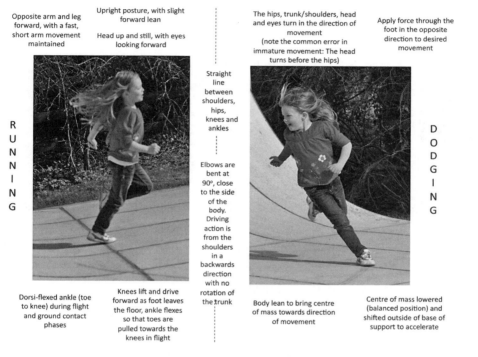

R U N N I N G

Opposite arm and leg forward, with a fast, short arm movement maintained

Upright posture, with slight forward lean

Head up and still, with eyes looking forward

Straight line between shoulders, hips, knees and ankles

Elbows are bent at 90°, close to the side of the body. Driving action is from the shoulders in a backwards direction with no rotation of the trunk

Dorsi-flexed ankle (toe to knee) during flight and ground contact phases

Knees lift and drive forward as foot leaves the floor, ankle flexes so that toes are pulled towards the knees in flight

The hips, trunk/shoulders, head and eyes turn in the direction of movement (note the common error in immature movement: The head turns before the hips)

Apply force through the foot in the opposite direction to desired movement

D O D G I N G

Body lean to bring centre of mass towards direction of movement

Centre of mass lowered (balanced position) and shifted outside of base of support to accelerate

Figure 10.6 The relatively mature running and dodging actions of a 5-year-old involved in playground games such as 'tag'.

In proposing a system for talent development in sports, Collins and colleagues proposed that the importance of early neuromuscular development is a key concept (Abbott *et al.*, 2002). Specifically, the programme was designed to equip individuals with a broad developmental base to aid sports participation for a healthier lifestyle and/or involvement in high-performance sport. Basic skills that underpin many sporting contexts, such as those highlighted in Table 10.3, are built upon by transitions that link skills progressively into sports-specific contexts (Figure 10.8). This can be paralleled with learning to write. First children learn to form letters, then words, then to link words into sentences; finally, they learn to develop these into writing paragraphs and stories.

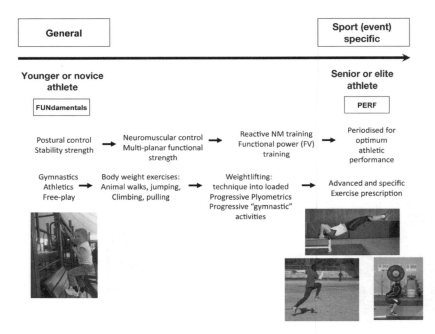

Figure 10.7 The progressive development of strength training throughout a child's development.

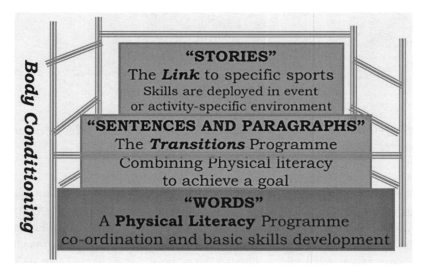

Figure 10.8 Developing physical literacy in children.

Source: *Developing the potential of young people in sport: a report for sportscotland by the University of Edinburgh*. Available at: www.sportscotland.org.uk.

Giedd *et al.* (1999) highlight that prior to puberty, the frontal lobes in the brain begin to reorganise and grow. This growth appears to represent millions of new synapses (connections between the brain cells) that process information. Then, around age 11, a significant pruning of these connections appears to take place, which continues into early adulthood. It would appear that the brain is optimising the efficiency of the neural system – strengthening those pathways that are most required and removing those that are least used. The implication for coaching here is clear: coaches should plan for sufficient variation in the young child's programme to ensure that a large number of neural pathways are retained, as the child may require them at later stages in their sporting career.

The speed of neural transmission is an important factor in both inter- and intramuscular coordination, and this depends not only on the junctions between nerve cells (synapses) but also on the structural properties of the connecting fibres (axons). One of the properties of the neural axons is that there is a layer of insulation around many fibres, known as the myelin sheath. Its function is to accelerate the speed of transmission of the nervous impulse between its origination in the CNS and the muscles. Before neurones receive their myelin sheath, they are considered immature and do not function well, but after myelination the neurones are mature and ready to fulfil their designated functions more efficiently. This is one reason why a toddler is less coordinated than a 9-year-old. Physically, the process of myelination is being completed by the biological age of 12. As this process is completed, it is important to emphasise activities that reinforce neuromuscular adaptation. This means that high-intensity speed work (short duration) and strength work through bodyweight and gymnastic-type exercises should form the basis of training activity development.

Different body segments experience different rates of growth, which, as was said earlier, leads to a change in the child's centre of mass and relative limb lengths during PHV (Philippaerts *et al.*, 2006). This is exacerbated by nerve growth being a developmental process that is not uniform; the rate of nervous impulse is different between some limbs and muscles. As muscles lengthen in response to bone growth, the nerves and muscles can become tightened.

Flexibility is known to be lost during this period. This is probably due to the long bones of the body having an accelerated growth compared to the flat bones and connective tissue. Total body posture control and strength training that encompasses full ranges of movement, accompanied by regular stretching, are important in children at this stage. Tight muscles often become weak muscles, and children develop compensations in their movement pattern to enable them to adapt their movements around such weaknesses (Seagrave, 2007). This can lead to many long-term problems relating to being able to control posture while moving. Regular musculoskeletal screening to identify muscle imbalances and promote ankle, knee, hip, shoulder and vertebrae alignment and range of movement should take place.

159

A PROGRESSIVE APPROACH TO COACHING CHILDREN'S PHYSICAL DEVELOPMENT

The process of growth and movement skill development is one that is relatively predictable in terms of universal principles and sequential progressions as children develop higher levels of functional competence. The key to successful coaching with children is to programme the appropriate coaching progressions to match these sequential development progressions. Planning for long-term development involves the logical and systematic sequencing of training factors in order to optimise specific training outcomes at predetermined times (Bompa and Haff, 2009). This process starts with helping children to develop basic movement skills such as agility, balance, coordination and speed. However, the overriding strategy of the children's coach must be to develop the all-round athlete before focusing solely on sport-specific development and, if appropriate, the highest level of performance.

Long-term programmes should always begin with a form of assessment in terms of how competent a child is. This should be followed by a focused coaching period aimed at skill mastery. As this is progressively learned, and the child demonstrates some consistency in skill execution, the volume of work that utilises this skill can increase. Following this, and after a further period of stabilisation, the volume should be reduced to accommodate higher levels of exercise complexity or intensity in terms of task demand (see Figure 10.9).

These progressions are not gradual increases in intensity (single-arm press-ups are very tough!), but illustrate how coaches can simply manipulate some variables to make an exercise easier or harder.

Think about how you manipulate the position of the centre of mass, the speed of the exercise, the muscles used, the number of body parts in touch with the floor, etc. to make another exercise easier or harder.

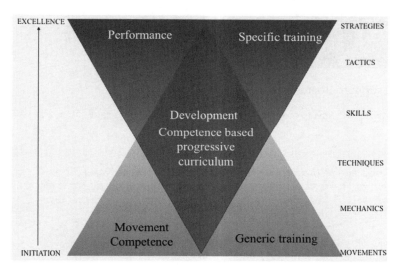

Figure 10.9 Progressive training curricula relate to the needs of the athlete at every stage of development.

Source: Adapted from Plisk (2008) and Seagrave (2007).

These progressions can take many weeks or months to accomplish, and should not be cut short or circumvented by impatient coaches looking to improve performance outcomes in the short term. The ability to execute basic, skilled athletic techniques, at optimum speed and under pressure, with power and precision, is key to successful physical performances (Plisk, 2008).

Skill progressions should be put in place to form progressive practices that enable the child to adapt over time. For example, Figure 10.10 and Table 10.4 illustrate different ways of presenting the competence-based approach (i.e. master one level of difficulty before progressing to the next) to being stable through single-leg-supported actions (Figure 10.10) and developing key skills relating to landing movements (Table 10.4).

Figure 10.10 Single-leg support progressions.

Source: Courtesy of Coachwise and sports coach UK. From Brewer (2008). Available at: www.1st4 sport.com.

Table 10.4 Competency-based landing progressions for jumping and hopping activities

Example competency stage	Key technical factors to emphasise (competency checklist) throughout stages
Double-leg landing and stick (stable flat-foot land and hold)	▪ Ankle dorsiflexed in preparation for landing
	▪ Flat-foot landing
Double-leg run, jump and stick	▪ Centre of mass lowered and directly above the base of support
Double-leg land, stick and throw	▪ Knees acting along the line of the toes
Single-leg land and stick	▪ Force absorbed through knee and hip flexion upon landing
Single-leg run, land and stick	▪ Evenly distributed landing across single foot and, where relevant, between both feet
Single-leg land, stick and throw	▪ Naturally straight (i.e. natural lumbar curve) spine with chest high

In taking time to understand the developmental processes that a child is experiencing, and applying some imagination to the progressions that are introduced into coaching practice, the coach can empower the child to develop sound movement skills that can then be developed to be performed more efficiently, more powerfully and more often, within specific sporting contexts.

C. Brewer

SUMMARY

Children and young people who experience well-planned, well-organised and systematically progressed programmes tend to achieve both success and longevity in their sporting careers. Children simply cannot be coached in the same way as adults. Coaches who can apply evidence-based practices that structure and monitor their training programmes to match the anatomical and physiological development processes of the child will be able to maximise the physical potential of their young participants. The aim of each stage in a logically sequenced programme is to develop the prerequisite movement skills and physical capacities to provide sound foundations for the following stages of progressive development.

Understanding how children develop physically is important for coaches as they can use this knowledge and their experience to devise imaginative practices that challenge the child in a positive way. This chapter has outlined how the child grows and develops structurally and physiologically, and the implications that the progression in their development has for the practising coach. A training programme that links maturation with the development of physical capacities in children and young people will result in a better-quality preparation of the individual for a lifetime of participation in sport.

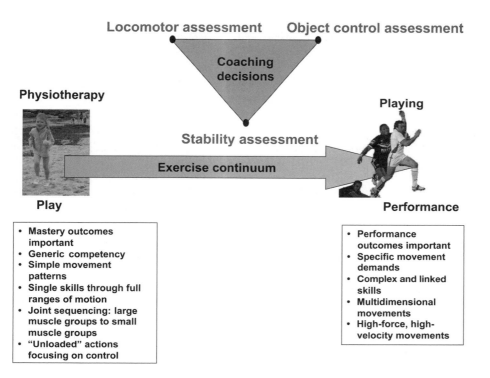

Figure 10.11 Coaching decisions are made by assessing individual competencies and biological development and aligning them to a continuum of progressive exercise difficulty.

The basis for taking part in sport is having the confidence and competence to perform basic sporting movements, such as the ability to run, jump, throw, change direction and exert or resist forces in a balanced and coordinated manner. These movement skills underpin many sport-specific skills. Coaches need to develop progressions for each of these skills that enable them to develop skill mastery, then progressively increase the complexity of the demand of the task. Skills can either be progressed by changing the complexity of the task, for example by linking skills, pressurising skills, or by making skills more challenging physically. This can be achieved by changing the position of the centre of gravity, reducing the base of support or changing the muscles involved in the exercise by altering the positions the joints are put in. A long-term perspective on the progression of children's movement skills and their physical development, and a process that encompasses assessment of progress along the way, is central to young participants' achieving their potential in sport.

THEORY INTO PRACTICE

A coach who has knowledge of how a child develops anatomically and physiologically will be able to design more effective and developmentally appropriate training programmes. The principles of training should all be considered when planning the programme that a young participant will follow. However, when designing the programme, the younger the child, the less important programme specificity actually is.

Coaches should develop programmes that, from an early age, are designed to promote mastery of the basic movement skills, such as running, jumping, landing, throwing, turning and dodging. A variety of coaching tools can be used to develop this, including games based practices. As skills are learned, progress these activities by combining skills into linked combinations, such as run, jump and land, or run and throw. These can then be progressed into sport-specific situational practices.

Coaches should structure training sessions into periods of short, high-intensity activities that enable optimum involvement from all children with lots of opportunities for self-directed rest within them. Small-sided games are ideal for this. Sessions should include aspects from a wide range of the 'fitness characteristics', such as elements of strength, speed, etc. This will enable the neuromuscular, musculoskeletal and bioenergetic systems to develop in tandem.

Coaches should plan progressions for each exercise, to make activities more challenging for those individuals who are able to execute the skill challenges that the coach presents. This will also enable coaches to make activities easier for children who find a particular skill too challenging, as they may not be strong enough, or coordinated enough, to perform the skill. Advancing skills too quickly can encourage children to develop movement compensations. Coaches should use their imagination to find different ways to challenge a child to perform the same degree of difficulty of a skill so that it does not become too repetitive or uninteresting.

C. Brewer

Puberty is a key marker in the physical development of a child. Prior to this important developmental marker, there is little difference between girls and boys in terms of their physical stature. Females typically reach puberty earlier than males, and there are differences between individuals as to when they go through puberty. Puberty causes key anatomical, hormonal and biochemical changes in individuals that can influence how the child should be coached and how they respond and adapt to exercise stimuli.

Prior to puberty, speed- and strength-based activities should be included in every session. These two elements encourage the development of the neuromuscular system, which develops rapidly from birth to late childhood. In the early years, coaches should plan activities that encourage distance over direction, for example in throwing or kicking skills. A well-developed neuromuscular system will enable the direction control aspects to be developed at a later stage.

Coaches can use basic methods, such as recording sitting height, to identify when a young participant is approaching peak height velocity. During this time, the volume of the training should be adjusted so that the body's energy can be conserved for growth. Coaches should ensure that there is variation in activities that stimulate muscle balance through a full range of movements, to avoid some common overuse injuries and postural mal-adaptations. At a time when many children are taking up a wide range of sports, this means achieving a balance between generic and sport-specific training and conditioning to support this. Prior to puberty, avoid over-exertion in children by limiting high-intensity activities to short durations with frequent recovery breaks. After puberty, encourage anaerobic system development through sustained high-intensity activities of differing and increasingly sport-specific durations.

Strength is a precursor to speed, power and movement economy, and relies on the individual's ability to recruit motor units. In the early years, this is best developed by activities that encourage neural development. Gymnastics-based activities, or strength balances such as handstands, are useful for this, as are skill-based techniques relating to activities such as jumping, throwing or lifting. After puberty, hormones facilitate muscle fibre development, and strength can be accelerated rapidly as testosterone 'floods' the child's system. Skill-based resistance training methods are ideal for this purpose. Coaches and parents should be reassured that these will neither stunt the child's growth nor significantly increase muscle bulk in the majority of individuals.

LEARNING MORE

About physical training methods:

- Brewer, C. (2008) *Strength and conditioning for sport: a practical guide for coaches.* Leeds: Coachwise.

About weight training in children:

■ Pierce, K., Brewer, C., Ramsey, M., Byrd, R., Sands, W.A. and Stone, M.H. (2008) Opinion paper and literature review: children and youth resistance training. *UKSCA Strength and Conditioning Journal*, July 2008 (www.uksca.org.uk).

About motor skill development in children:

■ Gallahue, D. and Ozmun, J. (2002) *Understanding motor development: infants, children, adolescents, adults*. Madison, WI: WCB Brown & Benchmark.

About anatomical and physical development in children:

■ Bar-Or, O. (1996) *The child and adolescent athlete*. Oxford: Blackwell.

About coaching fundamental movement skills:

■ Thompson, P.J. (2009) *Run–jump–throw: the official IAAF guide to teaching athletics*. Monaco: IAAF.
■ Association of Physical Education (UK) (2009) *Observing children moving*. Available at: www.afpe.org.uk.

About understanding how to plan physical training programmes:

■ Stone, M.H., Stone, M.E. and Sands, W. (2008) *Principles and practice of resistance training*. Champaign, IL: Human Kinetics.
■ Bompa, T.O. and Haff, G.G. (2009) *Periodization: theory and methodology of training* (5th ed.). Champaign, IL: Human Kinetics.

REFERENCES

Abbott, A., Collins, D., Martindale, R. and Sowerby, K. (2002) *Talent identification and development: an academic review*. A report for sportscotland by the University of Edinburgh. Edinburgh: sportscotland.

Association of Physical Education (UK) (2009) *Observing children moving*. Available at: www.afpe.org.uk.

Backx, F.J.G. (1996) The epidemiology of paediatric sports-related injuries. In O. Bar-Or (ed.), *The child and adolescent athlete*. Oxford: Blackwell.

Balyi, I. and Hamilton, A. (2001) Key to success: long-term athlete development. *Sports Coach* 23(1): 30–32.

Baquet, G., Berthoin, S., Gerbeaux, M. and Van Praagh, E. (2001) High-intensity aerobic training during a 10 week one-hour physical education cycle: effects on physical fitness of adolescents aged 11 to 16. *International Journal of Sports Medicine* 22(4): 295–300.

Baquet, G., Guinhouya, C., Dupont, G., Nourry, C. and Berthoin, S. (2004) Effects of a short-term interval training program on physical fitness in prepubertal children. *Journal of Strength and Conditioning Research* 18(4): 708–713.

Bar-Or, O. (1996) *The child and adolescent athlete*. Oxford: Blackwell.

Blimkie, J.R. and Sale, D.G. (1998) Strength development and trainability during childhood. In E. Van Praagh (ed.), *Pediatric anaerobic performance*. Champaign, IL: Human Kinetics.

Bompa, T.O. and Haff, G.G. (2009) *Periodization: theory and methodology of training* (5th ed.). Champaign, IL: Human Kinetics.

Bouvier, M. (1989) The biology and composition of bone. In S.C. Cronin (ed.), *Bone mechanics*. Boca Raton, FL: CRC Press.

Brewer, C. (2008) *Strength and conditioning for sport: a practical guide for coaches*. Leeds: Coachwise.

Casaburi, R., Daly, J., Hansen, J. and Effros, R. (1989) Abrupt changes in mixed venous blood gases following exercise onset. *Journal of Applied Physiology* 67: 1106–1112.

Coakley, J. (1996) Socialization through sports. In O. Bar-Or (ed.), *The child and adolescent athlete*. Oxford: Blackwell.

Collins, D., Brewer, C. and Martindale, R. (2007) Towards a new model for athlete development. Paper given at sports coach UK seminar on Athlete Development, Leeds.

Davies, C.T.M. (1985) Strength and mechanical properties of muscle in children and young adults. *Scandinavian Journal of Sports Science* 7: 11–15.

Fenoglio, R. (2003) The Manchester United 4 v 4 pilot scheme for U9s, Part 2: The analysis. *Insight – The FA Coaches Association Journal*, autumn.

Gallahue, D. and Ozmun, J. (2002) *Understanding motor development: infants, children, adolescents, adults*. Madison, WI: WCB Brown & Benchmark.

Giedd, J., Blumenthal, J., Jeffries, N., Castellanos, F., Liu, H., Ijdenbos, A., Paus, T., Evans, A. and Rapoport, J. (1999) Brain development during childhood and adolescence: a longitudinal MRI study. *Nature Neuroscience* 2(10): 861–863.

Hata, E. and Aoki, K. (1990) Age at menarche and selected menstrual characteristics in young Japanese athletes. *Research Quarterly for Exercise and Sport* 61(2): 178–183.

Herbert, D.L. (1991) Supervision of children. *Sports Medicine Standards and Malpractice Reporter* 3(4): 69.

Magill, R. (1993) *Motor learning: concepts and applications* (5th ed.). Singapore: McGraw-Hill.

Mahoney, C. and Boreham, C. (1992) Validity and reliability of fitness testing in primary schools. In T.J. Williams *et al.* (eds), *Fitness testing and primary school children, sport and physical activity*. London: E & FN Spon.

Meir, R., Colla, P. and Milligan, C. (2001) Impact of the 10-meter rule change on professional rugby league: implications for training. *Strength and Conditioning Journal* 23(6): 42–46.

Micheli, L. (1988) Strength training in the young athlete. In E. Brown and C. Branta (eds), *Competitive sports for children and youth*. Champaign, IL: Human Kinetics.

Musch, J. and Grondin, S. (2001) Unequal competition as an impediment to personal development: a review of the relative age effect in sport. *Developmental Review* 221(2): 147–167.

Philippaerts, R., Vaeyens, R., Janssens, M. *et al.* (2006) The relationship between peak height velocity and physical performance in youth soccer players. *Journal of Sports Sciences* 24(3): 221–230.

Pierce, K., Brewer, C., Ramsey, M., Byrd, R., Sands, W.A., Stone, M.E. and Stone, M.H. (2008) Youth resistance training. *United Kingdom Strength and Conditioning Association Journal* 10 (Summer): 9–34.

Plisk, S. (2008) Planning and periodisation de-mystified. Paper given at the UKSCA National Conference, Belfast, May.

Rogol, A.D. (1996) Delayed puberty in girls and primary and secondary amenorrhoea. In O. Bar-Or (ed.), *The child and adolescent athlete*. Oxford: Blackwell.

Seagrave, L. (2007) Mechanics of sprint technique. Paper given at the UKSCA National Conference, Inverclyde National Sports Centre, UK, May.

Seefeldt, V. (1979) Developmental motor patterns: implications for elementary school physical education. In C. Nadeau, W. Halliwell, K. Newell and C. Roberts (eds), *Psychology of motor behavior and sport*. Champaign, IL: Human Kinetics.

Seefeldt, V., Haubenstricker, J. and Reuschlein, S. (1979) Why physical education in elementary school curriculum? *Ontario Physical Education and Health Education Association Journal* 5(1): 21–31.

Small, G. (2006) Small-sided games study of young football athletes in Scotland. Independent consultation paper for the Scottish FA.

Stone, M.H., Stone, M.E. and Sands, W. (2008) *Principles and practice of resistance training*. Champaign, IL: Human Kinetics.

Tabata, I., Nishimura, K., Kouzaki, M., Hirai, Y., Ogita, F., Miyachi, M. and Yamamoto, K. (1996) Effects of moderate-intensity endurance and high-intensity intermittent training on anaerobic capacity and VO2 max. *Medicine and Science in Sports and Exercise* 28: 1327–1330.

Till, K., Cobley, S., Wattie, N., O'Hara, J., Cooke, C. and Chapman, C. (2010) The prevalence, influential factors and mechanisms of relative age effects in UK rugby league. *Scandinavian Journal of Medicine and Science in Sport* 20(2): 320–329.

Thompson, P.J. (2009) *Run–jump–throw: the official IAAF guide to teaching athletics*. Monaco: IAAF.

C. Brewer

CHAPTER ELEVEN

THE FAMILY FACTOR IN COACHING

TESS KAY AND DI BASS

CHAPTER OUTLINE

- The family as a support mechanism for youth sport
- Managing the coach–athlete–family relationship
- Learning more

INTRODUCTION

> *Well, you can't really succeed if you haven't got your family.*
>
> *(Swimmer, in Kay, 2000: 161)*

This chapter looks at an absolutely crucial part of the coaching system: the role played by families. Every coach knows how central families are to youth sport; without their input, coaching systems would simply fall apart. But although families play this crucial role, they can be surprisingly invisible within sport. The sheer familiarity of relying on parents and families is such a fundamental feature of youth sport that it tends to be taken for granted. Some sports do explicitly address the role of families and provide them with support, but on the whole families are not universally recognised, receive limited support and have little opportunity to influence how coaching systems develop (Kay, 2000). This is an important omission when young people's participation relies so wholly on families being able to support such systems.

This chapter therefore looks at the role that families play in facilitating young people's sports participation, and examines the implications these roles have for coaches. The chapter focuses on two elements of the family role that need to be understood by coaches:

- the support function provided by families: coaches need to be aware of the extent to which families invest in their children's sport, the challenges they may face in doing so, and the ways in which coaches can help families to support their child in the most appropriate and effective ways;

■ the role of family members within the coaching process: with families playing an active role in their child's sporting development, coaches need to consider how they can manage the coach–athlete–family relationship to everyone's benefit.

THE FAMILY AS A SUPPORT MECHANISM FOR YOUTH SPORT

In this section, we look at why families are so significant in supporting coaching in youth sport. In effect, families act as the 'glue' that holds these often complex systems together, giving young people the financial, emotional and practical support they need to progress within them. As sports talent development systems become more sophisticated and comprehensive, the role of families is becoming increasingly important.

Understanding family life today

To understand the role of families, coaches first need to be aware of some of the key features of family life today. Families are changing: the past three decades have seen rising divorce rates, increasing levels of lone parenthood, and growing numbers of 'reconstituted' families – family households produced after separation or divorce, when a parent forms a new 'step-family' with their children and new partner. Patterns of day-to-day family life have also been shifting, with more children being brought up in households in which both of their parents spend time in paid work. Yet we are also in an era of 'intensive parenting', when mothers and fathers are expected to be more actively involved in their children's activities than before (Coakley, 2009; Such, 2009). There are, however, cultural differences. For example, sport is highly valued by many North American and European parents, but given lower priority by many families of a South Asian heritage, who value education and family much more. There are, therefore, several pressures on families today that may affect their capacity and willingness to support their children's sport. It is useful for coaches to be aware of these different family situations as they may affect how well positioned families are to provide practical support for their children's sport, and also how much importance they attach to doing so.

How families support their children's sport

> I think the family, certainly from the initial detection point from when you first identify them, is the crux because if you don't get the parents on board and you don't get their support then you don't even get to work with the athlete do you . . . their role is critical.
> (National governing body representative, in Kay and Charlesworth, 2005: 10)

T. Kay and D. Bass

Families play a major role in children's initial socialisation into sport and their long-term participation. Young people do not have to be participating at a high level for sport to become a central component of family life and relationships, as Trussell's (2009) doctoral research has shown. Her study of sport among rural families in Canada showed how sport became a central activity through which parents and children related to each other and through which mothers and fathers met expectations of good parenting. Trussell coined the term 'Team Family' to capture the central role that sport took in defining family life.

The family's input becomes especially important for talented children who progress to high levels of performance. At this level, family life as a whole can be quite dramatically affected by the level of support that sports involvement requires. As a child's level of achievement rises, the demands made on the family inevitably increase. Daily routines are shaped by training schedules; shared family leisure time decreases; holidays are rearranged – and sometimes cancelled – to fit around competition schedules. Many parents adapt their work commitments to meet the time or money demands of sport; some change jobs, become self-employed or even give up work completely. Some families move house to be nearer specialist training facilities, while others remortgage or move to a smaller property to be able to meet the financial costs of support. It is perhaps unsurprising that a 2005 study therefore found that a third (36 per cent) of families described their child's sport as the 'main' influence on family life and another 49 per cent described it as a 'large' influence on it (Kay and Charlesworth, 2005). At this level of involvement, sport is no longer an 'add-on' to family life, but its defining feature:

> We have basically had to arrange our whole lives around swimming, and swimming has become our lives.
>
> (Swimmer's mother)

> Life is dictated by their sport.
>
> (Rower's father, in Kay, 2000: 162)

But not all families are able to support their children's participation to this extent. Children from low-income families, among which low-skilled workers, lone-parent households and ethnic minority families are all over-represented, are much less likely to be sports participants at the elite level (Sports Council, 1997). Many parents who are able to support their children recognise the difficulties faced by less affluent parents and believe that young people are being lost to their sport simply because their families are unable to provide the assistance that is needed:

> The main problem is the cost involved and the time. I fail to see how a child with full-time working parents – or parents out of work – who is not old enough to travel on their own could attend all necessary training.
>
> (Mother of athlete)

There were times in the past though where I can just remember thinking 'I just can't do this any more, it's way too hard'. I used to think it didn't matter how talented you were, you needed to be rich.

(Mother of gymnast, in Kay *et al.*, 2006: 9)

REFLECTION: THE DEMANDS ON FAMILIES

What sort of support does your sport need from families? For example:

- Does your sport demand a big time investment from parents?
- Does your sport demand a big financial investment from parents?
- Does your sport rely on parents to provide a lot of transport?

Are there any types of family who find it difficult provide the support that is needed – for example, families that might have too little time? Or families with a low income?

Does your sport need more support from parents as children get older and/or progress to higher performance levels?

Do you know whether children ever drop out because the practical demands on their families are too great?

Do you know whether children ever drop out because their families do not think sport is very important?

Supporting the supporters: how coaches can help families to play their role most effectively

It is important for coaches that families play their crucial role as effectively as possible, complementing coaches' own work rather than detracting from it. This section therefore considers how coaches can make sure families are best equipped to support their child's sport.

A series of research studies carried out in the United Kingdom provide some insight into the sort of support that families most need. In work conducted between 2003 and 2006, the Institute of Youth Sport (IYS) assessed the support needs of families of talented young sports performers in the sports of athletics, cricket, gymnastics, rugby, soccer, swimming and tennis (Kay and Charlesworth, 2005; Kay *et al.*, 2006). The overall finding of these studies was that what parents need most is better information about how to perform their role. They want guidance on what they should be doing to support their child's sport, and practical assistance to help them fulfil this function. The studies found that few sports had systematic mechanisms for providing advice on issues such as developmental pathways in their child's sport, lifestyle

adjustments, funding mechanisms and sports science information. Current support for families was described as 'well intended but relatively unstructured', 'minimal', 'informal', 'reactive rather than proactive' and 'ad hoc'. More than 90 per cent of the parents felt that they needed more guidance and help:

> I think we could do with more support . . . we are giving up a lot as well, and you know, we want to feel as though we have some support in return and that we are involved in what's going on.
>
> (Mother of tennis player)

> I can understand why a lot of people give up because you really don't get the assistance that is needed really.
>
> (Mother of athlete, in Kay and Charlesworth, 2005: 16)

Lack of support can lead to parental effort being wrongly directed. It is hard, for example, for families to judge whether tiredness during a period of intensive training is 'normal' or indicates a problem, or to know how to respond when their child's motivation flags during a period of poor performance. What families need are ways of accessing information that equips them to respond to such situations appropriately. They also want guidance on sources of external assistance, for example information on how to apply for grants, and advice on obtaining sponsorship. Across all seven sports covered in the IYS studies, there was high demand for four key types of information: information on dietary and nutrition needs, information on training, advice on funding mechanisms and sources of financial support, and information on the impact on family life. Although there was some variation between sports, overall around nine out of ten families wanted information in each of the areas listed.

Parents also wanted frequent feedback from sport on their child's progress; information on selection processes; advice on balancing academic and sporting commitments and demands; and early warning about training, competition and fixtures to allow them to plan for these.

It is important for coaches to be aware of these information needs because coaches are so often the primary interface between families and sport. Parents feel that good communication with coaches and sport professionals on these matters could make the job of supporting a young athlete that much easier:

Table 11.1 Information needs of parents of elite young performers (*n* = 484)

Type/format of information required	Percentage
Dietary/nutrition	95
Training	91
Funding/financial	90
Impact on family life	81

Table 11.2 Dissemination methods preferred by parents of elite young performers (n = 484)

Format of information required	Percentage
Factsheets/newsletters	87
Expert workshops	82
Websites	81

It would be very helpful if there was better communication between the parents and the coaches. Perhaps more advanced warning of, um, I would say holiday programmes, um, and you know, changes in training times, this sort of thing. Just better communication. I would like to know more; for me it's a grey area.

(Mother of gymnast)

When you first go into it, it's a case of you find out yourself how it all works, tournaments, what to enter, what not to enter, you know there is a lot to understand. What you get for wins and how that can affect you. There is like a rating system and you are really just left to get on with it, you know, learn by your mistakes. No one sits you down and says, 'this is a good tournament, don't bother with that one'. Um, you really are left to get on with it in that respect. I think I would have liked a bit more help at the beginning.

(Father of tennis player)

I think I would have liked a bit more help with the, with um, the physical side, the injury prevention. You got no advice on that, it was a case of if she picked an injury up we just found out for ourselves. I have learnt a lot now. If I was prepared when she first started, when she was say ten and she picked her first injury up. If I knew then what I knew now, she probably wouldn't have even got that injury, you know. But you didn't get nothing there as well, which was not right, I don't think.

(Father of tennis player, in Kay and Charlesworth, 2005: 16)

REFLECTION: HOW TO HELP FAMILIES TO HELP YOU

- What do families need to know in your sport?
- Do parents ever cause you problems by being uninformed? Could this be avoided?
- What are the best ways of getting information to parents?
- Do you offer parents specific chances to ask you questions, or do you assume that they will ask you anyway if they need to?

> ■ Do you operate any form of 'family forum' for parents, where they can meet together and share experiences, and also have the chance to question you and other sports experts?

The first section of the chapter has focused on the role families play in supporting their children's participation and the challenges they may face. It has particularly highlighted the important role of the coach in guiding families, by making sure they are well informed about what is required and how best they can fulfil their role. The next section will now look at the issues that coaches need to consider in dealing more directly with families within the coaching process.

MANAGING THE COACH–ATHLETE–FAMILY RELATIONSHIP

How should coaches handle the involvement of family members in their children's sport? Several authors emphasise that coaching is not just about appropriate coaches being appropriately skilled but also about the social relationships that are embedded in the coaching process. As Jones *et al.* explain, a coach's work is not done in isolation but 'is linked to a wide range of significant others' (2002: 35).

In youth sport, the relationships that are usually of primary importance are those between coaches, parents and athletes – what has been termed 'the primary family of sport' (Scanlon and Lewthwaite, 1988). To create an environment in which the young athlete can flourish, the coach needs to be aware of the many issues that may arise from the relationships between these three sets of people.

Key issues in coach–athlete–family relationships

Recent research has highlighted the following issues with regard to managing the coach–parent–athlete relationships.

Clarifying roles and expectations

The first issue that the coach must consider is that each person in this 'sporting triangle' (Byrne, 1993) has his or her own expectations about the coaching process and his or her role within it: 'Our social worlds offer no immunity to sport fields and gymnasia. Actions, beliefs, traditions and perspectives that define how we live in the world also define how we live and learn in sport' (Schempp, 1998: 1–2).

175

People fulfil roles in ways that reflect their beliefs and expectations (Jones *et al.*, 2002) about their own behaviour and the behaviour of others. Thus, 'sports coaching does not exist in a social vacuum but is subject, to varying extents, to the societal and sporting structures within which it operates' (ibid. 35). Bass's (2008) study of the coach–parents–athlete triangle in two swimming clubs involved particularly in-depth research of these relationships and provides multiple examples of the issues that arise. It showed that coaches, parents and swimmers were all heavily committed to the coaching process but often differed from each other in their expectations of their own and each other's roles. Coaches need to be aware that members of the sporting triangle do not come to a coaching situation value free but bring with them expectations, goals and hopes that they have gained through their own socialisation into the world of youth sport. These further develop through their experiences at a club and their interaction with others in that environment. In particular, new members joining the club, whether they be parents or athletes, may not be fully aware of what is expected of them until they are socialised into the mores of the 'community of practice' (Lave and Wenger, 1999). Coaches have an important role to play in developing the shared understanding in these relationships that is crucial to young people's experiences.

Working with the involved parents

Coaches can be critical of parents who put undue pressure on their child and interfere with the coaching process. It is important, however, for coaches to pay attention also to families who support their children in less conspicuous ways. Many of these parents are well intentioned but uncertain about what their role should be. As the first part of this chapter has shown, less knowledgeable parents would benefit from supportive guidance from a coach over how to fulfil their role as parents of a committed sportsperson and advice on how to approach some of the difficult situations they may face. In Bass's (2008) study, for example, one father described his regrets over reacting badly to what he considered to be a poor swim by his daughter:

> I made a very small mistake that caused quite a bit of upset for the rest of the day really. As she finished, being a backstroker, she looked straight up at the crowd. I looked at the clock – it wasn't a bad swim but it was disappointing after the 100 and I saw the time and went 'uggh' and my face was like . . . and she looked straight at me and that image and she thought 'Oh dear I've let him down' or whatever, 'he's going to be mad at me' or whatever went through her mind, I don't know, but we came home in abject silence . . . it was not a pleasant journey home and she . . . went straight to her bedroom and there was tears and real upset and it was just over split second facial expression.

Guidance from coaches may help parents be better prepared for such circumstances.

Many parents have been labelled 'over-involved' (Hellstedt, 1987), but sometimes criticisms are also voiced against those parents who do not attend club sessions and who thus may be

T. Kay and D. Bass

labelled 'under-involved'. However, parents who do not attend sports sessions are not necessarily less supportive of their children. Many fulfil their roles as 'supportive parents' by preparing meals, caring for their other children and doing other household duties that allow the family to function while their partner and child are heavily involved in the sport. It is helpful, therefore, for coaches to really get to know families in order to appreciate the complexities of the relationships that exist and the different ways in which parents provide, and may need, support.

Multiple roles: the coach-parent

Youth sport relies heavily on volunteers, and many parents therefore also take on the role of coach. There can be many positive benefits to this relationship in terms of levels of trust and support, but there may also be negative aspects such as additional pressure, emotions, frustration and lack of understanding (Weiss and Fretwell, 2005; Jowett et al., 2007). Bass (2008) found that although the swimmers in her study appreciated the knowledge their own parent-coach possessed, they were generally not happy about being coached by them. The pressures that this sometimes produced were described by a mother who reflected on her husband's role as their daughter's coach:

> There have been times when it's been kind of . . . been too much and I've felt that if she [the daughter] hadn't gone any more it would be OK because it was all getting a bit too intense with [the father] coaching her a bit and being so involved in the club as well – it all got a bit intense, but basic swimming – very happy with that.

This dual role of parent/coach could be problematic for parents as well as swimmers. One father in Bass's study declared that 'sometimes I play the role of the parent and the role of the coach very badly'. By working closely with parents, especially those involved in the club, the coach can help parents cope with what can be, at times, conflicting demands. Also, by ensuring that they know their athletes and parents, coaches are better positioned to make any organisational changes in terms of allocation of coaching duties that may be necessary.

Dealing with conflict

In an ideal situation, coaches, athletes and family members have shared expectations and collaborate effectively to achieve them. In reality, power struggles and conflict may occur as coach, parents and athletes act out their roles and variously 'position' themselves as they interact with other club members. Bass (2008) found that conflict within the sporting triangle occurred most when parents positioned themselves as 'experts'. If in this situation they also recognised and respected the coach as having 'expert power', then conflict did not necessarily arise. However, if parents positioned themselves as being more knowledgeable than the coach, then power struggles ensued, struggles that needed careful handling by the coach if relationships were to remain harmonious.

It is helpful for the coach to be aware that even at the familial level, conflict can occur. Both parents can be supportive towards their child's sport but, as Bass (2008) found, there can be variation in the expected levels of commitment. Within one family in Bass's study, the pressure that the father put on the daughter to attend sessions resulted in the child using the threat of giving up swimming as a weapon against her father. As the mother stated,

> [She] could . . . use it as a tool to threaten – she could say to him, 'If you make me do that, then I'm not going to go swimming any more', and it became a weapon. But it was a weapon she couldn't use on me because I didn't care.

Relationships between members of the sporting triangle can also be heavily affected by the context in which interactions took place. Within sports clubs, power often lies with the committee, and if the coach's goals are at odds with those of the committee and other members, then there is potential for conflict. Such conflict may become unmanageable, as in one of Bass's swimming clubs. Although both clubs in her study were at the 'development coaching' level (Lyle, 2002), they differed markedly in ethos, and this clearly affected the ways in which each coach could act out her role. In one club, the coach felt that, as it was a development club, emphasis should be on technique, but many parents wanted a stronger focus on performance. Eventually, the resulting pressure from this conflict led the coach to leave the club (Bass, 2008).

REFLECTION: MANAGING THE RELATIONSHIP IN THE SPORTING TRIANGLE

- What issues are faced by the coach when dealing with parents and their sporting children?
- What role or roles do parents play in the sporting career of their young athletes?
- How can a coach manage this situation in order to ensure that an environment is created that will lead to positive sporting experiences for those involved?

This section has emphasised the need to understand the coach–parent–athlete triangle and to appreciate that coaching is about more than just the technical aspects of the 'how' of coaching. If coaches are to manage the coaching process effectively, it would seem that they not only have to be clear about their own needs and expectations but also have to ensure that all members of the triad are aware of each other's individual sporting needs. Communication between all parties is therefore vital, for without it misunderstanding and conflict may arise, resulting in a less than ideal environment for the young athlete.

178

T. Kay and D. Bass

SUMMARY

This chapter has highlighted how significant families are to young people's sport overall and to coaching in particular. The research evidence in this area suggests that coaches should:

- recognise the pressures families can be under;
- help them to play their role as effectively as possible;
- actively manage their relationships with family members.

By doing so, coaches can do much to ensure that the 'sporting triangle' functions to the maximum benefit of young athletes.

LEARNING MORE

Coakley's (2009), Harrington's (2009) and Such's (2009) work on fathering and sport provide insights into the role of sport in family life in the United States, Australia and the United Kingdom respectively. Kay's 2000 article 'Sporting excellence: a family affair?' gives families' own accounts of how they support their child's sport and how family life is affected by their doing so. Hellstedt's 1987 article 'The coach/parent/athlete relationship' discusses the model of parental involvement Hellstedt devised to assist coaches in working with both athletes and parents. Jowett et al.'s 2007 article on dependence in the dual role parent/coach–child/athlete relationship explores the relationship between the parent and child when the parent is a coach. Jones et al.'s 2002 analysis of the coaching process discusses the importance of the social element within coaching.

REFERENCES

Bass, D. (2008) The coach–parent–athlete triangle: an investigation in age-group swimming. Unpublished doctoral thesis, Loughborough University, UK.

Byrne, T. (1993) Sport: it's a family affair. In M. Lee (ed.), *Coaching children in sport: principles and practice*. London: E & FN Spon.

Coakley, J. (2009) The good father: parental expectations and youth sports. In T.A. Kay (ed.), *Fathering through sport and leisure*. London: Routledge.

Cross, N. and Lyle, J. (1999) Preface. In N. Cross and J. Lyle (eds), *The coaching process: principles and practice for sport*. Oxford: Butterworth-Heinemann.

Harrington, M. (2009) Sports mad, good dads: Australian fathering through leisure and sport practices. In T.A. Kay (ed.), *Fathering through sport and leisure*. London: Routledge.

Hellstedt, J.C. (1987) The coach/parent/athlete relationship. *Sport Psychologist* 1: 151–160.

Jones, R.L. (2007) Coaching redefined: an everyday pedagogical endeavour. *Sport Education and Society* 12(2): 159–173.

Jones, R.L., Armour, K.M. and Potrac, P. (2002) Understanding the coaching process: a framework for social analysis. *Quest* 54: 34–48.

Jowett, S., Timson-Katchis, M. and Adams, R. (2007) Too close for comfort. *International Journal of Coaching Science* 1: 59–78.

Kay, T. (2000) Sporting excellence: a family affair? *European Physical Education Review* 6(2): 151–169.

Kay, T. (2003) The family factor in sport: a review of family factors affecting sports participation. In *Driving up participation*. London: Sport England.

Kay, T.A. and Charlesworth, H. (2005) Gifted and talented family support resource project: pre-implementation report. Unpublished report.

Kay, T.A., Charlesworth, H. and Smith, C. with Nuttall, J. (2006) Gifted and Talented Family Support Resource Project: report on the assessment of families' needs for support. Unpublished report.

Kirk, D., O'Connor, A., Carlson, T., Burke, P., Davis, K. and Glover, S. (1997) Time commitments in junior sport: social consequences for participants and their families. *European Journal of Physical Education* 2: 51–73.

Lave, J. and Wenger, E. (1999) Learning and pedagogy in communities of practice. In J. Leach and B. Mood (Eds.), *Learners and Pedagogy* (pp. 21–23). London: Paul Chapman Publishers.

Lyle, J.W.B. (2002) *Sports coaching concepts: a framework for coaches' behaviour*. London: Routledge.

Scanlon, T.K. and Lewthwaite, R. (1988) From stress to enjoyment: parental and coach influences on young participants. In E.W. Brown and C.F. Branta (eds), *Competitive sports for children and youth*. Champaign, IL: Human Kinetics.

Schempp, P. (1998) The dynamics of human diversity in sport pedagogy scholarship. *Sociology of Sport Online* 1. Available at: http://physed.otago.ac.nz/sosol/v1i1/v1i1a8.htm.

Sports Council (1997) *Development of Sporting Talent*, London: Sports Council.

Such, L. (2009) Fatherhood, the morality of personal time and leisure-based parenting. In T.A. Kay (ed.), *Fathering through sport and leisure*. London: Routledge.

Trussell, D. (2009) Organized youth sport, parenthood ideologies and gender relations: parents' and children's experiences and the construction of 'Team Family'. Unpublished doctoral dissertation, University of Waterloo, Waterloo, Ontario.

Weiss, M.R. and Fretwell, S.D. (2005) The parent–coach/child–athlete relationship in youth sport: cordial, contentious, or conundrum? *Research Quarterly for Exercise and Sport* 76: 286–305.

CHAPTER TWELVE

THE CHILD IN HIGH-PERFORMANCE SPORT

KARL WHARTON

CHAPTER OUTLINE

- Growth and maturational issues
- Key 'sensitive periods' for physical and skill development
- Psycho-social issues and goal setting
- Theory into practice
- Learning more

INTRODUCTION

The child in high-performance sport is one who has superior athletic talent; is subjected to long, arduous training programmes and early, intense competition schedules involving great sacrifice, effort and in many instances social isolation; receives expert coaching and support from sport scientists and medical staff; and, in many cases, is exposed to training camps and international travel away from family and friends. Child athletes are a unique athlete population who have different emotional, physical and social needs that vary depending on the athlete's particular stage of maturation. They demand specific and appropriate training programmes, expert coaching and support from a variety of services and appropriate competition schedules that ensure a safe and healthy athletic career, which promotes a future healthy lifestyle and well-being.

Development in high-performance sport has led to a situation that is characterised by:

- early talent identification and specialisation being more prevalent and structured, with children from an early age being faced with demanding training programmes involving long hours of intensive, repetitive training and in some cases strict dietary regimes;
- major competition commitments, and sometimes too much competition;

- the age of top athletes decreasing dramatically in many sports, and children at elite level in some sports;
- a significant increase in skill levels, mechanical loads, flexibility and strength requirements in many sports;
- substantially increased time devoted to training and preparation, and more repetition of skills;
- pressure and expectations to succeed from coaches, parents, governing bodies of sport and from the children themselves.

Many coaches may encounter problems of 'burn-out', serious overuse injury and substance abuse, all of which are associated with major athletic achievement (Côté and Fraser-Thomas, 2008). It could be argued that there is sometimes financial inequality among young performers, resulting in additional stress and a loss of enjoyment in sport.

Ryan (1999) describes how children in high-performance sport are sometimes exposed to excessive and undesirable coaching practice. Consequently, it is a duty of all coaches who are working in high-performance environments to be aware of the potential negative health implications (physical, physiological and psychological) and the impact on the young athlete's socio-cultural life within elite sport. Coaches must identify potential strategies and support structures that can be put in place to minimise such risks.

This chapter aims to provide the opportunity to develop knowledge of key issues that coaches face when dealing with 'elite' young athletes and how they may address these when coaching in a high-performance environment.

It is important that we make a distinction between the adult 'elite' athlete and the child in high-performance sport. In highlighting key differences, many factors come into play, most of which centre on the fact that a young athlete is not a miniature adult athlete but an individual with specific needs that are unique to children in high-performance sport.

GROWTH AND MATURATIONAL ISSUES

Coaches need to be aware that growth and maturation are not the same thing. Growth refers to the observable changes in physical characteristics such as height, weight and percentage body fat content, whereas maturation addresses the progression of the body towards 'maturity', including such developments as the conversion of cartilage to bone (Gordon, 2009).

Many sports still use age-based standards for performance levels and squad selection, such as under-11/13/15 years. However, these do not account for the considerable variability in the physical, psychological/emotional and intellectual maturity status of young athletes at any given chronological age. Therefore, coaches should not use an individual's chronological age as the sole measure of maturation or to plan an athlete's training programme, as doing so may place excessive demands on late-maturing individuals or leave early-maturing athletes

K. Wharton

uninterested and unchallenged. For these reasons, coaches need to be aware of the distinctions between:

- 'skeletal age' – a measure of the maturity of the skeleton determined by the degree of ossification of bone structure;
- 'chronological age' – the number of years and days elapsed since birth;
- 'training age' – the number of years for which an athlete has been specialising and training in a particular sport;
- 'developmental age' – a young athlete may be well developed physically – tall, strong and fast – but be less well developed than peers cognitively, socially or emotionally.

Normal growth in children after 24 months is steady until puberty, with height increasing by approximately 5 centimetres and weight by 2.5 kilos per year, with a unique intensity during the pubertal growth spurt or peak height velocity (PHV) (Wilmore and Costill 2004).

In order for coaches to fully individualise training for every young athlete, it is essential that they identify as closely as possible each athlete's PHV and assess their movement capabilities (strength, speed, endurance, skill and flexibility) to help establish a young performer's level of readiness for various training regimes and be able to set corresponding training loads (volume, intensity, duration, etc.) that are developmentally appropriate.

REFLECTION

During this rapid growth phase of PHV, there may be a period when young athletes' basic skills and abilities are impaired and they may look uncoordinated and clumsy. This is common and should not be a cause for concern. The body is just behind in learning to adapt to its rapidly changing form.

As a coach, what strategies would you adopt with an elite young athlete going through this stage?

Coaches need to exploit the onset of PHV, as it is considered a major movement skills learning period and provides a great opportunity to increase physical development and key movement functions (Jones et al., 2008).

Early versus late maturation

Even though every child passes through the same stages of development, the tempo and timing involved in passing through each stage are highly variable. There may be a difference

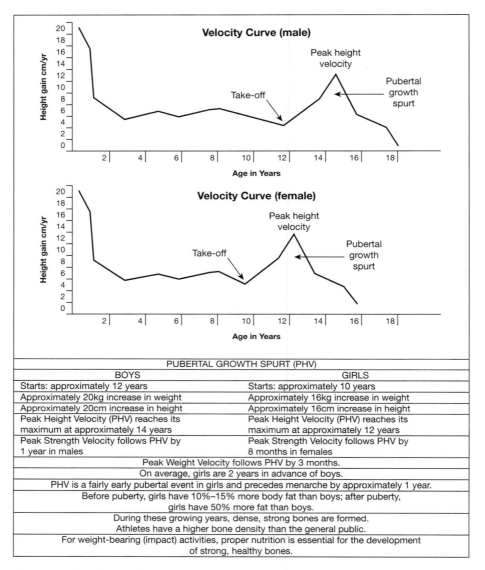

Figure 12.1 Pubertal growth spurt.

Source: Adapted from Russell (2006).

of plus or minus two years in development in maturity in a typical group of children of the same age (Stafford, 2005). For example, if we take a typical group of 13-year-olds, some may be operating developmentally more like a typical 11-year-old whereas others may be more like a typical 15-year-old, thus giving a potential overall difference of 4 years within such a group, which has obvious consequences for coaching practice and training programmes.

184
K. Wharton

Every coach has seen early-maturing children who tend to be several years in advance of the average, and in many cases they produce outstanding performances for their chronological age in the short term, but may struggle when peers catch up later. Coaches should be patient with late developers, who may be overwhelmed in some activities but will improve rapidly later. It is worthy of note that Michael Jordan, acclaimed as the greatest basketball player of all time, was cut from his sophomore varsity team because he was only 5' 9" (175 centimetres) tall at that time. But over the next two years he grew by 8 inches (20 centimetres) and developed enough skill and coordination while on the junior varsity squad to be on the varsity team as a senior in high school. Imagine if he had been disillusioned with the sport and decided to stop when he was cut from the team!

REFLECTION

How can the small, late-maturing athlete who is exceptionally skilled but lacks the physical characteristics to match more mature athletes be nurtured and in some cases protected so that he or she will persist in the sport?

Maturational differences

One of my colleagues, Su Stewart, works with British Fencing and took the photograph shown in Figure 12.2. The two boys are the same chronological age (16 years) but there is an obvious difference in their skeletal age. Su stated that there was more than 50 centimetres' difference in height and 45 kilograms' difference in weight between the two boys.

When there is considerable disparity in terms of the physical make-up of two athletes, this will have a direct implication for coaching practice in terms of specific individual training programmes, psychological and social support, and competitive success (Martens, 2004). In contact and collision sports, such as rugby, it is obvious that the boy on the right would be at considerable risk if he played against the boy on the left. In sports where speed, strength and power are likely to determine the outcome, it is obvious that the boy on the left would have an advantage. In contrast, young athletes with a smaller stature are likely to have more success in sports such as diving and gymnastics.

Coaches involved with development programmes need to be aware that the differences in the rate at which children mature can have a significant impact on optimal training loads and an individual's competitive career. The growing child and adolescent can be divided into pre-pubertal, pubertal and post-pubertal stages. In each stage, the young athlete will have different physiological characteristics, and hence training loads and competition exposure must be planned very carefully and in accordance with current knowledge of the growing athlete (Wilmore and Costill, 2004).

Figure 12.2 British National Under-17 Fencing Championships, 2005.

Source: Photo courtesy of Su Stewart.

Research suggests that early-maturing individuals are more likely to be selected through talent identification programmes than late-maturing players (Malina *et al.*, 2000). Therefore, there is an inherent bias towards stronger, more physically developed athletes. This can lead to late-maturing athletes missing out on elite coaching and/or dropping out of the sport at an early age. With this in mind, national governing bodies of sport and coaches should accommodate such differences by providing developmental programmes that permit and encourage both early and late entry into high-performance sport. This could involve competition 'age banding' of two or three years and selection onto development programmes based on potential rather than just on existing skill level. In addition, athletes should be monitored for progress and improvement rather than against a baseline score.

The timing of selection events can also be a limiting factor in selection. I know from my years in teaching that many of the boys selected for school soccer teams were born in the early part of the academic year, and their selection was related to their physical maturation. Some of the boys had up to 11 months' advantage over their peers born at the end of the academic year.

Coaches with great practical experience will tell you that, quite often, late maturers not only are superior performers but also, because they have not been involved in high-pressure competitive situations with the associated psychological pressures for as long as their early-maturing counterparts, tend to have a longer competitive 'shelf life' and a more positive outlook on their sport (Table 12.1).

REFLECTION

Research suggests that many sports systematically exclude late-maturing athletes and favour average and early-maturing athletes as chronological age and sport specialisation increase. Identify selection criteria to address this situation.

K. Wharton

Table 12.1 Characteristics of early versus late maturity

Early maturity	Late maturity
Generally taller than their peers.	Small stature.
Generally heavier than their peers.	Narrow hips.
Succeed at an earlier age in sports that require power and strength.	Low adiposity. High strength to weight ratio.
Early-developing children should be restrained or controlled in their training progress. The coach should ensure that their skill learning and development is not neglected or minimised in view of the relative success achieved by virtue of their advanced development.	Catch up to early maturers in height in late adolescence, but they do not catch up in weight.
Tend to have a shorter competitive career.	Tend to have a longer competitive career.

Ten years to create a world-class athlete – or is there another way?

Ericsson *et al.* (1993) implied that it takes a minimum of ten years to develop a talented athlete to world-class level. This 'ten-year plan' equates to 10,000 hours of training, deliberate practice and competition for approximately 3 hours a day for every day of the ten-year period. However, this is a contentious area within Ericsson *et al.*'s (1993) framework of deliberate practice and the theoretical belief that the probability of achieving excellence is increased with early specialisation. There are other experts who advocate a delayed approach to specialisation (Côté and Hay, 2002). One such approach is talent transfer. This is based on the assumption and observations that the skills and physical characteristics acquired by athletes in one sport can be transferred to another; for example gymnasts transferring to diving, or football players to other invasion games.

REFLECTION

Consider your own sport – think about the skills, tactics and physical requirements required to be a successful performer. What other sports require similar characteristics? Would you be willing to 'pass on' a young athlete who in your view would be better suited to another sport or have the potential to be more successful in a different sport?

Injury issues and maturation

As a senior athlete myself, I was very aware when I had an injury, but when I moved into coaching I found that on many occasions young athletes do not tell you when they have a niggle or strain; they put up with a lot of pain and feel as if they have few limitations. As a coach, you must be aware of this; dealing with child athletes is very different from dealing with adults, not only because of the child's physical immaturity but also because of their emotional and psychological needs. When you discuss injuries and training with a 12-year-old, it is very different from talking with a 25-year-old. The attitude of 'win at all costs' and 'try to work through your injuries' is unacceptable coaching practice and should be avoided at all times.

Why are child athletes more vulnerable?

The difference in the rate of growth between bone and soft tissue places the child athlete at a greater risk of overuse injury. Especially vulnerable are the apophyses, the articular cartilage and the physes (growth plates). The growth plate is the area of growing tissue near the ends of the long bones in children and adolescents. The growth plate is considerably weaker than the rest of the bone. These plates are the weakest areas of the growing skeleton – weaker than the surrounding ligaments and tendons – and therefore they are vulnerable to injury.

Coaches must be aware that growth plates are widest and most vulnerable to damage during the adolescent growth spurt. The types of training that coaches set for their young athletes may result in injuries to the epiphyseal and/or apophyseal growth plates. Coaches must be even more careful when working with late-maturing athletes, as they have growth plates for a longer period of time and are therefore more vulnerable to such injuries.

REFLECTION

You are coaching a group of 15-year-old athletes in your particular sport. What factors would you need to consider if you wanted to reduce the risk of growth plate injuries when planning their training programmes?

Implications for disordered eating

Young athletes, especially girls, are more vulnerable to the onset of eating disorders than are people in society at large, owing to the very nature of what makes for athletic success (Ryan, 1999). The required commitment to intense training, with its physical demands combined with the prospect of achievement, invariably attracts individuals who are competitive, and often perfectionist by nature. In almost every sport, as athletes progress to elite levels of competition they will experience an increasing emphasis from coaches and other support staff on the recording of personal data. Physical factors such as weight, the dimensions of the body, physique, and percentage of body fat become increasingly important as the 'competitive edge' is sought. This pressure to meet sometimes unrealistic weight goals may lead to problems associated with disordered eating, including anorexia and/or bulimia nervosa. These disorders may affect the growth process, influence hormonal function, cause amenorrhoea and low bone mineral density and other serious illnesses that may be life threatening (Wilmore and Costill, 2004). Table 12.2 identifies some of important points for the coach after he or she has read around the subject.

Anorexia and bulimia nervosa are serious health concerns that generally require someone close to the athlete – a coach, team-mate or family member – to recognise the warning signs and seek professional help.

Table 12.2 The signs of an eating disorder

Anorexia nervosa	Bulimia nervosa	Physical problems	Psychological problems
Pursuit of a thin body shape through strict dieting which leads to a drastic weight loss	Strong desire for thinness	Cavities and gum disease, osteoporosis	Feeling of low self-worth
Obsession for thinness is accompanied by a fear of being fat	Interrupted by episodes of binge eating	Gastrointestinal disturbance and dehydration	Social withdrawal
Obsession about food intake	Feelings of guilt and lack of control	Hair, nails and skin problems	Depression
Compulsive about exercise. Wearing of layered clothing	Eating is followed by efforts to avoid calorie absorption by vomiting, laxative abuse, excessive exercise or extended periods of fasting	Kidney damage, swollen salivary glands, electrolyte imbalance, irregular heartbeat, dizziness, fainting, headaches	Inability to identify or cope with feelings
Excessive self-criticism		Absence of menstruation	Mood swings and irritability
Unrealistic expectations		Water retention and bloating	Guilt and shame
Sleep disorders		Extreme sensitivity to cold	

KEY 'SENSITIVE PERIODS' FOR PHYSICAL AND SKILL DEVELOPMENT

For many activities, such as ice-skating, diving, gymnastics and swimming, establishing a broad repertoire of skills at an early age is vital, partly because world-class careers in those sports are often over by the age of 26. Many other sports also require an early acquisition of technical ability. This broad repertoire of skills should be taught correctly and appropriately from the start; how many times have you seen a talented athlete with ingrained poor technique?

For any young athlete, prior to the first major growth spurt there is a key period of skill acquisition and technical refinement. If there is a prolonged period of poor practice during this stage with little correction of errors, poor technique will result, and changing it will be very difficult.

Gone are the days of passing your talented performers from inexperienced coaches to more senior coaches and so on until they reach the high-performance coach several years later. We must adopt a more structured approach to the development of young athletes. The most valuable contribution that national governing bodies and high-performance clubs can contribute to the development of talented young athletes is the deployment of their best coaches to work with these young athletes from the start and a focus on key periods of opportunity for physical and skill development (Stafford, 2005).

Sensitive periods of development

The sensitive periods of development are important periods that refer to a point in the development of a specific behaviour or characteristic when training or practical experience can have the most beneficial effect on development. The same experience introduced at an earlier or later time may have little or no effect on or may hinder later skill development. All the energy systems are always trainable to some extent, but during the 'sensitive' periods accelerated adaptation should take place if the appropriate volume, intensity and duration of training are implemented (Table 12.3).

Table 12.3 Sensitive periods for physical and skill development

Element	Age and associated issues	
	Girls	Boys
Speed 1	Age 6–8: Speed/agility/quickness (SAQ) development	Age 7–9: SAQ development
Speed 2	Age 11–13 (anaerobic alactic power)	Age 13–16 (anaerobic alactic power)
Strength	Towards the end and immediately after PHV	12–18 months after PHV (testosterone spike)
Flexibility	Develop early and maintain	Develop early and maintain
Endurance	General training before PHV; the optimal trainability for endurance occurs after the onset of PHV (age 12–15)	General training before PHV; the optimal trainability for endurance occurs after the onset of PHV (age 14–16)
Skill	Age 8–11	Age 9–12

Source: Adapted from Russell (2006).
Note: PHV = peak height velocity.

REFLECTION

The belief expressed by many coaches that we must 'catch them when they're young' has been supported by a philosophy that in order to achieve success at senior level, it is necessary to start intensive training well before puberty (Baxter-Jones and Mundt, 2007).

At the 2008 Beijing Olympics, gymnast Oksana Chusovitina, who competed for Germany, took a silver medal on vault at the age of 33 and she said, 'I want to go to London in 2012 – I will only be 37!'

Reflect on both statements. Will either have any impact on your coaching practice?

Do children need to specialise in one sport early in their athletic career and will this give them a head start?

PSYCHO-SOCIAL ISSUES AND GOAL SETTING

When working with children in high-performance sport, coaches must be aware of the risks of 'burn-out' from physical and emotional stress, missed social and educational opportunities, and disruptions to family life. Since elite sport is mostly a phenomenon that occurs during late childhood and early adulthood, it is important to put this into a 'whole life' perspective. I remember one of my gymnasts telling me that 'my performance is more important than anything else in my life'. While his commitment has to be applauded and is a prerequisite of exceptional performance, what would have happened had he failed?

As coaches, we must be aware of the impact that elite sport has on young athletes and their personalities and motivational state. Their young performers being constantly put into competitive situations with resulting highs and lows associated with success and failure should be a major concern to coaches. Young athletes are under constant scrutiny and their performance achievements are highly visible to many 'significant others', sometimes on the world stage. These experiences will obviously have a great impact on athletes' self-worth and confidence, and will need careful nurturing by coaches and support staff.

We must remember that, as coaches, we have a significant impact on young athletes. They are so impressionable that what we say and do can often 'make or break' them. It is therefore imperative that the quality of these interactions is of the highest standard, and we must be aware that the enthusiasm generated can be such a key developmental force in a young athlete's career. The promotion of a 'win at all costs' ethic has both short-term and long-term detrimental effects on impressionable young athletes.

Evidence for the use of goal setting as an extremely powerful technique for enhancing performance has received considerable attention in the literature (Weinberg et al., 2000), but it must be implemented correctly. Coaches and athletes must set the right kind of goals, goals that provide direction and enhance motivation. We must help our athletes learn how to persevere and achieve aims by setting effective goals and designing appropriate programmes.

Be aware that:

- The early years of excellent training are crucial in helping to develop physical and mental competence.
- Achievement of early goals increases commitment to future goals and confidence in present ones.
- Coaches help increase confidence by being positive and having realistic expectations.

If coaches can make their training sessions enjoyable, then there is more chance of athletes having a 'good time'. I have seen young athletes accept discomfort, tolerate hard coaching sessions and fatigue, and be unaware of the length of the session just because they were enjoying themselves. This should prompt coaches to reflect on their coaching practice and session planning. Is it fun, enjoyable, varied and athlete centred?

192

In terms of letting young athletes have some form of childhood and social life, coaches must remember that young athletes are still children or adolescents and have the needs of such. If you always ban them from going out with their friends, attending parties or other social events, they are likely to feel resentment and their training will start to be affected. Coaches should be more athlete centred and flexible when designing training programmes and discuss issues such as the scheduling of sessions with their athletes so that a balance can be negotiated between training and having some sort of life outside sport. Therefore, coaches need to involve young athletes more in their own goal and programme planning so that a strict 'power/tell' relationship does not exist. It could be argued that effective high-performance training regimes necessitate the availability of the interconnecting disciplines and processes shown in Figure 12.3 in order to form a complete system to meet the sporting, social and emotional needs of the child in high-performance sport.

THEORY INTO PRACTICE

Practical implications for coaches

- Coaches should keep a regular check on athletes' weight and height so that they can identify growth spurts and restructure training programmes accordingly, but should demonstrate sensitivity with this issue, especially during the athletes' adolescence. Regular testing and monitoring of an athlete's performance and physical capabilities, against their own achievements, should be undertaken to keep coaches and young athletes informed of progress. Athletes should be grouped in terms of skeletal age rather than chronological age when taking part in physical conditioning and fitness work.
- Coaches should be prepared to change and adjust the training loads, methods and practices to fit the physical, psychological and performance outcomes as the athletes develop along the performance pathway.
- Skill development plans should be developed for each young athlete, and these should be discussed and agreed by you and the athlete. In conjunction with this, you will need to devise a specific and individualised training programme for each athlete, and this needs to be constantly reviewed.
- Remember that the social development of your athletes is just as important; there needs to be a balance of social and physical development. This may require some discussion and flexibility between you and your athletes in terms of altering training times and sessions occasionally so that your athletes can socialise with their peers.
- It is the coach's role to coordinate all the support systems, such as doctors, physiotherapists and performance analysts.
- Use simulation and modelling of various situations in the course of competition preparation, as this is very important for young performers.
- Do not take extreme decisions to 'drop' athletes from your squad before they reach the age of 16. Remember, big changes occur during PHV.

193

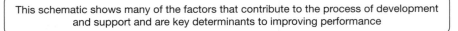

This schematic shows many of the factors that contribute to the process of development and support and are key determinants to improving performance

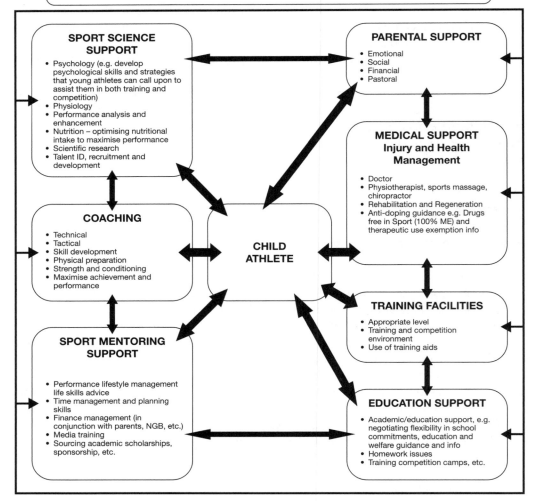

SPORT SCIENCE SUPPORT
- Psychology (e.g. develop psychological skills and strategies that young athletes can call upon to assist them in both training and competition)
- Physiology
- Performance analysis and enhancement
- Nutrition – optimising nutritional intake to maximise performance
- Scientific research
- Talent ID, recruitment and development

COACHING
- Technical
- Tactical
- Skill development
- Physical preparation
- Strength and conditioning
- Maximise achievement and performance

SPORT MENTORING SUPPORT
- Performance lifestyle management life skills advice
- Time management and planning skills
- Finance management (in conjunction with parents, NGB, etc.)
- Media training
- Sourcing academic scholarships, sponsorship, etc.

CHILD ATHLETE

PARENTAL SUPPORT
- Emotional
- Social
- Financial
- Pastoral

MEDICAL SUPPORT
Injury and Health Management
- Doctor
- Physiotherapist, sports massage, chiropractor
- Rehabilitation and Regeneration
- Anti-doping guidance e.g. Drugs free in Sport (100% ME) and therapeutic use exemption info

TRAINING FACILITIES
- Appropriate level
- Training and competition environment
- Use of training aids

EDUCATION SUPPORT
- Academic/education support, e.g. negotiating flexibility in school commitments, education and welfare guidance and info
- Homework issues
- Training competition camps, etc.

Figure 12.3 Multidimensional model for development and support for children in high-performance sport.

Educational issues

The combination of education and training in elite sport is an acute problem. When designing training programmes, coaches must consider academic demands on the child. Programmes should take into account academic loads, timing of exams and physical education activities. A good idea is to get a copy of the athlete's timetable and any forthcoming examination dates and work deadlines. This will allow you to plan ahead and limit or resolve any potential conflicts between the athlete's sporting and other commitments in advance. Wherever possible, training camps and additional training sessions should complement, not conflict with, major academic events at school. Coaches should be in regular contact with the school, the athlete and their parents to establish and maintain an effective support structure. Schools may have a policy for dealing with gifted and talented students, and this will outline how the school supports the additional demands made on child athletes. Some possible ways may include a flexible approach to curriculum delivery, homework, examinations, and distance learning, or athletes being excluded from certain aspects of the curriculum. With knowledge of key educational considerations, coaches and athletes can set realistic goals and plan more effective training programmes to reduce the pressure that many child athletes feel between school and sport.

CASE STUDY

Tom Daley (aged 15) became Britain's first world diving champion, in July 2009. However, he has had some difficult moments since he qualified for an Olympic final in Beijing. Daley was forced to move schools after being subject to bullying and is now settled in with a scholarship at Plymouth College. He said, 'Everything is going well because there are 50 other elite athletes there who understand the pressures of high-level competition so it's great to be among them and not stick out like a sore thumb.'

Plymouth College offers a flexible academic programme and timetable for international athletes, access to support services, smaller class sizes and individual support.

SUMMARY

Coaches must remember that there is great variability in the rates of athletic development. Most of the talented athletes I have worked with were multi-talented across a range of sports and transferred their skills and physical capabilities, some in less time than others. Coaches must not be restricted by historical viewpoints on talent development of elite child athletes but should remain open-minded to any opportunities that can enhance the talent development pathway and actually keep athletes on it long enough for them to reach their true potential. It is the coach's job to maximise child athletes' development by focusing on their physiological, psychological, technical, educational and social development in association with support structures by providing a holistic training environment that is coach driven and athlete focused. Remember, working with children in sport is a long-term investment. If we want the adult athlete stars of tomorrow, we must be patient and careful with the child athletes today.

LEARNING MORE

Further sources of information and guidance on several issues relating to child athletes are available for coaches in *Coaching Science* by Dan Gordon (2009), and a couple of articles by Istvan Balyi. Some resources have been produced specifically to support gifted and talented athletes in school and can be accessed at www.youthsporttrust.org and http://nationalstrategies.standards.dcsf.gov.uk/giftedandtalented?stakeholder=14. Issues related to talent transfer can be accessed at www.uksport.gov.uk. Information about athlete support is available at www.olympic.org/en/content/Olympic-Athletes/ Elite-Athletes, www.ausport.gov.au/ais and www.sportandstudy.org.

REFERENCES

Balyi, I. (1998a) Long-term planning of athlete development. *FHS* 1 (September): 8–11.

Balyi, I. (1998b) The training to compete phase. *FHS*, 2 (December): 8–13

Baxter-Jones, A. and Mundt, C. (2007) The young athlete. In N. Armstrong, N. Spurway and D. MacLaren (eds), *Paediatric exercise physiology*. Philadelphia: Churchill Livingstone.

Côté, J. and Fraser-Thomas, J (2008) Play, practice and athlete development. In D. Farrow, J. Baker and C. MacMahon (eds), *Developing sport expertise*. London: Routledge.

Côté, J. and Hay, J. (2002) Children's involvement in sport: a developmental perspective. In J.M. Silva III and D.E. Stevens (eds), *Psychological foundations of sport* (2nd ed.). Boston, MA: Merill.

Ericsson, K.A., Krampe, R.T. and Tesch-Römer, C. (1993) The role of deliberate practice in the acquisition of expert performance. *Psychological Review* 100(3): 363–406.

Gordon, D. (2009) *Coaching Science*. Poole, UK: Learning Matters

Jones, R.L., Hughes, M. & Kingston, K. (2008) *An introduction to sports coaching: from science and theory to practice*. London: Routledge

Malina, R.M., Pena, R., Eisenmann, J.C. and Horta, L. (2000) Height, mass and skeletal maturity in elite Portuguese soccer players aged 11–16. *Journal of Sports Sciences* 18: 685–693.

Martens, R. (2004) *Successful coaching* (3rd ed.). Champaign, IL: Human Kinetics.

Russell, K. (2006) Fédération Internationale de Gymnastique – Academy L3 Resource Manual. Lausanne: FIG.

Ryan, J. (1999) *Little girls in pretty boxes: the making and breaking of elite gymnasts and figure skaters*. London: Women's Press.

Stafford, I. (2005) *Coaching for long-term athlete development: to improve participation and performance in sport*. Leeds: Coachwise.

Weinberg, R.S., Burton, D., Yukelson, D. and Weigand, D. (2000) Perceived goal setting practices in Olympic athletes: an exploratory investigation. *Sport Psychologist* 14: 279–295.

Wilmore, J.H. and Costill, D.L. (2004) *Physiology of sport and exercise* (3rd ed.). Champaign, IL: Human Kinetics.

CHAPTER THIRTEEN

COACHING DISABLED CHILDREN IN SPORT

KEN BLACK

CHAPTER OUTLINE

- Systemic approaches and models of inclusion
- Sporting pathways: physical education to community to performance
- Real lives: some guidelines based on coach and participant experiences

---

INTRODUCTION

A plethora of practical and theoretical advice has been produced in the past 25 to 30 years about how to provide opportunities for young disabled people in physical activity and sport. This has included many books and manuals, academic papers in journals or conference proceedings, resource cards, videotapes, CD-ROMs and DVDs. This material has been developed by specialists in adapted physical activity, disability sport organisations, educationalists and practitioners from the higher, secondary, primary and special education fields, coach educators, and, more recently, an increase in sport-specific input from sports governing bodies, federations and related agencies. As a practitioner in inclusive physical activity and disability sport for the past 30 years, I have been fortunate to enjoy many practical sessions with coaches, physical educationalists, sports leaders and volunteers, working with them to share ideas and strategies to enable them to better include disabled children in their sports and programmes. A request common to all of these many sessions has been for practical models and methods and easy-to-grasp ways of making inclusion work. This request has helped shape the chapter, which will:

- highlight commonalities across a selection of these ideas and strategies, and offer practical suggestions that will enable the coach or coach educator to approach the inclusion of young disabled people with confidence and show that inclusive practice has benefits in any coaching and teaching situation;

197

- consider some examples of infrastructural models developed to create pathways in sport for young disabled people and the potential role of the coach in these systems;
- identify some coaching guidelines based on real-life experiences of disability sport coaches and current and former participants.

Throughout this chapter, discussions will be supported by the views of practitioners working within inclusive physical activity and disability sport.

SYSTEMIC APPROACHES AND MODELS OF INCLUSION

A parallel universe

Sport, whether for disabled or non-disabled participants, is often represented as a pathway starting with participation and basic skill acquisition in community or school, perhaps leading to local and club competition and ultimately, for the few, the achievement of high-level performance. The traditional 'pyramid model' of sports development is examined in detail in Chapter 3 of this book. In the area of disability sport, this pathway is combined with an element of separateness, the pinnacle of which, for many, is defined by the Paralympics, the ultimate arena within which disabled people can compete with their peers. However, in some ways it can be seen as a monument to segregation. Hargreaves (2000: 181, quoted in Thomas and Smith 2009: 120) said of the Stoke Mandeville Games (commonly held to be a Paralympic precursor):

> [I]t was not the sporting abilities of the athletes that was the raison d'être of competition, but rather it was their disabilities that created a sportsworld specifically for them – separate, spatially and symbolically, from the 'real' world of sport outside.

Although for the athletes this may have changed, media treatment has continued to focus on the 'superhuman' aspect of overcoming adversity, delivered in short bursts around high-profile events. For the vast majority of disabled children and adults, however, it is the everyday access to opportunities in physical activity and sport in school and community that restricts choice and defines difference. In a recent extensive consultation exercise conducted in Australia with the users of disability services, and the staff, parents and carers who support them, the lack of interface between sport and ordinary disabled people was still apparent (Australian Sports Commission, 2009). In developed countries such as the United Kingdom and Australia, only a few hundred disabled athletes achieve Paralympic status, a tiny proportion of the wider disabled population.

K. Black

REFLECTION

Thomas and Smith (2009) pose the following challenging questions:

- Has the limited coverage of elite disabled athletes . . . helped to challenge dominant perceptions of, and the issues surrounding, impairment, disability and disabled people's lives?
- Or has it resulted in consequences that . . . may well be the reverse of what was intended by the advocates involved?

What do you think? Reflect on the central issues involved here: does the emphasis on the achievements of the few deflect attention from the legitimate rights and desires of the many? It is important for coaches working with, or who contemplate working with, disabled participants, to consider this seemingly contradictory dichotomy.

See Hargreaves (2000) and Thomas and Smith (2009).

The accursed acronym

A number of models of inclusion targeting inclusive practice in physical education and school sport have emerged over recent years. In the United Kingdom, the Youth Sport Trust developed the STEP model (Youth Sport Trust, 2011) as a framework for activity differentiation on its TOP Sport activity cards and supporting material in 1997. For example:

- **S** – Space (e.g. change the space in which the activity is taking place);
- **T** – Task (e.g. change the nature of the activity);
- **E** – Equipment (e.g. change the type, size or colour);
- **P** – People (e.g. change the people – the numbers and/or ways in which they are involved, and how they interact with each other).

In a parallel development, the Australian Sports Commission (ASC), through its Disability Education Program, uses a similar device in the form of the TREE acronym (Australian Sports Commission, no date b):

- **T** –Teaching/coaching style (e.g. how the teacher or coach organises, leads and communicates);
- **R** – Rules and regulations (e.g. changes to the rules governing games and activities to promote inclusion);
- **E** – Environment (e.g. changes to the space, for the whole group or individuals within the group);
- **E** – Equipment (e.g. as in STEP, change the size, weight, colour, etc.).

199

A more recent ASC programme, Active After-school Communities, launched in 2005, uses the 'Change it' principle to assist teachers, coaches and sports leaders in finding ways of making activities different in order to promote inclusion of all abilities (Australian Sports Commission, no date a; see also Bee, 2008: 77–86, who applies it to coaching scenarios):

- **C** – Coaching style
- **H** – How you score
- **A** – playing Area
- **N** – Number of players
- **G** – Game rules
- **E** – Equipment
- **I** – Intensity
- **T** – Time.

'Change it' has also been adopted by a number of national sporting organisations (governing body equivalents) in Australia. The recently established Football Federation Australia has incorporated this model into its coach education system as a practical planning tool (Football Federation Australia, no date).

These acronyms are useful as an aide-mémoire for coaches, and provide vehicles for activity adaptation and modification. These models can be applied to assist coaches differentiate tasks and skill development practices with *any* group of developing players or athletes.

Functional and structural models

The Inclusion Spectrum was developed in the late 1990s in the United Kingdom to provide a structure for inclusion. It was initially aimed at teachers and support staff working in mainstream schools to help them to better include young people who had statements of special educational needs in physical education programmes (Stevenson, 2009; Black and Williamson, in press: chapter 7). The Inclusion Spectrum consists of five different approaches to the organisation of physical activity arranged in a continuum of participation. The most appropriate level of inclusion can be selected according to the situation, such as age, ability and composition of the group; the nature of the activity; the environment; the equipment; and the number of support staff.

Disability sport activities are associated with all the other approaches. This means that activities originally aimed at disabled children and adults are 'reverse-integrated' to include all and can be used as the basis for open, modified, parallel or separate activities.

While the Inclusion Spectrum focuses on delivery approaches, Kasser and Lytle (2005: 138) concentrate on the process of adaptation and modification, outlining a step sequence aimed at the inclusion of all abilities in physical activity, which they label the FAMME model (a Functional Approach for Modifying Movement Experiences). Using this process in a logical

200

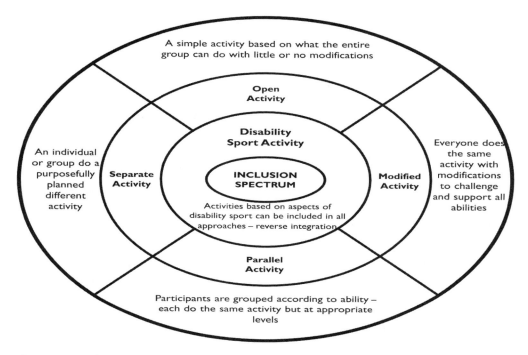

Figure 13.1 The Inclusion Spectrum model.

Copyright © Pam Stevenson and Ken Black, 2006.

way, coaches can apply their imagination and observational skills to modify activities appropriately for each participant.

FAMME sets out the following four-step procedure, and examples have been provided for greater clarity.

Step 1: Determine underlying components of skills – in other words, what components are necessary to perform a movement skill successfully. For example, moving to catch a ball involves eye–hand coordination, but it also involves speed, balance and spatial awareness. Differences affecting any of these components will require a modified approach. For example, in general, throwing and catching (or sending and receiving) are normally learned and practised together, as they are complementary. However, where an individual has coordination diffi-culties a large ball may be easier to catch and a smaller ball easier to throw. Therefore, for some children initial practices may involve coaching these skills separately using appropriate equipment.

Step 2: Determine current capabilities of the individual. For example, a difference in age will affect skill acquisition, with an 8-year-old child obviously having less strength, balance and coordination than an adolescent. A swimming coach might have less modification to consider with a swimmer who has a single lower-limb impairment than a coach working with a similar individual whose discipline is track athletics.

Step 3: Match modification efforts to capabilities. This means, for example, ensuring that modifications are necessary and support inclusion. If an individual is capable of holding a lightweight bat or racket, then their existing capabilities are reduced if the coach insists on attaching a full-size implement to the individual's arm using a glove-bat (an assistive device to enable a young person with an impaired or absent grip to participate in a racket sport).

Step 4: Evaluate modification effectiveness. Here the coach uses their powers of observation and analysis to check whether any suggested modification or adaptation is contributing to skill acquisition and development, or is failing to support, or even hindering, the process. For example, a coach observing the throwing action of a wheelchair user might focus on their arm action, when an adjustment in the positional angle of their wheelchair in relation to the direction of throw might enable the athlete to throw more freely.

Yet another inclusive activity acronym has been coined by Matt LaCortiglia, a physical educationalist at Perkins School for the Blind in Watertown, Massachusetts (LaCortiglia, 2009). This is an example of a process devised to meet the needs of a specific population, but with wider application in other settings. LaCortiglia's system, called FAIER, is essentially an individual-centred structure within which practitioners, such as coaches, can seek creative solutions, in progressive steps, to ensure the inclusion of young people in physical activity. The FAIER process is organised along a similar activity–modify–review process to that of Kasser and Lytle. Again, examples have been provided for greater clarity:

- *Foundation*. This involves identifying achievable goals for each participant, and the activities likely to lead to the goals being met. An example would be a strengthening activity leading to a long-term goal of improved performance in a throw. At this stage, it is also important to identify the strengths, capabilities and preferences of the individual, as these can be a starting point for the subsequent development of the activity. Finally, available resources required to conduct the sessions, such as space and equipment, are considered.
- *Awareness*. Here the coach takes into consideration any aspects specific to the individual. For example, certain communication methods may be required, such as 'finger Braille' for deaf-blind children, or regular reinforcement and repetition of key messages. These considerations should not be central to the process, but act more as 'supporting information'. For example, in a wider application a child who has an intellectual impairment may benefit more from an accurate demonstration of a skill than from a verbal explanation.
- *Implementation*. In this phase, the activity is constructed on the basis of the factors identified in the foundation and awareness stages. The activity or equipment used can be modified if this is necessary for the successful completion of the activity goal and progress towards the long-term goal.
- *Evaluation*. This is where the coach observes the individual's performance and suggests modifications or changes in technique or equipment. For example, manual guidance

may be needed to help reinforce verbal instruction. The safety of the activity can also be assessed.

- *Refinement*. The coach analyses the performance and suggests changes that might be required to challenge the individual further, or to develop a specific aspect leading towards attainment of the long-term goal.

These systems are designed to provide a structure against which teachers and coaches can apply task differentiation, where tasks are set and adapted, and support is provided to reflect the needs of the learner. The key factor is the flexibility of these systems, with potential application in any physical activity and sport scenario and across a range of abilities. The systems empower coaches, allowing them to change their approach or modify their delivery to provide optimum opportunities for the athletes. If the systems are truly participant centred, will they therefore not also empower the child as well as the coach?

REFLECTION

Find out more about these models in the texts and websites detailed in the References section:

- the TREE model
- the Inclusion Spectrum
- the FAMME model
- the FAIER process.

Compare their practical application and user-friendliness as tools of inclusion. Are they equally effective in the coaching environment, as opposed to supporting inclusion within physical education?

Would these models be inappropriate when working with *any* group of young people?

SPORTING PATHWAYS: PHYSICAL EDUCATION TO COMMUNITY TO PERFORMANCE

Ways and means

As discussed previously, models of inclusion have been consistently aimed at the inclusion of school-aged, disabled children in the physical education (PE) domain, although some question the nature and extent of inclusion within physical education or after-school provision (Thomas and Smith, 2009; Atkinson and Black, 2006). However, the various ways of achieving inclusion in practice will be less effective if they are not integrated within an infrastructure that creates an environment of opportunity, linking young disabled people to trained and motivated coaches and teachers.

A number of initiatives in different national sport systems have attempted to provide an interface between physical education and sport, connect young disabled people with participant pathways and provide a mechanism whereby coaches can develop inclusive practices. The following subsection highlights a few examples of best practice.

The Australian Sports Commission: Sports CONNECT

In Australia, the Disability Education Program (DEP), an education and training programme based on the creation of a network of coordinators and presenters in each state and territory, has been coordinated by the Disability Sport Unit at the Australian Sports Commission since 1995. Its aim has been to provide support to sport providers to assist them in creating opportunities for disabled people within their clubs, programmes and activities.

Acknowledging that the education and training focus had been mainly on the 'supply' side of the sporting equation, the DEP has been supplanted by Sports CONNECT (Australian Sports Commission, Disability Sport Unit, 2011), a national framework that works to build pathways for disabled people to get involved in sport by creating a positive and active interaction between sports and disability organisations and the people they support (the 'demand' side).

By 2009, Sports CONNECT had engaged with 25 national sporting organisations (NSOs), each funded for a period of five years and supported by a dedicated consultant, to develop inclusive policy and practice from board level to coaches working with athletes. This process encourages sports to take responsibility for *everyone* who wants to access their programmes. At state and territory level, the key relationship is with the departments of sport and recreation (within which most of the Sports CONNECT state or territory coordinators are based). One aspect of this relationship is to link inclusive practice NSOs with their state and territory equivalents. The Sports CONNECT network aims to create a supportive environment for local development, sometimes in targeted communities.

> I know of a disability sport club based in Tasmania that links children and adults into existing sport systems. It's designed to enable them to move on or remain within the club. Participation in open leagues enables better players to move on. However, the development of social and sports etiquette skills is just as important. Not all people go to clubs to achieve elite status.
> (Scott Goodman, Senior Coach, Athletes with Disabilities, Australian Athletics)

This system is leading to the embedding of inclusive coaching practice within mainstream coach education programmes. Where sporting bodies adopt this approach, coaches receive sport-specific inclusion information as part of their regular professional development. This

204

contrasts with the previous system in Australia, Coaching Athletes with Disabilities, and the inclusion modules offered by agencies such as sports coach UK, which are optional.

The Youth Sport Trust: Playground to Podium

In England, the Youth Sport Trust, in conjunction with Sport England, UK Sport and the British Paralympic Association, embarked on an ambitious project to form a pathway in sport for young disabled people that would take them from physical education, through community-based participation, to high-level performance and competition.

The framework, launched in 2006 and called Playground to Podium (P2P), has the ultimate target of discovering and preparing young disabled people for Paralympic representation, the initial target being the London Paralympics in 2012. However, it also hopes to broaden the participation base and provide opportunities at all levels.

Each component part of P2P is the responsibility of a different agency, linking school sport partnerships (community of primary, secondary and special schools clustered around a specialist sports college), county sport partnerships (networks of agencies promoting co-ordinating community sport at county level in England; see Sport England, 2011), national governing bodies of sport, sports coach UK (see www.sportscoachuk.org), and the English Federation of Disability Sport (see www.efds.co.uk). In this way, the participating agencies are encouraged to provide leadership and organisation within their sector, liaise with internal and external partners, and deliver agreed local and national outcomes.

> The process is a fairly simple one: high-quality PE; access to an enriched experience in school through events and on-site club; twin-track participation and coaching options, introducing a first competitive experience; higher-level performance coaching enabling progression and participation in regional events; a network of national events and squad systems underpinning selection for elite performance programmes.
> (Mark Botterill, Special Educational Needs and Inclusion Officer, Youth Sport Trust)

The P2P approach involves coaches at different stages along the pathway working with different levels of ability. However, the issue for them is to be aware of which agency is co-ordinating at each stage and providing them with a point of contact.

Disability Sport Wales

Disability Sport Wales (DSW; also known as the Federation of Disability Sport Wales) is accepted worldwide as an example of a successful and progressive national disability sport development model (see www.disabilitysportwales.org).

Following an initial pilot project in one local authority in 1997, the Sports Council for Wales utilised relaxed National Lottery funding regulations to initiate the recruitment of a specialist disability sport development officer in each of the 22 Welsh local authorities.

The pilot project had revealed two main issues:

- Locating a specialist disability sport development officer within a disability trust, and not within the local authority's own sports development team, left them 'outside the system' with reduced influence.
- There were no clear, identifiable exit routes from community level into competitive disability sport programmes.

Therefore, the Sports Council for Wales funded 50 per cent of the cost of the sports development officers, locating them within the sports development units and encouraging the local authorities to increase these to full-time appointments. By 2009, 70 per cent of the local authorities had created full-time posts.

A further review encouraged the local authorities to embed the work of these specialist officers within mainstream sports development programmes, treating them as a source of information and support rather than simply passing all disability-related issues in their direction.

The creation of a human resource network led to a subsequent vertical leap in participation, with only 1,200 opportunities per year for disabled people in 2002 but an impressive 320,000 opportunities by 2008.

The creation of an Academy programme in 2006 established a focus for a talent identification process, linking the increased grassroots opportunities to a player pathway for young disabled people. The Academy consists of three tiers:

- *Tier 3.* Emerging talent is identified, for example through DSW competitions or 'come and try' events held at community level. Athletes at this level are unlikely to have been classified for national or international disability sport.
- *Tier 2.* At this stage, at least six months into the programme, athletes have demonstrated achievement in competition and receive official sports classification. Tier 2 athletes receive support from Academy coaches and moderate financial support from DSW.
- *Tier 1.* These athletes have demonstrable talent and the potential to access the UK performance programmes (e.g. World Class potential through UK Sport). They will also receive enhanced support through the Sports Council for Wales.

The Academy programme identified 9 of 15 new athletes who achieved selection for the Great Britain Paralympic team for Beijing in 2008. In the Welsh system, coaches working with disabled athletes benefit from working within a clearly defined structure.

Big picture, narrow view

There are a number of important issues raised in these examples.

- Sports CONNECT is underpinned by an equity message, with a central aim of influencing sports providers to adopt inclusive policies and practices. However, it exists in parallel to the competitive sports focus of the Australian Paralympic Committee, with which it has only tenuous links. They each have independent relationships with the mainstream sport governing bodies.
- The Disability Sport Wales approach concentrated first on the creation of opportunities in physical activity and sport, followed by the development of a player pathway, leading towards a greater cultural understanding of inclusion as a result.
- Playground to Podium has a core philosophy of shared responsibility in order to achieve the goal of increased participation and talent identification, but is completely dependent on the ability and motivation of the constituent agencies to deliver their commitments.
- The funding that supports some of these programmes is linked directly to Paralympic sport pathways. However, Paralympic sport is open only to a minority of the disabled population.

Only 13 per cent (currently) of impairment groups in the UK can access Paralympic sport, which means 87 per cent of disabled people (as recognised by disability legislation) who can still access competitive sport may miss out.

(Ray Ashley, Regional Manager, English Federation of Disability Sport)

REFLECTION

Look again at the sports development models described previously (details of each can be explored through the specific references). What benefits are provided by each system for:

- the community coach;
- coaches working with higher-level athletes?

What does sports development need to consider at each level of participation? What is its most important resource?

REAL LIVES: SOME GUIDELINES BASED ON COACH AND PARTICIPANT EXPERIENCES

I gathered the views of a number of current and former Paralympic athletes, and those of individuals coaching and working in disability sport.

The coach

Most athletes expressed a preference for a coach who was:

- flexible
- a good communicator and listener
- knowledgeable
- patient
- prepared to share ideas
- trustworthy.

> Someone who doesn't think that they know everything. Someone who wants to learn. Someone who talks to athletes about their goals.
> (Baroness Tanni Grey-Thompson DBE, five-time Great Britain Paralympic athlete, winner of 11 gold medals, now retired)

The athlete

As expressed in the FAMME and FAIER systems previously described, it is important to know the existing skills, capabilities, knowledge and preferences of the participant. But it is also important to acknowledge that young disabled people may have had less opportunity to develop physical skills naturally than their non-disabled peers.

> The coach needs to establish the physical development and skill preparation of their athlete. It may be necessary to return to basics and spend time developing the fundamental movement skills that non-disabled children might develop through play.
> (Chris Nunn OAM, High Performance Manager, Australian Paralympic Committee)

The role of physical education varied according to individual experiences. Some athletes questioned did not feel that physical education had impacted on their later sports careers. Others felt that they had been included at primary level, but in the more competitive sport-specific environment of secondary school they spent more time on the sidelines.

> I had to fight to be included in the Talented Sports Program at high school.
> (Wade McMahon, current Australian Paralympic javelin athlete)

208

My parents encouraged me to take part in all activities, and this attitude was echoed by my school teachers and my peers.

(Don Elgin, former Australian Paralympic pentathlete)

One practitioner of long standing considered the issues from the viewpoint of the PE teacher, also suggesting how a two-way school–club process could be mutually beneficial:

Mainstream PE teachers face many challenges today: more behavioural and neurological conditions amongst schoolchildren; obese and passive children who struggle even with the basic motor skills because of too little daily activity; large group sizes; and lack of knowledge of mainstream PE teachers about disability sport. For all these reasons, teachers in inclusive settings are tempted to allow the non-participation of a significantly disabled child. We should work with schools to show them how their students can benefit from community sports programmes, how sports clubs can assist schools, and how the club coaches can learn from more contact with disabled children.

(Aija Saari, Development Manager, Finnish Disability Sport Association)

Motivation

There was a strong view about the role of the individual participant in terms of motivation.

Motivation should come from within; if it's not there in the first place, the coach cannot provide it.

(Fred Periac, former French/Australian Paralympic track and road athlete)

Another athlete supported the importance of self-motivation:

Sometimes when the coach is away for long periods, it can be hard to stay motivated and finish sessions. But training on your own does show how dedicated you are if you finish every session without taking short cuts.

(Wade McMahon, current Australian Paralympic javelin athlete)

Supporting continued participation

This view stresses the importance of continuing professional development mirroring the progress of the athletes.

A major barrier for young disabled people lies in the skills and capacity of people – teachers, coaches. Their level of expertise has to grow as the young person progresses through the coaching system.

(Mark Botterill, Special Educational Needs and Inclusion Officer, Youth Sport Trust)

When considering the content of this chapter, a conscious decision was taken to avoid a 'tips for coaches' approach. Instead, the author invites coaches to consider and use the models outlined above to challenge and question their current coaching practice, utilising their coaching expertise to expand opportunities for disabled children. The solutions lie with the enquiring mind and adaptable imagination of the coach.

REFERENCES

Atkinson, H. and Black, K. (2006) The experiences of young disabled people participating in PE, school sport and extra-curricular activities in Leicester-Shire and Rutland. Online, available at Leicester-Shire & Rutland Sport, www.lrsport.org – resource library section.

Australian Sports Commission (2001) *Give it a go: including people with disabilities in sport and physical activity*. Belconnen, ACT: ASC Publication Services Unit (previously published as *Willing and able: an introduction to inclusive practices*, 1995).

Australian Sports Commission (2009) 'Disability Sector Resource Project Consultation Phase Report. Online, available at: www.ausport.gov.au/__data/assets/pdf_file/0004/351265/Sports_CONNECT_Education_Report_FINAL.pdf

Australian Sports Commission (2011a) Active After-school Communities programme. Online, available at: www.ausport.gov.au/participating/schools_and_juniors/aasc (last accessed February 2011).

Australian Sports Commission (2011b) Participating in Sport, Disability, Resources. Online, available at: www.ausport.gov.au/participating/disability/resources (free activity card downloads showing TREE model; last accessed February 2011).

Australian Sports Commission, Disability Sport Unit (2011) Participating in sport: disability sport. Online, available at: www.ausport.gov.au/participating/disability (last accessed February 2011).

Bee, L. (2008) Inclusive coaching. In *Intermediate coaching: general principles manual*. Belconnen, ACT: ASC Publishing.

Black, K. (2008) Inclusive activities and games; slide presentation. Online, ICSSPE/CIEPSS, Berlin, available at: www.icsspe.org/index.php?m=13&n=80&o=114 (last accessed February 2011).

Black, K. and Williamson, D. (2011) Designing inclusive physical activities and games. In A. Cereijo-Roibas, E. Stamatakis and K. Black (eds), *Design for sport*. Farnham, UK: Gower.

Football Federation of Australia (2011) Inclusive planning. Online, available at: www.my footballclub.com.au/Inclusion/Pages/InclusivePlanning.aspx.

Hargreaves, J. (2000) *Heroines of sport: the politics of difference and identity*. London: Routledge.

Kasser, S.L. and Lytle, R.K. (2005) A functional approach for modifying movement experiences (FAMME). In *Inclusive physical activity: a lifetime of opportunities*. Champaign, IL: Human Kinetics.

K. Black

LaCortiglia, M. (2009) Adaptive physical education. Online, Perkins School for the Blind, Watertown, MA, available at: http://support.perkins.org/site/PageServer?pagename=Webcasts_Adaptive_PE_Matt_LaCortiglia (last accessed February 2011).

Sport England/county sport partnerships (2011) Online, available at www.sportengland.org/support__advice/county_sports_partnerships.aspx (last accessed February 2011).

Stevenson, P. (2009) The pedagogy of inclusive youth sport: working towards real solutions. In H. Fitzgerald (ed.), *Disability and youth sport*. London: Routledge.

Thomas, N. and Smith, A. (2009) *Disability, sport and society: an introduction*. London: Routledge.

Youth Sport Trust (2011) TOP Sportsability. Online, available at: www.youthsporttrust.org/page/top-sportsability/index.html (last accessed February 2011).

PART III

ON SPORT

CHAPTER FOURTEEN

GIRLS IN SPORT

RUTH JEANES

CHAPTER OUTLINE

- ▣ **Understanding girls' participation**
- ▣ **Girls' experiences of sport: a further constraint?**
- ▣ **Engaging girls in sport**
- ▣ **Theory into practice 1: involving girls in sport**
- ▣ **Theory into practice 2: retaining girls in sport**
- ▣ **Learning more**

INTRODUCTION

Girls' complex relationship with sport has been examined extensively by policy makers, practitioners and academics in recent years. At the heart of this analysis is the recognition that within the developed world, girls participate in sport less than boys. National surveys provide a mixed picture of girls' participation. While there has been a general increase in the number of girls involved in physical activity, overall, girls' participation rates consistently lag behind those of boys, particularly within organised sport. In the United Kingdom, for example, 75 per cent of boys frequently (ten times or more in the previous year) participate in sport outside of physical education (PE) lessons compared to 52 per cent of girls (Sport England/MORI, 2003). Female participation reduces significantly during the teenage years, with 40 per cent of girls dropping out of sport by the age of 14 (Youth Sport Trust/Office for Standards in Education, 2000).

Encouraging girls to participate in sport is a challenging process. However, some sports have been extremely successful at attracting large number of female participants. Football (soccer) in the United Kingdom, for example, has experienced a huge rise in the number of girls and women participating since the mid-1990s. The number of affiliated girls' teams rose from

80 in 1993 to over 8,000 in 2005 (FIFA, 2006), and it is now the most popular participation sport for both girls and women. It is evident, therefore, that while there are difficulties with both engaging and retaining girls in sports, in certain circumstances they can be willing and enthusiastic participants.

The purpose of this chapter is to enhance coaches' understanding of girls' relationship with sport and encourage them to think critically about how to involve them. There has been an extensive range of research detailing why girls are harder to engage than boys but the identified constraints emerging from this work can be divided into two overarching areas: reasons that prevent girls from getting involved in sport, such as wider social and cultural beliefs, and then, second, factors that turn girls off sport when they do take part, such as negative experiences in PE or poor sports leaders. This chapter provides an overview of both of these areas, what the implications are for coaches wishing to work with girls and how they can negate the issues raised to successfully involve girls in sport.

UNDERSTANDING GIRLS' PARTICIPATION

Cultural and social barriers

Encouraging girls to participate in sport can be a complex and challenging task. It is useful for coaches who wish to work with girls to be aware of some of the reasons why they may be reluctant to participate. The purpose of this section is to provide a brief overview of the broad social and cultural barriers known to limit girls' participation.

One of the major barriers to girls' participation is the dominant social belief that sport is a male pursuit and as a result is not part of an appropriate feminine identity (Cockburn and Clarke, 2002). Certain attributes associated with sport and athleticism (power, strength, speed and aggression) are considered masculine, which means that they are not associated with traditional feminine ideals and participation is neither an essential nor a relevant part of a female identity. As Duncan (2007: 49) explains, 'Gendering practices tend to promote limiting ideas of what behaviors are appropriate for girls; skill at sport and physical activity is not considered one of them.'

Girls are unlikely to see sport as an arena in which their femininity can be affirmed and therefore are less inclined to participate in sport than their male peers (Coakley and White, 1999). Reflecting this, only a quarter of girls believe it is 'cool' to be sporty or that 'being good at sport' is important for them (Institute of Youth Sport, 2000).

The potential conflict between developing an appropriate female body and the requirements of a sporting body has been identified as a further concern for girls and can reinforce the perception that if they participate in sport they will be seen as unfeminine. The slim, toned body image continues to prevail as the dominant ideal that females should be striving to achieve. Several studies have identified that girls dislike what sport 'does' to their bodies (that is, it makes

216

them sweaty and dirty, and develop muscle; Gorely *et al.*, 2003) and feel conflicts with their effort to develop an 'ideal' body. Women who do play sport, and particularly those with bodies that do not reflect the feminine ideal, are often perceived as butch, unfeminine and homosexual. Stereotypes that female athletes are lesbians still prevail and play a significant role in discouraging many girls from participating, particularly in non-feminine-appropriate sports.

Psychological barriers

Alongside these social and cultural barriers, analysis from a psychological perspective has identified a lack of confidence as undermining girls' desire to participate in sport regularly (Wigfield *et al.*, 1997). Girls from an early age are given less opportunity to play and explore their environment, and therefore do not develop core motor skills in the same way that boys do (Kane, 2006). When girls move into structured sports opportunities, it is quickly evident that they have lower skill levels than boys and develop perceptions about themselves as 'no good' at sport (Lee *et al.*, 1999). This in turn reduces their desire to participate and engage with sport: 'For some girls, such feelings of failure and inadequacy result in a life-long aversion to physical activity even if they started out interested in learning skills and playing sports' (Duncan, 2007: 37).

This lack of confidence can extend beyond sports ability to girls questioning their body shape and appearance when participating. Sport provides a setting where girls' body shape can be assessed and appraised (Evans, 2006). Dress requirements for sport can often perpetuate this feeling. Many girls discuss disliking PE because of the requirement to wear unflattering and often revealing kit (Choi, 2000). This can be important in discouraging girls from participating, particularly if they feel that their body does not reflect the slim, toned ideal. Whitehead and Biddle (2008: 256) describe how this is a key constraint for many girls:

> Their [girls'] acceptance of the prescribed norms relating to the 'thin ideal' or 'body beautiful' means that they feel embarrassed putting themselves 'on show' during sport and physical activity and do not like others to see them lest they do not measure up to the ideal body.

There is a common perception that girls are not interested in sport, and this reasoning is used to explain their lower participation rates. Illustrating the social, cultural and psychological constraints girls can experience assists with demonstrating the complexities of the problem. Girls are faced with a broad array of challenges that they must negate, and understandably this reduces the desire of many to pursue participation.

It is important to acknowledge that some girls are affected more than others by the barriers described. The constraints discussed can be particularly pertinent for girls from certain cultural and social backgrounds. Although it is identified that sport often does not hold a central position in Western girls' lives, for girls from ethnic minorities sport can have even less relevance. The following case study illustrates some of the challenges of working with diverse groups and how these can be overcome.

CASE STUDY: ENGAGING MUSLIM GIRLS IN SPORT

The 'Widening Access through Sport' project based at Loughborough University in the United Kingdom was developed to engage Muslim girls in regular sports opportunities. There was a recognition that girls from black and other ethnic minority groups participate less than other groups, and this project looked to address this recognition through a structured programme of sports opportunities. The project has successfully involved a group of Muslim girls who rarely participated in sport previously. A number of factors contributed to this success. Initially, deliverers discussed with girls why they disliked sport. The girls discussed problems with dress requirements for sport, a lack of support from parents, and inadequate changing and playing facilities. They were then asked to comment on how they felt these could be overcome and what activities they would find appealing to participate in. A programme of activities was developed shaped by their requests, and the girls were allowed to participate in their chosen clothing. Sports opportunities were organised in locations where the girls were able to access single-sex changing rooms and where rooms could be 'blocked off' to prevent male access. Female coaches were used for all activities and they were briefed by a community officer from the girls' local community, who was able to provide specific information on how to work with girls from Muslim communities and ensure their requirements were met. The girls have maintained their involvement and are now enthusiastic and willing participants in sport. For more information, see Lowrey and Kay (2005).

GIRLS' EXPERIENCES OF SPORT: A FURTHER CONSTRAINT?

Girls' disengagement with sport is influenced by the broader factors discussed, but increasingly research has highlighted that the experiences girls have when they do participate are also contributing significantly to female drop-out. Many girls would be willing participants but are being 'turned off' playing by negative and unenjoyable experiences when they do participate, particularly in school PE (Flintoff and Scraton, 2001).

It is important therefore to consider what contributes to poor participation experiences for girls and how coaches can avoid these within their own sessions. As this section will illustrate, leadership plays a pivotal role in engaging girls. Much of the research examining why girls have negative experiences of sport has focused on school PE (Wright, 1999). Available research highlights a multitude of reasons why girls dislike PE and subsequently attempt to avoid taking part in sport. In summary (Institute of Youth Sport, 2000; Garrett, 2004), these include:

- lack of inclusiveness: girls with lower ability being marginalised;
- overly competitive opportunities that highlight poor ability;
- teachers unsympathetic to girls' needs, and sports provided that do not reflect activities girls would like to take part in;
- teachers being overly critical of and aggressive towards girls;
- boys dominating mixed sessions and girls not having the opportunity to actively take part.

As the list indicates, many of the factors girls describe as putting them off sport emanate from poor leadership. The role of the coach in engaging girls is therefore a pivotal one (Biddle and Mutrie, 2001). Research examining girls' experience of PE is extremely useful for illustrating how poor experiences are created and what leaders should avoid when trying to encourage them to play sport. However, it also illustrates that when working with girls, coaches can encounter multiple demands, as Wiese-Bjornstal (2007: 7) highlights:

> Girls want coaches to provide good technical instruction and contingent positive feedback; allow them to participate in decision-making about goals, practices, and games; create positive team atmospheres; and develop warm interpersonal relationships with them. These characteristics of social relationships with coaches affect girls' continued participation through increasing their satisfaction with, and confidence in, their sport experiences.

The final section considers more specifically what creates positive sporting experiences for girls and how coaches can develop sessions that provide the requirements outlined.

ENGAGING GIRLS IN SPORT

Creating a 'girl-friendly' sports environment

As would be anticipated, girls are more likely to participate in sport when they find the experience enjoyable. Participating with friends is extremely important, and girls welcome sport environments that offer the opportunity to socialise and interact with other participants. As this teenage girl in my own research discusses, coaches who allow girls the chance to socialise in the sport setting are viewed positively:

> She [the coach] understands that we come because we want to spend time together and she lets us have a gossip and find out what's going on at the same time as doing stuff. When I went to netball it wasn't like that. The coach shouted at us all the time for talking and kept saying we weren't there to socialise but actually I was. I get to talk to lots of my friends in sport that I wouldn't normally see, that's why I like doing it.
>
> (Girl, aged 14)

A further factor girls discuss as contributing to enjoyment is how much competition is emphasised within sessions. Available research suggests that girls may differ in how much they require sports opportunities to be structured in a way that fosters competition and comparison. While it is recognised that many girls thrive on a competitive atmosphere, particularly those with high ability (Gorely et al., 2003), studies also suggest that some girls will only consider participating in informal, unstructured sessions that emphasise participation for its own sake (Whitehead and Biddle, 2008). Discussing this with girls, and tailoring sessions to reflect participants' desired outcomes and motivations for attending, is key to providing the 'right' environment for girls. From these conversations, coaches can determine how much girls require certain elements to be emphasised, such as competition, and construct sessions accordingly (Jones et al., 2004).

Coach–participant interactions: girls' preferences

How coaches interact with girls also contributes to their enjoyment of sports opportunities (Wiese-Bjornstal, 2007). Girls welcome coaches who are friendly, demonstrate a personal interest in them and are prepared to engage in a 'laugh and joke' with them (Jeanes and Kay, 2007). Lee (1993) indicates that effective coaches of young people are good communicators, and this appears to be a particularly important requirement for girls. Young athletes interviewed in Lee's research felt a sense of humour to be an essential coaching quality, something girls in my own research also discussed:

> It's [cricket sessions] just fun; he comes in and talks away to us then he asks how we are doing; then tells us what he's been up to and has a bit of a laugh with us. I just enjoy it; he makes you feel welcome and like he's interested in you.
>
> (Girl, aged 12)

As a result of the poor experiences many girls encounter in PE, it is important that coaches interact with girls differently than their teachers. Girls are extremely critical of coaches who are overly authoritarian and 'shout at them' when they make mistakes (Jeanes and Kay, 2007). In contrast, coaches who speak to them respectfully, facilitate participation in decision making and allow opportunities to influence sport session content are highly valued (Mageau and Vallerand, 2003).

Developing girls' sports skills

While girls want to participate in a supportive sports environment, they also place importance on skill improvement, regardless of initial ability (Martin et al., 1999). Girls comment favourably on coaches who facilitate skill development but within their capabilities and in a context where they are not required to compare their development with other participants'. A range of research suggests that coaches working with young people should look to foster a 'task-involving climate' that includes a focus on mastering skills and reinforcement for effort and improvement. Such an environment is more facilitative to producing enjoyment, satisfaction and motivation towards sport (Galloway, 2003). Girls reflect this need (Smith *et al.*, 2005), as one girl explained:

> I went along every week [to hockey coaching] but I don't think I got any better and I got bored . . . yeah, [the coach] was nice but she never told me really what I should be doing or how to do things better. She just got us doing things every week but never really said if we were doing them right or anything . . . I just got fed up and stopped.
>
> (Girl, aged 13)

It is recognised that coaches are highly competent in assisting participants with improving their sports skills. However, when attempting to address girls' other requirements for informality and non-pressurised learning, it can be easy to assume they have little desire to develop in their chosen sport. This can result in coaches simply providing space to engage in sport and not providing feedback and direction to support learning (Smith *et al.*, 2005). The important aspect emerging from my research in this area is that girls want to progress, regardless of ability. Girls with lower ability continually voiced their frustrations at being ignored by sports leaders and receiving only limited information on how they could improve. Coaches who provided regular feedback and delivered it in a way that did not highlight their lower ability were by contrast perceived to be good leaders and encouraged girls to continue participation (Weiss *et al.*, 1997).

SUMMARY

Encouraging and sustaining girls' participation is a complex process. Whereas previous research has tended to focus on the broader social and cultural barriers affecting girls and the need for coaches to overcome these, this chapter, while acknowledging the importance of this aspect, also suggests the need for a critical appraisal of the way sport is delivered if sports practitioners and leaders want to be successful at retaining girls in sport. It is important not to underestimate the cultural, social, psychological and physical constraints that have been identified as limiting girls' participation in sport. Equally, recognising the impact of ethnicity, social class and family circumstances on intensifying these barriers is critical. However, coaches must not consider these barriers insurmountable, and there is a growing body of evidence that suggests girls do negate them and when sport is delivered appropriately, they will willingly take part. Creating the 'right' environment can be difficult and frustrating for coaches but those who are successful are making significant contributions to challenging long-standing assumptions and values about women in sport as well as ensuring that girls access the numerous physical, psychological and social benefits that participating in sport can provide.

THEORY INTO PRACTICE 1: INVOLVING GIRLS IN SPORT

Although coaches may consider that many of the barriers discussed are outside their control, understanding what prevents girls from participating and the reasons they may drop out, and recognising that some girls face greater challenges than others, are important steps in addressing the issues discussed. Table 14.1 briefly outlines the key barriers and possible ways coaches can support girls in negating them.

The recommendations provided are only initial suggestions. Overarching all of these is the need for coaches to directly engage with the girls they are working with and allow them the opportunity to discuss any problems they feel they have with participating in sport. Such conversations allow coaches to be in an informed position when deciding how best to address the constraints girls face.

THEORY INTO PRACTICE 2: RETAINING GIRLS IN SPORT

There are a number of practical considerations emerging from research discussing girls' positive and negative sports experiences. The following list summarises how coaches can help bring about a positive sports environment for girls:

■ Consult with girls, understand their motivations for involvement and involve them in session planning.
■ Support girls to help them improve, and do not ignore those with limited ability.
■ Provide opportunities for 'chat' and socialising within sessions.
■ Communicate with girls respectfully and avoid being overly critical or aggressive.

R. Jeanes

Table 14.1 Involving girls in sport

Barrier/constraint	Recommendation for coaches
Perception of sport as unfeminine	▪ Encourage girls to discuss why they believe sport is inappropriate and encourage them to challenge this. ▪ Highlight a variety of female athletes as potential role models to illustrate that all types of women can and do play sport. ▪ Encourage girls to support and encourage one another to develop a belief that sport is an important and valuable part of their lives.
Lack of confidence, belief that sport 'is not for them'	▪ Structure sessions to allow girls to develop skills from a basic level. ▪ Reassure girls that skills can be developed and not having them currently is not an indication they are 'no good at sport'. ▪ Create a sports environment where individual accomplishments are valued rather than competition and comparison among girls.
Concerns about body image	▪ Allow girls as far as possible to participate in clothing they feel comfortable wearing. ▪ Ensure that any negative comments regarding girls' body shape are not left unchallenged.
Barriers for ethnic minority girls	▪ Facilitate discussions with girls to allow them to discuss their needs and structure sessions appropriately. ▪ Ensure appropriate changing facilities are available. ▪ Offer single-sex sessions where possible. ▪ Adjust clothing requirements to allow girls to remain fully covered if they wish.

Source: Adapted from the Women's Sports and Fitness Foundation's Barriers to Sport for Women and Girls factsheets, 2008.

LEARNING MORE

There is an extensive amount of information on the various barriers girls face that coaches can use in order to explore the issues highlighted in greater detail. A comprehensive overview is provided by the Tucker Center for Research on Girls and Women in Sport (Wiese-Bjornstal, 2007). More generic information and advice on involving girls in sport is provided by the Women's Sports and Fitness Foundation (2008a, b). For a more academic and theoretical perspective on the barriers discussed, see Scraton and Flintoff (2002). Specific information on involving girls from ethnic minorities is available from Kay (2006) and practical guidelines have been produced by Birmingham (UK) City Council (2008). Further detailed information on girls' experiences of PE and how this contributes to disengagement with sport is provided by Penney (2002) and Wright (1999). Coaches requiring further information on developing sessions that are appealing to girls should consult Jeanes and Kay (2007), the Tucker Center for Research on Girls and Women in Sport (Wiese-Bjornstal, 2007) and Mageau and Vallerand (2003).

REFERENCES

Biddle, S.J.H. and Mutrie, N. (2001) *Psychology of physical activity: determinants, well-being and interventions*. London: Routledge.

Birmingham City Council (2008) *Improving participation of Muslim girls in physical education and school sport: shared practical guidance from Birmingham schools 2008*. Birmingham: Birmingham City Council

Choi, P. (2000) *Femininity and the physically active woman*. London: Routledge.

Coakley, J. and White, A. (1999) Making decisions: how young people become involved and stay involved in sport. In J. Coakley and P. Donnelly (eds), *Inside sports*. London: Routledge.

Cockburn, C. and Clarke, G. (2002) Everybody's looking at you! Girls negotiating the 'femininity deficit' they occur in physical education. *Women's Studies International Forum* 25(6): 651–665.

FIFA (2006) *Big Count Survey Report*. Zurich: FIFA.

Duncan, M. (2007) Sociological dimensions of girls' physical activity participation. In Tucker Center for Research on Girls and Women in Sport, *Developing physically active girls: an evidence-based multidisciplinary approach*. Online, available at: www.cehd.umn.edu/tucker center/projects/TCRR/2007-Tucker-Center-Research-Report.pdf (accessed 5 May 2009).

Evans, B. (2006) 'I'd feel ashamed': girls' bodies and sports participation. *Gender, Place and Culture* 13(5): 547–561.

Flintoff, A. and Scraton, S. (2001) Stepping into active leisure? Young women's perceptions of active lifestyles and their experiences of school PE. *Sport, Education and Society* 6(1): 5–21.

Galloway, M.K. (2003) In the classroom and on the playing field: lessons from teachers and coaches for cultivating motivation in adolescence. *Dissertation Abstracts International* 64(9-A), 3188A (ATT no. 3104225).

Garrett, R. (2004) Negotiating a physical identity: girls, bodies and physical education. *Sport Education and Society* 9(2): 223–237.

Gorely, T., Holroyd, R. and Kirk, D. (2003) Muscularity, the habitus and the social construction of gender: towards a gender-relevant physical education. *British Journal of Sociology of Education* 24(4): 429–448.

Institute of Youth Sport (2000) *Towards girl-friendly physical education: the Nike/YST Girls in Sport Partnership Project final report*. Loughborough: Institute of Youth Sport (authors: D. Kirk, H. Fitzgerald, J. Wang and S. Biddle).

Jeanes, R. and Kay, T. (2007) 'She had to buy a football book to do it: issues in the leadership of physical activity for girls. *Physical Education Matters*, Summer: 32–36.

Jones, R., Armour, K. and Potrac, P. (2004) *Sports coaching cultures: from theory to practice*. London: Routledge

Kane, E. (2006) No way my boys are going to be like that! Parents' responses to children's gender nonconformity. *Gender and Society* 20(2): 22–44.

Kay, T.A. (2006) Daughters of Islam. *International Review for the Sociology of Sport* 41(3–4): 339–355.

Lee, M. (1993) Why are you coaching children? In M. Lee (ed.), *Coaching children in sport: principles and practice*. London: E&FN Spon.

Lee, A.M., Fredenburg, K., Belcher, D. and Cleveland, N. (1999) Gender differences in children's conceptions of competence and motivation in physical education. *Sport, Education and Society* 4(2): 161–174.

Lowrey, J. and Kay, T. (2005) Doing sport, doing inclusion: an analysis of provider and participant perceptions of targeted sport provision for young Muslims. In A. Flintoff, J. Long and K. Hylton (eds), *Youth, sport, and active leisure: theory, policy and participation*. Eastbourne, UK: Leisure Studies Association.

Mageau, G.A. and Vallerand, R.J. (2003) The coach–athlete relationship: a motivational model. *Journal of Sports Sciences* 21(11): 883–904.

Martin, S.B., Jackson, A.W., Richardson, P.A. and Weiller, K.H. (1999) Coaching preferences of adolescent youths and their parents. *Journal of Applied Sport Psychology* 11(2): 247–262.

Penney, D. (ed.) (2002) *Gender and physical education: contemporary issues and future directions*. London: Routledge.

Scraton, S. and Flintoff, A. (2002) *Gender and sport: a reader*. London: Routledge.

Smith, S.L., Fry, M.D., Ethington, C.A. and Li, Y. (2005) The effect of female athletes' perceptions of their coaches' behaviors on their perceptions of motivational climate. *Journal of Applied Sport Psychology* 17(2): 170–177.

Sport England/MORI (2003) *Young People and Sport Survey, 2002*. London: Sport England.

Weiss, M.R., Ebbeck, V. and Horn, T.S. (1997) Children's self-perceptions and sources of competence information: a cluster analysis. *Journal of Sport and Exercise Psychology* 19: 52–70.

Whitehead, S. and Biddle, S. (2008) Adolescent girls' perceptions of physical activity: a focus group study. *European Physical Education Review* 14(2): 243–262.

Wiese-Bjornstal, D. (2007) Psychological dimensions of girls' physical activity participation. In Tucker Center for Research on Girls and Women in Sport, *Developing physically active girls: an evidence-based multidisciplinary approach*. Online, available at: www.cehd.umn.edu/tuckercenter/projects/TCRR/2007-Tucker-Center-Research-Report.pdf (accessed 5 May 2009).

Wigfield, A., Eccles, J.S., Yoon, K.W., Harold, R.D., Arbreton, A J.A., Freedman-Doan, C. and Blumenfeld, P. (1997) Change in children's competence beliefs and subjective task values across the elementary school years: a 3-year study. *Journal of Educational Psychology* 89(3): 451–469.

Women's Sports and Fitness Foundation (2008a) Barriers to sports participation for women and girls. Online, available at: http://wsff.org.uk/sites/wsff.org.uk/files/Barriers_to_sports_participation_for_women_and_girls1.pdf (accessed 1 June 2009).

Women's Sports and Fitness Foundation (2008b) Muslim women in sport. Online, available at: http://wsff.org.uk/sites/wsff.org.uk/files/Muslim_women_in_sport.pdf (accessed 1 June 2009).

Wright, J. (1999) Changing gendered practice in physical education: working with teachers. *European Physical Education Review* 5(3): 181–197.

Youth Sport Trust/Office for Standards in Education (2000) *Sports colleges: the first two years: innovation in physical education and sport*. London: The Stationery Office.

R. Jeanes

CHAPTER FIFTEEN

DEVELOPMENTAL TRANSITIONS IN SPORT

MARK BRUNER, LEISHA STRACHAN AND JEAN CÔTÉ

CHAPTER OUTLINE

■ **Transition research in sport**
■ **Transitions for children in sport**
■ **An integrated approach to examining developmental transitions in sport**
■ **Theory into practice**
■ **Learning more**

INTRODUCTION

Sport has been heralded as a rich context for promoting physical, psychological, emotional, and social development for children (Fraser-Thomas et al., 2005). Despite the identified benefits of sport on children's development, surprisingly minimal research has examined how early developmental transitions in sport affect a child's participation in sport and psycho-social development. The purpose of this chapter is to identify and explore three important developmental transitions in sport: (1) entry into sport (approximately 5–7 years of age); (2) movement into performance-based sport participation (approximately 12–14 years of age); and (3) movement into recreational sport involvement (approximately 12–14 years of age).

TRANSITION RESEARCH IN SPORT

Transition research in sport dates back to the mid-1960s (e.g. Hallden, 1965). Since that time, the number of investigations into athlete career transitions has risen substantially (McPherson, 1980; Lavallee et al., 1998). The increased attention has brought about several key developments, including major shifts in research foci and theoretical frameworks, the consideration of contextual factors, and the publication of position statements on career transitions in sport (e.g. Alfermann and Stambulova, 2007; Stambulova *et al.*, 2009; Wylleman *et al.*, 1999). This growing body of research supports a 'holistic' perspective on the athlete's career (cf. Wylleman *et al.*, 1999) and the importance of psycho-social variables on athlete development during critical transitions in a sport career. Accordingly, researchers now hold a developmental perspective on athlete transitions.

While much of the early transition research in sport psychology focused on understanding how the transitions out of elite sport influence the athlete (e.g. Baillie and Danish, 1992; Ogilvie and Howe, 1986), recent studies upholding this developmental perspective on an athlete's career have begun to investigate how social (e.g. coaches, parents, peers) and societal (e.g. sport system, culture) influences contribute to athlete development and transitions (Stambulova *et al.*, 2007; Wylleman *et al.*, 2000). However, there is a lack of guidelines on children's transitions in sport and the effect of these transitions on a child's participation and psycho-social development.

TRANSITIONS FOR CHILDREN IN SPORT

Within the sport psychology literature, a number of athlete development models have been identified as highlighting key transitional stages and phases specific to young athletes (Bruner *et al.*, 2009, 2010). The identification of these critical time periods is vital to gaining an understanding of the issues that are pertinent to children and youth as they move through their sport experience.

Wylleman and Lavallee (2004) have put forward a 'holistic' developmental perspective highlighting an athlete's transitions over a sport career. The perspective conceptualises sport as one key facet of an individual's life transitions and includes four levels (athletic, psychological, psycho-social and academic/vocational). The athletic level consists of two types of transitions in an athletic career: normative and non-normative. Normative transitions are foreseeable events that may occur in an athlete's career (e.g. beginning intensive training in a sport; Stambulova, 1994). Contrarily, non-normative transitions are unpredictable and often involuntary occurrences that may happen in the course of an athletic career (e.g. injury, changing teams). Within the athletic level, children fall within the first two stages, initiation and development, which are based on previous work by Bloom (1985). The next layer is the psychological level and describes childhood and adolescence as the first two stages of development. The third layer is the psycho-social level, where Wylleman and Lavallee (2004) highlight the contributions of significant others (i.e. parents, siblings, peers and coaches) to the lives of young people. The final level, academic/vocational, denotes the educational progression that is expected in different phases of life (i.e. primary and secondary education). This model challenges researchers to consider the multidimensional nature of development and to consider all phases when examining children and youth in sport.

When examining athlete development in sport, perhaps one of the most researched models (see Bruner *et al.*, 2010) is the Developmental Model of Sport Participation (DMSP; Côté,

1999; Côté and Fraser-Thomas, 2007). This model suggests three trajectories that a child may follow as he or she progresses through sport. The first two trajectories will be the focus in this chapter, particularly the following stages: (1) entry into sport and sampling (approximately ages 5–7); (2) sampling to specialising (approximately ages 12–14); and (3) sampling to recreational (approximately ages 12–14). Sampling refers to a stage in development where a child participates in deliberate play activities and several different sport activities (Côté, 1999; Côté and Fraser-Thomas, 2007). As a child samples a variety of sports centred around playing, the focus in this stage is the growth of physical and motor skills as well as enjoyment. Further, sampling and playing has also been linked to the promotion of several developmental outcomes, including pro-social behaviour, a healthy identity and the accruement of social capital (Strachan et al., 2008). Upon entry into sport at approximately age 5, the DMSP contends that a child will participate in sampling, at least until age 12. At this time, a child will decide to either participate in the specialising years, where there is more emphasis on the development of skills in two or three specific sports, or enter the recreational years, which encourages the continuation of sampling through recreational sport participation. Although research has been conducted to examine personal and contextual factors *within* the trajectories (Strachan et al., 2009), there is a lack of research studying the transitions *between* the stages and trajectories of the DMSP. An integration of transition models used within (e.g. Wylleman and Lavallee, 2004) and outside of the sport context (e.g. Schlossberg, 1981, 1984) may help us to understand the transitions between these critical phases. Further, an inclusion of both stage-based and transition-based approaches will address recent calls in the sport psychology literature to explore the integration of stage-based and transition-based models to better comprehend the complexity of sport participation (Bruner et al., 2009).

Schlossberg's transition model

Nancy Schlossberg (1981, 1984) proposed an influential conceptual framework on career transitions that has been adapted and successfully used in a sport setting (e.g. Bruner et al., 2008; Pearson and Petitpas, 1990). Recently, this framework has been expanded by Goodman et al. (2006) to include four key factors that influence a transition. Collectively, these four factors are referred to as the 4 Ss: Situation (What is happening?), Self (To whom is it happening?), Support (What help is available?) and Strategies (How does the person cope?). The four factors can be regarded as potential assets and/or liabilities, and make a substantial difference to how an individual copes with a transition (Goodman et al., 2006).

The 4 Ss in developmental transitions in sport

Situation

The situation refers to four contexts of the transition: *trigger, timing,* perceptions of *control* and *stress* of the transition. The *trigger* reveals what set off the transition. Specifically, was the transition anticipated (e.g. moving up in an athletic age category) or unanticipated (e.g. getting dropped from an elite team)? The *timing* refers to how the transition relates to one's social clock (Goodman *et al.*, 2006). Did the individual initiate the transition or did it happen to him or her (e.g. making an elite team after try-outs, or being dropped from a team mid-season)? *Control* entails what aspects of the transition the young athlete can control. The final component pertains to the amount of *stress* the youth faces from the athletic transition and other facets of his or her life.

Self

Along with the situation, an individual's characteristics and psychological resources may influence the transition. Demographic characteristics that may enable or hinder the transition include age, gender, race, ethnicity, socio-economic status and culture (Goodman *et al.*, 2006). Pertinent personal characteristics may include psychological resources, ego development, outlook (e.g., optimism and self-efficacy), commitment and values, spirituality, and resiliency (ibid.).

Support

Support for the athlete is commonly classified into three different typologies (e.g. House and Kahn, 1985): (1) instrumental support – offering something tangible to assist the young athlete, such as a parent driving the young athlete to practices and games; (2) informational support – providing relevant information to help the young athlete cope with the transition, such as a veteran athlete offering advice to the young athlete based upon previous transition experience; and (3) emotional support – providing reassurance, caring and/or empathy to the young athlete, for example a coach reassuring the young athlete early in the competitive season after a poor performance.

Assessment of support for the young athlete during a transition may involve a series of questions: (1) Does the child feel that he or she is receiving enough support? (2) Does the child have a range of types of support – close family, coaches or friends? (3) Has the child's support system or 'convoy of social support' been interrupted by this transition (e.g. moving away from home to train)? (Goodman *et al.*, 2006).

Strategies

The final S, strategies, refers to an evaluation of the strategies an individual possesses to successfully adapt to a transition. For the remainder of this chapter, the strategies will refer to specific recommendations for coaches to help young athletes overcome issues presented within each of the other three Ss (situation, self, support) to foster development and continued participation in sport.

AN INTEGRATED APPROACH TO EXAMINING DEVELOPMENTAL TRANSITIONS IN SPORT

In an effort to address the previously identified need to integrate distinct athlete development approaches, we have integrated (where possible) the content of Wylleman and Lavallee's transition model (describing athletic, psychological, social and academic development in sport) into the three identified stages of Côté's (1999) DMSP: (1) entry into sport and sampling (approximately ages 5–7); (2) sampling to specialising (approximately ages 12–14); and (3) sampling to recreational (approximately ages 12–14). To provide a uniform structure to each transition, the three transitions will be further subdivided into Schlossberg's 4 Ss (situation, self, support, strategies).

Entry into sport

Situation

The *timing* of a child's first participation in organised sport usually occurs around the ages of 5 to 7 (Côté and Fraser-Thomas, 2007). A child's initiation into sport can be *triggered* by a number of social and/or environmental factors. Parents are usually the main social agents that activate a child's interest to first participate in sport (Jacobs and Eccles, 2000). The role that parents play in the development of their child's first participation includes providing the support to take part in an organised sport and 'playing sport' with their child. Environmental factors such as the opportunity to play basketball in a driveway, soccer in a backyard, or baseball in a school yard are also important triggers of a child's first experience with sport (Côté, 1999).

The perception that children have of their own competence and the *control* children have over their participation are important motivational variables during childhood that affect the level of *stress* experienced in a specific sport setting. Thus, in order to develop feelings of physical competence and control over their participation, children's first exposure to sport should be characterised by concrete mastery experiences with tangible outcomes (Chase, 1998). Large amounts of deliberate play and the opportunity to sample different sports in an enjoyable environment provide children with a diversity of settings to play sport that ultimately give them *control* over their experience and lower the *stress* associated with competitive participation in one sport. On the other hand, early specialisation and intense practice of one sport reduces children's control over their activity, increases stress and promotes a state of identity 'foreclosure' which occurs when a child's identity is prescribed to them by parents without sufficient exploration (Harter, 1999).

Self

A child's first exposure to sport is influenced by his or her personal characteristics, such as aptitudes, temperament, attitudes and motivation. Once again, parents play a major role in how children perceive themselves in sport. Research shows that children's self-perceptions are highly influenced by family characteristics (e.g. income and education) and personal characteristics (e.g. sex and age; Jacobs and Eccles, 2000). In other words, parents' perceptions of their children's ability and interest in sport will influence the support that parents provide to their children and ultimately affect their children's self-perception. Although a variety of terms have been used in the literature to describe the self, *confidence* is certainly the most-used term and the most important characteristic that should be valued by coaches and parents of children entering into sport. The way children perceive themselves and their level of confidence when they are introduced to sport have important implications for their persistence and future participation (Vealey and Chase, 2008).

Support

When children are first introduced to sport, adults' (parents and coaches) psycho-social support is probably the most important element in the development of the child's self-esteem. For example, parents' psycho-social support is positively correlated with a child's enjoyment of and enthusiasm for swimming (Power and Woolger, 1994). Through social and verbal encouragement, Bandura's (1978) self-efficacy theory provides theoretical evidence of the importance of parental and coaches' psycho-social support for a child's acquisition of positive values towards sport.

Strategies

Kleiber (1981) suggested that the 'fun' of sports for young children lies in its play qualities. Although sports have become more organised and institutionalised in the past few years, children's first experience in sport is still connected with the importance of experimenting with new or different means of doing things rather than attaining a goal (Côté et al., 2007a). Often, early participation in organised sport becomes distorted by adults who reward behaviours such as excessive competition, physical aggression against others, and cheating. Researchers (Côté and Fraser-Thomas, 2007; Kleiber, 1981) have argued that in order to keep sport enjoyable during childhood, adults should (1) limit competition and performance outcomes, (2) provide play experiences for all children, (3) limit the influence of spectators, and (4) provide choices to children. These guidelines should be at the forefront of a child's first experience of sport.

Sampling to specialising

Situation

During the transition from sampling to specialising, the age of the participant appears to *trigger* this transition. The *timing* of this transition should be athlete initiated. However, in many cases the timing is controlled by an adult, whether it is the coach or a parent. Giving these young athletes greater *control* over their participation in elite sports may allow them to feel more empowered, thereby enabling the development of positive outcomes (Strachan *et al.*, 2009). Further, because this transition occurs during another major transition for youth, adolescence, other stresses beyond sport (i.e. making or having a new group of friends) may add to the complexity of this situation (Allen, 2003).

Self

The development of the *self* is one of the key components of growth as young people progress through adolescence (Harter, 1999). The same is true for youth who participate in sport. Through this transition from sampling to specialising, there may be a shift in cognitive readiness, motivation and identity (Wylleman and Lavallee, 2004). Movement to the formal operations stage of cognitive development (Piaget, 1952) allows for the introduction of more abstract concepts in sport. In terms of motivation, an intrinsic perspective is of utmost importance to promote interest and persistence (Allen, 2003) as these athletes move into a new phase of sport involvement. Finally, a sport identity has been found to be a mediator between psycho-social and socio-environmental factors and sport participation (Lau *et al.*, 2006). Hence, identity plays a key role in promoting persistence in sport for youth. It is important to build a positive identity through sport; however, it is also crucial for youth to maintain a proper perspective so that they do not define themselves only as athletes. A reliance on sport identity as a means to define the self may have negative implications for the development of young people through sport (Coakley, 1992).

Support

As noted within the psycho-social level of Wylleman and Lavallee's (2004) model, *support* is another key factor to consider for youth going through this transition. Coaches need to support athletes by promoting enjoyment while assisting them with skill development (Côté *et al.*, 2007b). Parents play an important role in providing psycho-social support and modelling appropriate behaviours for their children (Côté and Fraser-Thomas, 2007). Lastly, peers provide a growing source of support for youth during this transition. The presence of positive peer groups in sport may enhance motivation, persistence and interest (Allen, 2003).

Strategies

There are a few *strategies* to offer to coaches who may be interacting with athletes beginning to specialise in sport. Coaches should provide these young athletes with opportunities to develop sport-specific skills and increase their competence. Côté and Fraser-Thomas (2007) further suggest that competitive experiences should be made available to athletes, as competition may not only help increase their opportunities to travel and to receive recognition but also enhance their life experiences. While enhancing their skill levels, coaches need to be cognisant of the need to provide athletes with some choice while encouraging positive peer and coach interactions. It is also crucial to always consider their age and stage of development (i.e. adolescence) so that their developmental needs can be addressed. By keeping this in mind, coaches have the opportunity to help youth develop a love for sport and sincerely enjoy their sport experience.

CASE STUDY

Larry is a 12-year-old boy who is currently involved in soccer, hockey, American football and swimming. He is thinking about specialising in soccer and his parents have asked for your advice. From what you have read in this chapter, how would you advise them to deal with this important transition?

Sampling to recreational

Situation

The transition from sampling to a recreational sporting context is often initiated by youth (aged approximately 12–14 years) electing not to pursue an elite developmental trajectory but to remain involved in sport to seek a context that promotes fun, challenge and enjoyment (Côté et al., 2007a). While for most youth the *timing* of this transition is normative, others may be forced into this trajectory when not selected for an elite athletic context. For those young athletes 'cut' or deselected at the beginning of a competitive season, the non-normative transition may be unanticipated and involuntary (Wylleman and Lavallee, 2004). The two distinct types of transitions may give rise to quite different perceptions of *control* and associated *stress* leading into a recreational setting.

Self

As children move into adolescence, they begin to embark on a critical period of growth and development, and engage in a number of activities, including sport, to build their personal identity (Wagner, 1996). It is also during adolescence that they begin to compartmentalise themselves as being 'different' people in different domains (Horn, 2004). This ability to develop higher-order abstractions about self permits adolescents to evaluate themselves as having differing levels of ability in different athletic contexts. In a recreational sport setting, this may involve young athletes feeling competent in one sport (e.g. volleyball) yet not in another

234

(e.g. basketball), or viewing themselves as being competent in one skill (e.g. serving) but not in another (e.g. spiking). However, this developmental process is not seamless and frequently involves adolescents' reconciling 'cognitive confusion' concerning themselves (Harter, 1999). It is during these trying times that young athletes look to their social support network, specifically the feedback of significant others such as coaches and peers, to resolve conflicting information about the self and form their personal identity (Horn, 2004).

Support

During key developmental transitions in sport, such as the movement to recreational sport, the sources and types of support often shift for the young athlete. Early athletic support for the child during the sampling years may be primarily derived from the family, specifically the parents, while in later elite or recreational years the important supportive roles of coaches and peers often emerge (Wylleman and Lavallee, 2004). In addition to changes in the sources of support, the type of support offered by each source may also evolve. For example, parental support may evolve over the different stages of athletic development (Côté, 1999).

Strategies

On the basis of the description of the previous 3 Ss (situation, self and support), it is recommended that recreational youth coaches devise a number of strategies to assist young athletes to cope with the transition into recreational sport. First, recreational youth coaches should be cognisant of the nature of each young athlete's transition (normative versus non-normative) in order to better understand an athlete's background and any challenges associated with the transition, particularly for those athletes experiencing a non-normative transition. Second, recreational youth coaches should attempt to promote a positive environment that fosters a sense of self for the young athletes. In addition, recreational youth coaches should evaluate the present support network for each athlete to assist and/or complement the athlete's support system.

DIRECTED TASK

Find a newspaper or magazine article that discusses the transition of an athlete. What caused the transition to occur for the athlete? What were the outcomes of this transition? Could this transition have been made smoother for the athlete, and if so, how?

THEORY INTO PRACTICE

In summary, when children initiate sport, coaches should focus on creating a sporting atmosphere that allows them to have fun, develop and maintain a positive attitude towards sport, and acquire fundamental motor skills. Coaches and parents involved in children's early participation in organised sport should be careful not to reward a child's negative behaviours, such as excessive competition, physical aggression against others, and cheating. A greater focus on play and enjoyment during the initiation phase into sport is in line with results of studies that investigate the motives for a child's participation in sport (e.g. Petlichkoff, 1993). After sampling several different sports, an athlete may elect to specialise in one or two sports or maintain involvement in several sports in a recreational setting. If a child decides to specialise, coaches should focus on providing opportunities for the young athlete to develop sport-specific skills and increase their competence. Elite youth coaches should also be cognisant of the developmental changes occurring during adolescence for the young athlete and ensure that the athletic environment is rich in positive interactions among peers and coaches. Similarly, recreational youth coaches should foster a sporting environment that builds a sense of self for the young athlete. In addition, recreational coaches should be sensitive to the nature of each child's athletic background (normative versus non-normative) to better understand the context leading to the child's decision to participate in recreational sport. Finally, recreational coaches should carefully monitor the support network of their athletes to ensure each athlete is receiving adequate instrumental, informational and emotional support to promote positive youth development and continued participation in sport.

LEARNING MORE

Several helpful resources are recommended for those wishing to learn more about the developmental needs of young athletes (Côté et al., 2010), developmental approaches to athlete transitions and performance (Côté et al., 2007a; Stambulova et al., 2009; Wylleman and Lavallee, 2004), effective coaching (Côté and Gilbert, 2009) and positive youth development in sport (Fraser-Thomas et al., 2005).

REFERENCES

Alfermann, D. and Stambulova, N. (2007) Career transitions and career termination. In G. Tenenbaum and R.C. Eklund (eds), *Handbook of sport psychology*. Hoboken, NJ: John Wiley.

Allen, J.B. (2003) Social motivation in youth sport. *Journal of Sport and Exercise Psychology* 25: 551–567.

M. Bruner *et al.*

Baillie, P.H.F. and Danish, S.J. (1992) Understanding the career transition of athletes. *Sport Psychologist* 6: 77–98.

Bandura, A. (1978) The self system in reciprocal determinism. *American Psychologist* 33: 344–358.

Bloom, B.S. (ed.) (1985) *Developing talent in young people*. New York: Ballantine.

Bruner, M.W., Munroe-Chandler, K. and Spink, K.S. (2008) Entry into elite sport: a preliminary investigation into the transition experiences of rookie athletes. *Journal of Applied Sport Psychology* 20: 236–252.

Bruner, M.W., Erickson, K., McFadden, K. and Côté, J. (2009) Tracing the origins of athlete development models in sport: a citation path analysis. *International Review of Sport and Exercise Psychology* 2(1): 23–37.

Bruner, M.W., Erickson, K., Wilson, B. and Côté, J. (2010) An appraisal of athlete development models through citation network analysis. *Psychology of Sport and Exercise* 11(2): 133–139.

Chase, M.A. (1998) Sources of self-efficacy in physical education and sport. *Journal of Teaching in Physical Education* 18: 76–89.

Coakley, J.J. (1992) Burnout among adolescent athletes: a personal failure or social problem? *Sociology of Sport Journal* 9(3): 271–285.

Côté, J. (1999) The influence of the family in the development of talent in sports. *Sport Psychologist* 13: 395–417.

Côté, J. and Fraser-Thomas, J. (2007) Youth involvement in sport. In P. Crocker (ed.), *Sport psychology: a Canadian perspective*. Toronto: Pearson.

Côté, J. and Gilbert, W. (2009) An integrative definition of coaching effectiveness and expertise. *International Journal of Sports Science & Coaching* 4: 307–323.

Côté, J., Baker, J. and Abernethy, B. (2007a) Practice and play in the development of sport expertise. In R. Eklund and G. Tenenbaum (eds), *Handbook of Sport Psychology* (3rd ed.). Hoboken, NJ: John Wiley.

Côté, J., Young, B., North, J. and Duffy, P. (2007b) Towards a definition of excellence in sport coaching. *International Journal of Coaching Science* 1(1): 3–17.

Côté, J., Bruner, M.W., Strachan, L., Erickson, K. and Fraser-Thomas, J. (2010) Athlete development and coaching. In J. Lyle and C. Cushion (eds), *Sport coaching: professionalism and practice*. Oxford: Elsevier.

Fraser-Thomas, J.L., Côté, J. and Deakin, J. (2005) Youth sport programs: an avenue to foster positive youth development. *Physical Education and Sport Pedagogy* 10: 19–40.

Goodman, J., Schlossberg, N. and Anderson, M. (2006) *Counseling adults in transition: linking theory to practice* (3rd ed.). New York: Springer .

Hallden, D. (1965) The adjustment of athletes after retiring from sports. In F. Antonelli (ed.), *Proceedings of the 1st International Congress of Sport Psychology, Rome*.

Harter, S. (1999) *The construction of self: a developmental perspective*. New York: Guilford Press.

Horn, T. (2004) Developmental perspectives on self-perceptions in children and adolescents. In M. Weiss (ed.), *Developmental sport and exercise psychology: a lifespan perspective*. Morgantown, WV: Fitness Information Technology.

House, J.S. and Kahn, R.L. (1985) Measures and concepts of social support. In S. Cohen and S.L. Syme (eds), *Social support and health*. New York: Academic Press.

Jacobs, J.E. and Eccles, J.S. (2000) Parents, task values, and real-life achievement-related choices. In C. Sansone and J.M. Harackiewicz (eds), *Intrinsic and extrinsic motivation: the search for optimal motivation and performance*. New York: Academic Press.

Kleiber, D.A. (1981) Searching for enjoyment in children's sports. *Physical Educator* 38: 77–84.

Lau, P.W.C., Fox, K.R. and Cheung, M.W.L. (2006) An analysis of sport identity as a predictor of children's participation in sport. *Pediatric Exercise Science* 18: 415–425.

Lavallee, D., Sinclair, D.A. and Wylleman, P. (1998) An annotated bibliography on career transitions in sport: I. Counselling-based references. *Australian Journal of Career Development* 7: 34–42.

McPherson, B.D. (1980) Retirement from professional sport: the process and problems of occupational and psychological adjustment. *Sociological Symposium* 30: 126–143.

Ogilvie, B.C. and Howe, M. (1986) The trauma of termination from athletics. In J.M. Williams (ed.), *Applied sport psychology*. Palo Alto, CA: Mayfield.

Pearson, R.E. and Petitpas, A.J. (1990) Transitions of athletes: developmental and preventive perspectives. *Journal of Counseling and Development* 69: 7–10.

Petlichkoff, L.M. (1993). Coaching children: understanding the motivational process. *Sport Science Review* 2: 48–61.

Piaget, J. (1952) Jean Piaget. In E.G. Boring (ed.), *A history of psychology in autobiography*, vol. 4. New York: Russell & Russell.

Power, T.G. and Woolger, C. (1994) Parenting practices and age group swimming: a correlational study. *Research Quarterly for Exercise and Sport* 65: 59–66.

Schlossberg, N.K. (1981) A model for analyzing human adaptation to transition. *The Counseling Psychologist* 9: 2–18.

Schlossberg, N.K. (1984) *Counseling adults in transition: linking theory to practice* (2nd ed.). New York: Springer.

Stambulova, N.B. (1994) Developmental sports career investigations in Russia: a post-perestroika analysis. *Sport Psychologist* 8: 221–237.

Stambulova, N.B., Stephan, Y. and Järphag, U. (2007) Athletic retirement: a cross-national comparison of elite French and Swedish athletes. *Psychology of Sport and Exercise* 8: 101–118.

Stambulova, N., Alfermann, D., Statler, T. and Côté, J. (2009) Career development and transitions of athletes: the ISSP Position Stand. *International Journal of Sport and Exercise Psychology* 7: 395–412.

Strachan, L., MacDonald, D.J., Fraser-Thomas, J. and Côté, J. (2008) Youth sport: talent, socialisation, and development. In R. Fisher and R.P. Bailey (eds), *Talent identification and development: the search for sporting excellence*. Berlin: ICSSPE.

Strachan, L., Côté, J., and Deakin, J. (2009) An evaluation of personal and contextual factors in competitive youth sport. *Journal of Applied Sport Psychology* 21: 340–355.

Vealey, R.S. and Chase, M.A. (2008) Self-confidence in sport. In T. Horn (ed.), *Advances in sport psychology*. Champaign, IL: Human Kinetics.

M. Bruner *et al.*

Wagner, W. (1996) Optimal development in adolescence: what is it and how can it be encouraged? *Counseling Psychologist* 24: 360–399.

Wright, A. and Côté, J. (2003) A retrospective analysis of leadership development through sport. *Sport Psychologist* 17: 268–291.

Wylleman, P. and Lavallee, D. (2004) A developmental perspective on transitions faced by athletes. In M.R. Weiss (ed.), *Developmental sport psychology: a lifespan perspective.* Morgantown, WV: Fitness Information Technology.

Wylleman, P., Lavallee, D. and Alfermann, D. (eds) (1999) *Transitions in the career of competitive athletes.* Lund, Sweden: FEPSAC.

Wylleman, P., De Knop, P., Ewing, M.E. and Cumming, S.P. (2000) Transitions in youth sport: a developmental perspective on parental involvement. In D. Lavallee and P. Wylleman (eds), *Career transition in sport: international perspectives.* Morgantown, WV: Fitness Information Technology.

CHAPTER SIXTEEN

THE HEALTH OF YOUNG ATHLETES

ROBERT M. MALINA

CHAPTER OUTLINE

- Definition of basic terms
- Potential health benefits of participation in sports
- Sport and other social outcomes with implications for health
- Potential health risks of participation in sports
- Theory into practice
- Learning more

INTRODUCTION

Sport participation has high social value in many societies, which is evident from the fact that sport is a feature of daily living for many children and adolescents the world over. The number of adolescents competing at national and international levels continues to increase, and significant numbers of children and adolescents begin systematic training and specialisation in a sport at relatively young ages with the goal of attaining elite status. There is a need to distinguish the talented few from the overwhelming majority of youth who participate in sport and never attain elite levels. Unfortunately, attention and often resources are focused on the elite!

Understanding the role of organised sport in the lives of youth is the focus of many chapters in this volume. This chapter considers the health of youth participants in sport from the perspective of potential benefits and risks for indicators of health status.

240

DEFINITION OF BASIC TERMS

Before we discuss potential benefits and risks for health of sport participation, we need to define three key words – sport, health and youth – recognising that definitions are generally operational.

Sport can be informal or formal. Focus is on formal, organised sports which imply the presence of a coach, regular practices and competitions during a season. Organised youth sports as known today are relatively recent. From relatively humble beginnings, they have become, for better or worse, a major feature in the daily lives of children and adolescents throughout the world. A major player in the expansion of youth sports is the sporting goods manufacturing industry.

Definitions of *health* range from a lack of disease to a state of physical, mental, social and emotional well-being. For the present discussion, health of sport participants is viewed in the context of health-related physical fitness and behaviours, risk factors for cardiovascular and metabolic diseases, injury, sudden death, and growth and maturation.

The term *youth* collectively includes children and adolescents between about 5 and 18 years. Children and adolescents are in the process of 'growing up', a process that encompasses: (1) *growth* – increase in the size of the body as a whole and of its parts and systems; (2) *maturation* – progress towards the biologically mature or adult state (an operational concept which varies with bodily systems); and (3) *development* – learning of appropriate cognitive, social, affective, moral and other behaviours expected by society. Growth and maturation are biological processes, while development is a behavioural process often subsumed in the term 'socialisation', which is specific to a culture. Motor development, the process of acquiring proficiency in movement skills, involves all three processes.

Growth, maturation and development are distinct, though related and interacting, processes. The processes are characteristically quite variable within and between individuals, especially during the transition into puberty and during sexual maturation and the adolescent growth spurt. Interactions among growth, maturation and development vary during childhood and adolescence, among individuals, and within and between cultural groups.

Organised sport is one of many demands placed on children and adolescents. Demands associated with family, friends, school, study, play and non-sport activities, among others, are realities of childhood and adolescence. Where does sport fit into the process of 'growing up'? Where does sport fit into the daily lives of children and adolescents?

POTENTIAL HEALTH BENEFITS OF PARTICIPATION IN SPORTS

Potential benefits of sport participation for indicators of health – in terms of physical fitness, body composition, and cardiovascular and metabolic risk factors – are associated with regular physical activity, and sport is a primary medium of activity for most youth. Potential behavioural health benefits, though less studied, are more dependent upon the sport environment and quality of adult involvement.

Regular physical activity

Data derived from diaries, accelerometry and doubly labelled water indicate that children and adolescents involved in sport have higher levels of moderate to vigorous physical activity, estimated daily energy expenditure, and energy expenditure in physical activity (Katzmarzyk and Malina, 1998; Wickel and Eisenmann, 2007; Ribeyre et al., 2000). Data derived from questionnaires are consistent in showing that adolescent sport participants report being more physically active than non-participants. Sports vary in intensity and continuity of activity. Team sports such as soccer, basketball, ice hockey and field hockey involve more or less reasonably continuous activity which varies in intensity during a match, while sports like baseball and American football involve intermittent activity among frequent periods of relative inactivity. Among individual sports, intermittent activity is characteristic of gymnastics, diving, racket sports and some field events in athletics, while continuous activity is a feature of swimming and running events in athletics.

Sport and movement skills

The development of general movement and sport-specific skills is a primary objective of youth sports programmes from the community level to more advanced programs that focus on a single sport. Improvement in sport skills is also a major motivation for children and adolescents to participate in sport. Children who are more proficient in movement skills are more likely to be more physically active and fit in adolescence (Barnett et al., 2008, 2009; Wrotniak et al., 2006).

Transfer of sport participation to adult physical activity

Participation in sports during adolescence tends to track at higher levels than other indicators of physical activity (Malina, 2001), while frequency of sport participation, membership in sport clubs, and sport club training and competition during adolescence in Scandinavian countries are significant predictors of physical activity in young adulthood (from the mid-twenties to the early thirties). Sport participation in childhood (time in sports) and adolescence (time in sports, kinds of after school activities) is also a significant predictor of sport and physical fitness activities in young American adults. It is likely that sports skills transfer readily to other skills that facilitate readiness for an active lifestyle. Sport programmes vary among countries and in accessibility, cost and participant selectivity, so that translation of sport participation during youth into an active lifestyle in adulthood needs study.

242

R.M. Malina

Improved physical fitness

Youth who are regularly active tend to have higher levels of aerobic fitness compared to less active youth. Aerobic fitness is especially well developed in adolescent athletes in sports with a high endurance component: distance running, swimming, cycling, soccer, ice hockey. Experimental aerobic and resistance training programmes are associated with significant gains in aerobic endurance and muscular strength and endurance, respectively. Although these data are not based on youth involved in specific sport programmes, both aerobic and resistance training are often recommended for participants in many sports.

Regulation of body weight and adiposity

Regular physical activity has the potential to favourably influence body weight, specifically adiposity. Youth who are relatively high in physical activity tend to have less adiposity. Adolescent athletes of both sexes have less relative fatness. Experimental activity programmes in normal-weight youth have a minimal effect on fatness, but are associated with reductions in overall and abdominal adiposity in overweight and obese youth. Beneficial effects of activity on fatness in obese youth are lost when interventions stop. Continued regular activity is essential, but the amount and intensity of activity needed for weight loss in obese youth are not known.

Organised sport is increasingly indicated as a potentially important context of physical activity to combat the epidemic of obesity among youth. For example, 'The International Olympic Committee, in an effort to fight childhood obesity and other problems associated with inactivity among children, on Thursday voted to stage Youth Olympic Games modelled after the Olympics' (Michaelis, 2007).

Yet it is not clear how an event for talented adolescent athletes will combat obesity in youth. As sport is presently organised and practised, it is very likely that overweight or obese youth will not have equal opportunities compared to normal-weight youth. Obese youth tend to be less proficient in movement skills and components of physical fitness. Excess body mass or fatness associated with obesity has a negative influence on most motor and fitness tests, specifically those requiring movement or projection of the body, whereas isometric and isokinetic strength are greater in obese compared to non-obese youth, reflecting the absolute size advantage of the obese.

Improved skeletal health

Bone is a feature of body composition that is currently a focus of attention in the context of preventing osteoporosis later in life. Regular physical activity has a beneficial effect on bone mineral content and density. This is apparent in studies of youth, including athletes and non-athletes, and retrospective studies of childhood and adolescent sport activity relative to adult bone mineral content (Strong et al., 2005). Retrospective studies of racket sport athletes highlight beneficial effects of early training on bone mineral accrual (Kannus et al., 1995).

Indicators of cardiovascular and metabolic health

Regular physical activity is generally accepted as having a beneficial influence on indicators of cardiovascular and metabolic health in children and adolescents. Results of a systematic review (Strong et al., 2005) suggest the following trends.

Considerable emphasis has been placed upon cholesterol, a wax-like substance that can build up on the walls of arteries. The build-up of cholesterol and fat (lipids) on the arterial walls can potentially interfere with or block the flow of blood; the latter is usually apparent in middle age. A goal of public health is to improve the cholesterol profile of youth. The cholesterol profile of an individual is usually viewed in three components: HDL (high-density lipoprotein), or 'good' cholesterol; LDL (low-density lipoprotein), or 'bad' cholesterol; and triglycerides, a form of fat (lipid) related to cholesterol.

A variety of intervention studies indicate a weak beneficial effect of physical activity on HDL cholesterol and triglycerides but no effect on total cholesterol and LDL cholesterol. A sustained volume of activity may be the key factor. School-based programmes are not generally effective in improving the lipid and lipoprotein profiles of youth.

Physical activity and blood pressures are not related in normotensive youth, but experimental activity programmes such as those that improve aerobic fitness have a beneficial effect on blood pressures in hypertensive youth. Aerobic programmes may also reduce the blood pressure of youth with mild essential hypertension.

Features of the metabolic syndrome (elevated triglycerides, blood pressure and fasting glucose, insulin resistance, abdominal obesity) have been documented in youth. Among non-obese youth, a better metabolic profile clusters independently with higher levels of physical activity and aerobic fitness and with lower levels of inactivity and adiposity. Observational and cross-sectional studies show a relationship between some elements of the syndrome and physical activity, more so in obese youth, among whom activity programmes are associated with reduced insulin and triglycerides.

Corresponding data relating cardiovascular and metabolic risk indicators to training in young athletes are not extensive. Young athletes between 9 and 18 years of age in several sports that included a significant endurance component showed, on average, a better cholesterol profile of blood lipids (lower triglycerides) and lipoproteins (higher HDL and lower LDL cholesterol) than the general population. The profiles of athletes, however, showed considerable variability, including some trained athletes with dyslipidaemia. Regular endurance training was not associated with a more favourable HDL cholesterol profile in adolescent

R.M. Malina

athletes (Eisenmann, 2007). On the other hand, a study of female athletes aged 9–15 indicated higher levels of HDL cholesterol and a higher HDL cholesterol/total cholesterol ratio in gymnasts compared to runners and non-athletes (Vasankari *et al.*, 2000).

Sport and psycho-social outcomes

Social interactions with team-mates, opponents and adults in and through sport are generally assumed to contribute to the psycho-social development of participants. Self-concept has received most attention. Self-concept refers to how the individual perceives or views him- or herself; it is not to be confused with self-esteem, which refers to the value one places on the view of oneself. In addition to global or overall self-concept, several domains are often assessed: academic, social, emotional, physical, sport competence and appearance. It is important to note that the structure of self-concept changes with age and becomes more clearly differentiated in the transition into puberty and during adolescence.

Physical activity is positively correlated with global and physical self-concept, but weakly correlated with social, emotional and academic self-concepts. Most data are based on quasi-experimental study designs ('quasi' means 'resembling' or 'approximately') in which groups of subjects are compared by physical activity status. Such studies are not strictly experimental designs in which subjects are randomly assigned to experimental and control groups and the relationship between a specific dose of physical activity and a particular outcome such as self-concept is directly examined. Results of quasi-experimental studies indicate strong positive effects of physical activity programmes on global self-concept, physical self-concept, appearance and sport competence; effects on the social and academic domains of participants are weak. Sport participation is positively associated with global self-concept and perceived sport competence. Sport also has potential for a negative influence that is dependent upon outcome (winning or losing) and quality of adult involvement, specifically coaches per se and coaching styles (Smoll and Smith, 2003).

SPORT AND OTHER SOCIAL OUTCOMES WITH IMPLICATIONS FOR HEALTH

Adolescent sport participation is associated with a reduction in the likelihood of involvement in delinquent and risk-taking sexual behaviours, pregnancies, and suicide ideation and attempts (Malina, 2007). Sport participation is also associated with greater likelihood of staying in school and fewer absences. Though interesting, the evidence varies in quality and is derived largely from interscholastic sport participants in the United States. The associations need to be more critically evaluated relative to the many factors that influence adolescent behaviours.

POTENTIAL HEALTH RISKS OF PARTICIPATION IN SPORTS

A risk refers to a person, situation or thing that suggests a hazard. In the context of sport, it implies potential for a negative outcome.

Risk of injury

Children and adolescents incur injury in organised and unorganised sport, in addition to many other activities. Injuries are classified as acute – fractures, sprains, strains, general trauma, and overuse (microtrauma associated with excessive repetition of specific sport activities). The latter receive considerable attention, given their increasing prevalence among youth, and organised sports are implicated as the primary cause, in particular year-round participation in a single sport. There is also increasing concern about head injuries. American football, with the potential for high-impact contact in tackling, and soccer, with opportunities for repetitive heading of the ball, are often singled out. Head injuries can occur in many sports, specifically those with potential for collision between players or between players and a fixed object. Potential for long-term problems associated with head injury in sport is a major concern.

The study of injury in youth sport is hampered by definition and method of reporting. Primary sources of data are case series based on convenience samples from emergency departments or sports medicine clinics; other data come from accident reports, insurance records, interviews and retrospective questionnaires. Such records largely provide information on major, acute injuries – that is, those sufficiently serious to require emergency medical care and insurance coverage. Less severe or minor injuries are more difficult to define and classify and may pass unnoticed in youth sports. There are relatively few prospective studies that monitor injuries as they occur in practice and competitions during a season. Prospective studies have a standard data collection system that provides accurate exposure data (the denominator or number of athletes exposed to the risk of being injured), record of injuries as they occur, and access to treatment by an athletic trainer or physician.

There is a reasonably extensive literature on the prevalence and incidence of injuries in youth sports or to young athletes. Summaries of estimated rates per athlete exposures for a variety of sports are available (Caine et al., 2006; McGuine, 2006).

Previous injury and/or inadequate rehabilitation from an injury are significant risks for subsequent injury. Evidence is consistent in studies of child and adolescent athletes and across sports (Emery, 2003). A critical issue for injured young athletes, especially at more elite levels, is pressure to participate before complete recovery. Such pressure may be self-generated but quite often comes from adults involved: coaches, trainers, parents and perhaps sport administrators.

Injury literature in youth sports often focuses on risk factors unique to the sport environment and the young participant. Sport-related risk factors are potentially manageable and modifiable, especially those related to training, equipment and playing conditions. Coach and parent

246

R.M. Malina

educational interventions and modifications of sports or their rules may also serve to reduce injury risk.

Proposed risk factors for injury associated with sport participants, such as strength imbalance, physique, skill, the growth spurt, and so on, are obviously related to normal growth and maturation and thus are very difficult to specify. Information on suggested player-risk factors is based largely on clinical observations and perhaps impressions. Status of an injured athlete at the time of injury or treatment is not ordinarily recorded. The focus of necessity is on treatment and occasionally rehabilitation. Information on athlete characteristics may be included in pre-participation physical examinations (height, weight, maturity status, muscular strength, etc.), but pre-participation examinations are not always required, especially with younger athletes, and even if they are carried out, observations are often not readily available for integration with clinical observations.

Most injuries sustained in youth sport are minor. However, increasing specialisation beginning at relatively young ages elevates the risk of exposure to injury, especially the overuse variety, e.g. tennis elbow, swimmer's shoulder, Little League elbow, stress fractures, low back problems in artistic gymnasts, and so on. Little League elbow refers to chronic elbow pain noted among 11- to 13-year-old baseball pitchers about 50 years ago. The pain and inflammation of the medial part of the elbow was associated with repetitive throwing (i.e. overuse) in the act of pitching a baseball; an additional factor in this overuse injury is poor pitching mechanics. Talented young athletes who continue to train and compete for many years are at greater risk of injury, especially musculoskeletal injuries.

The implication of injuries for the health of the athlete while a youngster and eventually as an adult needs study. Functional complications in adulthood associated with musculoskeletal injuries incurred in sport during childhood or adolescence periodically surface in the popular press.

There is considerable interest at present in sport-related head injuries, specifically concussions. Current discussion focuses largely on former professional American football players and more recently on professional ice hockey players. Delayed brain damage and perhaps cognitive impairment has been reported in retired professional American football players (Miller, 2009). The discussion in the press is filtering to youth levels (Brody, 2009). Dizziness and depression are frequently reported among youth and adults who have suffered sport-related concussion. Head injury in sport requires close monitoring, and potential long-term consequences of blows to the head in sport require closer attention and further study (McLeod *et al.*, 2006; Gessel *et al.*, 2007).

DIRECTED TASK

Injuries are a reality in sport and may affect the health of young athletes. A related issue is the recording of injuries and associated risks. How are injuries to youth monitored in your sport or perhaps your country? What on-field services are available for the injured young athlete? Who makes the decision on 'return to play' after an injury? Consider injuries to young athletes in your sport or country in the context of monitoring their occurrence, on-field treatment and 'return to play'.

Competitive stress

Discussions of potential psychological or behavioural risks associated with organised youth sport are often set in the context of competitive stress, which has been a concern since their inception. Stress is a physiological state and is beset with problems of measurement. Physiological measures (heart rate, galvanic skin response, hormonal levels) are not strongly correlated with paper-and-pencil scales commonly used in surveys of youth sport participants. Individual differences in the perception of stress are considerable.

Sport-related stress is generally transient, and is more accentuated in individual sports in which athletes compete as individuals before judges. The greater number of athletes and the highly interactive nature of team sports tend to diffuse responsibility so that the performance of any individual athlete is generally less conspicuous and performance evaluation is less of a threat. The buffer of team members may alleviate stress associated with mistakes and losing. There are, of course, situational exceptions such as the penalty shot in soccer and free throws in basketball. In contrast to actual competitions, it is more difficult to gauge stress in training or practice environments of specific sports which are under the control of coaches, each with their own style of teaching and training.

Potential consequences of competitive stress include lowered self-esteem, elevated anxiety, more aggressive behaviour, injury, 'burn-out' (see below) and perhaps others. Factors associated with stress include failure; negative performance evaluations by coaches, parents and peers; and unrealistic expectations by self, parents and coaches.

The influence of interactions between biological and behavioural characteristics of young athletes in contributing to stress and potentially negative outcomes associated with sport has not received attention. The transition into puberty as well as sexual maturation and the adolescent growth spurt include major physiological, physical and behavioural alterations. Puberty is often described as a period of physiological learning. These changes often occur at a time when there is considerable emphasis on sport selection and specialisation.

Social physique anxiety refers to feelings of anxiety experienced when there is a prospect or presence of interpersonal evaluation of an individual's physique (Hart et al., 1989). Social physique anxiety increases during adolescence and is associated with a decline in self-esteem. Young females in aesthetic sports are probably more at risk for social physique anxiety than participants in other sports, especially team sports. Among young female figures skaters, for

248

example, social physique anxiety was a significant predictor of risk of disordered eating (Monsma and Malina, 2004); social physique anxiety, age at menarche and physique were also related to appearance-related physical self-perceptions (Monsma et al., 2006).

Stresses associated with year-round training and competition in female gymnasts and swimmers may influence mental health. Three of 27 highly trained gymnasts and 4 of 16 moderately trained swimmers were described at risk for 'a manifest mental disorder over time' (Theintz et al., 1994).

Burn-out

'Burn-out' refers to withdrawal from sport due to chronic stress. It develops over time and is frequently associated with perceptions by a young athlete that he or she cannot meet the sport demands (physical, psychological) placed upon him or her. Reduction in sport accomplishments and associated rewards (no longer receiving them) are additional factors. Signs of chronic stress include behavioural alterations – agitation, loss of interest in practice, sleep disturbances; other manifestations include depression, lack of energy, skin rashes and nausea, and frequent illness (Gould and Dieffenbach, 2003).

The prevalence of burn-out is not known with certainty. Data are based largely on small samples, case series and retrospective surveys of participants largely in individual sports – golf, tennis and swimming – although evidence for team sports, specifically rugby, is expanding. Many factors are probably involved in the development of burn-out, but three are especially important: negative performance evaluations (critical rather than supportive), inconsistent feedback from coaches and officials (mixed message for the young athlete), and overtraining. Overprotection by coaches, trainers, parents and sport officials is an additional factor. Overprotection limits exposure to new situations and thus opportunities to develop coping mechanisms and social relationships, and may foster feelings of dependency, lack of control and being powerless. Self-perceptions of not being able to meet expectations imposed by self and/or others and injury are additional factors (Gould and Dieffenbach, 2003). Note that sport-related circumstances conducive to the development of burn-out in young athletes are superimposed on and interact with normal biological and behavioural demands of adolescence.

Compromised growth and maturation

Discussions of the merits of youth sport often include a caveat regarding potentially negative influences on growth (size attained) and maturation (timing and tempo of progress to the mature state). Given the expansion of youth sports to include year-round training, increased training demands and national and international competitions, it is periodically suggested that systematic training for some sports has a potentially negative influence on growth and maturation. Concern is expressed for young elite athletes, and for girls more than boys. Those who train at elite levels are a small, though highly visible, fraction of the large numbers of youth sport participants.

Later mean ages at menarche and the short stature and later maturation of female artistic gymnasts are often attributed to intensive training. Presently available data, however, are do not support these assertions.

Age at menarche data for adolescent athletes is very limited (9 prospective; 10 status quo; 6 are of gymnasts, 3 of swimmers). Most data are from late adolescent and young adult athletes and are retrospective (recall). Ages at menarche vary, on average, by sport and event or discipline within a sport, and not all athletes are late maturing. Intensive training before menarche is implied to 'cause' lateness, but the data are cross-sectional, which does not establish causality. Definition is a problem; 'taking up sport' is not equivalent to training, and girls who take up sport after menarche are excluded. Many factors influence menarche, including genotype, family size, home environment and diet, among others. The potential influence of coaches and the sport system is not known.

Data for female artistic gymnasts are short term and not sufficiently longitudinal to estimate parameters of the growth spurt for individual girls. The available data also do not control for other factors: selection, selective drop-out and persistence, coaching and training environment, and so on, in addition to normal variation in growth and maturation. Male gymnasts are also short and later maturing, and events for males are probably more strenuous than those for females. Overall, gymnasts of both sexes have the growth and maturity characteristics of short, normal, late-maturing youth with short parents (Malina, 1999). If there is a potential risk for growth and maturation in gymnastics and other sports, the environments of specific sports – specifically, interactions among compromised nutrition, coaching style and demands, unrealistic expectations (athlete, coach, parents) and associated stresses – need closer scrutiny.

Are programmes for the talented a health risk?

Elite young athletes face potential social, nutritional and chemical risks associated with the environments of their respective sports. Social manipulation is perhaps most evident in preferential treatment which may lead to overdependence on and/or control by coaches and sport organisations, altered social relationships with peers, parents and family, and perhaps arrested social development. A potential by-product of excessive dependence of young athletes upon coaches and sport officials (and often the blind faith and trust of parents) is potential for emotional abuse – verbal or non-verbal, physical abuse and sexual abuse and molestation.

Indirect and direct dietary manipulation is a concern in some sports. Pressures, at times subtle, to maintain or lose weight by young athletes, especially in aesthetic sports and wrestling, when the natural course of growth is to gain weight, can lead to disordered eating and clinical eating disorders. Direct dietary manipulation has been documented in the former German Democratic Republic, where gymnasts were on a dietary regime that included a negative energy balance

250

R.M. Malina

over time, targeting an optimal performance weight (Jahreis et al., 1991). Intentional energy deficit may border on chronic under-nutrition.

Chemical abuse by professional athletes is a common item on sport pages. Chemical manipulation with young athletes can take several forms, including supplements such as creatine and 'fat burners' with caffeine as a major ingredient, diuretics to make them lose weight, and of course performance-enhancing drugs, the use of which was well documented among adolescent female swimmers in the former German Democratic Republic (Franke and Berendonk, 1997). Use of prohibited performance-enhancing substances by young athletes is apparently not widespread, but a small but significant percentage of youth – both athletes and non-athletes – have tried or have been enticed into using these substances (Faigenbaum et al., 1998; Laure and Binsinger, 2005). It is of interest that parents, friends and even family physicians were indicated as the source of performance enhancers.

Sudden death in young athletes

Deaths in sport are rare, but awareness of the remote possibility of sudden death in sport and the need for shared responsibility for sports safety among athletes, parents, coaches and sport organisations is important.

Several examples should suffice. The clinical profiles of 25 youth aged between 3 and 19 who died from cardiac arrest after receiving an unexpected blow to the chest have been reported (Maron et al., 1995). Death ensued from commotio cordis ('cardiac concussion'), which may be related to the thinness of the chest wall in children and adolescents, causing it to yield to the force of the projectile or blow, thus facilitating the transmission of the force to the heart. A comprehensive analysis of 1,866 sudden deaths in competitive athletes aged 19 ± 6 years between 1980 and 2006 noted that the majority were related to cardiovascular conditions and disease (Maron et al., 2009). Major cardiovascular causes were hypertrophic cardiomyopathy (36 per cent), a pathological thickening of the walls of the left ventricle that obstructs blood flow from the left ventricle to the aorta, and congenital anomalies of the coronary arteries (17 per cent). Commotio cordis and heat stroke accounted for 3 per cent and 2 per cent of deaths, respectively.

What are the implications of studies of sudden death for youth sports? Parents, coaches and administrators should be aware of inherent risks in sport, including the rare possibility of death. There is much discussion of pre-participation physical examinations for young athletes, but such examinations on a large-scale basis may be impractical and do not guarantee that cardiovascular problems will necessarily be identified (Maron et al., 2007). On-field preventive measures, especially for non-cardiovascular causes of sudden death, include hydration of athletes, scheduling practices to avoid the hottest times of the day, awareness of lightning and thunderstorms in the area, and monitoring athletes on the field by awareness of 'red flags' as to who might be having trouble. And it is good sense to have an emergency plan in place for practices and competitions.

REFLECTIONS

Not all sport programmes for youth have access to on-field physiotherapists (athletic trainers in the United States) or medical personnel. As coach of a youth team, design a protocol for the monitoring and reporting injuries as they occur.

Coach behaviours are often indicated as risk factors for potentially negative consequences of participation in youth sport: injuries, lowered self-esteem, burn-out. Evaluate your coaching behaviours – training protocols, style of play, methods of evaluating performances and providing feedback, decisions on returning to play after an injury, and others – as they may relate to potentially negative influences on the enjoyment of sport by your players.

THEORY INTO PRACTICE

Involvement in organised sport has the potential for both positive and negative health outcomes for youth. At times, the line between some benefits and risks may be quite fine. Increased risk is often associated with adult behaviours and expectations (parents, coaches), and perhaps the system for some sports. Benefits outweigh risks, and participation in sports is a satisfying, healthy experience for the overwhelming majority of children and adolescents.

The responsibility of those who work with youth sport – coaches, trainers, teachers, and also parents – is to provide an environment in which potential health benefits can be realised and potential health risks are minimised.

Risk of injury, burn-out and manipulation of young athletes may be elevated in programmes for the elite or talented. Vigilance and systematic monitoring of coaching and training environments are essential.

CASE STUDY

Youth sport programmes, and especially behaviours of coaches, are often topics of critical media attention. Attention is often focused on potential health risks for youth participants – overuse injury, overtraining, burn-out, aggressive behaviours, among others – that may be related directly or indirectly to coach behaviours. In this context, your community or club asked you about your coaching style and how it might relate to the health and well-being of the young athletes under your charge. Develop an approach – based on currently available information – for use with the community or club that will provide a balanced view of potential benefits and risks of participation in sport for the physical and behavioural health of the young athletes.

252

The chapter is based on a lecture presented at the Annual Meeting of the American College of Sport Medicine, 2010.

REFERENCES

Barnett, L.M., van Beurden, E., Morgan, P.J., Brooks, L.O. and Beard, J.R. (2008) Does childhood motor skill proficiency predict adolescent fitness? *Medicine and Science in Exercise and Sport* 40: 2137–2144.

Barnett, L.M., van Beurden, E., Morgan, P.J., Brooks, L.O. and Beard, J.R. (2009) Childhood motor skill proficiency as a predictor of adolescent physical activity. *Journal of Adolescent Health* 44: 252–259.

Brody, J.E. (2009) Sports imperative: protecting young brains. *New York Times*, 24 August. Online, available at: http://query.nytimes.com/gst/fullpage.html?res=9502E1DD1131F93 6A1575BC0A96F9C8B63&scp=2&sq=jane%20brody%20%22sports%20imperative% 22&st=cse (accessed 25 August 2009).

Caine, D., Caine, C. and Maffulli, N. (2006) Incidenc e and distribution of pediatric sport-related injuries. *Clinical Journal of Sports Medicine* 16: 500–513.

Coelho e Silva, M.J., Figueiredo, A.J., Elferink-Gemser, M.T. and Malina, R.M. (eds) (2009) *Youth sports* (2nd ed.). Coimbra, Portugal: Coimbra University Press.

Eisenmann, J.C. (2002) Blood lipids and lipoproteins in child and adolescent athletes. *Sports Medicine* 32: 297–307.

Emery, C.A. (2003) Risk factors for injury in child and adolescent sport: a systematic review of the literature. *Clinical Journal of Sports Medicine* 13: 256–268.

Faigenbaum, A.D., Zaichkowsky, L.D., Gardner, D.E. and Micheli, L.J. (1998) Anabolic steroid use by male and female middle school students. *Pediatrics* 101(5): e1–e6.

Franke, W.W. and Berendonk, B. (1997). Hormonal doping and androgenization of athletes: a secret program of the German Democratic Republic government. *Clinical Chemistry* 43: 1262–1279.

Gessel, L.M., Fields, S.K., Collins, C.L., Dick, R.W. and Comstock, R.D. (2007) Concussions among United States high school and collegiate athletes. *Journal of Athletic Training* 42: 495–503.

Gould, D. and Dieffenbach, K. (2003) Psychological issues in youth sports: competitive anxiety, overtraining, and burnout. In R.M. Malina and M.A. Clark (eds), *Youth sports: perspectives for a new century*. Monterey, CA: Coaches Choice.

Hart, E.A., Leary, M.R. and Rejeski, W.J. (1989) The measurement of social physique anxiety. *Journal of Sport and Exercise Psychology* 11: 94–104.

Jahreis, G., Kauf, E., Fröhner, G. and Schmidt, H.E. (1991) Influence of intensive exercise on insulin-like growth factor I, thyroid and steroid hormones in female gymnasts. *Growth Regulation* 1: 95–99.

Kannus, P., Haapasalo, H., Sankelo, M., Sievanen, H., Pasanen, M., Heinonen, A., Oja, P. and Vuori, I. (1995) Effect of starting age of physical activity on bone mass in the dominant arm of tennis and squash players. *Annals of Internal Medicine* 123: 27–31.

Katzmarzyk, P.T. and Malina, R.M. (1998) Contributions of organized sports participation to estimated daily energy expenditure in youth. *Pediatric Exercise Science* 10: 378–386.

Laure, P. and Binsinger, C. (2005) Adolescent athletes and the demand and supply of drugs to improve their performance. *Journal of Sports Science and Medicine* 4: 272–277.

McGuine, T. (2006) Sports injuries in high school athletes: a review of injury-risk and injury-prevention research. *Clinical Journal of Sports Medicine* 16: 488–499.

McLeod, T.C.V., Barr, W.B., McCrea, M. and Guskiewicz, K.M. (2006) Psychometric and measurement properties of concussion assessment tools in youth sports. *Journal of Athletic Training* 41: 399–408.

Malina, R.M. (1999) Growth and maturation of elite female gymnasts: is training a factor? In F.E. Johnston, B. Zemel and P.B. Eveleth (eds), *Human growth in context*. London: Smith-Gordon.

Malina, R.M. (2001) Tracking of physical activity across the lifespan. *Research Digest: President's Council on Physical Fitness and Sports*, series 3, no. 14.

Malina, R.M. (2006) Weight training in youth-growth, maturation, and safety: an evidence-based review. *Clinical Journal of Sports Medicine* 16: 478–487.

Malina, R.M. (2007) Benefits and risks of participation in organized youth sports. In C.E. Gonçalves, S.P. Cumming, M.J. Coelho e Silva and R.M. Malina (eds), *Youth sports*. Coimbra, Portugal: Coimbra University Press.

Malina, R.M. (2010) Early sports specialization: roots, effectiveness, risks. *Current Sports Medicine Reports* 9: 364-371.

Malina, R.M. and Clark, M.A. (eds) (2003) *Youth sports: perspectives for a new century*. Monterey, CA: Coaches Choice.

Malina, R.M., Bouchard, C. and Bar-Or, O. (2004) *Growth, maturation, and physical activity* (2nd ed.). Champaign, IL: Human Kinetics.

Maron, B.J., Poliac, L.C., Kaplan, J.A. and Mueller, F.O. (1995) Blunt impact to the chest leading to sudden death from cardiac arrest during sports activities. *New England Journal of Medicine* 333: 337–342.

R.M. Malina

Maron, B.J., Thompson, P.D., Ackerman, M.J. et al. (2007) Recommendations and considerations related to preparticipation screening for cardiovascular abnormalities in competitive athletics: 2007 update. *Circulation* 115: 1643–1655.

Maron, B.J., Doerer, J.J., Haas, T.S., Tierney, D.M. and Mueller, F.O. (2009) Sudden deaths in young competitive athletes: analysis of 1866 deaths in the United States, 1980–2006. *Circulation* 119: 1085–1092.

Michaelis, V. (2007) IOC votes to start Youth Olympics in 2010. *USA Today*, 5 July. Online, available at: www.usatoday.com/sports/olympics/2007-07-05-youth-notes_N.htm (accessed 7 January 2008).

Miller, G. (2009) A late hit for pro football players. *Science* 325: 670–672.

Monsma, E.V. and Malina, R.M. (2004) Correlates of eating disorder risk among competitive female figure skaters. *Psychology of Sport and Exercise* 5: 447–460.

Monsma, E.V., Malina, R.M. and Feltz, D.L. (2006) Pubertal status and physical self-perceptions of competitive female figure skaters: an interdisciplinary approach. *Research Quarterly for Exercise and Sport* 77: 158–166.

Physical Activity Guidelines Committee (2008) *Physical Activity Guidelines Advisory Committee Report 2008, Part G, Section 9: Youth*. Washington, DC: Department of Health and Human Services, pp. G9-1–G9-33.

Ribeyre, J., Fellmann, N., Montaurier, C., Delaitre, M., Vernet, J., Coudert, J. and Vermorel, M. (2000) Daily energy expenditure and its main components as measured by whole-body indirect calorimetry in athletic and non-athletic adolescents. *British Journal of Nutrition* 83: 355–362.

Smoll, F.L. and Smith, R.E. (2003) Enhancing coaching effectiveness in youth sports: theory, research, and intervention. In R.M. Malina and M.A. Clark (eds), *Youth sports: perspectives for a new century*. Monterey, CA: Coaches Choice.

Strong, W.B., Malina, R.M., Blimkie, C.J.R. et al. (2005) Evidence based physical activity for school youth. *Journal of Pediatrics* 146: 732–737.

Theintz, G., Ladame, F., Kehrer, E., Plichta, C., Howald, H. and Sizonenko, P.C. (1994) Prospective study of psychological development of adolescent female athletes: initial assessment. *Journal of Adolescent Health* 15: 258–262.

Vasankari, T., Lehtonen-Veromaa, M., Möttönen, T., Ahotupa, M., Irjala, K., Heinonen, O., Leino, A. and Viikari, J. (2000) Reduced mildly oxidized LDL in young female athletes. *Atherosclerosis* 151: 399–405.

Wickel, E.E. and Eisenmann, J.C. (2007) Contribution of youth sport to total daily physical activity among 6- to 12-yr-old boys. *Medicine and Science in Sports and Exercise* 39: 1493–1500.

Wrotniak, B.H., Epstein, L.H., Dorn, J.M., Jones, K.E. and Kondilis, V.A. (2006) The relationship between motor proficiency and physical activity in children. *Pediatrics* 118: e1758–e1765.

CHAPTER SEVENTEEN

SPORT AND POSITIVE YOUTH DEVELOPMENT

NICHOLAS L. HOLT

CHAPTER OUTLINE

- The good and bad of youth sport
- Core concept: positive youth development
- Coaching and positive youth development
- Positive parenting practices
- Peer interactions
- Theory into practice: promoting positive youth development through sport
- Learning more

INTRODUCTION

A recent national survey from Canada showed that 87 per cent of children and adolescents failed to meet the guidelines published in Canada's Guide for Physical Activity: to accumulate 90 minutes of moderate to vigorous physical activity per day (Active Healthy Kids Canada, 2009). Similarly, many children and adolescents engage in too many sedentary behaviours such as watching television, playing video games or 'hanging out' with friends. Sedentary behaviours do little to promote healthy physical, social, psychological and cognitive development.

Healthy development can be enhanced by involving youth in structured, organised activities during their leisure time. For example, a study conducted in the US showed that when youth watch television or hang out with friends, they report high intrinsic motivation but low levels of concentration and effort, whereas during structured, organised activities (such as sport) they report high levels of intrinsic motivation, effort and concentration (Larson, 1994). Therefore, structured, organised activities such as sport can be intrinsically motivating *and* stimulate young people to promote healthy development. However, positive development does not automatically occur by simply registering a child in a sport programme (Petitpas

256

et al., 2008). The purpose of this chapter is to describe ways in which youth sport can be delivered and experienced in order to optimise youth development.

THE GOOD AND BAD OF YOUTH SPORT

As Tessa Jowell, then UK cabinet minister responsible for the London 2012 Olympic Games, has repeatedly argued in the media, 'A good sport policy is also a good education, health and anti-crime policy.' Although it is unlikely that simply providing sporting opportunities will solve such a range of social concerns, the idea that youth sport has the potential to positively influence society is widely appealing.

Before we examine how sport may promote development, it is important to bear in mind that debates over the merits of sport participation continue. Results of several large-scale studies (primarily but not exclusively conducted in the US) have associated numerous positive outcomes with youth sport participation. Typically, these questionnaire-based surveys have required respondents to indicate whether or not they participate in organised sport and then respond to health-related questions. Responses of sport participants and non-sport participants are then compared. Findings of these studies show youth sport participation can increase physical activity levels; improve self-esteem, grade point averages, emotional regulation, problem solving and teamwork; and provide opportunities for learning moral behaviours (e.g. Barber *et al.*, 2001; Dworkin *et al.*, 2003; Marsh and Kleitman, 2003).

But sport participation has also been associated with health risk behaviours. A study of US middle school students showed that boys who were sport participants were more likely to carry a weapon and be involved in physical fights compared with non-sport participants (Garry and Morrissey, 2000). Studies from countries such as France (Lorente *et al.*, 2004), the US (Rainey *et al.*, 1996) and Iceland (Thorlindsson, 1989) showed that athletes were more likely than their non-athlete counterparts to consume alcohol. Additionally, whereas athletes are less likely to regularly smoke cigarettes than non-athletes (Pate *et al.*, 2000), findings from studies in the US show that adolescent athletes are more likely to use chewing tobacco (Garry and Morrissey, 2000; Melnick *et al.*, 2001).

This chapter is based on the assumption that youth sport, when appropriately provided, has the potential to influence youth development in healthy positive ways. Sport, in and of itself, does not produce positive developmental outcomes (Petitpas *et al.*, 2008). Rather, the ways in which sport is delivered to and experienced by participants is the key issue in understanding how to optimise youth sport and positive development. The types of social interactions (with coaches, parents and peers) that contribute to healthy positive development through sport will be examined in this chapter.

CORE CONCEPT: POSITIVE YOUTH DEVELOPMENT

Positive youth development (PYD) is a strength-based conception of youth. Rather than youth being viewed as 'problems to be solved', they are considered as 'resources to be developed' (Roth and Brooks-Gunn 2003). From this perspective, positive development can be defined as 'the engagement in pro-social behaviors and avoidance of health compromising behaviors and future jeopardizing behaviors' (Roth et al., 1998: 426). Richard Lerner, a leading proponent of PYD, argues that *all youth* can experience positive development. Childhood and adolescence can be viewed as periods of growth during which young people can develop increasing competence along with knowledge of themselves and their place in society (Jones and Lavallee, 2009).

Lerner described PYD in terms of the '5 Cs' of competence, confidence, connection, character, and caring (or compassion). Competence is a positive view of one's actions in domain-specific areas. Confidence is an internal sense of overall positive self-worth and self-efficacy and one's global self-regard, as opposed to domain-specific beliefs. Connection refers to positive bonds with people and institutions. Character is respect for societal and cultural rules. Finally, caring or compassion refers to a sense of sympathy and empathy for others. Lerner et al. (2005) demonstrated empirical evidence supporting the 5 Cs model of PYD in a study of 1,700 fifth-graders and 1,117 of their parents recruited from 4-H clubs (clubs in rural areas that provide extra-curricular activities to help connect young people to country life). Essentially, the idea is that the more of these 'Cs' young people possess, the more positive their development.

A recent study examined the existence of the 5 Cs in sport contexts. Jones et al. (in press) used a sport-specific PYD measure to survey 258 youth athletes attending summer sport camps at a Canadian university. Although the full 5 Cs model was not supported, two broad factors conceptually consistent with Lerner's approach to PYD did emerge. The first factor was labelled 'personal values' and contained items originally designed to measure caring, character, family connection and competence. The second factor was labelled 'competence/confidence' and contained items designed to measure confidence, competence, and connection to peers. While the results of this single study did not fully support the specific details of the 5 Cs, it showed that these concepts were relevant to youth involved in sport.

CASE STUDY

Holt et al. (2008a) conducted a case study with a well-respected high school soccer coach in Canada. The coach was a teacher at a large school and voluntarily ran the senior team. He was well qualified and had been a university-level player. The school had a clear mission for its sport teams, a mission that aligned with the ideals of PYD. Similarly, the coach had a philosophy that involved having his athletes accept challenges,

N.L. Holt

persevere, and choose their own attitude and path in life. He also wished to impart to his athletes that they represented the school's tradition of sporting excellence.

Researchers attended practices and games and interviewed players at the end of the season. Players were asked whether and how they learned life skills through their involvement on the team. Players reported three types of life skills: learning to take initiative, respect, and teamwork/leadership. But the researchers did not observe the coach making extensive attempts to directly teach these life skills per se. Rather, he provided athletes with options and decision-making responsibilities, which allowed them to demonstrate initiative. Respect was 'taught' in the sense that students were punished if they failed to demonstrate respect during games. Students appeared to learn about teamwork through their peer interactions, which suggests that youth were 'producers of their own experiences'. The point here is that while the coach did not directly teach for positive development, his philosophy was clear and consistent with these ideals, and he created an atmosphere that enabled the players to thrive.

COACHING AND POSITIVE YOUTH DEVELOPMENT

Broadly speaking, there are two main ways in researchers have examined how to promote PYD through coaching in sport. Some scholars have developed instructional programmes with educational curricular designed to teach life skills. The idea of life skills parallels PYD, but life skills have been defined more specifically in relation to sport. That is, life skills are viewed as the skills required to deal with the demands and challenges of everyday life. They can be physical, behavioural or cognitive, and may be transferable from sport to other life domains (Papacharisis et al., 2005).

One example of a life skills programme is Danish's (2002) Sports United to Promote Education and Recreation (SUPER) approach. In SUPER, youth receive workshops in the form of sport clinics that include sport-specific skills as well as more general life skills. Papacharisis et al. (2005) used a quasi-experimental design to evaluate a modified version of SUPER with Greek children. Children who received the intervention improved higher goal-setting, problem-solving, positive thinking and sport skills.

Similar sport-based life skills interventions have been adapted for golf ('The First Tee' programme) and football ('Play It Smart') in the US. The First Tee programme is school based and has an academic focus, whereas Play It Smart is an after-school programme with a general life skills focus (Petitpas et al., 2008). These programmes provide promising practices for promoting PYD through sport. However, it is important to realise that such programmes are delivered by instructors specifically trained to teach life skills. As Gould and Carson (2008) argued, these instructional settings are most likely considerably different from 'everyday' school or competitive youth sport programmes.

259

One study that revealed more information about how coaches in 'everyday' programmes might attempt to teach concepts consistent with PYD was conducted by Gould *et al.* (2006). One hundred and fifty-four high school coaches from the US were surveyed and asked about their roles and responsibilities as a coach. Coaches reported that their most important objectives involved helping athletes with psychological and social skills plus teaching physical skills. However, common problems coaches faced included athletes' failure to take personal responsibility, lack of motivation or work ethic, poor communication and listening skills, poor grades, and problems with parents. These problems suggest that these coaches were not particularly effective in aiding athletes' psychological and social development.

Extending this initial study, Gould *et al.* (2007) interviewed ten outstanding high school football coaches about how they taught life skills. Rather than being 'run-of-the-mill' coaches, the participants in this study were selected because they had been nominated for the prestigious National Football League (NFL) Coach of the Year award. These coaches tended to view life skills as a central part of their coaching role and, while they were driven to win football games, they prioritised athlete personal development over winning. Therefore, these top-quality coaches had clear-cut and well-thought-out coaching philosophies that were compatible with the ideals of PYD.

REFLECTION

If you are a coach or instructor, think about your philosophy. Do you have a clear philosophy that you could easily explain in a few sentences (like the 'elevator pitch')? Do you prioritise youth development above all else? What factors make it difficult for you to prioritise youth development? Can you change these factors? What specific activities do you give to your players to promote their development? Can you use sport to teach them lessons that will be valuable in other areas of their lives?

POSITIVE PARENTING PRACTICES

Whereas coaches have vitally important roles in youth sport, the influence of parents on children's and adolescents' development cannot be overlooked. Coaches may see athletes for a few hours per week, but parents have by far the most powerful influence on the overall course of their children's physical, social, psychological and cognitive development (Bronfenbrenner and Morris, 1998). Parents are probably most important during childhood, and while they remain central in adolescents' lives, their relative influence on development moves somewhat into the background as peers become more important. In sport though, parents continue to play particularly important roles supporting their children during early adolescence (Côté, 1999).

N.L. Holt

Parenting can be thought of in two compatible but different ways. At the most general level, there is a parenting *style*. Parenting style is a broad concept that refers to the range of attitudes parents have towards their children and the emotional climate parents create (Darling and Steinberg, 1993). For example, some parents may have a general style of being strict and authoritarian. Within their general style, parents also display more specific parenting *practices*. Parenting practices reflect parents' goals for their children and have a direct influence on children's behaviours in specific contexts. For example, parents might give their children money for scoring a goal.

One recent study (Holt *et al.* 2009a) of parenting styles and strategies among 56 parents of female soccer players suggested that an *autonomy-supportive* approach may be effective. The autonomy-supportive approach is based on the work of Grolnick (2003). She suggested three elements to this parenting approach: autonomy-support versus control, structure and involvement:

- Autonomy-support versus control refers to the degree to which children feel that they initiate their actions rather than feeling forced to act in a certain manner. Autonomy-supportive parents provide children with the options to choose and solve problems on their own, and exert minimal pressure on them to act in a certain way.
- Structure is the extent to which parents provide clear and consistent guidelines, expectations and rules for their children's behaviours. Structure is often confused with control, but parents can provide structure in autonomy-supportive ways. For example, parents can explain the boundaries of a situation so that children know what to expect in response to their behaviour. Children can then make decisions within the limits set by their parents.
- Involvement is the extent to which parents take an active part in their children's lives. More involvement is generally better when parents provide children a sense of independence and appropriate structure. However, there can be too much parental involvement when that involvement undermines children's autonomy.

The Holt *et al.* (2009a) study showed that some soccer parents were autonomy-supportive, provided appropriate structure and allowed children to be involved in decision making. These parents were also able to read their children's mood and had open channels of communication. For example, they were able to chat with their children about soccer without tension or negative emotions. Other parents were more controlling. These parents did not support their children's autonomy, were not sensitive to their children's mood and tended to report more closed modes of communication. For example, these parents tended to have very tense conversations with their children about sport, and often the children did not want even to talk to their parents about games. These findings suggest that autonomy-supportive parenting may be an effective strategy for sport parents.

PEER INTERACTIONS

As was mentioned in the previous section, peers become increasingly important during the adolescent period. Through their interactions with peers, adolescents can acquire skills, attitudes and behaviours that influence their development (Rubin *et al.*, 2006). Sport psychology researchers have examined the idea of *peer friendships* in sport. Weiss *et al.* (1996) interviewed 8- to 16-year-olds from the US about their 'best sport friendships'. Friendship themes identified through content analysis included companionship and pleasant play, loyalty and intimacy, self-esteem enhancement and supportiveness, things in common, conflict resolution, and conflict. Subsequent research revealed that adolescent junior tennis players who reported a higher quality of sport friendships rated tennis enjoyment and commitment higher than players with lower-quality sport friendships (Weiss and Smith, 2002).

Recent PYD-related research has revealed on a fairly consistent basis that the most meaningful aspects of sport participation arise from peer interactions. In one study, young adult university students were asked about the types of life skills they learned through playing youth sport (Holt *et al.*, 2009b). Social skills relating to learning about teamwork stood out as being the most meaningful aspects of their sport experiences. Importantly, these social skills retained value in the participants' adult lives. For example, participants reported that through sport they had learned to work with 'different' types of people, and this helped them to engage effectively in team projects at work or at university. Another study showed that adolescent girls learned ways to manage conflicts through their involvement on sport teams (Holt *et al.*, 2008b).

It appears that sport provides a context in which to develop meaningful friendships. But in addition to this, playing on a team or training with a squad also expands youths' social network and almost 'forces' them to learn to deal with different types of people. These different types of people might not be part of the person's social group if it were not for their involvement in sport. Although peer interactions may not always appear to be going smoothly, the ways in which peers learn to deal with each other and manage difficult situations seems to have important implications for their social development, both within sport and beyond.

THEORY INTO PRACTICE: PROMOTING POSITIVE YOUTH DEVELOPMENT THROUGH SPORT

From a coaching perspective, while it is perfectly acceptable for coaches to strive to win, to promote PYD they should place the development of their athletes before the win/loss column. Top youth sport coaches appear to embrace this idea and have clear-cut philosophies that emphasise youth development (Gould et al., 2007). The practical implication is clear: encourage coaches to develop philosophies that promote athlete development ahead of winning competitions, while striving to create the most competitive and 'winning' teams possible. Easier said than done, perhaps, but the impetus for PYD must originate from coaches' philosophies. For coaches to develop such philosophies, they will need to operate in youth sport organisations that have missions consistent with the ideals of PYD.

From a parenting perspective, it appears that autonomy-supportive parenting approaches may be ideal for promoting PYD. Parents should be encouraged to take an active interest and be involved in their children's sport, but to do so in a manner that provides children with a sense of independence. Rather than commanding children what to do and controlling all their activities, parents can clearly identify certain boundaries and then allow children to make decisions within these limits. For example, parents could give their child the choice of playing either hockey or soccer but make it quite clear that whichever sport the child chooses, he or she must commit to attending all practices and games for the entire season (i.e. no quitting). In this case, the parents are setting up boundaries by providing a limited number of options (rather than telling their child 'you can do whatever you want'). The child is then empowered to make the decision about which sport she or he wants to play, which should foster a sense of independence. The parents' job is then to ensure they support their child's decision.

It is more difficult to provide practical implications from a peer perspective. Perhaps the most important thing is to arm practitioners with the knowledge that peer conflicts will occur on sport teams, but the ways in which athletes learn to interact with different types of peers and manage these conflicts are some of the most important and meaningful aspects of sport participation. These are the skills that appear to transfer most readily across different areas of adolescents' lives and retain value in their adult lives. The implication is that peers should be encouraged to make efforts to deal with different types of peers and manage conflicts, rather than shying away from such situations.

CONCLUSION

The argument put forth in this chapter is that sport has the potential to promote PYD, although I have acknowledged that PYD will not automatically occur simply as a result of sport being provided. A limitation of the practical implications set out in this chapter is that, although there is an emerging body of evidence, research examining how to promote PYD through sport remains in its infancy. It may also be relevant to consider that the majority of research has been conducted in North American contexts. The North American emphasis on PYD may be because of the turn towards adult-supervised activities as parents become reluctant to allow their children to engage in free play in their neighbourhood locales. Given these considerations, readers would be well advised to evaluate how well the ideas translate to their own situations.

Providing sport opportunities that promote PYD may help keep more youth involved in sport for longer and help combat the problems of insufficient physical activity in many societies. But sport is not a panacea for physical activity. In fact, sport may primarily serve the most active, most well-adjusted youth. Multifaceted approaches are needed to promote youth physical activity, and attention must be paid to providing safe play areas and other physical activity programmes. Nonetheless, youth sport has a certain allure that hooks children and adolescents. Our goal should be to ensure that more youth have more positive experiences in sport more frequently.

LEARNING MORE

Further sources of information on the general concept of positive youth development are available from Professor Richard Lerner's website, http://ase.tufts.edu/iaryd/about PeopleLernerR.htm, and Professor Reed Larson's website, www.youthdev.illinois.edu. For research on positive youth development through sport, see Holt's (2008) book *Positive Youth Development through Sport*. For an example of a sporting organisation that provides funds to low-income youth to access sport with the goal of promoting positive development, see www.kidsportcanada.ca.

REFERENCES

Active Healthy Kids Canada (2009). Report card on physical activity for children and youth. Active Healthy Kids Canada. Online, available from www.activehealthykids.ca (accessed 28 August 2009).

Barber, B.K., Bean, R.L. and Erickson, L.D. (2001) Expanding the study and understanding of parental psychological control. In B.K. Barber (ed.) *Intrusive parenting: how psychological*

N.L. Holt

control affects children and adolescents. Washington, DC: American Psychological Association.

Bronfenbrenner, U. and Morris, P.A. (1998) The ecology of developmental processes. In R.M. Lerner (ed.) *Handbook of child psychology*, vol. 1: *Theoretical models of human development* (5th ed.). New York: Wiley.

Côté, J. (1999) The influence of the family in the development of talent in sport. *Sport Psychologist* 13: 395–417.

Danish, S.J. (2002) *SUPER (Sports United to Promote Education and Recreation) program leader manual* (3rd ed.). Richmond, VA: Life Skills Center, Virginia Commonwealth University.

Darling, N. and Steinberg, L. (1993) Parenting style as context: an integrative model. *Psychological Bulletin* 113: 482–496.

Dworkin, J.B., Larson, R.W. and Hansen, D.M. (2003) Adolescents' accounts of growth experiences in youth activities. *Journal of Youth and Adolescence* 32: 17–26.

Garry, J.P. and Morrisey, S.L. (2000) Team sports participation and risk-taking behaviours among a biracial middle school population. *Clinical Journal of Sport Medicine* 10: 185–190.

Gould, D. and Carson, S. (2008) Life skills development through sport: current status and future directions. *International Review of Sport and Exercise Psychology* 1: 58–78.

Gould, D., Chung, Y., Smith, P. and White, J. (2006) Future directions in coaching life skills: understanding high school coaches' views and needs. *Athletic Insight* 8(3), article 3. Online, available from: www.athleticinsight.com/Vol8Iss3/CoachingPDF.pdf (accessed 7 March 2008).

Gould, D., Collins, K., Lauer, L. and Chung, Y. (2007) Coaching life skills through football: a study of award winning high school coaches. *Journal of Applied Sport Psychology* 19: 16–37.

Grolnick, W.S. (2003) *Psychology of parenting control: how well-meant parenting backfires.* Mahwah, NJ: Lawrence Erlbaum.

Holt, N.L. (ed.) (2008) *Positive youth development through sport*. London: Routledge.

Holt, N.L., Tink, L.N., Mandigo, J.L. and Fox, K.R. (2008a) Do youth learn life skills through their involvement in high school sport? *Canadian Journal of Education* 31(2): 281–304.

Holt, N.L., Black, D.E., Tamminen, K.A., Mandigo, J.L. and Fox, K.R. (2008b) Levels of social complexity and dimensions of peer experience in youth sport. *Journal of Sport and Exercise Psychology* 30: 411–431.

Holt, N.L., Tamminen, K.A., Black, D.E., Mandigo, J.L. and Fox, K.R. (2009a) Youth sport parenting styles and practices. *Journal of Sport and Exercise Psychology* 31: 37–59.

Holt, N.L., Tamminen, K.A., Tink, L.N. and Black, D.E. (2009b) An interpretive analysis of life skills associated with sport participation. *Qualitative Research in Sport and Exercise* 1(2): 160–175.

Jones, M.I., Dunn, J.G.H., Holt, N.L., Sullivan, P.J. and Bloom, G.A. (in press) Exploring the '5Cs' of positive youth development in sport. *Journal of Sport Behavior*.

Jones, M.I. and Lavallee, D. (2009) Exploring the life skills needs of British adolescent athletes. *Psychology of Sport and Exercise* 10: 159–167.

Larson, R.W. (1994) Youth organizations, hobbies, and sports as developmental contexts. In R.K. Silbereisen and E. Todt (eds), *Adolescence in context: the interplay of family, school, peers, and work in adjustment*. New York: Springer-Verlag.

Lerner, R.M., Lerner, J.V., Almerigi, J. *et al*. (2005) Positive youth development, participation in community youth development programs, and community contributions of fifth-grade adolescents: findings from the first wave of the 4-H Study of Positive Youth Development. *Journal of Early Adolescence* 25: 17–71.

Lorente, F.O., Souville, M., Griffet, J. and Grélot, L. (2004) Participation in sports and alcohol consumption among French adolescents. *Addictive Behaviors* 29: 941–946.

Marsh, H.W. and Kleitman, S. (2003) School athletic participation: mostly gain with little pain. *Journal of Sport and Exercise Psychology* 25: 205–228.

Melnick, M.J., Miller, K.E., Sabo, D.F., Farrell, M.P. and Barnes, G.N. (2001) Tobacco use among high school athletes and nonathletes: Results of the 1997 Youth Risk Behavior Survey. *Adolescence* 36: 727–747.

Papacharisis V., Goudas, M., Danish, S.J. and Theodorakis, Y. (2005) The effectiveness of teaching a life skills program in a sport context. *Journal of Applied Sport Psychology* 17: 247–254.

Pate, R.R., Trost, S.G., Levin, S. and Dowda, M. (2000) Sports participation and health-related behaviors among US youth. *Archives of Pediatrics and Adolescent Medicine* 154: 904–911.

Petitpas, A.J., Cornelius, A.E. and Van Raalte, J.L. (2008) Youth development through sport: it's all about relationships. In N.L. Holt (ed.), *Positive youth development through sport*. London: Routledge.

Rainey, C.J., McKeown, R.E., Sargent, R.G. and Valois, R.F. (1996) Patterns of tobacco and alcohol use among sedentary, exercising, nonathletic, and athletic youth. *Journal of School Health* 66: 27–32.

Roth, J. and Brooks-Gunn, J. (2003) Youth development programs: risk, prevention, and policy. *Journal of Adolescent Health* 32: 170–182.

Roth, J., Brooks-Gunn, J., Murray, L. and Foster, W. (1998) Promoting healthy adolescents: synthesis of youth development program evaluations. *Journal of Research on Adolescence* 8: 423–459.

Rubin, K.H., Bukowski, W. and Parker, J.G. (2006) Peer interactions, relationships, and groups. In W. Damon, R.M. Lerner and N. Eisenberg (eds), *Handbook of child psychology*, vol. 3: *Social, emotional, and personality development* (6th ed.). New York: Wiley.

Thorlindsson, T. (1989. Sport participation, smoking, and drug and alcohol use among Icelandic youth. *Sociology of Sport Journal* 6: 136–143.

Weiss, M.R. and Smith, A.L. (2002) Friendship quality in youth sport: relationship to age, gender, and motivational variables. *Journal of Sport and Exercise Psychology* 24: 420–437.

Weiss, M.R., Smith, A.L. and Theeboom, M. (1996) 'That's what friends are for': children's and teenagers' perceptions of peer relationships in the sport domain. *Journal of Sport and Exercise Psychology* 18: 347–379.

CHAPTER EIGHTEEN

CHILDREN'S SPORT IN POLICY CONTEXTS

MICHAEL COLLINS

CHAPTER OUTLINE

■ The Sports Council going solo, 1960s, 1970s, 1980s
■ Challenges of the 1990s
■ Children's sport: a double policy priority under new Labour
■ Current challenges to children's PE and sport
■ Learning more

INTRODUCTION

Across the world, and throughout the 150 years of modern sport's evolution in the voluntary, state and commercial sectors in turn, youth has been its strongest link (including in ministerial arrangements); even in the highest-participant states of Scandinavia, taking part declines after childhood, adolescence and studenthood (Sport England, 1999). Education policy was common to England and Wales until devolution, with different arrangements in Scotland and Northern Ireland, but now all four countries of the United Kingdom can do things differently at school age. For several decades, coaching was amateur, certainly at basic levels, but concern for international competitiveness and the need to cope with growing participation led to the establishment of the National Coaching Foundation (NCF), now more commonly known as sports coach UK, and the seeking of a 'professional vocation'. So, only recently has it been possible to talk of a policy for coaching, and one encompassing rather than separately identifying youth coaching. For brevity and simplicity's sake, this chapter will focus on England, setting school and youth physical education (PE) sport and coaching policies against the wider sports policy panorama since, and identifying trends and current challenges.

THE SPORTS COUNCIL GOING SOLO, 1960s, 1970s, 1980s

Sport had been a compulsory part of the curriculum in the United Kingdom since the 1940s, and took a noticeable share of time and resources (because of facility costs) in gyms and playing fields, and from the 1960s in sports halls and swimming pools, sometimes provided by and managed jointly with a local authority. The Central Council of Physical Recreation (Wolfenden, 1960) recognised that Britain was lagging behind other countries in elite sports performance (overwhelmingly by youth), that there was a large drop-out after leaving school, and that there was a shortage of facilities to enable youth and adult participation. After minor political tussles about whether there should be a national advisory body on sport (Coghlan, 1990), the Sports Council was formed, in 1966, and produced strategies and programmes that encouraged major facility developments with local authority partners in the fiscally encouraging years of the 1970s.

It became recognised that facilities were dominated by well-organised, mobile and relatively affluent groups, however, and direct outreach to more deprived groups was needed. Through an unplanned but helpful intervention in 1981 by sports minister Denis Howell, this was provided in the form of Action Sport workers, aimed initially at inner-city and later at rural youth (Collins, 2010), and soon more widely through Sports Development Officers country-wide. School leavers were the major target through the 1980s, but curiously, having started as an agency under the aegis of the Department of Education, for 30 years the Sports Council was not allowed to work in schools, except in the joint facilities already mentioned (ibid.). Coaching at this stage was fairly amateur, and focused on picking up the promising young performers from schools and clubs and developing their tactical, psychological and technical performance capabilities. Sport England recognised the need for leadership in coach education and preparation, and sponsored the formation of the National Coaching Foundation, in 1983. Sue Campbell, its second director, picked up ideas about technical and sports science education from Canada and Australia and improved upon them, but expected performance level to be the dominant element (Campbell, 1992). At this time, the only focused study was Martin Lee's (1993) *Coaching Children in Sport*.

Meantime, school PE and sport developed rather slowly, pressured by regularly changing political views on the volume of the overall curriculum, and the fact that it was not seen as an 'academic' subject when employable skills were seen as a necessary outcome of education. Moreover, the PE profession became divided three ways as to where emphasis should lie: in traditional, (mainly) team games (which resulted in less choice for girls and a dominant male and competitive ethos); or through a wider set of activities, many non-competitive, and suitable for continuation for a longer span of life; or generic skills for retaining fitness and conveying health. This debate still rumbles on (Green et al., 2005). Coaching was linked to the first, and somewhat to the second, of these. This was exacerbated by political moves in which the Greater London Council and other major (Labour-controlled) city education authorities took a stance against competition; many non-specialist teachers, pressed to carry out more paper-work for student profiling and records, refused to continue doing as much in voluntary support

268

M. Collins

of running curricular and non-curricular sport. The third arm of a hitherto unexperienced triple whammy was a major downturn in school populations, leading to school closures and reorganisations, ageing buildings and lack of investment, especially in the relatively costly sports facilities and their management, which was amateur compared to management in the local authority and commercial sectors (and to some extent still is).

At the same time, the concept that parents and local communities should have much more say in local school management stripped much control from the Department in Whitehall. A senior civil servant said to the author (then head of research, planning and strategy for the Sports Council) and his chief executive, 'The Department used to have power; now we do not even have much influence.' Also, unlike in several countries, primary schooling had no specialised PE teachers to guide growing youngsters in movement skills; some received just a few hours' training in their degree courses.

CHALLENGES OF THE 1990s

The 1990s brought a number of changes. School populations started to grow again slowly; it became obvious that many schools needed major refurbishing or even total rebuilding; the National Curriculum could not reconcile all aspects of the three philosophies, but more concordance on content did appear (e.g. Penney and Evans, 1999). The growth of sports sciences (physiology, psychology, biomechanics, nutrition and sociology) at university crept into GCSE and A level exams, and became popular (there were 22,000 A level candidates in 2008). Indeed, sports sciences were lauded by the Department and school inspectors as a subject with cross-disciplinary potential.

This provided a veneer of academic respectability, and better-qualified teachers were finding employment in secondary schools. For a fleeting couple of years, the Sports Council became a non-departmental government body of the Department of Education, unfortunately under the aegis of a minister, Robert Atkins, who was considered relatively ineffective, with sport being treated with 'an attitude which combined neglect, disdain and incomprehension' (Houlihan and White, 2002: 63). But it opened the door for continued working when the four domestic sports councils and a new UK Sports Council in charge of elite sport became some of a large number of non-departmental public bodies answering to the new Department of Culture, Media and Sport under the New Labour government. International competitiveness fuelled a focus on elite sport and the concomitant improvements in coaching in what De Bosscher et al. (2008) colourfully called 'the global sporting arms race'. The formation of sports coach UK was to transcend devolution and serve all four domestic sports councils.

In her three terms of office as prime minister, Margaret Thatcher had no interest in sport and declined to support Olympic bids. Her successor, John Major, was willing to support bids for major events, but a more significant act was to legislate the introduction of a National Lottery. This was unexpectedly popular and produced major sums of money for sport, for the first time providing the broken-time payments for professional training of elite athletes that the Olympic athlete Sebastian Coe and others had campaigned for. After relatively poor medal hauls for Britain in the Olympics in Sydney and Athens, in conjunction with commercial sponsorship, and investment in coaching and technology, this produced huge improvements in performance in the third cycle in Beijing in 2008, showing the gestation time needed for such programmes, a lesson not properly learned in support of mass participation.

One other factor was significant, and that was the emergence of a policy champion. Sue Campbell had been a PE teacher and performer and university lecturer before working for Sport England in the East Midlands. As was mentioned earlier, she became the second director of the National Coaching Foundation (NCF) soon after its formation, and set about learning lessons from and improving on the training of coaches from basic club level to national coach that she saw overseas, especially in Canada and Australia. The NCF's courses included courses in sports sciences and medicine, child pedagogy and support for adult competitors, and health and safety, and a Diploma rapidly became the gold standard internationally, attracting people even from those places from which earlier ideas had been culled. With the benefit of a ministerial Coaching Task Force (CTF, 2002), her successors in what is now sports coach UK are developing a five-tier National Coach Certification system that will be compatible with, but in advance of, developments elsewhere in Europe. Soon she moved on to fulfil a dream of improving school sport and PE offered by the patronage of businessman Sir John Beckwith to form the Youth Sport Trust (YST) in 1994, and rapidly developed short courses (backed by manuals and equipment bags) to help, first, the non-specialist primary teachers of PE and children's transition to secondary schools. These were hugely successful and soon she gained finance from both the National Lottery and the Exchequer. For a time she was, unusually, an adviser to ministers in both the Department of Education and the Department of Media, Culture and Sport. She became chair of the YST and then of UK Sport. The YST developed to oversee specialist sports colleges (SSCs), sport in special schools, and Step into Sport youth volunteering; SSCs grew in number to 400 sites, linked by a major annual conference. Meanwhile, UK Sport developed sporting champions and sport-in-development links with Third World countries. Baroness Campbell, as she became in 2008, has a first-hand knowledge of both the foundation and the pinnacle of sporting participation. These factors underpinned a remarkable transformation of school sport and PE, to which I now turn.

CHILDREN'S SPORT: A DOUBLE POLICY PRIORITY UNDER NEW LABOUR

In 2002, Houlihan and White could speak of three policy clusters. Two – elite sport and school and youth sport – were strong in terms of numbers of organisations, finance and political support; the third – adult sport in local communities – was weakly supported. The elite group, of course, was dominated by teenagers and young adults, with an increasing number connected with and training at higher education institutions through the Talented Athletes Scholarship Scheme, which after 2005 offered small bursaries to younger children.

270

M. Collins

In 1991–1999, the NCF introduced Champion Coaching, to provide accessible and affordable coaching sessions for young athletes in schools and clubs who wanted to improve. In over 100 local authority areas, it provided a basis for talent identification and coach training that was real (Bell, 2010), though never monitored or acknowledged by Sport England. But it was still dominated by children from middle-class households and non-deprived areas (Collins and Buller, 2000). On the one hand, it helped the Active Sports and national junior sports programmes (Enoch, 2010), and on the other it helped the professionalisation of coaching (Bell, 2010). The rebranded English Sports Council wanted to see 3,000 community sports coaches and funded bursaries; by 2009, sports coach UK was seeking another 93,000 coaches at all levels by 2016, identifying children's coaches as one of four groups (North, 2009), with coach education delivered by the national governing bodies and the YST.

In 2003, the then Department for Education and Skills and the Department for Culture, Media and Sport introduced the multi-strand Physical Education, School Sport and Club Links (PESSCL) programme, which put £1.5 billion into school sport over the next seven years. Its main outcomes have been:

■ 90 per cent of children getting two hours a week of quality PE and sport in and out of school (ahead of target, but lagging in years 10 and 11), and 50 per cent three hours (though nine-tenths of this was out of curriculum, and quality was self-defined);
■ better than average academic results in Specialist Sports Colleges (SSCs);
■ growing numbers involved in clubs, coaching and competition;
■ School Sport Partnerships helping primary PE (see Table 18.1).

It has been extended to 2011 and rebranded, with the notable and challenging addition of seeking 5 hours a week of quality PE and sport a week (see below), with a further £0.7 billion.

sports coach UK (2008) aims to provide 2 hours of 'guided sport' in school and an hour outside by 2016 for 99 per cent of all 5-year-olds, ranging down to 80 per cent of 15- and 16-year-olds (currently this age group was averaging 3.6 hours, peaking at 6 hours for the oldest cohort, involving 1.2 million coaching hours, 61 per cent of the total). The supply analysis, unfortunately, did not identify children's coaches, but sought overall a 5 per cent year-on-year increase in coached hours, with a major growth in extra-curricular or community coaching for children. There are scattered academic articles on coaching children, but even Lyle's (2002) seminal text includes nothing; Hagger (2003) on coaching young performers and Haskins (2010) on youth in general are manuals, Haskins arguing that coaching, through promoting the 5 Cs (competence, confidence, character and caring, connection, and creativity), can help positive development of young people in general, and not just those at risk of going, or actually going, 'off the rails'.

CURRENT CHALLENGES TO CHILDREN'S PE AND SPORT

For all that PE and school sport in England have been transformed in the past 15 years, there are weaknesses in and criticisms of what has happened and been achieved. I set out seven below.

Table 18.1 The Physical Education, School Sport and Club Links (PESSCL) and Physical Education and Sport Strategy for Young People (PESSYP) programmes, 2003–2008

DfEE 2003 elements (1)	Developments and PESSYP 2008 (2)
▪ PSA targets from 62% in 2003 of 75% of children having 2 hours' high-quality PE and sport a week by 2006, 85% by 2008; £1.5bn, 2003–8	▪ Exceeded 90% by 2007–8 ; but only 71% and 66% in years 10 and 11 (3); a five-hour target is being set (DCSF, 2008) with £755m for 2008–11
▪ 400 specialist sport colleges (SSCs) by 2005	▪ The Department for Education and Employment says exam results have improved; there is still a struggle between physical activity, competitive and lifelong recreation; help raise the floor rather than raising the ceiling (4); SSCs obtain above-average GCSE scores for five subjects graded A*–C (6)
▪ 450 School Sport Partnerships (SSPs) involving virtually all state schools	▪ SSPs do develop networks, help teacher development, and focus on neglected primary PE (5); £30m for coaches in SSPs 2008–11
▪ 3,200 school sport coordinators (SSCos) by 2006, linked to 18,000 primary teachers	▪ Appoint further education college coordinators (FESCOs) linked to SSPs
▪ Increase proportion entering clubs	▪ Club links increase from 5 to 7.6 per school, 2003–7, and volunteers from 12% to 16%
▪ Gifted and talented (G&T) development programmes including talent camps	▪ Those registered as G&T rise from 3% to 7%
▪ Step into Sport to encourage youth volunteering in 200 SSPs	▪ SSCs developing interest in sports leadership ▪ £45m for Playing with Success schemes with professional clubs to increase numeracy and literacy ▪ Create at least one multi-sport club for disabled children in each SSP

Sources: (1) Department for Education and Skills (2003); (2) Department for Children, Schools and Families (2008); (3) Quick *et al.* (2009); (4) Houlihan and Wong (2005); (5) Loughborough Partnership (2005); (6) Youth Sports Trust (2000).

Extra contact time, but intensity and quality?

Despite the growth in hours of school sport, much of it, at both primary and secondary level, involves only moderate physical exertion, and so does not set a benchmark for carrying into adult life protective activity against obesity and its attendant ills such as diabetes, coronary heart disease and strokes. Even the government-funded recent free swimming programmes for under-16s and over-60s in England are believed by many pool managers to benefit many who already swim rather than new swimmers (Shibli, 2008).

Still no recognised qualification for primary PE

Specialist qualification of primary PE teachers will not alone ensure the high quality of PE the government aspires to, but would provide a surer basis for community-based volunteer coaches to come in and work in partnership. A pejorative comment would be that TOPs is a sticking plaster on a long-term wound. (TOPs are Youth Sport Trust TOP programmes, which are intended to encourage all youth, from 18 months to 18 years, to make the most of PE and sport opportunities, including TOP Links to help them organise sport or dance festivals in primary schools, and TOP Sportsability to integrate youth with disabilities with their peers).

PE still offers inequitable choices for girls and disabled pupils

Girls are taking up activities that used to be the prerogative of boys, including soccer, cricket, rugby and boxing, but it is still true that PE and school sport is gendered; the choice is still narrower for girls, boys still get priority for equipment and space, and team games still predominate over the individual activities many girls prefer (Flintoff and Scraton, 2001).

It is very strongly true that opportunities for disabled pupils are very much poorer, despite principles of inclusion for mainstream PE in the curriculum: in 2001, 45 per cent of disabled schoolchildren spent less than an hour in PE lessons compared to 18 per cent of all pupils, while Thomas and Smith (2009: 107–114) claimed that disabled pupils spent less active time in a narrower range of activities out of school; most community coaches have no training or experience in supporting physically disabled athletes or, still more so, those with learning difficulties.

Volunteering

All surveys of sports volunteering in Britain show problems of getting enough volunteers as playing careers have extended into the veteran years, and ever more leisure attractions compete for time and energy, so the challenge facing sports coach UK should not be minimised.

The elephant in the room: childhood obesity

In 2012, we may expect 1 million British children to be obese, including 22 per cent of boys and 19 per cent of girls aged 2–15 (Central Office of Information, 2008). The doyen of exercise science, Jerry Morris, said, four weeks before his death aged 99, 'Just imagine what historians are going to say about the way we've allowed the epidemic of childhood obesity. "Disgrace" is a mild sort of word' (www.FT.com, downloaded 4 November 2009). If a political panic hits after 2012, elite sport could certainly suffer from transfer of funds.

Can the 'hinge' in the single system cope?

Lord Carter (2005) sought a single sports system backed by simple grant aid procedures. With any form of representative regional sport bodies abolished, the crucial link between national policy and local delivery are the 49 County Sports Partnerships, bringing together national governing bodies and clubs, schools and LEAs, district and unitary councils, and a host of other partners. With small staffs and core budgets and two changes of policy priorities in their brief lives, they are supposed to broker a wide range of programmes with education, health and community safety partners with deeper pockets and more political clout.

Reduced resources after 2012?

As always after the benefits of a home Olympics, support for elite sport will reduce markedly for the next quadrennial, even after a good medal tally, and will bring some squeeze on performance coaching spending. It is unclear what will happen to basic coaching if a Conservative government is returned at the next general election, but it is to be hoped that the government's commitments to coaching workforce development will hold.

Are things different in other parts of Great Britain? In Wales, under the Welsh Assembly government there are programmes similar to PESSCL (PES, Dragon Sport and Talented Athletes, and specialist colleges, though perhaps with less coordination) and Free Swimming. In Scotland, with greater devolution to the Scottish Executive, there has been no programme similar to PESSYP, and less progress in school PE and sport. Moreover, there are no specialist colleges (Thomson, 2010). Both countries have strategies (*Climbing Higher*; Welsh Assembly Government, 2005; and *Reaching Higher*; Scottish Executive, 2007) more like the previous English framework (Sport England, 2004), seeking sport for good, and implementing the Department for Culture, Media and Sport's (2002) *Game Plan*.

CONCLUSION

Both elite sport and PE and school sport in England have had unprecedented money, physical and human resources and have flourished, though not without issues. The former is tightly focused and rewards success; the latter is more multi-strand, kaleidoscopic and difficult to coordinate, and it remains to be seen whether the County Sports Partnerships can handle this task; already there are hints that it is not easy to hold school programmes, club work, physical activity promotion and performance sport in a flexible and changing balance (Henry *et al.*, 2009). Meantime, community provision flounders, with inadequate resources, coordination and leadership – not an encouraging environment for young people leaving schools or universities or seeking competitive careers. Coaching, like other social policy interventions, is multifaceted and requires complex partnerships and long-term programmes and patience, qualities many politicians and even some policy makers lack. Its outcomes are indirect and difficult to measure and attribute, so it is a ripe field for social research.

ADDENDUM

In 2010 the ConDem coalition came into power with manifesto promises to make swingeing public expenditure cuts and to reduce a huge deficit. It cancelled free swimming as 'unaffordable'; abolished Specialist Sports Colleges; threatened to cut all the PESSYP spending of £162m, but saved enough to pay SS coordinators one day a week instead of two after a vociferous campaign, including by Baroness Campbell; and imposed local authority spending cuts which exceeded the average for sport and culture, being non-statutory. At the same time, the reduced welfare benefits and increased unemployment amongst the low-skilled are going to accelerate the rich–poor gaps in income, health and discretionary/leisure spending.

REFERENCES

Bell, B. (2010) Building a legacy for youth and coaching: champion coaching on Merseyside. In Collins, M.F. (ed.), *Examining sports development*. London: Routledge.

Campbell, S. (1992) Coach education in the 21st century: a look into the future. In T. Williams, L. Almond and A. Sparkes (eds), *Sport and physical activity: moving towards excellence*. London: E& FN Spon.

Carter, P. [Lord] (2005) *Review of national sport effort and resources*. London: Department for Culture, Media and Sport.

Central Office of Information (2008) *Healthy weight, healthy lives: a cross-government strategy*. London: COI.

Coaching Task Force (2002) *The Coaching Task Force: final report*. London: Department for Culture, Media and Sport.

Coghlan, J. (1990) *Sport and British politics since 1960*. London: Falmer Press.

Collins, M.F. (2010) The development of sports development. In M.F. Collins (ed.), *Examining sports development*. London: Routledge.

Collins, M.F. and Buller, J.R. (2000) Bridging the post-school institutional gap in sport: evaluating champion coaching in Nottinghamshire. *Managing Leisure* 5: 200–221.

De Bosscher, V., Bingham, J., Shibli, S., van Bottenburg, M. and de Knop, P. (2008) *The global sporting arms race: an international study on sports factors leading to international sporting success*. Oxford: Meyer & Meyer Sport.

Department for Children, Schools and Families (DCSF) (2008) *PESSYP: creating a world class system for PE and sport*. London: DCSF.

Department for Education and Skills (DfES) (2003) *Learning through PE and sport: a guide to the PESSCL strategy*. London: DfES.

Department of Culture, Media and Sport (2002) *Game Plan: a strategy for delivering the government's sport and physical activity objectives*. London: DCMS.

Enoch, N. (2010) Towards a contemporary national structure for youth sport in England. In M.F. Collins (ed.), *Examining sports development*. London: Routledge.

Flintoff, A. and Scraton, S. (2001) Stepping into active leisure? Young women's perceptions of active lifestyles and their experiences of school physical education. *Sport, Education and Society* 6: 5–22.

Green, K., Smith, A. and Roberts, K. (2005) Young people and lifelong participation in sport and physical activity: a sociological perspective on contemporary physical education programmes in England and Wales. *Leisure Studies* 24(1): 27–43.

Hagger, M. (2003) *Coaching the young performer* (2nd ed.). Leeds: Coachwise.

Hardman, K. and Marshall, J. (2009) *Second world-wide survey of physical education*. Berlin: International Council of Sport Science and Physical Education.

Haskins, D. (2010) *Coaching the whole child: positive development through sport*. Leeds: Coachwise.

Henry, I., Harwood, C.G., Downward, P.M. and Robinson, L.A. (2008) *Sports partnerships promoting inclusive communities*. Loughborough, UK: Loughborough University Institute for Sport and Leisure Policy.

Houlihan, B. and White, A. (2002) *The politics of sports development: development of sport or development through sport*. London: Routledge.

Houlihan, B. and Wong, C. (2005) *Report on 2004 survey of Specialist Sports Colleges*. Loughborough, UK: Loughborough University, Institute of Youth Sport.

Lee, M. (ed.) (1993) *Coaching children in sport: principles and practice*. London: E & FN Spon.

Loughborough Partnership (2005) *School Sports Partnerships: annual monitoring and evaluation*. Loughborough, UK: Loughborough University, Institute of Youth Sport.

Lyle, J. (2002) *Sports coaching concepts: a framework for coaches' behaviour*. London: Routledge.

North, J. (2009) *The coaching workforce 2009–2016*. Leeds: sports coach UK.

Penney, D. and Evans, J. (1999) *Politics, policy and practice in physical education*. London: E & FN Spon.

Quick, S., Dalziel, D., Thornton, A. and Simon, A. (2009) *PE and school sport survey 2008/09*. Research Report DCSF-168. London: TNS-BMRB for the Department of Children, Schools and Families.

Scottish Executive (2007) *Reaching higher: building on the success of Sport 21*. Edinburgh: SE.

Shibli, S. (2008) Free swimming: will it work? Paper presented to ISRM conference, Alton Towers. Online, available from www.isrm.co.uk.

Sport England (1999) *Compass 1999: sports participation in Europe*. London: Sport England.

Sport England (2004) *Framework for sport in England: making England an active and successful sporting nation: a vision for 2020*. London: Sport England.

Sport England (2008) *Grow Sustain Excel: A strategy for 2008–2011*. London: Sport England.

sports coach UK (2008) *The UK Coaching Framework*. Leeds: Coachwise.

Thomas, N. and Smith, A. (2009) *Disability, sport and society*. London: Routledge.

Thomson, I. (2010) Sport in a devolved system: the Scottish experience. In M.F. Collins (ed.), *Examining sports development*. London: Routledge

Welsh Assembly Government (2005) *Climbing Higher: a strategy for sport and physical activity in Wales*. Cardiff: WAG.

Wolfenden, J. [Sir, later Lord] (1960) *Sport and the community*. London: Central Council for Physical Recreation.

Youth Sports Trust (2000) *Know the score: collection of evidence to support the impact of the Sports College Network*. Loughborough, UK: YST.

CHAPTER NINETEEN

THE YOUNG PLAYER AS A LEARNER

ANTHONY ROSSI AND RICHARD TINNING

CHAPTER OUTLINE

▪ **Young people**
▪ **Young people, learning and the technologised age**
▪ **Learning in sport**
▪ **So what does the evidence presented mean and how can it help?**
▪ **Learning more**

INTRODUCTION

There is a popular belief that contemporary sports coaches face increasingly complex problems when coaching young performers. These problems appear to be located around the idea that 'youth' in the twenty-first century are somewhat different from their counterparts who went before them. This issue was flagged a generation ago, in a paper titled 'Teaching and coaching today's kids'. In that paper, Shirley Willis (1994) related the story of a then well-known, experienced coach who admitted (on a radio interview) that he couldn't teach *today's kids* because they had a different sense of authority. They questioned things and often expected to be included in decision making. Moreover, they weren't impressed by the old-fashioned punishment methods such as push-ups. More recently, in considering young people as learners in a physical education context, Tinning (2007) wondered whether, because of the different social context and the increasing influence of digital media in their lives, young people were rather like 'aliens in the gym'. Tinning concluded, however, that as far as *physical competence* and *skill development* were concerned, young people are probably more like their parents than aliens. So even if the argument for contemporary youth being different holds, differences in sports technique learning may well be less obvious than other differences.

Increasingly, though, there is evidence in the literature that contemporary youth 'learn' and 'act' in ways that might seem at best unfamiliar and at worst anarchical and disruptive (see

A. Rossi and R. Tinning

Kenway and Bullen, 2001; White and Wyn, 2008). More likely, young performers fall (perhaps as they have always done) somewhere between these points. This nonetheless places the coach in an unenviable position: how to make sense of young people in ways that make coaching practices appealing and meaningful. In this chapter, we explore this notion by examining the concept of youth and youth identity and relating this to what the contemporary literature says about learning and learning theory. We also discuss the implications for coaching. Inevitably, such a discussion will include current discourses surrounding popular and popularised approaches to teaching and coaching.

YOUNG PEOPLE

There are perhaps two things that characterise enduring discourses related to the idea of youth. The first is that youth is seen as a transitional period or a stage on the way to something else that is arguably a more desirable state (Kenway and Bullen, 2001) – in other words, adulthood. The consequence of this is that no status of any significance is afforded to being young or being a youth. This is interesting in and of itself, given the barrage of advertising and marketing of products and procedures aimed at 'making' adults young (again), and the weight of advertising revenue directed at 'youth markets'. Second, the lack of status becomes inextricably linked with the idea of youth as a 'problem'. So, no matter what generational shifts there have been, these two things seem persistent and therefore warrant some attention. This discourse has largely emerged from the notion of youth subcultures, an idea developed at the University of Birmingham in the United Kingdom in the 1970s. It was predicated on the idea that a youth subculture was a culture of resistance to the dominant orthodoxy. Tait (2000) argues that while this produced some useful conceptual tools, it remained limited as a way of explaining how youth get on with their lives. Tait (ibid.) is more an advocate of the notion of youth as a constructed montage of problems brought about by the principles of governance and surveillance. Hence, Tait advocates a broader use of the work of Michel Foucault and his ideas about governmentality as a theoretical framework for understanding the notion of youth.

Even though this chapter is about young sport performers as learners, we have written it, unashamedly, from a critical youth perspective. The reason for this is that, in our view, children do not play or engage in sport in a social, political or economic vacuum. Young people in the twenty-first century (and perhaps since the beginning of organised youth sport) play sport amid social turmoil, political prejudice and varying levels of economic certainty. Young people (as a category) are, more than ever, overtly politicised, as is evidenced in the school reforms, control measures, surveillance and other forms of governance applied to them (see Roberts, 1996). Contemporary youth culture is shaped by government policy on education, on public expenditure for recreational spaces and facilities, and the increased 'medicalisation' of youth as sociopathic, troublesome, different and 'at risk' (Giardina and Donnelly, 2008). Young people are also, at least in developed nations, among the most marketised segments of society. Corporations spend billions of dollars trying both to connect to youth culture (as a market) and, at the same time, to help create it. This is nowhere more apparent than in sport and the connection of sport to broader cultural trends in music and fashion. Indeed, large companies no longer try to promote sport but rather promote the idea of sport; it is lifestyle, or at least the image of it, that is important (Rinehart, 2008).

Young people also have to deal with constantly shifting social circumstances and exist in a globalised economy shaped largely by neo-liberalism (sometimes called neo-conservativism; Klein, 2008) – that is, a political philosophy that extols the virtues of the free market, small government and individual responsibility. This has been the accepted political orthodoxy since at least the early 1980s, but in 2008 it came apart at the seams, causing worldwide financial crisis and economic hardship unprecedented since the depression of the 1930s. It is amid this social, economic and political turmoil that young people are meant to somehow make sense of the world. And it is against this backdrop that adults expect young people to embrace sport and, further, to become eager learners seeking fulfilment through improvement and moral fortitude. Given that young people have never known or experienced political or economic circumstances that are any different, we are mindful that we could be accused of just being whining baby-boomers. However, in our view the argument that young people, as a consequence of the circumstances in which they are growing up, are in many ways very different from preceding generations is a convincing one. Hence, it makes no sense to talk about young performers as learners without taking due cognisance of these circumstances. We therefore see the role of the coach, whether at the weekend volunteer level or at the elite youth level, as being profoundly important yet at the same time incredibly complex.

REFLECTION

If you are a student (physical education, coaching studies), then you are most likely to be one of the 'young' people referred to in this section! Does this seem a reasonable assessment of youth? Given that it is drawn from academic literature, it has 'authority', but to what extent is it true for you?

If you are an adult coach, to what extent do you sense 'difference' in the young people with whom you work . . . different from what, from whom? If you perceive levels of difference, what does this mean for your work as a coach? Does it present you with challenges regarding how to engage young people in learning activities you design in an effort to improve their performance? Do they connect with the tasks or do they just 'go through the motions'?

Youth: one moral panic after another

Since the start of the nineteenth century, about every 25–30 years or so, members of the 'older' generation begin to voice anxiety about the nation's (whichever nation's) young people

A. Rossi and R. Tinning

(Bramham, 2005). The young people do not share the same values, have different dispositions to work, have new leisure pursuits previously unavailable and live rather easily with advancing and rapidly changing technology. These 'differences' are often the cause for concern (rather than celebration) regarding the 'waywardness' of youth, and this in turn leads to a demonising of young people such that we (adults) are charged with the responsibility of making them 'better'. These circumstances are amply documented in literature dating from the late 1970s as well as in more contemporary work, for example in Australia by Johanna Wyn and Rob White (1997). Of course, such concerns are not distributed evenly across either gender or class divides. Historically at least, girls have been considered to be less of a 'problem' than boys, and certainly troublesome girls tend to be more easily privatised – that is, problems related to girls tend not to be sensationalised in the public domain in the same way boys' problems tend to be (Bramham, 2005). More recently, however, in both the United Kingdom and Australia, media coverage of problem youth has often included or been devoted to young girls, particularly around issues related to binge drinking, eating disorders and substance abuse (see Barham, 2004; White and Wyn, 2008). Much has also been written about the influence of class, with rather simplistic connections being made between troublesome youth, class and income levels, and geographical location (see Weller, 2006). Similarly, race or ethnicity is rather carelessly attached to the concept of youth.

The best that we can say is that 'youth' is socially constructed. The meaning of the word 'youth' is entirely contextual and is better considered as a relational concept (see Wyn and White, 1997) in that it tends to be most commonly understood in relation to the concept of adulthood, which is often regarded as the 'arrival' state. As a consequence, 'youth' can only ever be a state of becoming, and this tends to limit our understanding of 'youth culture'. As a consequence, youth are most often seen as needing guidance and assistance to become an adult, and it is adult 'expertise' that ensures this is conducted correctly.

YOUNG PEOPLE, LEARNING AND THE TECHNOLOGISED AGE

According to White and Wyn (2008), there is widespread support for the idea that immersion in digital communication technologies is one of the principal defining features of what became known as Generation Y (Generation Y was preceded by Generation X and before that the baby-boomers). It is likely that such defining principles will continue. In Australia, by the early 2000s, 80 per cent of 15- to 17-year-olds had their own mobile (cell) phone (Tjong et al., 2003), with 14 years being the average age for first mobile (cell) phone ownership. A poll in the United Kingdom (Gibson, 2005) indicated that close to 35 per cent of 14- to 21-year-olds had their own online content via social networking sites and blogs. As a point of contrast, older people tend to refer to such communication technologies as 'new', whereas for younger persons they are simply a taken-for-granted fact of life (White and Wyn, 2008).

What does this mean for learning?

It is difficult to write definitively about what all this means for learning, and one of the reasons is that youth generations of a (post)modern era, particularly in the developed world, are regarded as a generation with choice. One of the things they tend to choose is to mix work (as in paid work) and schooling, suggesting that there are serious and increasing shifts in how young people make sense of and use formal education and other learning opportunities (Ball *et al.*, 2000). This confirms Raffo and Reeves's (1999) finding, that young people are exercising choices which make them part-time children and part-time adults, making adult decisions based on wants, needs and desires. Whether such a process of decision making is based on Maslow's (1954) needs hierarchy (though perhaps with less linear structure) or the classic supply and demand economic model is not clear. What we can say with more confidence is that linear notions of educational experiences, and transitions in and out of them, are no longer tenable. So, while schooling is saddled with the structural constraints of the industrial revolution, young people manage their way in the world with far greater complexity and creativity and much less linearity. It is not too long a bow to draw to suggest that how young people go about learning is similarly neither linear nor predictable, is likely to involve multi-media, be spread across multiple locations and have varying levels of independence and intensity. The problem for a sports coach of how to create meaningful learning experiences that connect to young people in the way that they experience and live in the world must seem like a mighty challenge.

CASE STUDY

One of the abilities attributed to young people is their capacity to multi-task. So, it would not be uncommon to see a young person at home doing their homework, watching the TV and listening to their iPod. Does this kind of behaviour manifest itself in your coaching situations? That is, do young performers talk to each other while you are coaching, answer their mobile (cell) phones and yet still know how to perform the task or activity you are working on? These may not be the actual things they do, but do they multi-task in coaching contexts? Try to observe this and make a mental or even a written note about it. If possible, make more than one set of observations; perhaps observe your performers over the course of a few sessions.

Reflect on your observations. Consider these questions:

- Was it apparent that your young performers were multi-tasking?
- If so, do you think it made any difference to their performance?
- If not, why do you think that is? Were they focused, did the tasks demand lots of attention, were they too busy trying to stay warm (or keep cool)?

A. Rossi and R. Tinning

LEARNING IN SPORT

Two very short and incomplete personal stories

The issue of learning in sport is a minefield where many now fear to tread unless they have some particular barrow to push. We enter this 'minefield' through some modest (potted) personal histories that might get us started.

Story 1: Learning about learning and teaching

Though the authors of this chapter are nearly ten years apart in age and have grown up on opposite sides of the world (Richard in Melbourne, Australia, and Anthony in London, England), there is a remarkable similarity when it comes to our teacher education experience. For both of us it was dominated by the prevalence of physical activity learning (we did lots of practical classes), and we learned about 'learning' through courses in what was called at the time 'skill acquisition' (or derivations thereof). Much of this would have been founded on work in experimental psychology, which was finding a new place in the study of sport. These courses would have been dominated by information processing theory and were underpinned by much of what had been developed out of behaviourism, in particular through the legacy of Thorndike (1932) and Hull (1943) and the important influence of Skinner (1938). In our field of physical education (PE), behaviourism emerged in the work of Knapp (1964), Whiting (1969) and Oxendine (1968), and then others who followed, such as Singer (1975) and Sage (1971). The core concepts of study would have been practice, feedback and the transfer of training. In addition, we would have learned about 'stage theory', which was about how children pass through definable stages of development, physically, cognitively and emotionally. All of this pointed to a very linear model of learning, which required a very linear form of teaching and coaching.

Against this dominant behavioural conception of learning physical activity, there were some practical courses that may have troubled such ideas about learning. For example, Educational Gymnastics or Movement Education was much more driven by play theory, 'discovery' learning and the educational ideas of John Dewey. Some of the work on games by Liz Mauldon and Betty Redfern (1969) took a similar approach. Such inconsistencies, however, were largely glossed over.

Story 2: Moving on

By the early 1980s, Richard Schmidt's schema theory (first published in 1975) had gained traction within motor learning courses and was being widely tested by doctoral students across the United States (and perhaps beyond). Its principal feature was the power of variable practice as significant contributor to learning. At around the same time, in more esoteric quarters, ecological psychology and dynamical systems of *motor control* (the language change is important here), founded on earlier work by Nikolai Bernshtein (1967), were showing empirical promise. In Britain, also in the early 1980s, Dave Bunker and Rod Thorpe, two teacher educators at Loughborough University, thoroughly dispirited with the teaching of games they were witnessing in schools, came up with a new pedagogical model that placed *understanding* at the heart of the teaching process. Their model, Teaching Games for Understanding (TGfU) (Bunker and Thorpe, 1982) was somewhat slow to catch on (and actually remained so for some time), but some enthusiastic teachers took it up. By this time, Anthony (an enthusiast) was a secondary (high) school PE teacher, and Richard was impressed by what he saw of TGfU when he was a visitor on sabbatical to Loughborough in 1988.

Relevance

So what use do these personal potted histories serve? Well, conventional teaching and coaching of skills based on the teacher education (and research efforts beyond) for both of us were dominated by a *demonstrate, explain and practice* (DEP) model. The basis of this has been the idea we alluded to earlier, that learning motor skills is largely a linear process, controllable through the practice arrangements and the conditions of feedback provided. This model has proved remarkably resilient and resistant to change, and it will be commonplace, we suspect, in the home countries of all the authors in this book in both school PE and sports coaching. OK, nothing unusual so far, except that back at the beginning of this chapter we described how young people who inhabit an increasingly complex world are thought to learn differently – not in linear fashion but in complex multi-modal ways. Moreover, we suggested that learners now want to be decision makers; indeed, we often hear about the production of intelligent performers (i.e. decision makers) in sport. So, this would suggest that models of linear coaching might not be best, regardless of the sport or activity. Indeed, Paul Potrac highlights this in his stories of coaching in a chapter with Tania Cassidy (2006). The vignette used by Potrac and Cassidy must resonate with many coaches. It largely focuses on two things: the seeming lack of receptiveness of the players and the lack of carry-over of drills and practices into game scenarios. And while this may be a feature of invasion games coaching, it would seem that the phenomenon is more widespread. The authors then proceed to argue that an approach based on Vygotskian theory might better facilitate understanding and at the same time include the athletes in the learning process not as passive recipients but as active con-structors of the learning. We do not want to engage in a critique of the use of Vygotsky here, but suffice it to say the learning process is considered more collaborative, enables decision making, and uses problem-solving and scaffolding techniques (a process of building on what

A. Rossi and R. Tinning

has gone before and then using this to take the next step – which, importantly, is made reachable rather than impossible) provided by the teacher or coach. Hence, the athlete is very much more involved in the learning process and attempts to solve game play scenarios or event scenarios to better contextualise the learning process.

MEMORY TASK

Think back to your school days (for some readers that might be quite a while ago!). Does this approach to skill learning sound familiar to you? Can you remember any alternative approaches to coaching where, for example, you were asked to contribute your views or ideas? The collective coaching communication literature tends to suggest that communication is very much one-way (coach to athlete). Does this strike you as true? What are your communication strategies when coaching young performers?

Joining up some widely scattered dots

This approach has gathered enormous support within the field of coaching sport and teaching physical education, and one of the key reasons for this is that, for many, it connects a few dots. First, it brings some justification to (albeit little evidence for) TGfU as a model; it is entirely consistent with the principles of the model – what the early enthusiasts came to refer to as 'teaching the game though the game'. This 'constructivist' approach (if we can add to the overuse of this term) also connected with (but perhaps was seldom recognised by) advocates of the dynamic systems of motor control, who suggest that motor behaviour is the result of the interaction between three constraints: the learner, the environment or context, and the nature of the task – what is being increasingly referred to as 'constraints-based pedagogy' (Davids *et al.*, 2007). In some respects, we are left wondering whether TGfU became a model in search of a theory, particularly in the way TGfU has been almost evangelised since about 2000 – but that is a debate to be had elsewhere. This may be uncharitable, but one gets the sense that finally we have some theoretical underpinnings to our pedagogical practices and we can now consign the old behavioural stuff to the theoretical trash-can. Indeed, one of us (Anthony) is guilty of suggesting that in sport pedagogy our greatest allies might be the dynamical systems researchers; at least they do have some evidence (Rossi, 2003). For both of us, there is a sense of familiarity with current thinking about how young people learn, and it was manifest not in what we understood about learners through our training but in the 'educational' pedagogical practices we were exposed to in movement education or educational gymnastics classes as students and the advent of the early work on TGfU.

This, though, might be a limited, if not weak, justification for certain teaching and coaching practices. Our thinking is again more along the lines of the earlier sections of this chapter about young people. If young people are complex, multidimensional learners, intent on making decisions and choices about what they do – and don't do, then young athletes are unlikely to respond to highly linear and structured learning contexts. Indeed, in some of our research with the Australian Football League (the Australian Rules Football code) (Mallet *et al.*, 2006) it was clear that some coaches were at times bewildered (and more than just a little frustrated) by younger players in the squad who wanted to question everything and maintain a degree of independence in their learning of tasks, moves and strategies!

The Vygotskian-inspired approach advocated by Potrac and Cassidy (2006) may well match the attitudes, sense of purpose and ways of learning of young people. However, we suggest that there should be some caution in dispensing with all that has gone before as if it is past its sell-by date. Some things may benefit from a highly linear learning structure – perhaps abseiling, pole vaulting, a gymnastics routine, or even a gymnastics move. Environments that have much more unpredictable dynamics are likely to benefit from a non-linear structure. In this sense, we find there is still much to be gained from Lusted's (1986) ideas about pedagogy because they are inextricably linked to what it means to learn. As Lusted (1986) argues, it is entirely artificial to separate the task and the learner, and to illustrate this he calls on the words of Stuart Hall's dictum: pedagogy is a bit like horses for courses. This idea of pedagogy is about *pedagogies*, and as such can incorporate a multitude of DEP models and learning contexts that are collaborative and progress from the carefully scaffolded learning opportunities and activities created by the 'more capable other' – the Vygotskian term used by Potrac and Cassidy (2006) to refer to the coach.

SO WHAT DOES THE EVIDENCE PRESENTED MEAN AND HOW CAN IT HELP?

To deliberate on such questions, we need to return to what we said earlier, because we made the case that learning in sport does not occur in a social, economic or political vacuum. Young people are clearly complex and multi-layered, have new sets of concerns with which to contend (the environment, unstable employment conditions, etc.) and make decisions in different ways based on different things compared with generations that went before. While we cannot be absolutely sure how young people learn (or how anyone learns, for that matter), we can be reasonably confident that they *approach* learning differently. Such approaches to learning appear not to be static or stable, and certainly not predictable. This suggests that there is no one 'right' way to coach young performers, and coaches probably need to be as open to alternative sport pedagogies as their young performers are to approaches to learning.

We appreciate that some readers might be rather disappointed in that we offer no definitive, gold standard account of how young people learn, thereby enabling a choice on how to coach. We make no apology for this; to suggest that young performers' learning is so static that coaching can proceed in the way one might use a recipe book is just asking for trouble. When Tinning (2007) asked if our young people were 'aliens in the gym', he was provoking a consideration based on Green and Bigum's (1993) 'aliens in the classroom'. These authors

A. Rossi and R. Tinning

suggested that young people are aliens in two senses: first, there is a sense of their being different; and second, there is a sense of their being alienated from adults and still more so from society. In regard to school PE, Tinning concluded that it was probably the curriculum that was the alien rather than the students. It is probably not unreasonable to suggest that coaches need to grasp the gravity of this before making their coaching decisions. We should not be at all surprised that young people see things differently from older ones. As adolescents have increasingly produced their own biographies, particularly, paradoxically, through social media, the capacity to individualise their leisure time has intensified. Given sport's firm place as a leisure-time decision for many of our young people, it would appear that learning in sport is part of that individualised biographical production. In this sense, coaches probably need understand the part they play in this process.

LEARNING MORE

Robyn Jones's edited book *The Sports Coach as Educator* (2006) is useful in that it squarely identifies the educative role a coach has. In addition, we would recommend reading some of the contemporary youth literature to get a sense of youth cultures. You may be surprised to find that, in such texts, sport and physical activity are invariably missing. Nonetheless, a cultural understanding is helpful. More recent publications about how skills are learned are also useful, and the work drawing upon 'constraints', while potentially challenging, may provide some food for thought about your coaching practices.

REFERENCES

Ball, S.J., Maguire, M. and Macrae, S. (2000) *Choice, pathways and transitions post-16: new youth, new economies in the global city*. London: Routledge.

Barham, N. (2004) *Dis/connected: why our kids are turning their backs on everything we thought we knew*. London: Ebury Press.

Bernshtein, N.A. (1967) *The coordination and regulation of movements*. Oxford: Pergamon Press.

Bramham, P. (2005) Habits of a lifetime: youth, generation and lifestyles. In P. Bramham and J. Caudwell (eds), *Sport, active leisure and youth cultures*. Brighton: Leisure Studies Association.

Bunker, D. and Thorpe, R. (1982) A model for the teaching of games in secondary schools. *Bulletin of Physical Education* 18(1): 5–8.

Davids, K., Button, C. and Bennett, S.J. (2007) *Acquiring movement skill: a constraints-led perspective*. Champaign, IL: Human Kinetics.

Giardina, M.D. and Donnelly, M.K. (2008) Introduction. In M.D. Giardina and M.K. Donnelly (eds), *Youth culture and sport: identity, power, and politics*. New York: Routledge.

Gibson, O. (2005) Young blog their way to a publishing revolution. *Guardian* (London), 7 October: 9.

Green, B. and Bigum, C. (1993) Aliens in the classroom. *Australian Journal of Education* 37(2): 119–141.

Hull, C.L. (1943) *The principles of behaviour*. New York: Appleton-Century-Crofts.

Jones, R.L. (2006) *The sports coach as educator: re-conceptualising sports coaching*. London: Routledge.

Kenway, J. and Bullen, E. (2001) *Consuming children: education – entertainment – advertising*. Buckingham, UK: Open University Press.

Klein, N. (2008) *The shock doctrine*. New York: Penguin.

Knapp, B. (1964) *Skill in sport*. London: Routledge & Kegan Paul.

Lusted, D. (1986) Why pedagogy? *Screen* 27(5): 2–14.

Mallet, C., Rossi, A. and Tinning, R. (2007) *Coaching knowledge, learning and mentoring in the Australian Football League*. A final research report submitted to the Australian Football League Research Board (April).

Maslow, A. (1954) *Motivation and personality*. New York: Harper.

Mauldon, E. and Redfern, B. (1969) *Games teaching: a new approach for the primary school*. London: Macdonald & Evans.

Oxendine, J.B. (1968) *Psychology of motor learning*. New York: Appleton-Century-Crofts.

Potrac, P. and Cassidy, T. (2006) The coach as a 'more capable other'. In R.L. Jones (ed.), *The sports coach as educator*. London: Routledge.

Raffo, C. and Reeves, M. (1999) Youth, school-to-work transitions and social exclusion: individualised systems of social capital, situated learning and developments in the agency/structure debate. *Journal of Youth Studies* 3(2): 147–156.

Rinehart, R. (2008) Exploiting a new generation: corporate branding and the co-optation of action sport. In M.D. Giardina and M.K. Donnelly (eds), *Youth culture and sport: identity, power, and politics*. New York: Routledge.

Roberts, K. (1996). Young people, schools, sport and government policies. *Sport, Education and Society* 1(1): 47–58.

Rossi, A. (2003) Linking games for understanding with dynamical systems of skill acquisition: old milk in new bottles or have we really got a new research agenda in physical education and sport? In J. Butler, L. Griffin, B. Lombardo and R. Nastasi (eds), *Teaching games for understanding in physical education and sport: an international perspective*. Redmond, VA: NASPE.

Sage, G.H. (1971) *Introduction to motor behaviour: a neuropsychological approach*. Reading, MA: Addison-Wesley.

Schmidt, R.A. (1975) A schema theory of discrete motor skill learning. *Psychological Review* 82(4): 225–260.

Singer, R.N. (1975) *Motor learning and human performance*. New York: Macmillan.

Skinner, B.F. (1938) *The behavior of organisms: an experimental analysis*. New York: Appleton-Century-Crofts.

Tait, G. (2000) *Youth, sex and government*. New York: Peter Lang.

A. Rossi and R. Tinning

Thorndike, E.L. (1932) *The fundamentals of learning*. New York: Teachers College, Columbia University.

Tinning, R. (2007) Aliens in the gym? Considering young people as learners in physical education. *ACHPER Health Lifestyles Journal* 54(2): 13–18.

Tjong, S., Weber, I. and Sternberg J. (2003) Mobile youth culture: shaping telephone use in Australia and Singapore. Paper presented at the ANZCA 03 conference, Brisbane, July.

Weller, S. (2006). Skateboarding alone? Making social capital discourse relevant to teenagers' lives. *Journal of Youth Studies* 9(5): 557–574.

White, R. and Wyn, J. (2008) *Youth and society* (2nd ed.). Melbourne: Oxford University Press.

Whiting, H.T.A. (1969) *Acquiring ball skill*. London: Bell.

Willis, S. (1994) Teaching and coaching today's kids. *Aussie Action Sport* 3(3): 12–13.

Wyn, J. and White, R. (1997) *Rethinking youth*. Sydney: Allen & Unwin.

INDEX

Please note page numbers ending in 'f' refer to figures and ending in 't' refer to tables.

291